THE CHANGING TERRAIN OF RELIGIOUS FREEDOM

Edited by

Heather J. Sharkey

and

Jeffrey Edward Green

PENN

UNIVERSITY OF PENNSYLVANIA PRESS

PHILADELPHIA

Published by
University of Pennsylvania Press
Philadelphia, Pennsylvania 19104-4112
www.upenn.edu/pennpress

Printed in the United States of America on acid-free paper
10 9 8 7 6 5 4 3 2 1

A catalogue record for this book is available
from the Library of Congress.
ISBN 978-0-8122-5337-5

To Rogers Smith,
for his scholarship,
leadership,
and example

CONTENTS

INTRODUCTION

The Landscape of Religious Freedom

Heather J. Sharkey and Jeffrey Edward Green

This volume offers theoretical, historical, and jurisprudential perspectives on religious freedom, while examining what it may entail as an experience, a value, and a right. We start from the premise that the terrain of religious freedom never has been easy or smooth. Across societies, defending or contesting principles of religious freedom has required compromise, balancing, and wrangling with the law. On rocky ground—to continue the environmental metaphor—people have had to push through or maneuver around obstacles, or struggle to keep their footing. Drawing examples from the United States and the world, the essays in this collection illustrate these challenges. They sketch the contours of current debates while showing how the landscape has shifted.

In recent years, scholars have taken impassioned stances on how to understand religious freedom. Writing from the perspective of U.S. history, one group of scholars has argued that we should understand religious freedom as a legal goal that has been impossible, misleading, or subject to the designs of dominant players.[1] In the domestic sphere, they understand religious freedom as the subject of myths that states, groups, and individual citizens have told to conjure civic and other communities that promote certain groups while sidelining others.[2] In foreign policy, they maintain, religious freedom has formed the basis for agendas that states and corporations (both religious organizations and businesses) have used to meddle abroad or to advance self-serving causes.[3]

Taking a more sanguine position, another group has argued that we should see religious freedom within the constellation of human rights.[4] Members of this group see religious freedom as a goal—perhaps a measurable one[5]—worth striving for, even if states and societies often fall short in reaching it.[6]

These scholars see law as a positive tool in the mediation between claimants to religious freedom and advocates for equality in arenas like marriage.[7] Those who approach religious freedom within the framework of human rights tend to see religion itself as a social good, a structure for ethical systems, a special category of existence worth respecting, and a godsend (so to speak!) for helping people cope with the joys, sorrows, and anxieties of living and dying.

We recognize these multiple perspectives while approaching claims to religious freedom as political ventures. By calling them "political," we do not suggest that such claims are cunning or manipulative. We call them political because they involve bids for influence or recognition among those whose interests often collide. Whether religious freedom itself is impossible to achieve is not a point we argue. Instead, we contend that understanding religious freedom is hard because it means grappling with conflicting and perhaps irreconcilable claims (not least about what counts as religion), while appreciating when and why some views prevail over others.

We begin in the next section by explaining ideas and questions that propel our inquiry. We continue in the chapter by considering tensions that have pressed on claims to religious freedom. We conclude by surveying lessons from our collective endeavor. By approaching religious freedom as a series of struggles in distinct places and contexts, as well as in the realm of ideas, we hope to stimulate discussions about how religion, politics, and freedom have mixed in the past and how they mix today in our turbulent times.

Investigating Religious Freedom: From States to Terrains

During the 2017–18 academic year, the Andrea Mitchell Center for the Study of Democracy at the University of Pennsylvania sponsored the program that led to this book. Titled "States of Religious Freedom," this program began with an opening panel discussion at the National Constitution Center in Philadelphia, and thereafter continued on the University of Pennsylvania campus with monthly lectures by solo presenters followed by an end-of-year symposium. The program gathered specialists in law, history, sociology, anthropology, political science, theology, and religious studies. Participants included activists and practitioners, ordained religious leaders, and committed atheists. Still others were legal scholars who had participated in some of the court cases referenced in discussions.

The series organizers started from the premise that ideas about religious freedom have shaped past and present constructions of national cultures and foreign policies. Exemplifying this circumstance, in the United States, was the International Religious Freedom Act (IRFA) of 1998, which committed the State Department's Bureau of Democracy, Human Rights, and Labor to compiling annual watchdog reports on every country in the world, except the United States itself. By exempting the United States, these reports led the organizers to consider whether or how the United States was *exceptional*—exemplary in its own record of religious freedom or merely distinctive—relative to other countries. What the organizers had originally envisioned as a program that would situate U.S. experiences within a comparative international context became something that was unequivocally global in its scope of inquiry.

From here, the Mitchell Center encouraged participants to engage with various questions. What had the U.S. record been in accommodating religious freedom in the past, and what new debates surrounding religious freedom were affecting democracy, citizenship, and constitutionalism worldwide during the early twenty-first century? How had other countries, informed by their own histories and circumstances, negotiated terrains of religion, statehood, and citizenship? What was the status of religious freedom around the world amid controversies over gender roles and sexuality, religiously motivated violence, the rights of religious minorities relative to dominant groups, and the establishment of official religions? We wanted to understand how states, as political entities, enabled or hindered religious expression and culture, and how social conditions and attitudes—states of collective being—affected practices and understandings of religious freedom.

Several contributors responded to these questions by citing non-state agents and forces that shape terrains and climates of religious freedom. In doing so, they reflected on the geography of religious freedom—the "where" of challenges to beliefs, values, and practices, and of threats to persons. Law courts, unsurprisingly, have been one recurring venue for staging religious freedom. Other venues where disputes over religious freedom or its violation have occurred include university campuses and office buildings, butcher shops and bakeries, school buses and cafeterias—run-of-the-mill places where people have lived their daily lives. Commenting on this spatial and experiential dimension of religious freedom, Jolyon Thomas, a contributor to this volume, observes that many sites of disputes have been local and of small scale. They have often been, too, extralegal—outside the gaze of the law, too trivial for authorities to notice. Thomas suggests that we can fruitfully think about "microclimates" of religious freedom, occurring far below the level of the nation-state, region, or municipality. He gives the example of harassment that might occur along a street—even something as minute as an odd look or a sneer that could make people feel uneasy or unwelcome as they walk.[8]

While "States of Religious Freedom" was the name of the original program, the canopy of states became too small to cover our unfolding debates. States have limits, but religion, or the lack of it, seems boundless, even amorphous—perhaps because religion as a concept is so hard to capture and grasp. For this reason, we turned to the metaphor of ground to express what became the central premise girding this volume: namely, that religious freedom has had, and still has, a tricky and shifting terrain.

Whether contributors engaged in face-to-face conversations or by reading each other's work, their exchanges have lent this book its coherence. And yet, readers will quickly see that *The Changing Terrain of Religious Freedom* is a polyvocal collection. We do not discuss religious freedom with one voice because we hold various views and take different approaches. We do not start from consensus, but we *do* start from mutual respect and from a keen, shared interest in the issues at stake. We believe that this diversity in outlook is a strength of the volume and that it can stimulate productive debate.

Mapping the Terrain

To appreciate how complex the religious freedom landscape can be, consider the example of RFRA—the Religious Freedom Restoration Act, which was passed into law by the U.S. Congress with near-unanimous support in 1993. On the face of it, this statute affirms a national value that Americans have long celebrated and trace to the Pilgrims: defense of religious freedom, especially by nonconformists. Declaring that the government could not restrict individuals' religious practices without good reason, the act enabled people who experienced infringements to seek redress in court. For example, in *Singh v. Carter* (2016), an American Sikh military officer cited RFRA to successfully challenge his employer, the U.S. Army, for having pressured him to comply with its dress code by removing the turban and beard that expressed his religious identity. While this particular case made few waves, others provoked stormy debates. Indeed, in May 2019, reflecting on the quarter century that had passed since RFRA's enactment, the American nonprofit media organization, National Public Radio (NPR) (which itself was created by an act of Congress), observed that consensus around the act had evaporated. The religious freedom that RFRA embodied was "no longer a bipartisan issue" in Congress, no longer a sentiment uniting the country at large.[9]

What changed? Reflecting on RFRA in 2018, a legal scholar pointed to "tectonic shifts" that had occurred "in the doctrine and political valence of laws protecting religious exercise" in the United States.[10] Eroding consensus were debates over whose religion or ethics should prevail in cases of conflict, which issues properly fall within the purview of religious freedom, and even what counts as religion in the first place. Then, too, culture wars heated up around specific U.S. Supreme Court cases that invoked provisions of RFRA. Flashpoints included *Burwell v. Hobby Lobby* (2014), involving owners of a company who cited Christian ethical objections to paying for potentially post-conception forms of birth control, such as the "morning-after pill," within employee insurance packages, and also *Masterpiece Cakeshop v. Colorado Civil Rights Commission* (2018), which arose from a 2012 incident in which a business owner declined to make a wedding cake for two male customers on the grounds that gay marriage contradicted his Christian beliefs. RFRA had become "both a shield and a sword," in the words of another scholar; it was inciting a series of "rancorous identity wars" in the United States.[11]

As cases that involved birth control coverage and cake baking, *Burwell v. Hobby Lobby* and the "Cake Case" (to use a convenient shorthand for *Masterpiece Cakeshop v. Colorado Civil Rights Commission*) may seem different from the instances of egregious and sometimes violent repression that so often have concerned advocates of religious freedom. For example, political scientists Daniel Philpott (a contributor to this volume) and Timothy Samuel Shah reflect on the "real and widespread cases" of violent repression that justify recognizing religious freedom as a fundamental human right. "In great numbers, all over the world," wrote Philpott and Shah in 2016, "human beings are killed, tortured, imprisoned, detained, robbed of their property, deprived of their houses of worship, and denied jobs, economic opportunities, and positions in public service on account of their religion."[12]

In describing people of conscience who suffer, often in bodily ways, Philpott and Shah may have been thinking of a historical figure like Mary Dyer, a Quaker woman who lived more than a century before the United States became an independent republic. In 1660, Puritan authorities in Massachusetts hanged Dyer from an elm tree on Boston Common for professing heretical views. (In fact, Dyer had been convicted and nearly hanged once before for the same crime, namely, insisting on the greater importance of internal faith, over outward appearance and behavior, as a route to salvation.)[13] Or, to take a current example, Philpott and Shah could have been thinking of the million-plus Uighur Muslims in western China who now languish in mass internment camps, reportedly, in some cases, subject to torture. According to Amnesty International, the Chinese government has deemed all of these people potential separatists and terrorists who require "re-education."[14]

To be sure, the Uighur case—like nearly any example one could raise in a discussion of religious freedom—is laden with ambiguity. The Uighurs' religion, their Muslim-ness (however they practice or profess Islam), may differentiate them from the majority of Chinese people, but their language, ethnicity, history, and geographical concentration in the country's far west also figure in their distinction. Religion forms just one part of their story, suggesting that religious freedom or its violation is likely to form only part of their treatment as well. How much religion, and religious freedom, makes a difference in shaping lives and informing people's plights is one of the conceptual challenges we face in a study like this one. Can we quantify religion or religious freedom? Can we assign it a dosage?

Relative to the incarcerated Uighur Muslims of China, or the Rohingya Muslims of Myanmar (who experienced waves of persecution and displacement beginning in the late 1970s, and more intensely since 2017),[15] Jack Phillips, the Colorado baker at the center of the Cake Case, experienced no physical coercion. As a test of religious freedom, the Cake Case looks very different from the Uighur experience—not least because the Colorado dispute occurred in the open, with the public able to follow its judicial procedures. Recall that the baker, Phillips, maintained that helping to celebrate a gay marriage by preparing a cake for the wedding reception would have caused hardship by violating his Christian beliefs. Ultimately, the U.S. Supreme Court delivered a judgment in his favor, which rested, not on broad considerations of how to reconcile the free exercise of religion with anti-discriminatory legal norms, but on a narrow assessment that the Colorado Civil Rights Commission had demonstrated "clear and impermissible hostility" toward the religious beliefs of the baker when he explained the values that underlay his refusal to provide service. Observers continue to debate the meaning of this judgment, which, as Leslie Kendrick and Micah Schwartzman argue, grounded itself in the alleged anti-religious animus of the Colorado Civil Rights Commission and thus failed to sort out "the principles for determining whether religious liberty authorizes discrimination against gays and lesbians in the marketplace." To this extent, the judgment "ducked [the] central questions raised by that conflict."[16]

How compelling is the Cake Case in the annals of religious freedom? Not very, one American writer recently implied; by constantly "crying 'religious freedom'" in courts, some American litigants may be "bleaching meaning from the phrase" while pressing frivolous lawsuits.[17] Quite serious, maintains Joshua Matz, one of the contributors to this volume. *Masterpiece Cakeshop v. Colorado Civil Rights Commission*, he argues, bears on topics like sexual agency and the making of families while bringing public commerce into religious freedom disputes.[18] Anthropologists would probably agree that the Cake Case, like the Hobby Lobby case (again, *Burwell v. Hobby Lobby*), *is* serious, because it blends three things—sex, kinship, and trade—seminal to the human condition. Even Karl Marx—were we to resurrect him to seek his opinion—would likely agree that these two recent U.S. Supreme Court cases mix a potent brew of production (involving workers) and capital (involving the consolidation of private wealth), along with a heavy dose of the "opium of the people," as he famously (or infamously!) called religion. It is important to note that we do not need to agree on the merits or conclusions of various disputes to agree on the seriousness of their underlying concerns and their relevance to debates about religion and freedom.

Part of what makes religious freedom so complex as a field of inquiry is that agents in disputes can be hard to identify and reconcile. In the section below, we discuss some of these agents along with recurring tensions that arise from their claims.

People, States, and Walls of Separation

Claims to religious freedom often expose tensions between individuals, groups, and governments, especially when such claims undermine public policies that states want to pursue. For example, Article 9 of the European Convention on Human Rights guarantees individuals' rights to freedom of religion, thought, and conscience, but it advises that freedom of religion may be limited by the interests of "public safety . . . [for] the protection of public order, health or morals, or for the protection of the rights and freedoms of others." Negotiating limits between individual freedom and public order then becomes a major source of debate. A related tension has historically arisen in countries that aspire to democratic ideals while privileging certain religions, either explicitly (by instituting a state religion) or implicitly (by favoring one religion and its adherents in policies and practices). To venture beyond North America and Europe, we could cite Egypt as an example. Iterations of the Egyptian constitution, beginning in

1923, have affirmed individual religious freedom along with the state's duty and right to maintain public order (much like the European Convention on Human Rights). At the same time, though, Egypt has routinely asserted the primacy of Islam as a source of values and laws—including laws that privilege Muslims over non-Muslims, especially in family matters like marriage and inheritance.[19] In this sense, Egypt's claims regarding religion and freedom have been contradictory—even (one might be tempted to say) impossible.

Obviously, Egypt has not been alone. We could look elsewhere to see how balancing individual rights and collective well-being—combined with the privileging of majoritarian religions and groups—has challenged religious freedom. In Asia, for instance, majority privilege is visible in Israel vis-à-vis Judaism and Jews; in Myanmar, toward Buddhism and Buddhists; and, in Malaysia, regarding Islam and Muslims. By examining India, where the politics of cow slaughter and beef-eating has become a flashpoint, Cassie Adcock shows in this volume how Hindu majoritarian dominance has built momentum even as the religious, and religious freedom, dimensions of cow-and-beef controversies remain ambiguous and contestable.

A puzzle facing liberal states entails determining what neutrality toward religion should mean. One possibility is to neither support nor restrain religion in public policy. John Locke advanced this idea in his essay *A Letter Concerning Toleration* in 1689. Thomas Jefferson similarly called for a "wall of separation between Church and State" in 1802.[20] The question of the proper role of religion within liberal states still generates heated debate in countries around the world. Indeed, given the dramatic expansion of the modern state in so many areas of public life, such as health care and education, it is hard to see how state policies would not affect religious life in some ways. For this reason, some scholars have questioned both the desirability and possibility of a "wall of separation," advancing instead a competing notion of supporting equal accommodation and treatment of religions.[21]

In the United States, religious organizations have long worked with the government to provide social services, both at home and abroad.[22] (In fact, one scholar dates this history of collaboration to the early colonial era, specifically, to 1636, when the Commonwealth of Massachusetts enacted a tax to fund Harvard University as it trained clergy.[23]) The question of church-state separation loomed large as the twentieth century ended, especially after 1996, when federal and state governments began to promote "faith-based initiatives." These initiatives made it easier for enterprises run by recognized religious institutions—day-care centers, nursing homes, hospitals, and more—to compete for and receive government funding, that is, to overcome, as a White House website explained, "statutory, regulatory, and bureaucratic barriers" that had previously blocked religious institutions from garnering government support.[24] American evangelical groups pushed hard to advance these measures, a goal of which, they claimed, was to "unleash the armies of compassion" by enabling programs centered on faith.[25]

In a similar manner, many other democracies support religion while claiming to hold secular principles. France, for example, has supported religiously affiliated schools, maintained certain churches, and recognized Catholic holidays like All Saints' Day and Ascension Day on public-school calendars, even as it has restricted the wearing of religious symbols in public schools following a law enacted in 2004.[26] The latter policy, which especially affects Muslim females who may wish to wear headscarves, has led many to challenge the neutrality of France's policies and to question the state's treatment of religious minorities.[27] Using examples from France, Canada, and Germany, Lori Beaman shows in her essay within this volume how state and municipal authorities, as well as local citizens, often have justified projections of majoritarian religions—the display of crucifixes in public offices in Bavaria, for example—by insisting that they reflect "culture" and "history" instead of religion.

Religious Freedom, Individual Rights, and the Public Good

When do individual religious rights impede a state's pursuit of legitimate public policy? This question arose in the United States in a landmark case, *Wisconsin v. Yoder* (1972), involving parents who invoked religion to withdraw children from school at younger ages than their home state allowed.[28] The U.S. Supreme Court decided that Amish youth (belonging to a traditionalist sect rooted in Swiss-German Anabaptist Christianity) did not have to attend public school after eighth grade (approximately age thirteen), despite a Wisconsin law that mandated attendance until sixteen. Like other states, Wisconsin set this standard to develop human capital, boost the social and economic potential of youth, and cultivate critical thinking and with it the capacities of citizenship. Judges sided with the Amish litigants, reasoning that Wisconsin failed to prove how two extra school years made a difference in creating productive citizens. They reasoned, further, that Amish people had a record of law-abiding behavior (suggesting that socialization through schooling was not urgent) and that Amish families offered a de facto vocational education to youth after age thirteen, through training in skills like farming and carpentry. *Wisconsin v. Yoder* recognized the rights of adults, claiming to act from religious convictions, to impart principles to children and to chart their educational paths. In the jurisprudence on religious liberty, this case illustrates the importance of *exemptions* from state laws, while stoking debates about how exceptional exemptions should be.[29]

A current example of this tension between individual rights and the so-called public interest involves parents who refuse to vaccinate children. In 2018 and 2019, many news outlets drew attention to an ultra-Orthodox Jewish community in New York, some of whose members rejected vaccinations because their serums were potentially non-kosher.[30] These anti-vaxxers contributed to the resurgence of measles, which had disappeared in the United States by 2000 but returned with epidemic force in 2018. While demographic data on anti-vaxxers may be incomplete, the vast majority of Americans not vaccinating appear *not* to be ultra-Orthodox Jews; they come from a broad range of the population, diverse in its religious orientation, geographic origin, and political outlook. At the same time, the anti-vaccination movement is not only a U.S. phenomenon; it is growing in countries like the United Kingdom, Ireland, and Italy, among those who express doubts about safety, often citing a now-discredited but persistently influential medical research paper.[31] Thus the religious dimensions of refusal have actually been somewhat limited both in the United States and abroad.

If U.S. religious objectors, like the ultra-Orthodox Jews of New York, have been of special interest to both the anti-vaccination groups that cultivate the objectors and the media outlets that lambaste them, it may be because observers realize that religious refuseniks are likely to draw more sympathy from courts than their nonobservant counterparts. Again, *Wisconsin v. Yoder* (1972) is relevant. In that case, justices grappled with how to differentiate religious from nonreligious—or "conscientious"—objections. Justice Warren Burger, writing for the majority, distinguished "philosophical and personal" objections from specifically "religious" ones, arguing that the U.S. Constitution awarded only the "religious" special protection. Many U.S. states still make this distinction: In 2016, forty-seven out of fifty states recognized "religious" exemptions for opting out of vaccinations, while fewer than half recognized exemptions based on "philosophical, conscientious, or personal belief."[32] By valorizing religion more than conscience or philosophy, U.S. state and federal laws raise questions about what religion and "being religious" mean.

Ultra-Orthodox Jewish anti-vaxxers may also be easy targets in a large but scattered field in which white, upper-middle-class, and non-Jewish people far outnumber them.[33] This point raises the prospect that anti-Semitism may also explain the disproportionate attention that ultra-Orthodox Jewish anti-vaxxers have received, as members of an extremely small, visibly different, and highly observant non-Christian minority.

Adults Versus Children: Religious Freedom for "Majors" and Minors

Studies of religious freedom often use the terms "majority" and "minority" to refer to dominant and subordinate religious groups. We could speak about, say, the Muslim majority relative to the Baha'i, Christian, and Jewish minorities in Iran. Yet, majority can also cover the state of being full age, or adult, just as minority can mean being under age and subject to guardianship. Because disputes over religious freedom often involve babies, children, and adolescents, it makes sense to use the terms "majority" and "minority" in this age sense as well.

Consider Denmark. In 2018, a public petition prompted Danish legislators to consider a ban on male circumcision—or, more accurately, a ban on circumcising males younger than eighteen. At the end of 2020, the debate was still continuing. Since relatively few Danes of Christian background practice circumcision, any ban would affect mostly Denmark's small Jewish and Muslim communities, who traditionally and routinely circumcise boys. (Jews circumcise newborns, typically at eight days old; among Muslims, the age for circumcision ranges from birth to age ten, with age seven having been typical but with newborn circumcision apparently becoming more common).[34] Some Muslim and Jewish groups have argued that circumcising boys is critical to their religious identity and that attacks on the practice therefore amount to attacks on them. Advocates for the ban have argued that each owner of a foreskin should be able to decide whether to keep it or cut it off—and that he should be able to choose as an adult, free of parents; hence, their proposal for a minimum age.[35] Even more controversial today, worldwide, is the practice of cutting girls' genitals by either clitoridectomy or more severe operations, as Kristina Arriaga considers in her essay in this volume.

What rights do adults possess over children in families? When do rights and practices deserve recognition as "religious" and therefore warranting protection? And how should societies treat cultural practices when they involve the bodies of infants and children? A further question arises in cases like Denmark's: When is a policy humanitarian, intent on defending children, and when does it stray into attacks on minority and immigrant groups?

Children pose a jurisprudential puzzle for liberal philosophy. On the one hand, they are free citizens whose rights and liberties states should protect. On the other hand, though, minors do not yet enjoy rights of consent and are subject to parents' or guardians' choices. How one understands the position of children to some extent determines one's posture toward religious freedom, along with rights of states to intercede on behalf of minors. Liberals eager to protect the autonomy of minors may be less willing to grant religious exemptions to parents and guardians whose practices could be seen as impeding children as they mature into adults, either because of the severity or irreversibility of such practices (as with male circumcision and female genital cutting) or because of their potential undermining of future autonomy (as in exemptions from mandatory schooling).[36] Indeed, this has been the position of many Danes who now advocate for the ban on boys' circumcision; as a Danish Muslim supporter of the ban put it, "There is too much emphasis on the parents' religious and cultural rights."[37]

Thorny questions about what parents and states can do to, or for, children have generated heated debate when religious freedom comes into play. Consider another Supreme Court case from the United States, *Jehovah's Witnesses of Washington v. King County Hospital* (1967), which involved adult members of a Christian sect who cited religious objections to blood transfusions. The case went to court after hospital authorities in the state of Washington overrode objections from Jehovah's Witness parents by declaring their children wards of the state so that doctors could administer blood. The court ruled for Washington, concluding that parents had the right to "train and indoctrinate children in religious matters"—to shape their minds—but could not expose children's bodies to grievous danger.[38]

Far from being perennially passive parties in religious freedom debates, minors sometimes have staked positions themselves. Consider children who refused to salute the American flag or recite the associated Pledge of Allegiance in classrooms.[39] In the 1930s, an eight-year-old boy named Carleton Nicholas—also a Jehovah's Witness—refused to perform the pledge in Lynn, Massachusetts, whereupon school authorities expelled him. His example inspired a case that Jehovah's Witnesses later advanced in Pennsylvania, which led to the U.S. Supreme Court decision of *Minersville School District v. Gobitis* (1938). This case, in turn, informed *West Virginia State Board of Education v. Barnette*, following an instance in which West Virginia authorities threatened to send non-flag-pledging children to a school for juvenile delinquents. In 1943, the court ultimately decided that forcing children to salute the flag—like demanding unanimity of opinion—is unconstitutional.

Is Religious Freedom Only for Humans?

Increasingly today, many are asking not only *who* has freedom but *what* has freedom. Bearers of rights may include sacred places, along with elements of what the United Nations Educational, Scientific, and Cultural Organization (UNESCO) calls tangible and intangible heritage. Once again, we return to the "where" issue of religious freedom, involving questions about the geography of religion and the stages and props for its performance.

In North America, examples from the history of native peoples stand out. In a process that began in the 1880s, accelerated in the 1920s, and continued in the past century, Native Americans in the United States struggled to win recognition for cultural practices that often occurred in spaces and landscapes that they deemed sacred. They resisted the U.S. government's assimilationist efforts, which in the late nineteenth and early twentieth centuries included appointing Catholic and Protestant missions to Christianize Native Americans and imposing "Civilization Regulations," which banned their traditional dances. In the late 1920s, as Tisa Wenger has shown, Pueblo Indians successfully contested this ban by pushing the U.S. government to recognize their dances as acts of religion.[40] Later, other groups—notably, she argues, Catholics and Jews—enhanced their legitimacy in the eyes of Protestant power-holders by similarly casting cultural practices as religious enactments, and, in the Jewish case, also by framing Jewishness as a religious and not a racial identity.[41]

In 1978—twenty years before the International Religious Freedom Act declared religious freedom a priority of foreign policy—the U.S. Congress passed the American Indian Religious Freedom Act (AIRFA), which guaranteed "rights of Native Americans to exercise their traditional religions by ensuring access to sites, use and possession of sacred objects, and the freedom to worship through ceremonials and traditional rites." Almost immediately, AIRFA encountered what one of its drafters called a "stunning defeat" for the Native American cause,[42] leading some analysts to reflect that the act was more cosmetic than substantive. This defeat occurred in the court battle of

Lyng v. Northwest Indian Cemetery Protective Association (1988), which arose when the U.S. Forest Service proposed to build a road through a national forest to facilitate timber harvesting. Native Americans objected because the road crossed lands that they considered sacred and on which they performed rituals. Writing for the majority, Supreme Court Justice Sandra Day O'Connor decided for the Forest Service, reasoning that for the Native Americans, building a road would "compel . . . no behavior contrary to their belief."[43]

Lori Beaman argues that Native Americans in the *Lyng* case stood at a disadvantage because "the space they identify as sacred does not resonate with the religious views of the Christian mainstream" and because the ways they express their causes "fall outside of the acceptable framework of rights claims."[44] In other words, the U.S. court privileged a religion of belief over a religion of ritual and sacred terrain. Tensions between "Indian tribes" and "Native Hawaiians" on the one hand, and U.S. government agencies, on the other, have persisted, often over hunting and fishing rights that become ensnared in debates on religion. It is telling that a U.S. federal agency like the National Oceanic and Atmospheric Administration's Office for Coastal Management currently posts the text of AIRFA on its website.[45]

Canada has had a similar history of state repression and religious assimilation of native peoples, much of which once occurred (as in the United States and Australia) in state-subsidized Christian boarding schools that forcibly enrolled generations of children.[46] Canadian history has also witnessed continual resistance and pushback from indigenous groups, whose members have increasingly demanded recognition through advocacy and legal action based on claims to religion.[47] In *Ktunaxa Nation v. British Columbia* (2017), for example, members of the indigenous Ktunaxa Nation contested a proposed private ski resort in British Columbia, which would occupy land that they associated with the Grizzly Bear Spirit—a spirit central to their beliefs and cosmology.[48] In fact, they had been resisting the proposed resort for twenty-five years.[49] Invoking claims to religious freedom, they argued that the resort would threaten the habitat of bears and drive out the Grizzly Bear Spirit. The court disagreed, concluding that Ktunaxa claims to religious freedom, or "aboriginal" interest, did not exceed "state" interest in developing the region. "In short," the chief justice wrote in the judgment, which recalled the U.S. *Lyng* case of 1988, "the [Canadian] Charter [of Rights and Freedoms] protects the freedom to worship, but does not protect the spiritual focal point of the worship."[50]

Laws and cases can go other ways, however. In 2017, New Zealand ratified a law that granted Whanganui, a river that many indigenous Maori people consider sacred, the same legal status as a human being.[51] In Nainital, India, the High Court of Uttarakhand state ruled early in 2017 that both the Ganges and Yamuna Rivers should have the same rights as "living human entities," in response to the urgent need to reduce pollution in two waterways considered sacred by many Hindus. Worried about the accountability of the state government vis-à-vis claims that people could lodge on behalf of the rivers in case of floods and the like, local authorities appealed the decision to the Indian Supreme Court, which overruled the order a few months later.[52] Today, as ecological and environmental concerns increasingly arise in religious discussions, religious freedom claims to spaces and natural resources are likely to multiply—although how courts will respond remains to be seen.[53]

The Business of Religious Freedom

In the United States, the case of *Burwell v. Hobby Lobby* (2014) was a watershed. The U.S. Supreme Court recognized the rights of a profit-making corporation to enjoy religious liberty, holding that some for-profit companies could deny contraception coverage to employees on the basis of a religious objection.

There are many kinds of corporations, including religious institutions, which have long enjoyed recognized rights to religious freedom. The Roman Catholic Church and the Southern Baptist Convention are examples; these Christian organizations are "corporations" in the sense of being bodies of congregations or parishes that possess central leadership. Hobby Lobby is another kind of corporation; it is a money-making business, a chain of arts-and-crafts stores. The fact that it is also a family-run business proved significant because when the U.S. Supreme Court decided that Hobby Lobby did not have to support all forms of contraceptives in the health plan it offered its 13,000 or so employees,[54] it limited the ruling to "closely held" companies—not publicly traded corporations.[55]

Burwell v. Hobby Lobby recalls questions that the anthropologist Greg Urban poses in a collection of essays titled *Corporations and Citizenship* (which belongs to the same Penn Press/Mitchell Center series as this volume). To what extent have states treated corporations as citizens, endowed with rights like freedom of speech? What visible and invisible powers do corporations and the people who run them wield in democratic political systems? And how do corporations' profit-driven goals conflict with or undermine the rights and needs of individuals?[56] Questions like these are beyond the scope of this study. And yet, as controversies intensify over corporate entanglements in democratic societies, we should heed them as we assess debates on religious freedom.

Of course, there is a longer history of business entanglements with religious freedom, as the historian William Schultz reminds us in this volume, in his examination of the "I AM" religious movement, which flourished in the United States during the 1920s and 1930s. Conveying a message of self-improvement mixed with the occult ("What you think and feel you bring into form . . . what you meditate on, you become"[57]), the leaders of "I AM" devised a mail-order business to sell their inspirational books. An "important truth about American religious freedom," Schultz contends, "is that in the United States, religious freedom is inseparable from financial practices" and often occurs in the arena of commerce. However, it was the U.S. Postal Service, and not the U.S. Supreme Court, that entered the fray when it pursued Edna Ballard and her son Donald, the movement's leaders, for mail fraud—ostensibly to save the American public from tricksters and religious fakery. Contrasting the interwar-era "I AM" case with the Colorado Cake Case of 2017, one could argue that while U.S. authorities avowedly protected the religious freedom of *consumers* in the former instance, the U.S. courts protected the religious freedom of business *owners* in the latter. We return here to the idea that an emerging feature of the religious freedom terrain may be the growing power of business corporations as holders of rights.

Religious Freedom for Nonbelievers, "Nones," and Ambivalents

Burwell v. Hobby Lobby involved, again, a family firm—a business owned and closely run by the billionaire David Green and his children. The Greens, who identify as evangelical Christians, opened the Museum of the Bible near the National Mall in Washington, D.C., in 2017; they also have supported reintroducing a Bible-centered curriculum in U.S. public schools.[58] The Greens have expressed a desire to see *more* of the Bible in American public society. In this way, they contrast with activists in U.S. legal history who have insisted on the right to see *less*.

One of those who argued against religious intrusion was Ellery Schempp, a teenager living in Pennsylvania during the late 1950s, who objected to the Bible reading and prayer that his public school expected him to perform. His parents agreed and filed suit. From a Philadelphia district court, their case reached the U.S. Supreme Court in 1963 as *School District of Abington v. Schempp*. Schempp's parents argued that public-school-led Bible reading and prayer violated the Establishment Clause of the First Amendment of the U.S. Constitution, which bars Congress from making any law "respecting an establishment of religion." They claimed, further, that these practices conflicted with their own observance as members of a Unitarian Universalist Church. The Supreme Court decided for the Schempps, reasoning that not establishing religion meant neither inhibiting nor promoting it. In this volume, Leigh Schmidt's essay shows how, in the mid-twentieth-century United States, the road for dissenters and nonbelievers stayed rocky even if cases like *Schempp* signaled the death knell for public-school prayer.

How should we balance the rights of those who believe with those who do not? This question, which figured centrally in the Schempp case, stands to loom ever larger in countries like the United States, which claim not to establish or privilege religions while nevertheless enshrining special protections for religious belief and believers.

Today, growing numbers of people reject religious identities or strictures, identify as atheists or agnostics, or claim no attachment to a particular religious tradition or community. Such people are sometimes now called nonbelievers and "nones," even if both terms are problematic as negative appellations that may imply that religious belief and profession are positive, normatively superior alternatives. The term "nones" can also mislead in a different way: Many people may have no religious affiliation even if they *do* hold "religious" or "spiritual" convictions (such as belief in a deity) or engage in practices like prayer. This may be another way of saying that "nones" may be religious without having religion! A 2012 report from the Pew Foundation assessed those whom it called religiously "unaffiliated" and found that 7 percent of unaffiliated adults in China, 30 percent in France, and 68 percent in the United States professed belief in God or a "higher power." In terms of ritual, 7 percent of those in France and 27 percent in the United States attended religious services at least once a year, while in China, 44 percent of the unaffiliated reported engaging in graveside worship.[59] A more recent study by the Pew Research Center, in 2017, reported that more than a quarter of U.S. adults (27 percent) described themselves as "spiritual but not religious."[60]

The study of nonbelievers and the unaffiliated highlights the significance of what the philosopher Jürgen Habermas calls "postsecularity." By postsecularity, Habermas intends to describe the contemporary situation in which both "religious" and "nonreligious" groups, more than ever before, recognize each other as permanent and co-equal constituencies, with neither side contemplating the eventual disappearance or obsolescence of the other. Habermas calls on religious communities to accept the norms and values of liberal democracy and modern science and calls on nonreligionists to recognize that the "secularistic belief that religion is destined to disappear" is neither sociologically nor morally credible.[61] Similar ideas are expressed by Charles Taylor, in his influential study *A Secular Age*, in which he argues that we should move beyond traditional conceptions of secularism as the reduction of religious belief or the neutrality of the state toward religion, and recognize a third meaning of secularism to account for a world in which devout people increasingly must navigate within contexts that make no reference to God, gods, or other explicitly religious ideas. In other words, the religious, more than in the past (in the West at least), must live in a world where religion does not operate uncontested but is practiced with awareness of, and frequent confrontation with, nonreligious alternatives.[62]

What Taylor does not so much emphasize, but what is nonetheless consistent with his analysis, is the opposite movement: nonreligious people, too, must live in a world increasingly aware that their lack of religion is itself a *choice* (an existential stance), not a *truth* supported by external reality.[63] From this perspective, confident assertions of nonreligiosity as being somehow a mark of progressive modernity—uniquely consistent with the "fate of the times," as the sociological theorist, Max Weber, described it[64]—miss the mark. There is nothing inexorable or inevitable about either religion or irreligion as societies march forward in time.

The theories of Habermas and Taylor have certain limits: They reflect self-conscious biases rooted in Western Christian cultures; and they gesture toward a past that they seem to think was more "religious," or timelessly traditional, without always citing evidence to back up their claims. Taylor muses, for example, about why it was "virtually impossible not to believe in God in, say, 1500 in our Western society [sic], while in 2000 many of us find this not only easy, but even inescapable."[65] With its focus on the West, Taylor's observation overlooks ancient, nontheist traditions within what we would now call Buddhism and Hinduism, along with skeptical and universalist elements found in Islam. We could point, for example, to the Rig Veda's claims about the origins of the universe in the Nasadiya Sukta (Hymn of Creation), which is more than three millennia old; or to the thirteenth-century Sufi Persian poetry of Jalal al-Din Rumi, such as his poem that declares that he is: "Not Christian or Jew or Muslim, not Hindu, Buddhist, sufi, or zen; Not any religion or cultural system; I am not from the East or West . . . my place is placeless, a trace of the traceless."[66]

It is worth noting here, in response to Habermas and Taylor as well, that numerous scholars, writing from the perspective of Muslim history, have begun to question assumptions about what secularism is and how it works. For example, writing specifically about Egypt, Hussein Ali Agrama and Saba Mahmood each argue that state-led claims to secularism in the late twentieth and early twenty-first centuries—far from eliding religion in the public sphere—often masked religious sectarianism or sharpened sectarian sentiments within society at large.[67] As a set of ideas and practices, they show, secularism has been elusive, unpredictable, and less neutral in terms of religion than observers often assume—a point that Cassie Adcock advances in her essay in this volume with regard to agricultural science in India.

Whatever we call them—"nones," nonbelievers, atheists, skeptics, the unaffiliated, or the ambivalent—the number of people who hold no firm religious profession or communal identification is growing quickly, especially in states that are disinclined to enforce, promote, or privilege particular religions. In the United States alone, the number of "nones" jumped from 16 percent in 2007 to 23 percent in 2014 (with much of the drop in religious affiliation among Christians).[68] If this trend continues, the result is likely to be greater fluidity of identity, including intermittent conversions to, from, and among religions—as well as movements in, out, and around bounded communities. Affiliations are likely to become shakier, attesting to fluctuations and uncertainties in categories that many may have once assumed to be fixed or traditional, while complicating what it can mean to be "practicing" religious freedom.

The Impossible and the Possible in the Quest for Religious Freedom

In a book called *The Impossibility of Religious Freedom* (2005), Winnifred Fallers Sullivan advances a crisp argument, which has driven debates ever since. Because there is no way to assess what counts as sincere or valid religion or religious belief, she writes, religious freedom is impossible to promote or achieve.

Sullivan drew on her experience as an expert witness in *Warner v. City of Boca Raton*, a 1999 case involving a Florida municipal cemetery that required grave markers to sit flat with the grass. The dispute arose when the municipality, having ordered people to remove objects that violated the code, authorized demolishing the assorted crosses, Stars of David, candles, flowerpots, and other items that sat atop graves. Citing Florida's Religious Freedom Restoration Act—one of many state-based analogues of the federal RFRA legislation— litigants insisted on their right to install these items as religious acts and objects.[69] The case immersed the judge in nitty-gritty details about what religious expression might look like and when it deserved protection.

In 1964, U.S. Supreme Court Justice Potter Stewart famously declared in a case about pornography, "I know it when I see it." Sullivan suggested that the judge in *Warner v. City of Boca Raton* seemed to approach religion with a similar confidence.[70] Sullivan emerged from the case convinced of the tendency in the American public sphere to favor what she called a generic lower-case-*p* "protestant" understanding of religious freedom, based on capital-*P* Protestant Christian understandings of religion as a "private, voluntary, individual, textual, and believed" phenomenon that privileged inner conviction or faith over an attachment to, say, rituals, objects, or places. She concluded that "the law probably cannot get it right" in defining religion for the sake of determining what is "authentic, and therefore legally significant."[71] It would be better to "forsak[e] religious freedom as a legally enforced right" and instead judge cases on broader principles of nondiscrimination. In the U.S. context, she continued, this altered jurisprudence not only would prevent bias against those who do not identify as religious (and thus are ineligible for exemptions currently only provided on religious grounds) but free courts from tussling with the definition of true religion.

In an article styled as a defense of religious freedom, Daniel Philpott and Timothy David Shah strenuously reject Sullivan's claim that religious freedom is "impossible." They lament the efforts of a "phalanx of individuals" to discredit religious freedom, especially in Western societies. They also object to the way that these scholars and critics portray claims to religious freedom as a "projection of ideology, an interest of factions, [and] a colonial and imperial pursuit."[72]

Debates over religion and religious freedom can certainly give rise to doubts. One doubt relates to measuring the religious element in multifaceted cases—balancing religion relative to factors like ethnicity, age, class, and the like. Recall, again, the case of the Uighurs in China. Even determining which elements of an issue count as religious can be difficult. Cassie Adcock illustrates this point vividly in her essay in this volume about India's post-independence policies against cow slaughter, which authorities have claimed to base on cutting-edge agricultural research. At the same time, some elements that observers claim as religious may arise from other impulses, as Randall Balmer shows in his essay here about the "myth of origins" of the Religious Right in the United States during the 1980s. Rejecting the now-standard narrative associating the emergence of this movement with opposition to *Roe v. Wade* (1973) and the politics of abortion, Balmer argues that racial bias—including hostility toward the desegregation of schools and the dismantling of state laws that banned interracial dating and marriage—was decisive in launching the Religious Right among those who claimed to be acting on the basis of Christian values. In another vein, William Schultz in this volume addresses the question of when a religion is real or fake, flagging a concern with authenticity that has recurred in U.S. history. At the same time, he connects his study of religious freedom to the study of capitalism and corporations, which has become a flourishing field of historical inquiry, as well as to comparative studies of religion and fraud.

Still other doubts about religious freedom have sprung from concerns about its interaction and potential competition with other personal liberties—that is, with how religious freedom may squeeze out different values and claims. Concerned about such possibilities, the social theorist Alan Carling advocates for a value of "social equality of religion and belief" in lieu of a narrower conception of religious freedom. He calls this value "serob," turning an acronym of the phrase into a word. "Serob," he explains, would rest upon state neutrality toward religion and nondiscrimination on religious grounds, but it would also entail nondiscrimination between religion and other facets of identity, notably "gender, ethnicity, race, age, disability, sexuality or social caste."[73]

As if the debate over religious freedom were not hard enough, some scholars find themselves stuck on the possibility, or impossibility, of pinning down the religious. "What *is* religion, anyway?" they ask. Considering the history of religion as a social phenomenon, for example, Brent Nongbri, a specialist in the history of early Christian manuscripts from the eastern Mediterranean, has argued that "'religion' as a sphere of life ideally separated from politics, economics, and science" has not been "a universal feature of human history" insofar as "the act of distinguishing between 'religious' and 'secular' is a recent development." "The very idea of 'being religious' requires a companion notion of what it would mean to be 'not religious,'" Nongbri suggested, "and this dichotomy was not part of the ancient world."[74]

Kevin Schilbrack, a philosopher of religion, tackles this issue from another direction, by asking, "What *isn't* religion?" Schilbrack is dissatisfied by how religion in his view has become a vague catch-all, sometimes even applied in a quasi-serious way to explain things like the team loyalty of passionate soccer fans. Schilbrack seeks "a workable sense of where that variety [in religion] begins and ends." He surveys various theories, flagging the school of Émile Durkheim, who suggested that beliefs and practices amount to religion when they unite people into a community, and the school of Edward Tylor, who argued that religion involves spiritual beings. He concludes that religion "happens" when a person or group senses a reality "authorized by the nature of things," even if one "sets aside the belief in superhuman beings." Thus "religion" need not contain a sense of gods or spirits. The make-or-break feature of religion, for Schilbrack, is the presence of a "superempirical character of reality." This definition has the advantage of covering nontheist (even atheist) systems, such as Theravada Buddhism and Confucianism, under the umbrella of religion, even if Christianity remains an archetypal—or, dare we say, canonical—example.[75] His notions also recall the legal philosopher Ronald Dworkin's sense of religion as reflecting a sense of "cosmic mystery" (meaning awe toward and respect for the world's wonders) as well as a commitment to the objectivity of value (that human life and nature have intrinsic worth), neither of which necessarily requires belief in God.[76]

In 2010, the sociologist Martin Riesebrodt advanced another compelling theory of religion in his book *The Promise of Salvation*. Standing at the heart of religion, Riesebrodt argued, are "liturgies," established interventionist practices leading to "meaningful action," whereby people try to avert, mitigate, and live with circumstances over which humans lack control.[77] If living with religion happens through liturgies, as Riesebrodt suggests, then another sociologist of religion, Meredith McGuire, argues that these are likely to be neither collective nor fixed but, instead, personal, even idiosyncratic.[78] "Lived religion," as she calls it, entails individual, highly variable practices and understandings.[79] McGuire's ideas are especially useful in the context of debates over religious freedom because they help to make sense of religion's microenvironments or, to think about it another way, the religion of real people and not abstract collectives.

Just as defining religion can lead scholars into a thicket, so can defining spirits, the spiritual, and spirituality. In 2018, the Pew Research Center declared that, for the purposes of a report it conducted on religion in Western Europe, spirituality referred to "beliefs or feelings about supernatural phenomena, such as life after death, the existence of a soul apart from the human body, and the presence of spiritual energy in physical things such as mountains, trees or crystals." It used this definition to devise categories with which it asked people to identify in polls: "both religious and spiritual," "religious but not spiritual," "spiritual but not religious," and so on.[80] Another Pew survey, this time of the United States, devised a more complex typology by classifying Americans as "God-and-Country Believers," "Diversely Devout," "Spiritually Awake," "Solidly Secular," and more—and then by explaining each descriptor.[81] The dizzying array of labels across these studies points to the challenge of capturing religious identities and sentiments.

Roadmap

Where do these arguments about the nature of religion and religious freedom ultimately take us? Not to a rejection of the concepts but to an awareness of how hard it is to pin down terms and reach conclusions as particular cases and controversies arise. They return us to an argument we advanced at the outset: that promoting and ideally achieving social justice amid religious freedom claims has been and will remain a hard task. It will require grappling with diverse, conflicting, and perhaps irreconcilable claims; appreciating when and why some claims prevail while others fail to persuade; and accounting for changing cultural values and political circumstances. It will mean navigating the changing, bumpy terrain of religious freedom.

The ten essays that follow illustrate the scope of these challenges. They reflect the diverse methods and disciplinary foundations of the contributors, who approach their subjects from political science, philosophy and theology, law and advocacy, history, sociology, and religious studies. While the volume as a whole asserts no singular definitions of religion and religious freedom, readers will see that individual contributors may be advancing their own conceptions of what religion and religious freedom entail. As we suggested at the outset of this chapter, grappling with religious freedom makes its political engagement unavoidable.

The essays fall into three parts. Part I, "Ethical Arguments," advances religious freedom as a right in theory and practice. Approaching the subject as a political scientist, Daniel Philpott sets out to defend religious freedom as a universal principle and distinct human right. He responds to a trend that worries him: the refusal or inability of some influential academics to recognize religious freedom as, what U.S. Supreme Court Justice Robert Jackson called it in 1943, a "fixed star" in the "constitutional constellation" of the United States and, by extension, of the international landscape with regard to human rights. Philpott mounts a defense of religious freedom in philosophical terms, "as a universal principle, accessed through reason alone, grounded in human nature and human dignity."

Drawing on his background as a philosopher, historian, and theologian, Heiner Bielefeldt examines "freedom of religion or belief," or FoRB, as a principle of universal validity upheld in Article 18 of the United Nations Universal Declaration of Human Rights (UDHR) of 1948 and, in a more elaborate form, in the International Covenant on Civil and Political Rights (ICCPR) of 1966. Bielefeldt defines FoRB and affirms its viability, all the while acknowledging that it has been and continues to be a universal right in the making, a work-in-progress with imperfect application so far.

Part II, "The Social Contingency of Religious Freedom Disputes," offers five case studies illustrating the historically and socially contingent nature—and messy character—of religious freedom disputes.

Jolyon Thomas examines the history of U.S. involvement in the Territory of Hawaii and post-World War II Japan, especially vis-à-vis Buddhists, to argue that "the U.S. promotion of religious freedom, both on the continent and beyond . . . consistently happened under the aegis of American empire and with the aid of the country's military might." Religious freedom was not an abstract legal principle, he continues, but a project and set of claims on the part of U.S. authorities who attempted to "secure material resources, moral authority, and political advantage" in Hawaii and Japan. Thomas uses a meteorological metaphor in his essay, citing "microclimates" of religious freedom to suggest how "religious freedom discourse [was] constantly shifting, inevitably determined by local circumstances, and simultaneously subject to macro-level forces."

Sociologist Lori Beaman examines legal disputes from Germany, Canada, and the United States where, as she puts it, "religion is transformed into culture" in ways that affirm the power of dominant groups. She cites, for example, a dispute in Quebec City that arose over the display of crucifixes in a government-funded hospital that had been founded by Catholic nuns. Critics argued that the crucifixes had no place in this public institution because they privileged Christian religion; defenders insisted that the crosses should stay as cultural symbols and statements of Quebecois heritage. Beaman contends that the "de facto establishment" of religion, which she detects in cases like this one, privileges dominant groups in heterogeneous societies while undergirding tiers of belonging.

Leigh Schmidt questions the history of "irreligious freedom" by considering the experiences of outspoken atheists in the mid-twentieth-century United

States, such as members of one family, the De Young family, as they moved from Delaware and Minnesota to Iowa, Texas, and Kansas in search of stability and social acceptance. Schmidt follows the "potholed" route to freedom that American nonbelievers like the De Youngs had to travel, despite legal protections that the U.S. Supreme Court upheld, and concludes that commitments to religious freedom in the United States have left those who reject religion at a disadvantage. School buses and workplaces—not only courtrooms—figure in his study as the battlegrounds for freedom. Schmidt's study casts light on the role of small-scale and low-grade persecution, in the form of bullying or harassment, that can make the violation of religious freedom a chronic, almost ordinary affair.

Cassie Adcock draws attention to the history of postcolonial India. She assesses how popular attitudes, customs, and state policies inhibiting the slaughter of cows and the sale and consumption of beef are or have been a "religious" question associated with Hindu majoritarian dominance and the accommodation or exclusion of non-Hindus. At the same time, Adcock shows how cow protection debates often have arisen in scientific and public policy forums relating to animal husbandry and agriculture. "In the case of cow protection," she concludes, "religious freedom and secular agriculture are not discrete alternatives, they are two sides of the same coin." Debates over cow protection have had profound consequences for Indian politics by reifying sectarianism while feeding into a culture of Hindu nationalism and chauvinism that often has targeted Muslims. These debates also show how controversies over religion and religious freedom can become entangled in ostensibly secular discussions about agriculture and science more broadly.

In the last essay of Part II, William Schultz turns to the issue of commerce by considering "the long American tradition" of conducting debates over religious freedom in the language of consumer protection by means of "religious muckraking" designed to expose fraudsters. He studies the "I AM" movement, founded by an American couple in the 1920s, which promoted a message of positive thinking, self-help, and spiritual awareness. In the 1930s, the I AM movement claimed some one million followers, many of whom bought inspirational books, phonograph recordings, and other paraphernalia. The fact that its leaders sold these items by mail for profit prompted the U.S. Postal Service to press charges of racketeering against them. What counts as a valid religion, as opposed to a cult or a fraud? And who has the power to say? The case of the now largely forgotten I AM movement raises these big questions about religious validity.

Part III, "The (Mis)application of Religious Freedom," includes three essays that grapple with ongoing legal debates and culture wars within the United States. Referring to specific cases, the authors question the validity of claims to religion and religious freedom that have made their way to the courts.

This part begins with an essay by Randall Balmer, who studies how "religious freedom has been construed, misconstrued, and weaponized by [American] evangelical leaders since the late 1970s." Balmer challenges what he calls the self-mythologizing of the Religious Right as a force in American lobbying and electoral politics. Far from having arisen, as its supporters eventually claimed, in response to the case of *Roe v. Wade* that legalized abortion, the Religious Right grew in the crucible of racial politics and white supremacy. The legal case more centrally involved in the Religious Right's origins was another U.S. Supreme Court case from 1970, *Green v. Kennedy*, which rejected the tax-exempt status of institutions that evaded desegregation. Just as the U.S. Postal Service emerged as a protagonist in Schultz's study of the "I AM" movement, so here an unlikely public entity—the Internal Revenue Service (IRS), the tax-collecting bureau of the U.S. government—challenged Bob Jones University, an evangelical institution that excluded black students and forbade interracial dating. Balmer's study suggests, finally, how claims to religious values and ethics may obscure social antipathies such as those, in this case, that grew out of racism.

In her essay, Kristina Arriaga negotiates the line where the protection and the violation of religion, human rights, and women's rights collide. She does so by examining a legal dispute in Michigan involving a doctor who allegedly performed genital cutting on as many as one hundred girls over the course of twelve years, at the request of the girls' parents. The doctor belonged to the Bohra Ismaili community, most of whom trace South Asian origins, and who practice a religion that historically developed from an offshoot of Shi'i Islam. The doctor, and some of her supporters, defended the practice of excising part of girls' clitorises on the grounds of religious freedom. Claiming that the practice was a religious tradition akin to male circumcision and associated with bodily cleanliness, supporters of the practice also defended it as helping to ensure female sexual propriety. Arriaga rejects these claims. She calls the practice "a form of violence against women," not equivalent to male circumcision, which has "no medical benefits" but instead aims "to control women's sexual conduct" by reducing their capacity for sexual sensation. Even if courts accept that a practice is religious, she argues further, a religious freedom claim or exemption need not come into play. That is because "in U.S. jurisprudence it is clear that if the state has a compelling interest, such as protecting children from harm, the state can take measures to reject a religious freedom claim." Drawing on her own experience as an advocate in cases bearing on religious freedom in the United States, and convinced that this case may set precedents that reverberate onto the international stage, Arriaga argues that female genital cutting should not qualify as a religious practice that warrants protection.

Joshua Matz, a practicing lawyer, concludes the volume by examining three recent Supreme Court cases in the United States. In addition to *Masterpiece Cakeshop v. Colorado Civil Rights Commission* (2018), which was discussed earlier in this chapter, he considers *Trump v. Hawaii* (2017) (for which he filed an amicus brief) and *Dunn v. Ray* (2019). *Trump v. Hawaii* challenged the order of President Donald Trump, blocking travel into the United States of people from several Muslim-majority countries, on the grounds that the order expressed a religious animus against Muslims. *Dunn v. Ray* involved a Muslim man on death row who wanted an imam, not the Christian chaplain that the state of Alabama exclusively authorized, to be at his side as state authorities executed him by lethal injection. In the Cake Case, recall, the court recognized an element of religious animus against an evangelical Christian baker. In the other two cases, however, the court rejected similar findings of bias against Muslims. "These decisions," Matz concludes, "all recognized the principle that government may not act on the basis of anti-religious animus." And yet, in these decisions "the court applied the principle inconsistently." Matz expresses concerns about the potential for religious freedom claims and associated legal judgments to be partisan and inconsistent and to discriminate against religious minorities. He worries, in particular, that the Cake Case may amount to "merely the first step in a larger constitutional agenda to authorize discrimination throughout American life, so long as it is based on religious belief." His essay recalls arguments that Beaman and Adcock raise in their essays about the power of religious majorities to make demands and claim greater privileges. At the same time, Matz offers a rejoinder to the essays by Philpott and Bielefeldt by pointing to religious freedom's parochial, not universal, dimensions in practice.

Conclusion: Lessons and Takeaways

The authors of most recent studies of religious freedom seem split between skeptics and believers; there does not seem to be much middle ground. If some view religious freedom as a posture, an agenda, or a myth, others see it as an incontrovertible human right, a sphere deserving special protection. This book tries to clear ground for discussion between the two camps by gathering essays that grapple with thorny debates and by acknowledging divergent positions.

Part of what makes religious freedom so difficult to grasp and achieve is that religion itself is so murky. What is religion, and what isn't it? A matter of faith, belief, and inner conviction? A set of practices? A declaration of communal belonging? A connection to place—whether a piece of land, body of water, or site of veneration? Then, too, there is the question of how religion relates to God, gods, or no gods; to intermediaries like angels, bodhisattvas, and bear spirits; perhaps to objects like relics and crystals. Several commentators have noted the tendency in the United States, for example, to project normative Protestant Christian understandings of religion in ways that push other understandings aside. Disagreements and uncertainties about the nature, content, and practice of religion, quite simply, complicate efforts to wrangle with religious freedom.

Nonbelievers and "nones"—people who lack formal community allegiances—complicate discussions of religious freedom. One can belong to no church, for example, and still pray to Jesus; one can avoid eating pork, out of respect for the Jewish culture of one's forebears, and yet reject the Jewish concept of God. All of these possibilities add subtlety and ambiguity to debates over what it means to have a religion, and to be religious, or not. They also make it harder to know how best to respect religion while also not subordinating the interests and concerns of the irreligious.

The impossible part of religious freedom may be the prospect of satisfying everyone. "Your rights stop at the tip of my nose," a common expression goes; but what does that mean in practice? Balancing the claims of individuals, especially when they want exemptions (not baking a cake for gay people, for example, or not vaccinating a child), is hard to achieve when those claims collide with collective interests, run counter to public policies, or challenge the majority's assumptions about how things should work. Religious freedom is a juggling act made more complicated when the objects being tossed keep changing.

The law looms large in discussions of religious freedom, but it has limits in how much it can do. Laws cannot cover or anticipate all situations. They often fail to make the stretch from the courts to, say, the school bus or classroom—especially when no sympathetic authorities are there to stand watch. Changing laws is one thing, but changing attitudes is another. The French historian

Michel Winock appreciates this difference in explaining the persistence of anti-Semitism in modern France, reasoning that "discrimination [against Jews] disappeared from the law, but not from mentalities" in the century that followed the French Revolution.[82] We can detect a similar disjuncture between changed laws and persistent attitudes by examining, say, the history of atheists in the United States, or the history of Christian, Jewish, and other non-Muslim minorities, such as Yezidis, in Iraq.[83] For this reason, scholars should be careful not to privilege studies of law too much in the sphere of religious freedom: the law (or laws) can be abstractions. Seen in isolation, the existence of laws can mislead observers who want to understand how things are really working on the ground.

Religious freedom can mean different things depending on the subject to which it applies. For a person or group of people, it can refer to rights to practice, profess, or think in particular ways—to declare oneself a convert to Baha'ism, for example, or to insist on wearing the turban as a mark of one's Sikh-ness. For a society, religious freedom can refer to a climate of acceptance of, or hostility toward, diversity. For a corporation, it can mean the right to pursue certain policies (not to fund a form of birth control, for example). For a river, it can mean a recognition of sacred status and a consequent right to its freedom from mistreatment by humans.

When we focus only on humans, we should be clear when we make assumptions based on factors like age and gender. Many laws and customs work on the assumption that adults are the true bearers of religious liberties: what grown-ups want, they can impose on their children. It is not surprising, therefore, that recent disputes invoking religious freedom have often involved tensions between the relative power of "majors" and "minors." Likewise, in numerous countries in the world, laws bearing on religion privilege men over women, for example by recognizing only men as holders of clerical power (as priests, rabbis, imams, and so on) who have the authority to decide on matters of family law. In effect, such laws allow religious organizations to discriminate.[84] In some countries, laws only give either fathers or mothers (but not both) the right to pass on their religions, at least in the eyes of the state.

When we started the program that gave rise to this volume, we grappled with a question that placed the United States front and center: How exceptional has the United States been, meaning either exemplary in its own record of religious freedom or merely distinctive relative to the rest of the world? In response to this question, we can advance some conclusions as well.

The United States has been exceptional in the degree of its preoccupation with religious freedom. We can trace this keen interest to the longer history of European settlement by diverse and often nonconformist Christian sects, going back to 1620 when the Pilgrims disembarked from the *Mayflower*. Key thinkers in U.S. history reflected deeply on the issue, including James Madison, who witnessed the persecution of Baptists by Anglicans (Episcopalians) in Virginia,[85] and Thomas Jefferson, who contemplated the separation of church and state. In the twentieth century, U.S. courts waded into debates about the "establishment of religion." The legal record attests to their efforts. Decisions ranging from *West Virginia State Board of Education v. Barnette* and *Lyng v. Northwest Indian Cemetery Protective Association* to *Masterpiece Cakeshop v. Colorado Civil Rights Commission* have responded to cultural debates over the place of religion in U.S. public life. Finally, in the late twentieth century, at a time when immigration was making the U.S. religious landscape increasingly diverse (expanding the number, for example, of Hindus, Buddhists, and Muslims),[86] legislators professed their commitment by framing acts, commonly known by acronyms such as IRFA, AIRFA, and RFRA, to enshrine or promote religious freedoms. These acts inspired state-level analogs across the country from Alaska to Florida.

And yet, while the U.S. government and the American people may have been exceptional in their preoccupation with religious freedom, the United States has not always been exemplary in its record of accommodating dissenters and minority groups. We can look to Philadelphia, the City of Brotherly Love and the hometown of the Andrea Mitchell Center, for illustrative examples. On the one hand, William Penn, who founded the city, welcomed people of various sectarian and religious persuasions. Eighteenth-century Philadelphia became home to a Sephardic Jewish synagogue and a Roman Catholic church, both still flourishing, located little more than a stone's throw from what later became known as Independence Hall. On the other hand, in the nineteenth century, as waves of Irish immigrants flooded into the United States (many of them escaping famine), Philadelphia became home to a Protestant "crusade" movement that opposed the growth of Catholic communities.[87] In 1844, in a part of the city that was a quick walk away from where the University of Pennsylvania then had its campus, Protestant agitators rioted against Irish Catholics and targeted the church buildings where they worshipped; scores of people died. The fact that rioters spared two nearby *German* Catholic churches points to the ethnic dimensions of this conflict.[88] Anti-Catholic protest in the United States did not end with these events. As late as 1927, further to the northeast, in Queens, New York, the Ku Klux Klan led an anti-Catholic parade, which, again, largely targeted Irish people.[89] These cases show how anxieties over immigration—blending nativism, xenophobia, and anxieties about competition for jobs—mixed religion into the brew. By pointing to the history of intra-Christian or Christian sectarian conflict in the United States, these cases also remind us of the need to approach history with nuance, and to question the nature and even existence of religious "majorities."

Religious freedom is not a final achievement. Religious freedom is not even a concrete or tangible "thing." Religious freedom is, instead, an idea, a process, and an aspiration. Thinking internationally, the theologian, philosopher, and human rights advocate Heiner Bielefeldt—a contributor to this volume—describes it as a set of options among which people can choose.[90] Religious freedom, he adds, like religious identity for an individual, always amounts to a work in progress. Another of the volume's contributors, Jolyon Thomas, who approaches his subject as a specialist in Japanese religion and cultural history, describes religious freedom as a set of arguments that are "born in moments of conflict and compromise." Approaching the subject from the perspective of law, Douglas Laycock observes, in a similar vein, that "religious liberty is not needed when no one disagrees."[91] Debates over religious freedom are never a done deal. As Thomas remarks, "We invent them over and over again."

In the autobiography that he wrote toward the end of his life, Thomas Jefferson reflected proudly on the Virginia Statute for Religious Freedom of 1786, which he had drafted. The statute, he observed, was "meant to comprehend, within the mantle of its protection, the Jew and the Gentile, the Christian and Mahometan, the Hindoo, and Infidel of every denomination."[92] Jefferson's universality remains inspiring for our day, and sets a high standard to follow in its inclusive vision of what religious freedom can mean.

PART I

Ethical Arguments

CHAPTER 1

A Right of Its Own

A Case for the Human Right of Religious Freedom

Daniel Philpott

Religious freedom is one of the most widely violated human rights in the world. Since 2009, the Pew Research Center has reported consistently that about three-quarters of the world's population lives under a regime that heavily violates religious freedom.[1] In recent years, the Chinese government has cracked down on the practice of religion with an intensity not seen since the Cultural Revolution of 1966–79, interning a million or more Uighur Muslims, destroying and disbanding Christian churches, and even removing children from worship services. Hundreds of thousands of Rohingya Muslims in Burma have suffered violence and heavy discrimination at the hands of a Buddhist nationalist state and Buddhist armed militant groups. Governments in several Muslim-majority countries have restricted heavily and even outlawed sects that they consider heretical, including Ahmadis in Pakistan and Indonesia and Baha'is in Iran. The scope of religious freedom is increasingly restricted in Western Europe and North America, as well; though the curtailment is not nearly as harsh, the sources of the restriction are ideologically diverse, the issue is openly contested, and the contestation is ongoing and its outcome uncertain. Anti-Semitism is on the rise; Muslims have come to face increasing restrictions on dress, immigration, and the construction of mosques; and Christians have faced challenges to their liberty to conduct commerce, education, and civil society services like hospitals and orphanages compatibly with traditional norms of marriage and sexuality.[2]

Against this vector of restriction stands the wide consensus of countries and institutions that espouse religious freedom as a fundamental civil and human right. Among the world's liberal democracies, religious freedom has been for decades an element of the "standard package" of rights and privileges that are said to characterize just institutions. No country considers religious freedom more foundational and integral to its liberal democratic vision than the United States. Justice Robert Jackson opined in 1943 that "if there is any fixed star in our constitutional constellation, it is that no official, high or petty, can prescribe what shall be orthodox in politics, nationalism, religion, or other matters of opinion or force citizens to confess by word or act their faith therein."[3] An American narrative of religious freedom accords great weight to the principle's articulation in the First Amendment to the Constitution and proceeds with a litany of communities who were persecuted and rejected elsewhere but found a home in the United States: Mennonites, Mormons, Muslims, Baptists, Jews, Huguenots, Catholics, Jehovah's Witnesses, Amish, Quakers, Seventh Day Adventists, Scientologists, and atheists. In the 1990s, the United States Congress demonstrated and advanced this consensus by passing two bills with overwhelming bipartisan majorities: The Religious Freedom Restoration Act of 1993, which protected the conscience rights of religious people, and the International Religious Freedom Act of 1998, which mandated the promotion of religious freedom in American foreign policy.

Religious freedom is also ensconced in international law. It is articulated in Article 18 of both the Universal Declaration of Human Rights (UDHR) and the International Covenant on Civil and Political Rights (ICCPR), and even more thoroughly in the Declaration on the Elimination of All Forms of Intolerance and Discrimination Based on Religion or Belief of 1981. Europe, too, has taken up the cause. Several European countries and the European Union have followed the United States in incorporating religious freedom into their foreign policies in the past decade and a half.

Yet, despite this momentum, recent years have also seen the consensus on religious freedom within the West weakening. A bevy of voices, including prominent intellectuals, has been calling the principle into question, so much so that Justice Jackson's "fixed star" now risks becoming a battleground in a culture war. Heather Sharkey and Jeffrey Green render this battleground the central theme of their introductory essay for this volume and it frames the essay at hand. "The terrain of religious freedom," they observe, is "rocky ground" and has seen "impassioned stances on how to understand religious freedom" among scholars in the last fifteen years. Yes, the principle is in the

U.S. Constitution, some ask, but why? On what basis does religious freedom deserve a right of its own, warranting special recognition among other human rights?[4] Others ask whether religion is even a coherent enough phenomenon to be applied in law. They do not believe it is a genus of which there are species, or a stable, definable concept.[5] Still others—such as the writers known as the New Atheists—consider religion to be pernicious, an irrational atavism that inevitably begets instability and violence.[6] Another set of critics casts these doubts internationally and asserts that religious freedom is a product of Western modernity and should not be prescribed for non-Westerners who think differently about religion and its place in society, particularly Muslims living in Muslim-majority states, who are most often the object of Western scorn.[7]

Contestation begets innovation, and so the times call for a new defense of religious freedom. What is critically needed, I believe, is a fresh argument for religious freedom as a universal human right, not only in the positive, legal sense—that is, stipulated by conventions, constitutions, and courts—but also in the moral, pre-political sense—that is, as a natural right. Indeed, today's critics contend that it is precisely the lack of a universal grounding for religious freedom that casts doubt about the principle's place in law, whether it be international conventions or the constitutions of countries. Many of the major defenses of religious freedom available today argue from the premises of a faith tradition, which can help to establish the principle among members but will do little to forge consensus internationally or in pluralistic domestic settings.[8] Much reasoning about religious freedom also takes place within constitutional traditions—a large literature accompanies the U.S. Constitution—but such reasoning assumes the framework of the constitution in question. Here, by contrast, I seek to sketch the outlines of a defense of religious freedom as a universal principle, accessed through reason alone, grounded in human nature and human dignity.

What one may worry is an excessively large ambition is in fact bounded by clarity about what this inquiry is not. To assert that religious freedom is a human right and that its violation is globally widespread is not to deny that these violations, as well as conflicts over religion, are intertwined with ethnicity, demography, race, economics, the legacy of colonialism, nonreligious political pursuits, and other factors. Cassie Adcock's essay on the controversy over cow protection in India; Sharkey and Green's discussion in their introductory essay of Uighur Muslims; and discussions elsewhere of conflicts involving Rohingya Muslims in Burma, Fulani herdsmen in Nigeria, and other groups in other sites testify to this enmeshment. Such accounts are broadly sociological or anthropological and thus contrast with the argument at hand, which is focused on and limited to a question of practical reason: Why ought we respect the religious freedom of every person?

Nor will an assertion of a human right of religious freedom resolve, or come close to resolving, conflicts between religious freedom and other goods and principles, and even sometimes conflicts between claims of religious practice, such as Adcock's essay details. Such conflicts are real, are often difficult to resolve, and are the stuff of case law in the tradition of the U.S. Constitution, the laws of many other countries, the European Union, and international law. Several essays in this volume revolve around such conflicts and differ from the present inquiry, the question of whether there is a core universal human right to religious freedom that has prima facie status in legal conflicts but which nobody has asserted is absolute.

If this essay does not directly engage in these other analyses, though, it has implications for them. If religion is believed to be a basic human phenomenon and a subject of human rights, it will have far more weight in both kinds of inquiry. Assessments of religion's relative role in a conflict will be less likely to conclude that religion is illusory, epiphenomenal, or peripheral, even while its role in any particular conflict remains an open empirical question. Legal reasoning will favor religion far more in balancing it against other goods and principles if this reasoning does not presuppose that religion is indistinguishable from generalized conscience and speech rights or that the meaning of religious freedom is impossible to know. The question here remains narrower: Are there grounds for religious freedom as a universal human right?

Religion: Something for Everyone

I contend that religious freedom is indeed a distinct human right, just as it is articulated in international law (often in juxtaposition with thought, conscience, and belief) and in the constitutions of about 90 percent of the world's sovereign states.[9] I argue further that the basis of the human right of religious freedom is human dignity and thus follow the lead of the preamble of the Universal Declaration of Human Rights, which begins with a "recognition of the inherent dignity . . . of all members of the human family."[10]

Dignity alone, though, does not ground the specific rights found in the international conventions, except, perhaps, the right to life. On what basis do all human beings have rights to work, education, free speech and expression, ownership of property, assembly, health care, and the like? I shall argue further that human beings possess worth not only *simpliciter* but also with respect to certain basic goods through which they flourish. To violate a basic good is to violate a dimension of a person's dignity. Thus, human beings have rights to these goods. For instance, to deny a person her right to speech or education would deny her the ability to grow in knowledge, a fundamental way in which her worth is realized. Can religious freedom also be tied to human dignity, and thus, human rights, in this way? If so, then we would say that the human right of religious freedom protects a human good, one that instantiates human flourishing. But what is that good? Religion, I propose.

A problem arises. Many scholars are convinced that there is no coherent, universal entity called religion that is practiced by human beings as such. There are different versions of this skepticism. Some point out that definitions of religion exclude cases of what most people regard as a religion. For instance, if religion is defined in terms of worshipping God, then certain versions of Buddhism, Hinduism, and Shamanism, for instance, would be excluded. Others discover the opposite problem: Definitions of religion end up being too wide, applicable to so many phenomena that the concept loses coherence and tractability. If religion is defined in terms of the sacred, the luminous, or the spiritual, then it would have to include ardent nationalism, fervent environmentalism, fanatical devotion to Marxist revolution, and attending a Guns N' Roses concert. "Some people dilute [religion] to the point of futility," observes Martin Riesebrodt, the late scholar of religious studies at the University of Chicago, "considering barbecues with guitar music, soccer games, shopping in supermarkets, or art exhibitions to be religious phenomena."[11]

Some scholars hold that religion as a general concept arose in Western modernity, especially through the influence of the Protestant Reformation, the Enlightenment, colonialism, and Christian missions. On this reasoning, religion, far from being universal, is a product of a certain time, a particular context, and, most of all, the interests of the powerful.[12] Still others are skeptical that there is a robust concept of religion just because they believe that religion is senseless. Earlier, I mentioned the New Atheists, who follow in a tradition of Enlightenment thought that views religion as the product of premodern superstition that will eventually melt under the light and heat of science, democracy, free thought, economic and technological progress, education, and historical criticism. For thinkers like Karl Marx, Friedrich Nietzsche, and Sigmund Freud, religion is an alien force that distorts and confines true human interests: an oppressive superstructure, a slave mentality, an illusion.

Yet, some scholars persist in viewing religion as universal.[13] One is Riesebrodt, who, in his 2010 book, *The Promise of Salvation*, developed a way of defining and understanding religion that arguably avoids the typical pitfalls of other conceptions and identifies the core of what religions are about.[14] Riesebrodt's approach is ingeniously simple. Innovatively, he focuses on what ordinary people do when they practice religion and on why they do it and what they expect to get out of it. Whereas, in recent decades, scholars have approached religion as a system of beliefs, an expression of ultimate meaning, or the realm of the sacred, and have run into problems of excessive inclusion or exclusion, Riesebrodt's stress on practices holds promise for zeroing in not only on what is distinct about religion but also on how its practitioners themselves understand it. Sociologist Christian Smith, a prolific scholar of religion, was captivated by Riesebrodt's approach and sought to develop and refine it further in combination with some of his own commitments.[15]

Here is Smith's definition of religion, inspired by Riesebrodt: "Religion is a complex of culturally prescribed practices, based on premises about the existence and nature of superhuman powers, whether personal or impersonal, which seek to help practitioners gain access to and communicate or align themselves with these powers, in hope of realizing human goods and avoiding things bad."[16] The noun that defines religion here is *practices*, which Smith defines in turn as "culturally meaningful behaviors that are intentionally repeated over time."[17] They include prayer, burning incense, reading sacred texts, consulting oracles, repeating incantations, and scores of other behaviors that are enacted, repeated, endowed with meaning, and prescribed by a community that exists over time.[18] The distinguishing feature of these practices—what Smith calls the "pivotal idea" in the definition—is their orientation toward superhuman powers. Religions center on entities that their members believe are neither fashioned by humans, either individually or collectively, nor dependent on humans, yet can "make things [in which humans have a strong interest] happen or prevent them from happening." Smith is careful to say (following Riesebrodt) that superhuman is not necessarily supernatural. Religion may, but does not necessarily, involve "God, gods, spirits, higher beings, holy, numinous, ultimate concern, and sacred," but rather may locate its powers in nature or other energies and dynamisms. Smith offers the example of dharmic religions, such as Hinduism, Buddhism, Sikhism, and Jainism, as ones that feature impersonal powers—for instance, Hinduism's Brahman, which is the creator of all that exists but lacks personhood.[19] All religions, though, also contain premises about superhuman powers, beliefs that range from implicit, presupposed meanings to elaborate and explicit statements of doctrine. Smith's inclusion of beliefs is important. In contrast to other scholars of religion, Smith does not make beliefs the central focus of religion, yet, in contrast to still others, he does not contend that beliefs are unique to certain religions like Protestant Christianity. Beliefs, Smith argues, are inescapably a part of religion but also inevitably intertwined with practices.[20]

Through practices in which humans align themselves with superhuman powers, they gain benefits—blessings, goods, rewards—and avoid evils—ills, curses, punishments. The benefits and avoidances of evil may be everyday matters like success on an academic examination, a sunny day, or help in living virtuously; or larger, life-defining matters like healing from a terminal illness, avoiding financial ruin, or the flourishing of one's children; or important spiritual matters like redemption from one's past sins, enlightenment, nirvana, happiness, entering heaven, or union with God. There is nothing esoteric about these benefits. The benefits the religion delivers and the evils that it avoids are the kind that concern everyone.

This definition of religion is the sort that a sociologist or an anthropologist would propound in an effort to describe human beings and their social world soundly. It does not describe in depth the beliefs and practices of any one religion. Nor is it the work of a theologian. It says nothing about whether religion is good or valuable for human beings or whether the beliefs of all, some, or one religion are true or truer than the rest. It says nothing about whether superhuman powers of any sort—God, gods, spirits, energy centers—really exist. If Smith is correct, though, that his (and Riesebrodt's) definition is "fully adequate"—properly inclusive, properly exclusive—then it succeeds in identifying a distinct human activity in a general, universal way, the first step in arguing for a human right of religious freedom.

Glosses

Several glosses on this definition clarify and deepen it. First, the ability of this definition to distinguish religion from other phenomena that can sometimes look like a religion—taking on sacred qualities or inspiring life-giving devotion—can be accentuated. Nationalism, Marxism, environmentalism, a person's work ethic, devotion to sports and other phenomena can be adhered to "religiously"—that is, they can share in certain qualities of religion—but none of these meet the present definition of religion. Consider nationalism, for instance, an ideology that champions the political program of a nation, which a wide consensus of theorists agree is a collection of people who live on a common plot of land; share a language, culture, and history; and aspire to govern themselves, often in the form of an independent state.[21] In contrast to religion, nationalism requires no practices through which the members of a nation relate to superhuman powers; rather, it is a set of commitments that the members of a nation share regarding who belongs in what territory, under what political regime, and on what terms. True, nationalism may come to look like a religion when the members of a nation treat the nation as an object of worship and national leaders as possessors of superhuman powers.[22] Worship and deification, though, are not intrinsic to nationalism. They are not a part of its definition and are absent in the actual practice of millions of people who manifest patriotism, or "civic nationalism," characterized by a commitment to the nation that is real but relative, sincere but circumscribed. For many people, nationalism is conditioned by religious faith; those people follow their nation only to the extent that their religious commitments will allow.

That nationalism and religion are different phenomena is also evidenced by the distinction between forms of nationalism that combine with religion—Hindu nationalism in India, Buddhist nationalism in Sri Lanka—and those that do not and may even take a decidedly secular form, for instance, that of the Jacobins who led the French Revolution or of Kemal Ataturk, the founder of the Republic of Turkey. The phenomenon of "religious nationalism," the subject of several important scholarly analyses, is only intelligible if there is also an unreligious form of nationalism.[23] The adjective and the noun denote different entities and do not necessarily coexist.

The logic runs much the same for Marxism, environmentalism, and the like. According to Smith's definition (derived from Riesebrodt), Marxism is not religion since it holds that only the material world is real and that religion is an illusory projection. Like nationalists, of course, Marxists can invest their leaders with god-like status—recall the enormous posters of Vladimir Lenin and Mao Zedong—but this investment is not intrinsic to the ideological doctrine.

Not only does Smith's definition render religion distinct from other phenomena that sometimes resemble it, but also, as Riesebrodt points out, members of most religions have themselves understood their religion to be distinct from other spheres of life—economic, cultural, political, familial, and recreational.[24] This is not to say that religion is sealed off from these other spheres. Religious people will say that their faith governs what they do in the marketplace, in the political realm, in the workplace, in all that they do. If religion interpenetrates other realms, though, it is still distinct from them.

The second gloss is this: Other characteristics of religions that are not part of Smith's definition help to fill out the picture of why people practice religions. I am persuaded that Smith's definition is adequate. Although these other features do not define religion, they add content to what religion is and typically does. Religion provides answers to what may be called "the grand questions of life." Where do we come from? Where did the universe come from? What is the basis of our moral convictions? Why do we suffer? Is there help for us in our suffering? What happens to us after death?[25] Smith does not include answers to these questions in his definition of religion because he says that people also practice religion to gain help in everyday matters.[26] But if such answers are not all that religion provides, they are still central to what people across an extraordinary diversity of times and places have sought in religion and what they have hoped superhuman powers will provide.

Other characteristics of religion deserve mention. Riesebrodt places a central emphasis on worship, or the liturgies through which people seek direct access to superhuman powers.[27] Worship does not add to Smith's definition; it is a practice of the kind he describes. It is an especially important practice, though, because of its direct and intentional focus on superhuman powers. Most religions contain a caste of clerics, a corps of people whose vocation is to help others establish relationship with superhuman powers. Religions embody a community, a cohesive group of people who practice the rituals together and orient their lives around them. Important, also, is a moral code that is associated closely with the superhuman power. Not every religion that fits Smith's definition contains all of these characteristics, but most contain most of them.

A third gloss, one that buttresses Smith's argument, is that people and peoples across an astonishingly diverse array of cultures, geographic locales, and historical epochs have practiced religion that fits Smith's definition.[28] Smith argues that the practice of religion can be found in every society. Vividly illustrating religion's extraordinary historical reach is the recent discovery of the Göbekli Tepe, an archaeological site in Turkey dating back to 9600 BCE, which some experts argue is a place for worship that predates agriculture.[29] The site suggests that religion is at the origin of human experience.

A fourth, related, gloss, also buttressing Smith's case, is that the concept of religion also has a long history among philosophers and theologians. Riesebrodt and Smith's view that religion is human and universal may be novel in the university today, but it is hardly new or exclusively modern. In the western tradition, the Roman philosopher Cicero; early Christian thinkers like Augustine, Lactantius, and Tertullian; and the medieval Christian philosopher Thomas Aquinas wrote of religion as a general human phenomenon—long before the modern world ever came to be.[30]

A fifth gloss is that most religions, both ancient and modern, have understood themselves to be one among several other religions—a general category, different forms of which other humans practice. This is clear in the cases of Judaism, Christianity, and Islam, the latter two of which explicitly differentiated themselves from their predecessor(s). Riesebrodt maintains that Buddhism, Jainism, Sikhism, Daoism, and Shintoism also contain writings by authors who conceived of their religion as one in a world also inhabited by other religions (though they did not use the word *religion*).[31] Of course, the ways in which religions have regarded and related to other religions have varied enormously, including through conquest, assimilation, friendship, dialogue, syncretism, and proselytism. The idea that religion is a genus of which there are species, though, is as old as religions themselves.

A sixth, and final, gloss: Religion does not seem to be disappearing or proving to be an atavism as predicted by proponents of the secularization thesis, who dominated the academy only a generation ago. During the twentieth century—when the secularization prediction reached its acme—the share of the world population adhering to Catholic and Protestant Christianity, Islam, and Hinduism jumped from 50 percent in 1900 to 64 percent in 2000. The World Values Survey finds that in the early 2000s, 79 percent of people surveyed in fifty countries across the globe reported belief in God, whereas 73 percent reported the same in the late 1980s and early 1990s.[32] Global poll numbers are admittedly rough and do not capture unusually unreligious regions like northwestern Europe or the recent rise of the "nones," or the religiously unaffiliated, in the United States.[33] A global and historical perspective, though, suggests far more strongly that religion is universal rather than that it is a primitive phenomenon in secular decline.

Religion Is Basically Good

To say that religion is a universal human experience, though, does not establish it as one that merits protection through a universal human right. A further step is needed—an argument that religion is a human good that manifests human dignity.

Aristotle taught that there are some goods that humans seek as instrumental to other ends and other goods that they seek for their own sake.[34] Money is almost always an instrumental good. Apart from coin collectors, people seek it as a means to what it can purchase. Goods sought for their own sake include knowledge, life, health, play, work, aesthetic appreciation, and friendship, among others. Some of these goods, like work or knowledge, can also be instrumental to other goods, but what is important is that they can be final ends. I follow the lead of philosophers who call them basic human goods.[35] While much more can be said about these goods and their place in moral reasoning than space allows, what is important here is that basic goods are fundamental constituents of human flourishing. By supplying humans with something of intrinsic benefit, they offer a basic reason for action. A basic good presupposes that humans are rational and that their acts are free and always oriented toward an end. Some goods are realized through the cooperative activity of two or more persons who act for its sake together. Friendship, for instance, can only be realized through cooperative activity. Knowledge can sometimes be realized through cooperative activity, as in a classroom.

Humans apprehend the basic goods through reflection on their practical experience. One looks at one's actions and asks, What am I doing? Why? To what end? The answers point to basic goods. The goods are not derived from logical demonstrations or from prior premises but rather are grasped through an act of the intellect. Goods are not the same as moral norms (do not lie, do not murder); rather, moral norms are derived from goods and call for respecting them.

I argue that religion as defined by Smith is a basic good.[36] Seeking right relationship with superhuman powers (shorthand for gaining access to, communicate with, and align with, to convey Smith's terms), which is the key end of religious practices, is a final end, one that humans seek for its own sake. A variety of experiences can serve as prompts that lead people to religion—an encounter with the beauty of religion as practiced by a person or a community, a grasp of the truth of a particular religion, an attraction to religion as an answer to suffering, a relatively unreflective continuation of one's upbringing, or a desire to support one's religious spouse. Once people do take up religion, though, orienting themselves toward superhuman power, they will usually find intrinsic fulfillment in religion, at least to some degree.

Again, basic goods are grasped through reflection on action and are not proved or derived. One of the best ways to confront skepticism of a basic good is to ask, If X is not a basic good, then to what is it instrumental? If it can be shown that a good is not plausibly instrumental to another good, then the case for its basic character will be strengthened. Some goods can be both instrumental and basic. Knowledge, again, can be instrumental to other purposes but also sought for its own sake. The case for a basic good depends on the possibility of its also being sought for its own sake.

It might seem that one aspect of Smith's definition risks rendering religion an instrumental good. Namely, he says that practices that elicit right relationship (communication, access, alignment) with superhuman powers are performed "in hope of realizing human goods and avoiding things bad." Is this not precisely instrumental? I think Smith is correct in incorporating the hope of receiving goods and of avoiding ills into his definition of religion. These hopes are essential to why people engage in religious practices. Undoubtedly there are people who engage in religious practices in order to gain benefits in the most crassly instrumental or transactional sense. Perhaps they think they can manipulate the superhuman powers—or simply the other members of the community—in order to elicit material prosperity. Even the more typically sincere religious person, though, anticipates manifold benefits from her practice of religion. As noted above, these range widely and might include the healing of a relative, success on an examination, friendship and community, peace with God, enlightenment, nirvana, and union with God. Is religion therefore only an instrumental good?

Such a conclusion, I contend, is a distortion of what religion is and does. To say that A is instrumental to B is to say that A and B are separate entities and that A is a means of achieving B. Do the practices through which a religious person seeks harmony with a superhuman power and the benefits that the person hopes to result from (or ills to be avoided through) this harmony match this description? In fact, authentic religion does not easily fit this picture of instrumentality. The benefits (and the avoidance of ills) are better seen as part and parcel of the practice of religion rather than effects that are produced by a cause. Earlier, I substituted the term "right relationship" as shorthand for Smith's three terms of "communication," "access," and "alignment." Relationship connotes something important about these terms, which is the two-way traffic that they describe between humans and the superhuman, in which humans petition, entreat, honor, and seek to please, and the superhuman supplies, bestows, and blesses. In this sense, religion is a common good shared not only among the members of the religious community but also between these members and the superhuman power. The benefits and the evils—asking for them, receiving them, being saved from them—I submit, are part and parcel of the relationship, which people conceive as an end in itself.

Helpful here is an analogy with another basic human good that is enacted in common, friendship, which is instantiated through a relationship between people mutually willing one another's good. This willing often involves the bestowing of benefits. One friend lends the other money, looks after his children when he is gone, offers advice, buys him a beer, and so on. Yet, at least if the friendship is a strong one, we would be missing the mark if we say that the friends view their relationship merely as a means to these goods. It is more accurate to say that they will these goods as an expression of their friendship. The same is true with the relationship between humans and the superhuman power that is religion. The practices through which humans seek to be right with a superhuman power and the reciprocal actions of that power together constitute a good that they value for its own sake. It is just because religion has this relational character that we may describe the crass instrumentalist as one who misunderstands and malpractices religion.

Corroborating my view of religion as a basic good, grasped by the intellect, pursued through the will, Smith cites a "surge of new scientific work on religion" in the last couple of decades showing that religion fulfills human capacities for perception, recognition, and explanation. "Because of the nature of ordinary minds, religious expression in beliefs and practice is nearly inevitable in most people," as one of the most prominent of these researchers, Justin Barrett, puts it. Barrett's own work shows that in the first five years of development, children typically come to believe that behind the visible world is an agent who is responsible for causing it. Children are even directed by their reason toward believing in a God who is invisible, omniscient, omnipotent, and immortal.[37]

As a human good, a basic aspect of human fulfillment, religion is a dimension of human dignity. Dignity can mean either intrinsic worth or excellence due to one's station. In the present argument, intrinsic worth is most immediately relevant. Human beings should not be violated because they have intrinsic worth. Their religion is a dimension of this intrinsic worth; to violate it is to violate their dignity. In a certain sense, though, excellence is important, too—not the excellence of this or that class of human beings but the excellence of all human beings by virtue of what sort of creature they are. Human beings are excellent because of their free will, their intelligence, their capacity for interpersonal love, and, I would argue, their resultant capacity for realizing basic goods, which are intrinsically valuable. Excellence is, in fact, closely tied to worth. Humans have worth because of their excellence.

A final point on the basic human good of religion: It is not diminished by the fact that some persons elect not to practice it, whether they are atheist, agnostic, or passively indifferent. The argument at hand makes no judgment of the validity of reasons for nonpractice. These persons may be unconvinced that superhuman powers really exist; they may find religion unjust or wrongly restrictive; or perhaps they have experienced religion in a negative way.[38] Neither the definition of religion nor the argument for religion as a basic good, though, makes a claim about the reality of any or all superhuman powers. Were it known for certain that they do not exist, then one might conclude that the good of religion is illusory and void of value. I know of no convincing argument, however, that they certainly do not exist, no proof of atheism.[39] Whether and when religious practices are unjust is beyond the scope of the definition as well. Doubtless, people practice religion corruptly, manipulatively, and abusively; it is not in the ambit of this essay to define what the standards are. However, only if it were demonstrated that all religious practices were, say, unjustly exclusive or subordinating, would such practices justify skepticism of the good of religion. Again, I know of no such demonstration. Nothing in the argument at hand denies that people have bad experiences of religion, but these experiences do not encompass religion itself. Religion remains a basic good for human beings even if all human beings do not choose it.

From Religion to Religious Freedom

The dignity of the person with respect to the practice of religion is the core of the human right to religious freedom. From the fact that religion is a basic good, a fundamental, intrinsic, noninstrumental dimension of human flourishing, arises the moral norm that no person, faction, militant group, community, or government may interfere with a person's practice of religion (including his religious practice in coordination with others in a religious community).

Important to this case is the incommensurability of human goods. Basic goods—religion, play, work, knowledge—cannot be weighed against one another, substituted, or compared in quality.[40] Each instantiates flourishing in a unique way that is not reducible or subordinate to the others. It cannot be said that one good contains everything that another good contains plus more. The mistaken view that goods can be weighed in this fashion often motivates curtailments of religious freedom. Religion should be marginalized and suppressed, some dictators have argued, because it stands in the way of economic development, which in turn brings improved health, education (knowledge), and other goods. Apart from whether a dictator's secularist ideology is correct, however, it is wrong to restrict religion insofar as it is a freestanding basic good.

There is one other critical reason why religion must be free that is implicit both in Smith's definition of religion and in the account of religion as a basic good. That is, virtually all religions place a critical stress on interior commitment—the will, the heart, the enlightened mind, sincerity, authenticity, and right motive. This interior commitment is not a part of the definition of religion that I am employing here. Rather, it is a quality that properly accompanies the practices and beliefs that are a part of the definition, and one that most religions emphatically stress. They stress it in a variety of ways. Many religious faiths place strong value on a basic profession of faith both on the part of children who are brought up in the religious community and on the part of people who enter the community from the outside. The value of such a profession is tied to its sincerity; those going through the motions, doing only what they are told, or committing themselves mindlessly are considered less virtuous. Further still, all religions place central stress on interior cultivation, whether it be the engagement of the heart and the soul, growth in virtue, practicing true worship, exercising sincere belief and faith, achieving enlightenment, surrendering to God, or practicing loving kindness. Of course, religions also invoke criteria for outward conformity, whether this pertains to moral norms, the practice of virtues, dietary matters, ritual, or numerous other activities. External behavior, though, is to be performed with sincerity and right motive. Finally, simply insofar as religion is a basic good in the way that I describe above, it engages the will and the understanding. It is chosen, like all basic goods that are chosen, through a deliberate and knowledgeable act. Outward behavior and inward commitment, then, are inextricably linked.[41]

If this interior commitment is to be genuine, it cannot be coerced. Were it coerced, or were it adopted out of fear of harm at the hands of others, for social approval, or to avoid shame, the commitment would not be a commitment at all. So, too, the search for and the ability to reject such commitments out of conscience is entailed in the very same freedom. The early Christian writer, Lactantius, made the argument vividly: "Torture and piety are widely different. . . . For if you wish to defend religion by bloodshed and by tortures, and by guilt, it will no longer be defended, but will be polluted and profaned. For nothing is so much a matter of free-will as religion; in which, if the mind of the worshipper is disinclined to it, religion is at once taken away, and ceases to exist."[42] In a very different time and place, the first president of post-Suharto, democratic Indonesia, Abdurrahman Wahid, connected internal assent to religious freedom thusly:

> The fact that the Qur'an refers to God as "the Truth" is highly significant. If human knowledge is to attain this level of Truth, religious freedom is vital. Indeed the search for Truth (i.e., the search for God)—whether employing the intellect, emotions, or various forms of spiritual practice—should be allowed a free and broad range. For without freedom, the individual soul cannot attain absolute Truth, which is, by Its very nature, unconditional Freedom itself.
>
> Intellectual and emotional efforts are mere preludes in the search for Truth. One's goal as a Muslim should be to completely surrender oneself (*islâm*) to the absolute Truth and Reality of God rather than to mere intellectual or emotional concepts regarding the ultimate Truth. Without freedom, humans can only attain a self-satisfied and illusory grasp of the truth, rather than genuine Truth itself (*haqq al-haqiqi*).[43]

Wahid points to the central conclusion of the argument here: If religion is of highest importance to humans and their flourishing, and if the authentic practice of religion must be free, then it would be unjust to coerce, prevent, interfere with, or unduly restrict it and manifestly just to protect it with the force of law. More formally, religious freedom is the civic right of all persons and religious communities to express, practice, and spread their religion in all of its public and private dimensions and to be free from heavy discrimination on account of their religion.[44] In essence, religious freedom means that no person, alone or in community, should have to pay a material penalty for the practice of her religion.

Religious freedom is not an absolute right. This right does not give religious people license to do anything they like in the practice of their religion. All of the major human rights conventions, as well as important statements of the right—such as the Catholic Church's landmark declaration of 1965, *Dignitatis humanae*—make this point. Religious people may not curtail the religious freedom of others in the name of their own religion. Religious people may not violate other human rights, either. To take some obvious (though, sadly, genuine) examples, religions may not practice child sacrifice or lead their members in committing suicide, as at Jonestown. Of course, there are controversies. Polygyny and female genital mutilation are examples of religiously authorized practices that many believe violate other human rights but that are globally disputed. Then, there are the numerous controversies that make up the subject matter of constitutional law in developed democracies, where judges decide how religion is to be balanced against other goods.

Again, resolving these many controversies is not my task here.[45] Rather, it is to outline an argument for why religion deserves to be enumerated as a distinct right, and the boundaries of its practice then need to be delineated. The grounding for the right of religious freedom that I have offered, however, does imply that religion ought to be afforded wide deference and a presumption against restriction. The concept of basic goods indeed helps us decide where the boundaries of this deference and presumption lie. Again, one ought not to violate or destroy one basic good in the pursuit of another. If religion damages life, bodily integrity, the pursuit of knowledge through education, or other basic goods, then it may justly be restricted or regulated. Short of this, its practice ought to be respected.

I have been arguing for a moral right of religious freedom—a natural right, a human right. Such a right is pre-political, meaning that it does not require enactment in positive law for its validity. But the value of this right urges just such an enactment. So, it may be considered a great historical achievement that this right has been incorporated into the major human rights conventions, the constitutions of developed democracies (and many other countries), and the European Union. It is the 1981 Declaration on the Elimination of All Forms of Intolerance and of Discrimination Based on Religion or Belief that articulates the most full-bodied concept of the right, enumerating a remarkably wide range of dimensions of religious practices that merit protection, including worship, public expression of beliefs, religious education, the construction of buildings, and many other activities that individuals and communities undertake.

The purpose of the human right of religious freedom is to protect these phenomena—consistent with the definition endorsed here, they consist of practices, not merely beliefs—and thus to protect a wide diversity of ways in which humans relate to powers that are beyond human and live out answers to ultimate questions. Here, I have sought to articulate a manner in which this human right might be grounded and defended. To the degree that religion enjoys such a grounding and defense, it merits a right of its own and ought not simply to be folded into other rights like speech, belief, conscience, or expression or assimilated into broad principles like equality and democracy. While this argument alone cannot show how religion is to be balanced against other goods and principles, it purports to answer contemporary critics who claim either that religion does not merit a right of its own in law and policy or, more strongly, that religion is pernicious and ought not to be protected at all. Religion, I maintain, is a dimension of human dignity whose free pursuit, according to conscience, ought to be protected.

CHAPTER 2

Can Freedom of Religion or Belief (FoRB) Be Universal?

Heiner Bielefeldt

From their beginnings in the late eighteenth century, human rights have been exposed to political, legal, and intellectual contestation.[1] Among the various matters of controversy, the claim of universal validity inherent in the very concept of human rights sticks out as arguably the most disputed issue. It continues to trigger fierce debates. According to a definition proposed by James Griffin, a human right is "a right that we have simply in virtue of being human."[2] This implies that human rights are due to *all human beings equally*, across geographical, political, cultural, religious, ideological, and other boundaries. Such an understanding also undergirds the 1948 Universal Declaration of Human Rights (UDHR), in which the first article famously proclaims: "All human beings are born free and equal in dignity and rights." Likewise, the preamble of the UDHR professes "recognition of the inherent dignity and of the equal and inalienable rights of all members of the human family." Freedom of religion or belief (FoRB), enshrined in Article 18 of the UDHR—and in a more elaborate form in Article 18 of the International Covenant on Civil and Political Rights (ICCPR)—is part of that universalistic enterprise. It protects no less than *everyone's* freedom in the broad area of religious or nonreligious convictions and related individual and communitarian practices.[3] This is a high aspiration, indeed. In the eyes of some critics, FoRB may aim too high to be sustainable.[4]

In this essay, I try to make sense of FoRB as a universal human right. When doing so, I take into account various critical "deconstructions" to which human rights have been subjected. In the twenty-first century, human rights can no longer plausibly base their authority on "self-evident truths," metaphysical certainties, or trans-historical notions of "natural rights." Before tackling FoRB specifically, I therefore briefly sketch a critical understanding of human rights in general, which among other things refers to the pragmatic necessity to secure the preconditions of meaningful communicative interaction across boundaries. Subsequently, I take issue with three specific objections raised against the universalistic nature of FoRB. The most far-reaching objection assumes that FoRB cannot function without singling out certain religions, which are "worthy" of such protection, as opposed to others, which are not. This criticism amounts to unmasking FoRB as inherently and irredeemably discriminatory. A more subtle criticism points to clandestine theological or anthropological presuppositions, which underlie the rights-based approach in handling religious diversity. Given those presuppositions, FoRB may still implicitly privilege certain religious expressions over others, for instance "Protestant" types of religiosity or an understanding of religion as a commodity within a neoliberal market model of spiritual items. When defending FoRB against those objections, I at the same time assume that normative universalism can never exist in a "pure and simple" format. I concur with the editors of this volume, who pointed out in their introduction that the critical discussions brought together in this book should not lead "to a rejection of the concepts but to an awareness of how hard it is to pin down terms and reach conclusions as particular cases and controversies arise."[5] Seen from this angle, reforms and adaptations, in response to ever-new challenges and based on critical discourse, will always be necessary to promote and develop FoRB as a universal human right or, more precisely, as *a universal right in the making.*

Universalism and Contextuality in Human Rights Practice

Whoever invokes universal human rights will do so by using a particular language, by speaking within a particular context, by referring to particular historical experiences, and by moving within particular traditions, including their various particular concepts, narratives, and metaphors. In short, universal human rights can never be above particularities. Universalism pure and simple may exist in mathematics (even that may be controversial), but it certainly does not exist in the areas of morality, politics, and law. Particular interests, worldviews, class positions, and other particularities not only are part of human rights *practice* but also permeate the *very concept* of human rights.[6] In historical retrospective, we clearly see that the imagined rights holder—the abstract "human being as such"—typically displayed quite specific features. In the eighteenth century, the supposedly universal subject of human rights was usually imagined as having a particular sex (male), a particular skin color (white), and a particular social status (property owner). Why should this be different today? Is it not merely realistic to assume that future generations will shake their heads in wonderment about particularistic biases, which still permeated the basic normative concepts of the early twenty-first century?

It seems obvious that human rights, notwithstanding their universalistic aspiration, cannot be above historicity and contextuality. Assuming that this is true, however, what are the practical consequences? One option is to give up normative universalism in toto and discard the idea of universal rights as an irredeemably naïve or hypocritical project. Another option, to which I subscribe, is to try to reconstruct the idea of universal rights in a context-sensitive manner, which at the same time attempts to do justice to the awareness of the historicity of all normative constructs.

The first option—simply giving up the aspiration of normative universalism—has certain advantages. To admit that after considering all other options everyone will remain stuck in their various particularistic interests, contexts, and biases, which he or she will never be able to fully overcome, may sound just realistic. After all, no one can claim to have an untainted, objective overview of all the cultural, religious, and other factors that shape their outlook on things. Openly endorsing this undeniable fact at least has the charms of epistemological realism and normative modesty. However, conceding to each other our various biases and inescapable particularities may be an honest and indeed modest starting point for a discussion; yet, to conclude the discussion by declaring that the parties involved can do no more than merely agree to disagree usually indicates a diplomatic disaster. Hence, the obvious downside of the skeptical position is that the disparities of particularistic positions, worldviews, and interests would remain the ultimate and insuperable political reality. According to such a view, there would be no possibility—not even in theory, let alone in practice—to critically appeal to any other norms than the standards that just happen to exist within the various particular political and other entities.

The second option—reconstructing normative universalism critically—likewise starts on the assumption that we live in a world characterized by inescapable differences of context, interest, and worldview. The main difference from the first option is the clear insistence that we nonetheless have to *interact communicatively* in order to negotiate the terms of coexistence in our complicated common world.[7] The various particularities within which we live should at least be communicatively articulated, with the intention to avoid serious misunderstandings and potentially fatal consequences that may arise from a lack of communicative exchange. This pragmatically motivated insistence on communicative interaction across boundaries is the starting point in an attempt toward recapturing normative universalism. From there, we have to move toward reflecting certain normative preconditions of meaningful communication. One of these preconditions is respect for the responsible agency of human beings as potential participants of communicative interaction. Such respect for people's potential of responsible agency, I will argue, can become the entry point for conceptualizing a modern, secular concept of human dignity.

When referring to the concept of responsible agency, what counts is the *potential* of such agency, which we have to attribute to all human beings. Human dignity, thus understood, goes deeper than the appreciation of a person's *actual* performances. It precedes any concrete normative actions, efforts, or accomplishments whatsoever as their implicit sine qua non. Normative claims and obligations of any kind, ranging from personal promises or civil law contracts to constitutional norms and international conventions, necessarily presuppose that human beings, at least in principle, have the potential of responsible agency. Even those individuals who actually fail to live up to the expectation of responsible conduct are usually held "responsible" for their shortcomings,[8] which illustrates the indispensable nature of this presupposition. Accordingly, the recognition of the potential of responsible agency cannot depend on empirical qualities, skills, merits, or performances of this or that individual. Rather, it defines a fundamental status position, which is to be respected in all human beings equally, simply because they are "members of the human family," to cite again from the preamble of the UDHR. Human dignity, thus conceptualized, can only be an inclusive and egalitarian status position—or it fails to make any sense.

At the beginning of this essay, I cited the first sentence of Article 1 of the UDHR, which states: "All human beings are born free and equal in dignity and rights." The article goes on to declare that all human beings "are endowed with reason and conscience."[9] Although the first sentence of Article 1 is the most frequently quoted sentence within the UDHR, the subsequent sentence has attracted comparatively little attention. This may be because the formulation is not easy to understand. What does the endowment with reason and conscience imply? One might even worry that the wording used here could invite moral perfectionism, which ultimately might create a hierarchy of different degrees of dignity, in conjunction with different degrees of ("reasonable") moral performance or perfection. However, this would stand out as a flagrant discrepancy relative to the inclusive and egalitarian spirit of the UDHR.

So, what can be the meaning and what is the epistemological status of declaring all humans to be "endowed with reason and conscience"? Reading this proposition as a mere description leads to insuperable problems. After all, Article 1 of the UDHR makes an all-inclusive claim by covering no less than "all human beings." If this is to make any sense, however, the endowment with reason and conscience cannot depend on particular empirical qualities, skills, and performances of individual persons. Interpreting the article as a *descriptive* proposition thus does not seem to get us very far. Now, if we read the formulation as a *prescriptive* proposition—that is, as a kind of "moral appeal"—we end up with even bigger problems of interpretation because any moral appeal implicitly presupposes that the addressee already possesses something like reason and conscience. A moral appeal would be pointless without the assumption that the addressed individual is generally receptive to moral pleas, emotions, and arguments. However, this very receptiveness is captured in the words "reason and conscience." A moral appeal that aims to create moral receptiveness to exactly such an appeal would be circular and thus self-contradictory. It looks like we are again at an impasse. Yet, there is a third possibility of understanding the sentence. Instead of entertaining a descriptive or prescriptive interpretation, I would like to propose to read Article 1, second sentence, of the UDHR in an *ascriptive* way. The point is that the international community *ascribes* to all human beings a potential, without which meaningful normative interaction would be unthinkable.

Given the fundamental status of responsible agency for any meaningful normative interaction, this potential must be ascribed to all humans equally.[10] It is not an empirical skill or quality, which individuals may have in different degrees, but it defines a *fundamental status position*, in relation to which all human beings are to be considered as strictly equal, including those who, owing to mental impairments or other contingencies, are unable to actually unfold their responsible agency. No individual has to "prove" through particular moral actions, efforts, performances, or merits that he or she is actually capable of responsible conduct. It is exactly the other way around in that the international community commits itself to treating all human beings equally as responsible subjects, which is tantamount to respecting their human dignity.[11] The various human rights, from freedom of expression to habeas corpus guarantees and from freedom of assembly to the right to education, are mutually complementary ways of institutionalizing the due respect for human dignity; FoRB, too, is part of that broader enterprise.

Normative universalism, thus reconstructed, is not simply above contextual particularities. It can only be a *universalism within*. Human life inevitably takes place within particular historical, cultural, political, and other contexts. This is a truism. Human rights cannot change, and they do not even aspire to change, that fundamental reality. However, they can promote respect for people *within* their contextual life worlds. In order to realize this function, human rights consistently address people in their potential of responsible agency. This means that the rights holders themselves have actively to voice their specific human rights-related interests, needs, wishes, and yearnings. As Michael Ignatieff has put it, "Human Rights matter because they help people to help themselves. They protect their agency."[12]

Without superseding contextuality (which would be impossible), human rights can contribute to broadening options and opportunities, opening up spaces, shifting boundaries, and crossing previously sealed borders. If successfully implemented, human rights can thus liberate people within their various contexts. At the same time, these contexts may change in line with the self-articulated wishes of the concerned individuals and groups. Within such historically open processes, however, human rights themselves will likewise change. Taking seriously contextuality in human rights practice must have repercussions also on the human rights theory—that is, on the understanding of normative principles and guiding ideas, which thus remain historically fluid.

In retrospect, we actually see how the contours of human rights have always been exposed to changes, reforms, and far-reaching adaptations, often initiated by previously marginalized groups, who have appropriated the language of human rights for their own struggles. Women's rights activists have succeeded in broadening the human rights discourse by exposing violations occurring in the private sphere, which in a traditional understanding remained largely outside human rights politics. People with disabilities have articulated their experiences of exclusion and established an international human rights convention that specifies their aspiration to a future barrier-free and inclusive society.[13] More recent nondiscrimination clauses include sexual orientation and gender identity within the lists of prohibited grounds of unequal treatment. Moreover, historians have begun to reconsider the genesis of human rights by challenging problematic Eurocentric ownership claims.[14] This critical business remains unfinished. Its purpose is to enhance the plausibility of universal human rights in a never-ending process of responding to new articulations of experiences of exclusion, discrimination, and repression. The normative universalism underlying human rights will thus always remain a historically open *universalism in the making*. Now, the question is how FoRB fits into that understanding of human rights.

Singling Out "Good Religion"?

Many of the controversial issues around FoRB mirror the dispute over human rights in general. At the same time, FoRB harbors a number of additional complications because FoRB has to do with religion, which is a controversial issue in itself. While the human rights approach has its contextual path dependencies and thus remains inextricably involved with a broad bundle of "particularisms," the same is certainly true for religion, too. As Cassie Adcock persuasively emphasizes in her essay in this volume, "There is, and can be, no stable definition of religion that stands outside history or politics."[15] Given the enormous diversity of faiths, beliefs, and concomitant individual and communitarian practices, none of the proposed definitions of what constitutes religion has ever found unanimous endorsement among scholars. If this assessment is true, however, does it not necessitate a negative answer to the initial question about whether FoRB can plausibly claim universal validity?

Some critics of FoRB seem inclined to draw that negative conclusion. Among them is Winnifred Fallers Sullivan, whose monograph carries her scathing message in its title: *The Impossibility of Religious Freedom*.[16] According to Sullivan, the right to religious freedom presupposes a definition of religion: "Legal protection for 'religion' anywhere demands a definition of religion."[17] She further contends that any definition of religion will necessarily mirror partisan interests: "The right kind of religion, the approved religion, is always that which is protected, while the wrong kind, whether popular or unpopular is always restricted or even prohibited."[18] This statement amounts to the charge that discrimination not only is a factual side effect of any practice of religious freedom but also defines the very core of the FoRB project, with the result that the idea of universal religious freedom appears to come close to an outright oxymoron.

Sullivan would be right if FoRB were to aim at the protection of religion (or the right kind of religion). This is the underlying assumption of her verdict.

However, at a closer look this assumption becomes more than questionable. Against a widespread misunderstanding, FoRB does not legally protect religion in itself; rather, it protects *human beings* in their individual and communitarian freedom.[19] FoRB is a multifaceted right, which covers a broad range of aspects: conscientious positions, profession of faith, and individual and communitarian practice, in addition to having private as well as public dimensions.[20] Yet what runs through all these various dimensions is its consistent focus on human beings as right holders. No less than any other human right—say, freedom of expression, freedom of assembly, the right to education, or the right to health—FoRB empowers human beings—that is, individuals as well as organized or unorganized groups of people. A slogan sometimes used is that FoRB protects believers (and nonbelievers) rather than beliefs. Even though one may wonder whether the term "believers" can make sense without considering their beliefs, it remains true that FoRB always approaches the variety of beliefs and concomitant practices from the angle of believers—that is, the human carriers of religious beliefs as well as religious practices.

The guiding idea undergirding human rights is that all human beings deserve respect regarding their dignity, freedom, and equality, and that international law should institutionally back up such respect. In keeping with that logic of the human rights approach in general, FoRB consistently focuses on human beings as the decisive holders of rights. They are the ones benefiting from the legal protection provided by FoRB—always in conjunction with other human rights. Consequently, it is only through the eyes and voices of human beings that religious issues can even become matters of human rights concerns. This, however, means that FoRB does not require a prior definition of "good religions" worthy of protection, as Sullivan suggests; instead, it provides an open space for the unfolding of diverse self-definitions of human beings in the broad field of religious convictions and practices, be they individual or communitarian and be they private or public. In keeping with the human rights approach, FoRB leaves the responsibility of defining what matters in the area of religion to the right holders themselves. It falls upon them to declare who they are; how they want to be treated; which practices they wish to see respected; and which support measures, if any, they may need from state or society. Respecting the self-understanding of human beings must remain the starting point and the overarching principle for any universalistic conceptualization of FoRB. Without taking that crucial premise systematically and seriously, any criticism of FoRB will miss the mark.

What is the reason for this focus on human beings as right holders of FoRB? Paradoxically, the starting point comes pretty close to the observation on which Sullivan herself bases her critique, namely, the numerous, often irreconcilable differences that characterize the vast field of religious convictions and practices. While some religions cherish holy books transmitted through divinely chosen prophets, other religions do not entertain any notions of prophecy, scriptural revelation, or even God. What is sacred for one community may remain opaque to another community; and the values that one group holds in high esteem may simply look strange and incomprehensible to others. For this reason, legal recognition within the framework of human rights cannot immediately be accorded to the particular contents of religions or beliefs—their truth claims, holy persons, scriptures, practices, for example—but only to human beings as the responsible agents who hold, cherish, develop, and possibly try to live up to such convictions.[21] In other words, FoRB does not protect religious traditions but instead *facilitates* the free search and development of faith-related identities in the broadest sense of the word. Rather than promoting specific religious norms and practices, FoRB's purpose is to ensure equal respect for all human beings as agents of faith-based practices. Instead of directly recognizing different worldviews, FoRB, alongside other human rights, aims at providing a practical recognition of everyone's equal dignity, with the consequence of opening up the space for the unfolding of religious or belief-related diversity.

Against another possible misunderstanding, which can easily arise in this context, it is important to stress that this focus on human beings does not necessarily imply an anthropocentric ideological standpoint. After all, human rights are about freedom. Taking freedom seriously, however, requires respect for people's most diverse orientations, including theo-centric, cosmocentric, and other obviously non-anthropocentric religious worldviews and related practices. The human agency that receives protection under FoRB actually covers a broad range of convictions and practices. It also includes voluntary acts of surrendering oneself to God by becoming a member of a monastic order—that is, positions that stand in the starkest possible contrast to a stereotypically anthropocentric attitude. A person may likewise believe that personhood is a mere illusion, which one should remove as an obstacle on the path to higher wisdom. Moreover, the legal recognition of human agency, as a part of human rights practice, does not necessarily presuppose a theology or philosophy of agency on the side of the right holders.

To be able to provide the space for such a vast diversity to unfold freedom, human rights themselves cannot assume an overarching quasi-religious or post-religious doctrinal authority. Michael Ignatieff correctly insists that the idea of human rights "is not a creed; it is not a metaphysics. To make it so is to turn it into a species of idolatry: humanism worshipping itself."[22] Any human rights idolatry would obfuscate the specific normative profile of human rights—that is, their intention to respect and empower human beings in their freedom. Thus, FoRB plays an important role as a custodian-right against the ever-lurking danger of turning human rights into a comprehensive doctrine, for example into doctrinal anthropocentrism, according to which the human being is the ultimate "measure of all things."[23]

Back to Sullivan's objection that religious freedom presupposes singling out certain religions worthy of protections. What she does not take fully into account is that FoRB, as a human right, consistently follows the logic of the human rights approach with its consistent focus on human beings. Accordingly, FoRB only *indirectly* relates to religions or beliefs, by approaching them through the lens of human beings. They are the right holders of FoRB, after all. The significance of that indirectness for an adequate understanding of FoRB can hardly be overrated. It is a space-providing indirectness in the service of human freedom and requires that human beings always have to step in and define what matters to them in the vast area of religious beliefs and practices. The indirectness, which defines the relationship between human rights and religion(s), furthermore creates the space for considering contextuality, again based on the articulation of the concerned human beings themselves. As a result of this, the precise contours of FoRB must remain historically open and fluid.

Yet another consequence of the focus on human beings is that the scope of protection provided by FoRB must be broad, indeed much broader than any predefined lists of "recognized religions" as they exist in many countries.[24] To quote the UN Human Rights Committee, which is the expert body in charge of monitoring the ICCPR: "Article 18 protects theistic, non-theistic and atheistic beliefs, as well as the right not to profess any religion or belief. The terms 'belief' and 'religion' are to be broadly construed."[25] The committee's clarification goes on: "Article 18 is not limited in its application to traditional religions or to religions and beliefs with institutional characteristics or practices analogous to those of traditional religions."[26] One should add that freedom of religion or belief equally covers the rights of members of large or small communities; minorities and minorities within minorities; conservatives as well as liberals; converts or re-converts; dissenters or other critical voices; and, last but not least, women who only have marginalized positions within many religious traditions. Moreover, the Convention on the Rights of the Child clarifies that children, too, are right holders of freedom of religion or belief.[27]

This broad and open conceptualization of FoRB can give rise to yet other questions. To pick up just one pressing issue: How does the broad understanding fit with the frequently invoked need to restrict certain religious practices if necessary—for instance, in the interest of public order or securing the rights of others? In some situations, it may actually be inevitable to limit certain manifestations of a religion—for example, if those clearly and directly endanger the fundamental rights of other people. The purpose of limitation clauses, such as the one specified in Article 18, paragraph 3 of the ICCPR,[28] however, is not to rule out "bad religion," as Sullivan seems to suggest, but to facilitate peaceful coexistence in a religious and belief-related pluralistic society based on equal respect for all human beings. This is a different logic. As a human right, FoRB cannot justify practices that amount to a direct violation of the human rights of other people. Against a widespread misunderstanding, I would furthermore like to emphasize in this context that limitation clauses like the ones contained in Article 18 of the ICCPR do not grant states a general permission to impose limitations in ways they see fit. It is the other way around in that the state, when trying to justify limitations, has to overturn a high threshold defined by a combination of important caveats.[29] The list of caveats includes presenting compelling empirical and normative arguments, issuing a formal law, persuasively demonstrating the need for such a law for the pursuance of a legitimate purpose, keeping limitations to the necessary minimum, avoiding any discriminatory side effects, and being willing to defend all of this to the democratic public and, as necessary, before courts. These caveats serve the purpose of securing the substance of FoRB (and likewise other human rights) to the maximum degree possible, even in situations of conflict or crisis. At the same time, they help to keep the conceptual space open for the articulation of a broad variety and of ever-new human rights concerns.

Implicit "Protestant" Bias?

So far, I have argued that FoRB does not presuppose any particular definition of religions worthy of protection, as some critics appear to believe. Rather, the competence of definition remains left to human beings, who are the relevant right holders in the area of FoRB. They are the ones who may define what protection, if any, they need in relation to their convictions and practices. My argument, however, will most likely give rise to another type of objection. If FoRB attributes the competence of definition to human beings, does this not implicitly privilege certain forms of religiosity, namely, "Protestant" expressions of religiosity with their emphasis on individual agency and faith, at the expense of those manifestations of religiosity or spirituality that focus more on collective ritual practices?[30] In related debates, the term "Protestant" frequently figures as a typological concept. Beyond the Christian context, in which the term originally emerged, "Protestant" forms of religiosity in this broader understanding may also cover reform movements within Islam, Buddhism, Hinduism, and other traditions. Those who invoke the "Protestant" paradigm often focus on three features: (1) the primacy of the internal sphere of believing as opposed to external ritual practice, (2) the emphasis on the individual person, and (3) the organization of religious community life in close analogy to freely chosen associations. I will now briefly discuss those three aspects with regard to whether FoRB actually presupposes a "Protestant" type of religiosity, thus understood.

Prioritizing Internal Faith?

Article 18, paragraph 2, of the ICCPR provides that the person's inner sphere of holding and forming a religious or belief-related conviction (the *forum internum*) receive *absolute* protection against any coercive interference: "No one shall be subject to coercion which would impair his freedom to have or adopt a religion or belief of his choice." At first glance, this wording seems to sufficiently illustrate an existing hierarchy between internal and external dimensions of religion. However, the picture changes once we consider that the cited paragraph is not the only human rights norm carrying such an absolute prohibition. To mention just two other examples, the ban on torture and the prohibition of slavery enjoy a similarly unconditional status; they, too, stand above any justifiable limitations, thus demarcating the ultimate boundaries, which the state can never legitimately cross. Inhumane practices, such as torturing an individual, trading human beings like cattle, or exposing human beings to coercive "brainwashing," can never be justified, not even in situations of crisis or emergency. When dealing with the "Protestantism" charge, it is important to bear in mind that the legal status of the *forum internum* dimension of freedom of religion or belief is by no means unique; it is not the only case of an absolute prohibition within the ICCPR.

Moreover, the jurisdiction of international courts and UN bodies, as well the advocacy work of international nongovernmental organizations (NGOs) are far from obsessed with the *forum internum* of FoRB. To a much larger extent, they deal with *forum externum* manifestations. Examples include the insistence on wearing religious garments in public life, the presence of religious symbols in public institutions, the performance of ritual male circumcision, religious initiation and socialization rights, the possibility to obey religious diets and fasting periods during work, discriminatory implications of public religious holidays, the handling of diversity in public and private schools, conditions for religious communities to obtain the status of a corporate legal entity, administrative permissions for building houses of worship, regulations concerning the ringing of church bells or the Muslim prayer call, autonomous recruitment of clergy, the running of church-owned cemeteries, state subsidies for religious organizations, legislative measures against collective religious hatred, fair participation in state-funded interreligious dialogue projects, affirmative action programs for members of religious minorities, and the running of religious charity organizations. This non-exhaustive list of examples should suffice to illustrate that FoRB does not focus mainly on issues of "internal" believing. In practice, it facilitates many visible and audible—and thus "external"—manifestations of religious life in all spheres of life.[31]

Individualistic Bias?

Another argument often invoked to demonstrate a "Protestant" understanding of religiosity allegedly underlying FoRB is its focus on individuals instead of groups. There is an important element of truth in that assumption. Unlike entitlements that are connected with particular group memberships, human rights must be respected in all human beings equally, prior to and independent of citizenship, family background, or membership in a specific religious community. In that sense, one can indeed say that human rights are rights of each individual. However, rights held by the individual are not necessarily "individualistic" in the sense of focusing on the isolated individual while ignoring or marginalizing the community aspects of human life. Confusing rights held by individuals with an individualistic way of life has become the source of countless misunderstandings, from Hegel and Marx to the "Asian values" debate of the 1990s, when some Asian governments claimed a communitarian ethos for Asian societies, as opposed to an allegedly one-sided individualism of Western societies. Such antagonistic constructions, however, do not survive serious scrutiny. Actually, human rights, albeit held by individuals, always presuppose communities in order to become a reality. To give just a few examples, freedom of expression can only flourish in a discourse community of speakers and listeners. The rights to freedom of peaceful assembly and association are, by definition, exercised jointly with others. Habeas corpus rights guarantee the maintenance of certain social ties even in situations of arrest and detention, and the right to form trade unions facilitates solidarity among colleagues in the workplace. Perhaps the most obvious example is the right to marriage and family life. As the wording of Article 18 in both the UDHR and the ICCPR testifies, FoRB, too, has a strong community dimension; it protects manifestations of religion or belief "in worship, observance, practice and teaching," which may be exercised "either individually or in community with others and in public or private."[32] Human rights are directed not against communitarian solidarity but against the various forms of authoritarianism in state and society. By challenging authoritarian practices in political life, family life, and religious community life—from political censorship, to forced marriages, to forced conversion—human rights can even become a positive factor for promoting communitarian solidarity based on respect for everyone's equal freedom. Thus, they do not reflect an abstract primacy of the individual over the community aspects of religious life.

Promoting "Free-Church-Type" Membership Associations?

Yet another version of the charge of a "Protestant" bias assumes that FoRB fosters voluntary associations based on individual membership.[33] This may represent a more sophisticated version of the "individualism" charge. Instead of accusing FoRB of privileging the isolated individual, the focus shifts toward a particular form of organization based on individual voluntary membership, as epitomized by Protestant "free churches." Again, the assumption proves questionable at closer analysis. FoRB actually recognizes many types of organizations, ranging from loose networks to membership-based free associations to hierarchical bodies. Respect for diverse types of organizations also includes the recognition of different understandings of what constitutes membership. The criteria for entering a community—such as by birth, adoption, marriage, conversion, initiation rites, and faith exams—largely fall within the autonomy of religious communities.[34] When Orthodox Judaism presupposes that a Jew is normally born from a Jewish mother, while other ways of becoming a Jew remain exceptional, this is fine from the perspective of FoRB. Traditionally, Alevites, Yezidis, and Druze stick to even stricter rules by only accepting birth as the way of joining the community. Many indigenous people, too, closely link spiritual practices to the idea of a common ethnic origin. Against a widespread misunderstanding, FoRB does not intend to alter any of this. It respects the diversity of membership concepts and admittance criteria. In particular, it does not vest the state with the authority to enforce an opening up of communities with the purpose of allowing converts into all of them. Reforms of membership or admittance criteria remain entirely left to the various communities themselves—provided they wish to embark on such a course.

Hence, even a short look at the practice of FoRB suffices to cast doubt on the ascription of a "Protestant" bias; at least it loses much of its prima facie plausibility. The actual practice of FoRB often concerns external manifestations of religions rather than one-sidedly focusing on the internal dimension of faith alone. Given the clear appreciation of community life in the wording of FoRB provisions, the assumption of an "individualistic" bias likewise proves questionable. And instead of propagating one particular type of organization akin to the Protestant "free church" model, FoRB actually accommodates a broad range of different types of religious organization, including different membership and admittance criteria.

A Neoliberal Market Model of Religiosity?

Objections come from yet another angle. Quite a number of critics have objected that FoRB actually propagates a neoliberal market model of religiosity, which eventually leads to a thorough commodification of faith and spirituality. A term that seems to support that reading is "choice," which even occurs twice in Article 18 of the ICCPR. While already paragraph 1 provides that everyone should be free to "have or adopt a religion or belief of his choice," paragraph 2 reinforces that guarantee by giving it a status beyond any justifiable limitations. Does the term "choice" not stem from the world of the shopping malls? If so, do we have to conclude that FoRB treats religious issues like items in a neoliberal spiritual wellness market? Talal Asad belongs to those holding that view. In his opinion, America sees it as its mission to "free beliefs as it frees property, that is, as an object that can be negotiated and exchanged without any legal obstacles."[35] In a similar vein, Elizabeth Shakman Hurd assumes that the hidden agenda underneath international religious freedom is the worldwide propagation of an open market "where the believer or nonbeliever can shop for, among other things, religion."[36] She furthermore contends that FoRB privileges a particular notion of religious agency: "Contemporary international religious freedom advocacy both presupposes and produces the neoliberal religious subject of the religious economies model: a rational, voluntary religious actor who seeks out the religious options that suit her best."[37] When seen from this viewpoint, FoRB merely mirrors a particularistic understanding of religiosity, largely modeled on the U.S. religious landscape, thus certainly forfeiting its claim to universality.

What the cited critics fail to acknowledge is the specific legal function that the term "choice" fulfills in the ICCPR and other international human rights instruments: It demarcates a sphere that should remain strictly free from any coercion. Given the ubiquitous risk of coercive interferences, the practical significance of providing such legal protection can hardly be overemphasized. Hence, FoRB empowers people against dangers of manipulation, intimidation, threats, or force. It is in this sense that everyone should be able to claim his or her right of free choice. However, while "choice" remains indispensable as a *legal* term, it is apparently much less useful in religious anthropology or religious phenomenology.[38]

Many religious believers may feel that categories like "destiny" or "calling" would much more adequately capture the identity-shaping quality of their religious convictions, which to them are not just a matter of subjective preference, taste, or "choice." Experiencing an urgent "calling" apparently differs very much from making a "choice" in the everyday understanding of the word; the experience of a calling can even come close to the subjective feeling of having no choice anymore. Whereas "choice" makes a lot of sense when used as a technical legal term, the term may prove much less adequate when it comes to describing existential experiences in the area of religion, worldview, or spirituality. After all, legal terminology has its inherent limitations and it is good to be aware of that fact. The language of law, including human rights law, is not suitable for expressing the manifold facets of human experience, least of all emotions, feelings of deep attachment, or existential concerns. However, criticizing legal terms for failing to reflect the deeper dimensions of human life would be not less mistaken than criticizing poetry for its lack of technical precision. Thus, any criticism of legal terminology must be based on an appreciation of its specific legal functions. It is important to note that we actually have different languages at our disposal, which can complement each other. When seen in this light, there is ultimately no contradiction between exposure to unconditional religious demands (beyond mere "choice"), on the one hand, and insisting on the legal entitlement to one's personal "free choice," on the other. For example, a Jehovah's Witness objecting to serving in the military may feel compelled to follow the "dictates (!) of his conscience" (in that existential sense, not just making a choice), while at the same time claiming his legal right to freedom of "choice" against the government. Fortunately, human life is not one-dimensional.

There is nothing mysterious in the observations just made. They analogously apply to other spheres of human life. Take the example of marriage or partnership. Many people will agree that "choice" is a somewhat awkward category when it comes to creating a lifelong relationship upon which so much depends. "Choosing" a spouse like an item from a catalog would certainly strike most of us as at least a little frivolous. Nonetheless, to have a guaranteed human right of "free choice" in matters of partnership and marriage remains highly important, given the reality of forced marriages or child marriages in many parts of the globe. If a young woman, who feels under pressure to marry a person imposed on her by her family, demands respect for her right to make her personal "choice" of a spouse, this obviously does not mean that she thereby implicitly subscribes to a full-fledged neoliberal market logic.

The same holds true for FoRB. Elizabeth Shakman Hurd mistakenly confuses a specific *legal* category designed to ensure strict noncoercion with a comprehensive neoliberal ideology and concomitant anthropology.[39] This also betrays a lack of familiarity with the actual practice of FoRB. Numerous people across the continents suffer serious consequences just because they wish to hold onto their religions, beliefs, or other existential convictions despite political or societal pressure. As a result, many of them experience discrimination, stigmatization, or even persecution. Those people obviously do not behave like consumers who just shop around in the spiritual wellness market to find the options that suit them best. Hurd's language could not be more remote from the real struggles for FoRB, in which countless people take enormous personal risks. When claiming their right to FoRB, including free choice of a religion or belief, they thus do not subscribe to a neoliberal market ideology, which some of them might even explicitly reject.

Universalism as Work in Progress

My responses in this chapter to some recent examples of FoRB criticism do not aim at a simple refutation, and my claim is certainly not to have "proven" the universalistic nature of FoRB. Normative universalism can be practically demonstrated as a useful, meaningful, and, in that sense, plausible concept; it cannot be "proven" in a quasi-mathematical fashion. Its epistemological status is that of a reasonable demonstration, not of a rationally proven certainty. When defending FoRB as a meaningful part of human rights, I moreover assume an understanding of normative universalism that remains historically open for further developments. Universal human rights can only make sense as a never-ending work in progress, which requires constant self-criticism, including the readiness to also listen to criticism voiced from outside the human rights community. Rather than discarding the idea of universal rights, which in my view would be a grave political mistake, criticism of human rights may also help to bring about a more context-sensitive understanding of normative universalism. What is true for human rights in general also applies to FoRB. Rather than speculating about an alleged "impossibility" of religious freedom, a critical analysis of existing tensions, gaps, blind spots, and unquestioned presuppositions can help to come up with more sophisticated conceptualizations in order to make the right to FoRB more plausible, more inclusive, and more realistic.

Human rights concepts and institutions have their historical path dependencies and thus can never be "universalistic" in a naïve sense of simply being above particularities, biases, and blind spots. This is also true for FoRB. Practical commitment on behalf of religious freedom will never be above the risks of ignorance, complacency, neglect, biases, or blind spots. How could it be otherwise? For this reason, criticism and self-criticism remain imperative. However, radical alternatives to religious freedom so far have failed to provide any practical guidance as to how to cope with contested issues. Controversies around headscarves in public schools, ritual male circumcision, crucifixes in public-school classrooms, religiously motivated asylum claims, conversion and missionary activities, and more will not mysteriously disappear once we get rid of the aspiration to secure religious freedom for everyone.

Much work remains ahead, not only at the level of practical implementation but also at the level of awareness building and adequate conceptualization. Here are a few examples: Although the inclusion of atheists and agnostics has received unequivocal endorsement in the theory of international FoRB, this has not yet consistently materialized in the actual human rights practice. It is time to change this in favor of an adequately broad strategic approach. Another issue that so far has received comparatively little attention is the religious freedom of migrant workers, in particular female migrant workers, who frequently remain "invisible" when taking employment in private households. Many of them face daily discrimination because of their religious beliefs without having adequate, if any, access to remedies. One of the biggest challenges concerns indigenous spiritual practices. There are good reasons to assume that the established categories of FoRB, as they have developed so far, fall short of accommodating adequately the needs and wishes of many indigenous peoples. Even the presupposition of agency, free self-definition, and free articulation, on which human rights practice is largely premised, may produce unintended side effects, thus possibly leading to new forms of exclusion.

Universal human rights can only exist on probation. This is also true for religious freedom. The defense of FoRB thus requires listening skills in a spirit of openness, not least in order to accommodate forms of articulation outside of the discursive mainstreams in academia, law, and politics.

PART II

The Social Contingency of Religious Freedom Disputes

CHAPTER 3

Microclimates of Religious Freedom

Global Norms Meet Local Conditions in Territorial Hawai`i and Occupied Japan

Jolyon Baraka Thomas

Within the city limits of Philadelphia lies the Wissahickon Valley Park, an extensive ravine where visitors can wander networks of walking paths that feel eerily distant from the city. Hiking trails traverse decrepit sewer pipes and pass under massive works of highway engineering, where vaulted bridges arch like cathedral ceilings and the sound of traffic zooming by above resonates like the voices of some unearthly choir. The crumbling infrastructure and vibrant graffiti reveal layers of the area's history as a long-standing center of American political and religious life.[1]

At a particular spot on the eastern side of the river, a massive statue of a man stands atop a rock outcropping, gazing west. A single word, "Toleration," is inscribed in the base. Erected in 1883 as a tribute to religious tolerance, the statue marked approximately a century of American experimentation with the concept of religious freedom in law, from the Virginia Statute for Religious Freedom (1786) to the Bill of Rights (ratified 1791). Perhaps it is one of these seminal documents that the unnamed Quaker man holds in his hands.

Like most statues, Toleration is silent. But the single word etched in its base and the westward gaze of its subject volubly tell a story that purports to be as old as the United States itself. That story imagines a nation founded by religious minorities who crossed the Atlantic to escape religious persecution. It places the origins of the United States in Europe rather than in the vast and diverse civilizations that predated Europeans' arrival on the American continent. And just as the word *toleration* implies a social center that arrogates to itself the right to include or exclude, the familiar story of American religious freedom privileges whiteness by erasing the abhorrent transoceanic passage of the enslaved human beings who crossed the Atlantic as cargo in the holds of ships rather than as pilgrims in pursuit of freedom.[2]

The transatlantic story of religious freedom is no doubt reassuring to some Americans because it suggests uninterrupted progress from Anglican religious oppression to American religious freedom. It furthermore implies that the American continent was an unconquered wilderness that white settlers tamed with the civilizing forces of democracy and freedom. The most recent iterations of this story boast that Americans who had perfected religious freedom at home were ideally situated to broadcast freedom to others abroad. This high-minded rhetoric positing the American birth of a universal freedom conveniently elides the fact that the U.S. promotion of religious freedom, both on the continent and beyond, has consistently happened under the aegis of American empire and with the aid of the country's military might.[3]

Rather than looking east across the Atlantic to the oppression "we" left behind, in this chapter I look instead at what Americans did with the concept of religious freedom as they moved across the continent and began extending this "American" ideal across the Pacific. Through examples drawn from the American Territory of Hawai`i and U.S.-occupied Japan, I show that religious freedom is not a universal *principle* discovered by Americans and then magnanimously granted to benighted others; rather, it is a *project* in which Americans and their non-U.S. interlocutors battled over operative terms in attempts to secure material resources, moral authority, and political advantage.[4] Inspired by the editors' operative metaphor of religious freedom as terrain, I use the meteorological metaphor of the *microclimate* to show that religious freedom discourse is constantly shifting, inevitably determined by local circumstances, and simultaneously subject to macro-level forces. Stakeholders' conflicts over resources and prestige are volatile tempests born from the ever-shifting fronts between religion and not-religion, driven in turn by the prevailing winds of social convention and geopolitical norms. Religious freedoms are born when concrete material circumstances dictate how these ambient ideological gusts collide and swirl. Religious freedoms emerge in places and moments where quotidian things like labor disputes meet global practices of imperialism or where policy initiatives like land reform encounter—and sometimes even help create—universalist ideals like human rights.

My historical examples in this chapter come from areas that were situated at the margins of America's Pacific empire; both were of great strategic and economic importance to the mainland United States. Together, the two cases show that religious freedom was never simply an abstract ideal that Americans brought to new territories. Rather, stakeholders beholden to U.S. hierarchies of race and Protestant-centric understandings of religion constructed uneven models of religious freedom, while non-Americans mobilized religious freedom talk in their attempts to secure equal treatment (Japanese Buddhists in territorial Hawai`i) or to reform religion according to their preferred criteria (Japanese elites in occupied Japan). Territorial Hawai`i and U.S.-occupied Japan were microclimates of religious freedom because their social and political terrain dictated how global discourses of white supremacy, liberalism, and civilization manifested in localized squalls over rights, resources, and privileges. In each case, white Americans and their non-U.S. interlocutors invented religious freedom anew. These newly constructed understandings of religious freedom privileged some types of religious being and belonging over others.

Religious Freedom: Map or Model?

What does it mean to discuss *the changing terrain of religious freedom*? To refer to religious freedom as "terrain" suggests that religious freedom marks or makes territory. It implies that religious freedom *has* a territory, that some places have religious freedom and others do not. To treat religious freedom as terrain also posits religious freedom as static, like the earth.

Yet, to liken religious freedom to the earth while also referring to change is to suggest that the concept can undergo seismic shifts. I appreciate this aspect of the territorial metaphor because it suggests that something seemingly stable and perennial—a universal human right, a founding principle of the United States—can disconcertingly move beneath our feet (as Heather Sharkey and Jeffrey Green argue in the introduction to this volume). The territorial metaphor furthermore suggests, quite reasonably, that religious freedom is an epistemic space that we all occupy. We now live in a world where macro-level questions of who gets foreign aid and micro-level questions of who is exempt from vaccinations are similarly dictated by the term "religious freedom."

But to render religious freedom as terrain runs the risk of making religious freedom something, like the earth, that predates human activity. Religious-freedom-as-terrain is subject to change, to be sure, but treating religious freedom as the ground beneath our feet runs the risk of naturalizing it, reifying it. Terrain does indeed shift, but orogeny and erosion are generally slow processes that are trackable only across millennia and centuries. It is only in their most violent expressions that these processes are visible to an unaided human eye observing change happening in real time. And, to briefly invert my line of argumentation, an additional complication that attends the terrain metaphor is that religious freedom disputes often dictate how stakeholders perceive territory itself: To one party, this place is just a mountain; to another, it is hallowed ground.[5]

I think that religious freedom is far more mercurial and much more artificial than the terrain metaphor suggests. Just as "conflict makes religions," we bring religious freedoms into being in moments of conflict and compromise.[6] We invent them over and over again. We do so because we label this thing *religion*, that thing *superstition*. We call this practice *oppression*, that other practice *emancipation*. We do not agree on these terms. Even when the concept of religious freedom is fixed in national charters, international treaties, and declarations of human rights, the question of what counts as religion remains unanswered.[7] The question of what is *not* religion becomes just as important. Who has standing to make a religious freedom claim? What sort of practices are legible *as religion* to cops, expert witnesses, judges?[8] What counts as religious repression, and what counts as the reasonable maintenance of peace and order?

To focus on these discursive questions is not to dismiss religious freedom as immaterial. Like religion, the concept of religious freedom is a "socially dependent fact" that has real-world, material impacts on places, objects, and human bodies.[9] Religious freedom can determine whether a monument is sited on public ground or private property.[10] In some parts of the United States, public-school teachers may lead schoolchildren in (Hindu?) postural yoga but not in Christian prayer.[11] These rules appear inconsistent because they are only as good as the definitions of "religion" and "freedom" that inform them. Interpretations of the religious freedom idea are also only as robust as legal understandings of the liberal subject and theological conceptions of the religious believer, with similarly material consequences. A corporation has a religious conscience even though it lacks a body that can suffer violence; a laborer does not deserve religious freedom because business owners and legislators render that worker's racialized body as less than human.[12]

Taking a cue from anthropologist Michael Lambek, I use a set of meteorological metaphors to describe this dynamic relationship between what stakeholders treat as "religion" and "not-religion."[13] If geopolitical norms (e.g., human rights) and national charters make religious freedom part of the broader legal-political *climate* (which is, of course, subject to anthropogenic change), the distinction between religion and not-religion can be thought of as a *front* capable of moving over terrain but also subject to shifting internal dynamics that reflect local conditions. Just as weather is local while climate is global, stakeholders' disputes over resources and privileges are localized manifestations of the ever-shifting religion/not-religion distinction. Local *squalls* are indicative of broader regional trends; they can also have knock-on effects on other local systems far afield.

Why *climate*? First, in its most basic usage, *climate* refers both to material circumstances and to the subjective experience of those circumstances. The Hawai`ian climate, for example, is a product not only of volcanic orogeny and prevailing trade winds but also of imperialist fantasy and leisure travel advertising. Second, climate is inherently contested. Metaphorically, we talk about the *political climate* when discussing circumstances that make taking a particular position on an issue either feasible or career suicide. More concretely, the topic of *anthropogenic climate change* remains a hotly disputed topic: who bears responsibility, what is to be done about it, whether it is a thing at all.[14] In its scientific sense, *climate* is also appealing for my purposes because it is determined only in the abstract by amalgamating mean measures of temperature, wind velocity, and precipitation across periods of thirty years or more: We never actually touch "the climate," but we can describe it through an imprecise yet accurate set of analytical tools such as computer models.[15] Finally, as the topic of anthropogenic climate change suggests, for all of its abstractions, the climate can pose exigent threats to human flourishing. A hostile climate may beget droughts, sea level rise, and the extirpation of species, but the very *idea* of a changing climate also provides rationales for increased securitization, militarization, and technocratic interventions that protect some human populations at the expense of dehumanized others.[16]

The same points are true of religious freedom, which similarly reflects material circumstances and subjective interpretations about embodiment, landscape, architecture, and the production of space.[17] Like climate, religious freedom can be ambient as a shared (if contested) ideal.[18] Like climate, religious freedom exists in the abstract as a composite of operative definitions, legal decisions, and informal arrangements. Like climate *change*, the anthropogenic quality of religious freedom as a legal norm can be masked with naturalizing rhetoric (e.g., religious freedom as a "God-given right"). Just as a copacetic climate can be conducive to human flourishing while a hostile climate can hinder it, religious freedom regimes can foster or threaten human lives. Just as the threat of climate change lets stakeholders rationalize technocratic fixes and militaristic interventions, interested parties can use the global discourse of religious freedom to designate specific "Countries of Particular Concern" or to describe target populations as threats or victims.[19]

There is always a risk of being too fond of one's own metaphors. For example, religious freedom is fully anthropogenic, whereas climate has both natural and artificial aspects. But I use climate as an operative metaphor because I want to emphasize how religious freedom emerges from a combination of material circumstances and discursive trends. I find the idea of climate useful because even though religious freedom exists as a global norm, local circumstances always dictate what counts as religion and who counts as a subject deserving freedom. I therefore focus on what scientists describe as *microclimates*: localized patterns dictated by the specific circumstances of terrain, the built environment, and ecology (by which I mean the interaction of biotic populations with each other and with the natural and artificial landscape).

I like the idea of the microclimate because microclimates are not merely natural phenomena. Certainly, they *are* natural: Microclimates can be created by a stand of trees or a depression in the landscape; they can pop up overnight or develop over millennia. But microclimates also exist in the built environments of cities (the cool shade and wind tunnels provided by high-rise buildings or the heat island caused by too many air conditioners pumping hot air out of homes and businesses). Microclimates are always local and are often artificial, but they are also fundamentally subject to broader weather patterns and slowly shifting climatic forces.

In both academic scholarship and practitioner literature on religious freedom, in political rhetoric and policy initiatives, religious freedom often appears as a static principle: It may be attenuated, distorted, recovered, established, or deviated from, but religious freedom itself seems timeless and unchanging.[20] For politicians appealing to the myth of America's founding, religious freedom is the very earth beneath our feet. For human rights advocates, it is an intrinsic quality of being born *Homo sapiens*. But in the actual embodied experience of living religious freedom rather than abstracting it, the icy gusts or high humidity of one spot as compared to another matches the ways that this party benefits from religious freedom (or even thinks in terms of religious freedom) while that other party does not. The point is not that religious freedom is present in some places and absent in others. The point is that religious freedom discourse is globally pervasive but still subject to the grubby politics of who gets which resources, who counts as human, and which bodies will survive and thrive.

The Trade Winds of Hawai`i

The Hawai`ian island of O`ahu is dotted with microclimates.[21] On one of my favorite hiking trails, for example, one first walks through a humid subtropical forest filled with diverse flora before entering an extensive stand of ironwood (*Casuarina*) trees, their brown needles soft on the forest floor. Several hundred meters up, the ironwoods give way to a clearing of barren red rocks before the flora changes yet again: invasive strawberry guava stand near at hand while a sea of uninterrupted green cascades down valleys to the left and right of the trail. Each of these stages on the hike has its own air quality and distinctive feel. When one pushes up the excruciating last few stairs into the clouds perpetually situated atop the Ko`olau Mountains and looks down on the beach far below, the icy gusts from the windward side of the island make the heat of the lower sections of the trail a distant memory.

Or one can think of hiking around O`ahu's undeveloped Ka`ena Point, a nature preserve situated at the end of the Farrington Highway. If one walks along the rutted grooves left by dirt bikes and off-road vehicles on the dirt path that extends past where the highway ends, there is a particular spot next to an albatross nesting ground that makes an ideal picnic location. There, one can look out over the Pacific Ocean to see a straight line in the water where colliding currents form an oceanic front. Polarized lenses make the fixity of the line mesmerizing, as the incessant motion of the waves leaves this seemingly artificial divider miraculously untouched as it stretches out to meet the horizon. So, too, the religion/not-religion divide.

The Farrington Highway that extends from both ends of the Ka`ena Point State Park is named for a former governor of the American Territory of Hawai`i, Wallace R. Farrington (1871–1933). In the summer of 1921, Farrington appeared as an expert witness alongside Chairman of the Hawai`i Emergency Labor Commission Walter F. Dillingham (1875–1963) and Hawai`ian Sugar Planters' Association (HSPA) lobbyist Royal D. Mead (b. 1876) in Washington, D.C., where the U.S. House of Representatives held a series of hearings on the subject of "Labor Problems in Hawaii."[22] At issue was a perceived labor shortage in Hawai`i's lucrative sugar economy, a roughly two-billion-dollar-a-year industry in today's dollars.

The problem the three men outlined in their collective testimony appeared at first blush to be a simple matter of staffing. But beneath their presentation lay an ugly truth. The problem with Hawai`i's sugar industry was not a lack of labor but rather the fact that 60 percent of sugar plantation laborers were using their racial solidarity to call for higher wages. When this Japanese majority called for increased wages, the men argued, Hawai`i's whole economy slowed. Japanese laborers were particularly intractable not only because of their putative tendency for collectivism but also because of the pernicious influence of Buddhist priests, who allegedly held control over the entire Japanese population on the islands. The expert witnesses argued that the government could address this problem by bringing in Chinese laborers to replace the uppity Japanese, who, in Dillingham's words, were "determined to use [their] money and the strength of [their] numbers to leave the established industries without necessary labor and enter into competition . . . with these established industries or actually acquire them."[23] According to Dillingham, Japanese intransigence diminished Big Sugar's annual earnings by about $50 million (approximately $740 million in today's dollars). Something had to change.

The problem Farrington and Dillingham identified was a direct outcome of the collision between America's racial hierarchies (Japanese workers served as part of America's surviving plantation economy, a legacy of slavery) and its nominally egalitarian federal laws (birthright citizenship as provided by the Fourteenth Amendment). Disputes took place in the form of strikes and strikebreaking, but behind the battles between labor and capital lay white suspicion about the ideological power of Buddhism and concerns about how far to extend the American ideal of religious freedom.[24] In the microclimate of territorial Hawai`i, the question of whether Buddhists really deserved religious freedom was intimately bound up with the question of whether Japanese laborers' demands for economic justice would be heard. Transoceanic material flows and ideological currents dictated how the denizens of territorial Hawai`i answered both questions: Commodity chains, eugenicist science, and equal rights were all at stake.

In the late nineteenth and early twentieth centuries, many Japanese laborers had emigrated to the Kingdom, and then Territory, of Hawai`i, where they earned paltry wages that allowed white plantation owners to pocket enormous profits. Technically, these migrant workers were on short-term contracts and were expected to eventually return to their Japanese homeland. In practice, Hawai`i's perennial growing season and agreeable climate saw many laborers settle permanently on the islands. By the last years of the nineteenth century, there was enough of a permanent Japanese population on the islands that the heads of Japan's Buddhist sects began dispatching chaplains to minister to the ritual needs of the laborers who had settled there.

Although the 1907 Gentlemen's Agreement between the United States and Japan had curbed Japanese immigration as a way of assuaging white Americans' fears about rapid demographic change, the practice of recruiting Japanese "picture brides" for male Japanese laborers contributed to a rapidly swelling Hawai`i-born Japanese population. Soon, the Japanese became the numerically dominant ethnicity on the archipelago. Since the U.S. empire had formally incorporated the Territory of Hawai`i in 1900, birthright citizenship law guaranteed these second-generation Japanese (*nisei*) not only the right to vote but also the right to own property. White landowners soon feared that these *nisei* would remain unassimilated and would use the privileges of birthright citizenship to snap up valuable real estate and ultimately control the lucrative sugar industry on behalf of the Japanese empire.

Nisei were technically Americans, but their first-generation (*issei*) immigrant parents sought to keep them connected with their Japanese roots by setting up Japanese language schools so that they could learn their parents' tongue. The parents' approach was pragmatic. Children growing up on multicultural plantations spoke a creole (commonly called *pidgin*) that amalgamated words from Chinese, English, Hawai`ian, Japanese, Korean, and Tagalog. Running Japanese language schools ensured that *nisei* developed fluency and literacy in their parents' native tongue. Voluntary associations of Japanese parents organized the schools, but many of them relied on school buildings, teachers, and other instructional infrastructure provided by local Buddhist missions. Effectively, most of the language schools were Buddhist institutions.

When a flood of patriotic sentiment known as "Americanism" swept the United States during World War I (1914–18), members of Hawai`i's white landowning class began claiming that the language schools posed a dire threat to the delicate caste system of racial and religious difference that undergirded Hawai`i's plantation economy. Equating Japanese Mikadoism (emperor worship) with Buddhism and Buddhism with the Japanese language, these white elites argued that ideologically unassimilable *nisei* threatened whites' fragile hold on Hawai`i's valuable real estate. Because Hawai`i's future prosperity demanded that Japanese Americans stay in their "proper" place as docile workers, they argued, Buddhism had to go.[25]

In January 1919, for example, College of Hawai`i professor of biology Vaughan MacCaughey (1887–1954) argued that the Buddhist-run Japanese language schools interfered with the crucial project of cultural assimilation: "The variety of Buddhism dominant in Hawai`i is medieval, ultra-superstitious and intensely Japanese. Mikado-worship and veneration of antique superstitions are prominent features of the system. Its inimical effects on the efforts of the public schools toward genuine Americanization are obvious, even upon cursory examination," MacCaughey wrote in the education journal *School and Society.* "The ideals and political life of the United States depend ultimately and absolutely upon the Christian American home," he continued. "True Americanization can not bloom in a Buddhist Oriental household. Hawai`i can not be American until she truly Christianizes her population, and makes dominant *the Christian home.*"[26]

Little in MacCaughey's published research suggests that he was an education expert, although his oeuvre does reveal his racist leanings and evangelical bent. His publications from this period included eugenicist disquisitions on "race mixture in Hawaii" alongside relatively dispassionate observations of the local flora and geography. Despite MacCaughey's evident lack of educational expertise, Charles J. McCarthy (1861–1929), governor of the Territory of Hawai`i, appointed MacCaughey as superintendent of the Territorial Department of Instruction shortly after the *School and Society* piece appeared. MacCaughey immediately invited a commission from the Department of the Interior to survey the islands' school system with the transparent objective of concocting a rationale for eliminating the Buddhist-run language schools once and for all.

The timing of the commission's visit in late 1919 would crucially affect its final report. In December 1919, the Japanese-language *Nippu Jiji* (*Japan-Hawai`i Times*) newspaper reported that Japanese workers had formed a new labor union to overcome the unfair conditions of Hawai`i's "slavery system" (*dorei seido*).[27] In a petition submitted to the Hawai`ian Sugar Planters' Association, union members wrote that, although it was "a great privilege and pride to live under the Stars and Stripes, which stands for freedom and justice, as a factor of this great industry and as a part of the labor of Hawai`i," nevertheless they were suffering under a paltry wage of seventy-seven cents a day.[28] Initially rebuffed by the HSPA in their polite request for higher wages, the new Japanese laborers' union continued to press its demands. The landowners were unrelenting.

The Japanese labor union had initially broached the topic of higher wages, but other workers took drastic action first. On January 19, 1920, Filipino workers struck. But, whereas workers of other ethnicities had previously been used to diminish laborers' power, this time Japanese laborers joined the Filipino workers in a striking moment of solidarity. Because Japanese plantation hands began refusing to work just one day after prominent Buddhist priests had submitted a letter to the HSPA asking the planters to accommodate the workers' demands, HSPA representatives concluded that Buddhist agitators were the masterminds behind Japanese workers' intransigence.[29] Plantation owners responded to the strike with cruelty, evicting laborers from plantation cottages just as a virulent influenza swept the islands. The flu sapped the workers' vitality and left many dead. The workers were only able to extract paltry concessions from the HSPA before they returned to work out of desperation in July 1920.

The education commissioners who had been called from the mainland submitted their report on the state of education in Hawai`i just as this high-stakes debate over labor drew to its dismal close. The report singled out the Buddhist-run Japanese language schools as serious obstacles to assimilation. Although a minority of white schoolteachers interviewed by the commissioners argued that the schools were forces for good in their communities, overall these teachers' sentiments toward the language schools were antagonistic. As the list of damning quotes gathered by the researchers suggests, many teachers saw the language schools as Buddhist, the Buddhists as Japanese nationalists, and the nationalism of the Buddhist schools as a contributing factor in strife between Japanese labor and the capitalist class: "The Japanese schools, under cover of religious instruction, teach the children loyalty to their Emperor and country. The Japanese language schools must go, if we are to teach the young Japanese to become Americans," one teacher argued.[30] Another said that some Japanese teachers may appear to "lean the right way," but that "the older ones, whose schools are a part of the Buddhist mission . . . teach a kind of divided allegiance theory, which fits a child to be an American for the time being—a Japanese should the occasion arise."[31]

These critiques must be understood in the light of the labor disputes of the day and the aforementioned fears on the part of white landowners that enfranchised *nisei* might snap up valuable plantation land. Though the July 1920 report's torturous diction was infelicitous, Superintendent MacCaughey must have been particularly happy with one line that unambiguously supported his pet project: "Although the commission recognizes the inherent right of every person in the United States to adopt any form of religious worship which he desires," the authors intoned, "nevertheless it holds that the principle of religious freedom to which our country is unswervingly committed does not demand that practices and activities must be tolerated in the name of religion which make the task of training for the duties and responsibilities of American citizenship a well-nigh hopeless one. The commission, therefore, . . . [recommends] that all foreign-language schools be abolished."[32]

Eliminating the Japanese language schools outright was politically impractical in a territory where Japanese people constituted 40 percent of the total population and held considerable social clout. Because the Department of the Interior report had clearly indicated the commissioners' awareness that abolishing the schools constituted a potential violation of Buddhists' religious liberty, there was also a fine legal line to walk between eliminating institutions associated with a particular religion and protecting an "American" way of life. In November 1920, the white-dominated Territorial Legislature got around this issue by establishing onerous restrictions on the schools, which technically allowed them to exist but made it nearly impossible for them to operate. Thanks to Act 30 of the Territorial Legislature, teachers now had to pass an ideological purity test, parents had to pay an exorbitant annual tuition fee, and pupils could not register until they had received a minimum amount of "proper" patriotic education in Hawai`i's English-language public schools.[33] Because the language schools remained permissible on paper, representatives of the white landowning class could claim, quite disingenuously, that Japanese parents' right to educate their children at the schools had not been violated.

Even as these legislative changes made it increasingly difficult for the extracurricular, purely voluntary language schools to operate, Hawai`i's white elites continued to stir up fears that Japanese language schools threatened not only Hawai`i but mainland America as well. In the House of Representatives hearings in the summer of 1921, Dillingham, Farrington, and Mead had presented the Japanese as intractable and irredeemable and had argued that Buddhist priests were directly responsible for fostering these immutable racial traits. Later that year, Governor McCarthy, who had signed the anti-language school Act 30 into law, complained similarly in the *Los Angeles Times*: "The intractability and hostility of the Japanese as a class toward the American community was forcefully demonstrated during a strike of Japanese plantation laborers on the island of Oahu during 1920. This strike, it has been sufficiently proved, was planned and fomented by the Japanese language press, the language schools, and the Buddhist priests."[34] An accompanying graphic depicted the archipelago's shifting demographics by showing a Japanese laborer towering over other ethnicities, while a simple map of the Pacific showed how Hawai`i could serve as a forward base for a Japanese invasion of the American mainland.

To challenge the anti-Japanese offensive, prominent Honolulu-based Buddhist priest Imamura Yemyō (1867–1932) wrote deftly argued tracts in both English and Japanese, stressing that the U.S. promise of religious freedom extended to Japanese Americans and guaranteed their right to maintain the language schools.[35] In his 1921 Japanese-language tract *On the American Spirit* (*Beikoku no seishin o ronzu*), for example, Imamura acknowledged that the constitution granted others the right to critique Buddhism, but he exhorted his *issei* and *nisei* readers to mobilize the constitutional principle of religious freedom in defense of their faith.

His readers listened. Led by Honolulu-based newspaperman Fred Kinzaburō Makino (1877–1953), with white attorney Joseph Lightfoot's (1864–1927) fees partially funded by Imamura's own Buddhist sect, Japanese American parents of language-school students filed a case against Governor Wallace R. Farrington in December 1922.[36] The plaintiffs, led by T. Tokushige (d.u.), won their case at the Ninth Circuit Court. (They were forced to appeal to the U.S. District Court when their initial case got bogged down by the foot-dragging tactics of the local civil courts.) The parents eventually went on to win again at the U.S. Supreme Court (*Farrington v. Tokushige*, decided on February 21, 1927). But even though anti-Buddhist animus was clearly central to white landowners' discriminatory agitation against the language schools, the courts bypassed the issue of religion entirely. The Ninth Circuit Court, for example, found for the Japanese by addressing the question of whether the territory's "police power" (suppressing potential insurrection) superseded citizens' constitutional rights. It did not mention religion at all.

When Japanese Americans finally won their case at the Supreme Court, they did so without the help of religious freedom. The court, citing the Fourteenth Amendment, upheld Japanese Americans' right to run language schools as they wished. But by ignoring the religious animus that drove territorial education policy, it reaffirmed Japanese Americans' place as second-class citizens who did not actually deserve religious freedom.

The court's decision reflected the fact that for many Americans at the time, Japaneseness and Buddhism (not to mention whiteness and Protestantism) were inextricably linked. The ruling protected Japanese Americans' right to create and operate voluntary organizations, but it did not explicitly protect their religious freedom as Buddhists. The court's silence on the issue left open the possibility that Buddhists did not actually have standing to make religious freedom claims. Making a religious freedom argument may have been unnecessary for the parents to win their case, but the upshot was that Buddhism did not count as a religion that deserved protection under constitutional law. Ultimately, although his sect had provided money for the legal fees, Imamura's eloquent arguments about the American promise of religious freedom were immaterial to the case.

What can we take away from this story? How do we make sense of labor migrations, commodity chains, competing conceptions of liberties and obligations, and eugenicist theorization about religion and race? Territorial Hawai`i was a site where material conditions like the value of land and anxieties about the costs of labor dictated how the gusts of conflict over rights and resources swirled. The prevailing winds of imperialism, trade, and racism determined how the ever-shifting front between religion (the Christianity of the landowning class) and not-religion (Buddhism, in this case) moved across the archipelago, resulting in local squalls and at the same time affecting practices far afield. The commission dispatched from the Department of the Interior argued that Japanese people in Territorial Hawai`i did not deserve religious freedom because Buddhism was inimical to Americanism. But twenty-five years later, U.S. military personnel would argue that the citizens of defeated Japan desperately *needed* religious freedom.

Behind the Front

At the heart of present-day Tokyo lies the impressive Meiji Shrine. Completed in 1920 to commemorate the death of the Meiji emperor Mutsuhito (1852–1912, r. 1867–1912), the shrine's architecture gives the impression of timeless tradition. Indeed, it is one of Tokyo's top tourist sites, and visitors today eagerly snap photos of the magnificent wedding processions that periodically pass through the picturesque shrine grounds. Compared to the frenetic energy of the adjacent fashion districts of Shibuya, Harajuku, and Omotesandō, the serene graveled paths of the shrine precincts make it easy to overlook the shrine's origins as an ideological symbol binding Japanese citizens to an apotheosized emperor who oversaw aggressive imperialist expansion. (Recall that Hokkaidō, Okinawa, Taiwan, and Korea fell under Japanese control during his reign).

Immediately adjacent to the Meiji Shrine lies a sprawling open area of a sort that is rare in crowded Tokyo. Just as the Meiji Shrine precincts incorporated classical ideals about the layout and species composition of sacred forests (*chinju no mori*) while also reflecting the designers' cutting-edge urban-planning ideas about shrines as leisure spaces, the area now known as Yoyogi Park began as a military parade ground (*renpeijō*) that doubled as a recreation area for picnics and kite-flying when it was not actively in use.[37] The linkage between the sacred forest and military spectacle, between Shintō shrine and relaxation, was typical of early twentieth-century Japan.[38]

Shortly after U.S.-led occupiers entered Japan to begin the process of reforming the country at the close of the Pacific War (1941–45), they transformed Yoyogi Parade Ground into Washington Heights, a subdivision housing American military personnel and their families. The training films these soldiers watched as part of their orientation to the Occupation mission suggest that they understood their task in pedagogical terms. Whereas wartime propaganda films like Frank Capra's *Know Your Enemy: Japan* had taught them that the Japanese were subhuman enemies who demanded outright eradication, orientation films like *Our Job in Japan* (written by Theodor Geisel, better known as Dr. Seuss) suggested that the "Japanese brain, like our brain, can be taught."[39] Building on this shared biology, the occupiers were to teach the formerly dehumanized Japanese "how to make sense."

Following the Potsdam Declaration of July 1945, initial post-surrender policy for Japan focused on demilitarizing and democratizing the country. Due to a widespread presupposition among the Allies that Japanese militarism derived from a quasi-religious form of emperor worship, reforming religion was a crucial part of this effort.[40] The occupiers were to proclaim religious freedom for all, ensure that militarist organizations did not "hide behind the cloak of religion," and instill "a desire for religious freedom" in the Japanese populace.

Proclaiming religious freedom through the October 4, 1945, Civil Liberties Directive turned out to be the easy part. The much harder task involved figuring out what exactly religious freedom was. The occupiers had not bothered to define religious freedom when the Occupation began, and serious differences of opinion between personnel confused the issue. Some, like Supreme Commander Douglas MacArthur (1880–1964), interpreted religious freedom as essentially the freedom to be Christian. Others, like chief of the Religions and Cultural Resources Division William K. Bunce (1907–2008), interpreted religious freedom as the right to choose one's personal faith rather than having it dictated by familial sectarian affiliation. Crucially, both the religious-freedom-as-Christianization and the religious-freedom-as-personal-choice models prioritized Protestant understandings of religion as private and elective.[41]

Occupation officials working in the Religions and Cultural Resources Division (part of the Civil Information and Education Section) rationalized reforms in the area of religion by suggesting that prewar and wartime Japan had been dominated by a national religion that they came to call "State Shintō." Appearing as both a "bad religion" (because it was ideologically coercive) and a "heretical secularism" (because it allegedly improperly fused religion and politics), the concept of "State Shintō" served as a rhetorical foil that helped the occupiers' inchoate (and frequently incoherent) understandings of religious freedom make sense.[42]

Thanks to this conceptual sleight of hand, the occupiers generally assumed that they had religious freedom and the Japanese did not. But telling this story meant overlooking the fact that Japanese people had been vigorously debating the meaning and scope of the religious freedom clause in the 1889 Meiji Constitution for decades before the occupiers arrived. Long before the occupiers "brought" religious freedom to Japan, Japanese people had been delivering speeches, writing impassioned op-eds, lobbying their elected representatives, and protesting legislation in the name of protecting religious freedom. Ignoring this history and assuming that religious freedom was a uniquely American export, the occupiers claimed to be teaching Japanese people how to understand "real" religious freedom for the first time.[43]

Ironically, the occupiers' policy of promoting religious freedom sometimes made life more difficult for the very people it ostensibly aimed to protect. Part of the problem was that the U.S. military government comprised numerous agencies pursuing diverse agendas. Sometimes these initiatives were aligned, but, just as frequently, different Occupation units pursued policies that worked at cross purposes. For example, the Intelligence Section and Public Safety Division encouraged local police to violently crack down on marginal religious movements that they deemed threats to peace and order even as officials in the Religions Division ordered the Occupation rank and file to treat all religious groups with respect.[44]

Less violently but no less importantly, when the Natural Resources Section single-mindedly pursued a land-reform policy in which all large parcels of land were to be divided into tracts no larger than 2.5 acres for single-family use, it placed religious institutions in dire straits. Many Shintō shrines and Buddhist temples had leased large properties from the Japanese government in a centuries-old custodial arrangement in which government lands served as sources of revenue thanks to farming, logging, and subleasing. Because the state could no longer materially support religious institutions under

Japan's new occupier-drafted constitution, clerics were suddenly only entitled to keep a tiny fraction of their traditionally held lands. Formerly expansive temple properties and shrine precincts were reduced to the footprints of the buildings that were directly used for what the occupiers thought of as "real" religious practices.

The upshot was that in the name of promoting religious freedom in Japan, the occupiers made it much harder for some religions to operate. In the question-and-answer column of the monthly journal *Shūkyō jihō* (*Religion Times*) published by the Religious Affairs Office of the Japanese Ministry of Education, for example, perplexed shrine and temple administrators wrote in with frantic queries about how much of their land they were entitled to keep and how to report their finances under the new taxation regime.[45] The Americans understood their project as "freeing" Japanese religions from state control; however, from the perspective of many clerics, the occupiers had simply replaced one type of statutory oversight with another that actually constrained religions in a new set of bewildering rules under the banner of "religious freedom."

The situation was further complicated by the fact that governmental authority and jurisdiction were ambiguous during the Occupation. Technically, two governments were in charge of the same territory and population: The American military government dictated policy; the Japanese government enforced it. This ambiguity created a conundrum concerning religious freedom. On the one hand, religious freedom was a civil right granted to Japanese citizens by their state under a brand-new constitution. On the other hand, the punitive nature of the Occupation made it clear that the Japanese state could not yet be trusted to guarantee this right. This curious jurisdictional situation combined with a wartime propaganda phrase to give birth to a new conception of religious freedom as a human right.

First, the propaganda. Months before the conflict between Japan and the United States broke out with the surprise attack on Pearl Harbor in December 1941, U.S. president Franklin Delano Roosevelt (1882–1945) had made one of the most important foreign policy speeches of his career. Exhorting Americans to redouble their efforts in providing support to allies fighting against totalitarianism abroad, in his January 1941 State of the Union address Roosevelt outlined what he called the "Four Freedoms": freedom of speech, freedom for everyone to "worship God in his own way," freedom from fear, and freedom from want. Thanks in part to a series of Norman Rockwell prints that appeared in the *Saturday Evening Post* and then recirculated as propaganda posters, after the United States entered the war, the "Four Freedoms" served as an aspirational encapsulation of the ideals for which Americans were fighting and dying abroad.

Human rights entered the conflict thanks to a Rooseveltian rhetorical flourish. "This nation has placed its destiny in the hands and heads and hearts of its millions of free men and women; and its faith in freedom under the guidance of God," Roosevelt intoned at the end of his famous speech. "Freedom means the supremacy of human rights everywhere. Our support goes to those who struggle to gain those rights or keep them. Our strength is in our unity of purpose. To that high concept there can be no end save victory."[46]

Roosevelt threw in the line about human rights as a last-minute fillip. Many people, including his own speechwriters, were mystified as to what the phrase actually meant.[47] But over the course of the war, this inchoate concept solidified as shorthand for "why we fight." By the time the Occupation began in September 1945, officials regularly justified their reformist project by claiming to protect "human rights."

Why would the occupiers refer to religious freedom as a human right when the perfectly suitable concept of civil rights would have served just fine? Human rights discourse solidified in Japan because it solved the jurisdictional problem I outlined above. Mere civil rights were granted to citizens by their governments, which meant that untrustworthy governments might get them wrong. By contrast, human rights transcended governmental purview. By making rights innate, universal, and timeless, the occupiers could claim that they were not merely imposing American values on the defeated country. At the same time, because the concept of human rights implicitly called state sovereignty into question by allowing the global community to police states for violations of their own citizens' rights, the occupiers could forestall the possibility that the Japanese state might coerce Japan's vulnerable citizens in matters of conscience. In other words, the police power of the Occupation and the emancipatory rhetoric of liberty combined to generate the concept of religious-freedom-as-human-right. Crucially, this concrete instantiation of religious-freedom-as-human-right discourse took place in Japan out of operational necessity and before religious freedom was included in the 1948 UN Universal Declaration of Human Rights.[48]

This human rights project could appear both rational and natural because the occupiers benefited from close collaborations with Japanese legal experts and scholars of religion who served as their local advisers. Many of these local experts provided Japanese-language essays and op-eds that supported the occupiers' project, even as they used their close connections with the occupying forces to advance their own understandings about what constituted "real religion" and how Japanese clerics and laypeople should understand religious freedom. For example, illustrated primers to Japan's new constitution like Kitaura Keitarō's (1887–1954) *The Constitution, Illustrated and Explained* (1947) depicted the new normal by showing three members of the same family simultaneously engaged in three different types of religious practice, highlighting the unprecedented notion that religious affiliation would be a matter of personal choice rather than family background.[49] Scholar of constitutional law Minobe Tatsukichi (1873–1948) provided his own interpretation of the new constitution by suggesting that the universal human right to religious freedom was an antidote to the particularism of what the occupiers had termed "State Shintō."[50] Perhaps most strikingly, University of Tokyo professor of religion Kishimoto Hideo (1903–64) wrote a series of op-eds in popular newspapers that dismissed clerics as ignorant while promoting a humanistic, psychologized understanding of religion as a balm for human suffering. For Japanese people to get religious freedom, they had to "get" religion as Kishimoto understood it: private, rational, and functional.[51]

Between the active roles played by Japanese elites during the Occupation and the historical fact that Japanese people had engaged in long-standing debates over religious freedom for decades before the Americans even arrived, it is impossible to say that the Americans simply bequeathed religious freedom to the Japanese people. Rather, collaborations between Japanese elites and American officials created the notion that all people are naturally religious from birth and that each individual must ultimately choose just one religion. This model of freedom, imposed under military occupation, created a new conundrum: In a country where most people did not have exclusivist understandings of religious affiliation, now they were not only *able* to choose their religions. They had to.[52]

The birth of religious-freedom-as-human-right during the Allied Occupation of Japan exemplifies the existence of what I call *microclimates of religious freedom*. The nascent global discourse of human rights, not yet solidified in the UN Universal Declaration of Human Rights (1948), was an atmospheric current that flowed through post-defeat Japan, pushing the ever-shifting front between religion and not-religion this way and that. As the occupiers' conflicting initiatives collided and swirled with Japanese elites' pet objectives, new conflicts erupted between clerics and academics, bureaucrats and diplomats. Some of these local squalls were tempests in teapots, as when indignant

Christian missionaries complained to the occupiers that egalitarian religious freedom policy interfered with the *real* work of converting Japanese people to Christianity.[53] Others, like the devastating economic blow to shrine and temple finances brought on by land-reform policies, were more consequential. But my point is that these moments of conflict cannot be understood simply as instances of the presence or absence of religious freedom. Rather, they were born from the material conditions of the Occupation (who had guns, who was allowed to hold land) and the ambient ideological winds of the postwar moment (the question of how to universalize rights and freedoms as a bulwark against authoritarian excess). Americans did not bring religious freedom to Japan. Rather, in localized interactions with Japanese people, Americans invented religious freedom, all over again, for the first time.

The point here is that each instance of religious freedom theorizing and policy making is new because stakeholders must account for the particular ways that global norms collide with local conditions. Religious freedom is not just "out there" waiting to be discovered or applied. Religious freedoms are made when people need them to solve specific problems. In occupied Japan, the concept of religious-freedom-as-human-right served as a convenient foil for "State Shintō," justifying the occupiers' presence and sublimating their policy initiatives with lofty rhetoric.

Conclusion

The two parts of my story are interlinked not only because they involve debates between Japanese and American people over the contentious topic of religious freedom, but also because they took place in places with ambiguous jurisdictional status situated at the margins of U.S. empire. The United States forcibly acquired territorial Hawai`i and made the archipelago into a plantation economy structured by American hierarchies of race, where the profits of the lucrative sugar industry superseded the rights of the foreign-born laborers who helped it function. Second-generation Japanese (*nisei*) were subject to conflicting claims about whether the religious freedom ideal protected the Buddhist-run language schools where they learned their parents' tongue. Because it ignored the religious animus that drove the language-school dispute, the Supreme Court decision in *Farrington v. Tokushige* (1927) effectively denied religious freedom to these Japanese Americans even though it protected their right to run voluntary language schools. The point would be driven home fifteen years later when race and religious affiliation became pretexts for the mass incarceration of Japanese people after the bombing of Pearl Harbor.[54]

In occupied Japan, American policy makers disagreed with one another about what religious freedom was, but they all agreed that Japanese people lacked it and desperately needed it. With the aid of local elites, the occupiers took it upon themselves to bestow "real religious freedom" on the Japanese people. But the religious freedom these parties collaboratively invented used the still-inchoate language of human rights to rationalize and justify a series of reforms that often hurt religious institutions rather than helped them. As in territorial Hawai`i, in occupied Japan religious freedom talk worked to protect the political and economic interests of the powerful. There, too, local circumstances combined with global norms to birth new understandings of religious freedom.

It might seem counterintuitive to address the material conditions of religious freedom by invoking something as ethereal as climate. But, like climate, religious freedom is something that ineluctably affects all of us. Like climate, those effects can be measured in the abstract when we talk about religious freedom as a universal principle or as a human right. But in practice, *religious freedoms* are born in microclimates that pop into existence when stakeholders battle over resources, try to secure territory, or appeal to shared ideals. At times, the language of religious freedom is wholly unhelpful because interest groups cannot agree on whether something like Buddhism counts as "real religion." At times, the language of religious freedom is immaterial because technocratic reforms like land redistribution interfere with free exercise. At other times, the language of religious freedom becomes indispensable because abstract catchphrases like "human rights" have to become concretized. My meteorological metaphor is admittedly imperfect and probably cannot be universally applied, but it helps bring religious freedom down to earth by suggesting that religious freedom is not the terrain of our shared political life but rather the tempestuous product of localized conflicts over territory, resources, and privilege.

CHAPTER 4

The Protection of Religion as "Culture" and "History"

Three Case Studies

Lori G. Beaman

In April 2018, the prime minister of Bavaria, Markus Söder, announced that "Christian crosses [are] to be publicly displayed in all of its official buildings."[1] Prime Minister Söder claimed that "the cross is a fundamental symbol of our Bavarian identity and way of life."[2] The regional bishop of the Evangelical Lutheran Church in Bavaria and chairman of the Council of the Evangelical Church in Germany, Bishop Heinrich Bedford-Strohm, opposed Söder's decision.[3] The head of the German Bishops' Conference, Cardinal Reinhard Marx, also objected to Söder's order, arguing that such a display of the cross "amounts to 'expropriating the cross in the name of the state'" and that the cross represents more than a cultural symbol.[4] A survey conducted by the German newspaper *Bild am Sonntag* shortly after Söder's announcement revealed that 64 percent of the German population opposed the display of crosses in public buildings.[5]

Across the Atlantic in 2017, the board of directors for Hôpital du Saint-Sacrement in Quebec City, Canada, removed a crucifix following a complaint made by a patient. The board intended to give the decommissioned crucifix to the Sisters of Charity, the religious order that founded the hospital. According to news reports, the motivation for the removal of the crucifix was twofold: first, the decision of the Supreme Court of Canada in the *Saguenay*[6] case of 2015 meant that religious symbols could not be displayed in public institutions; and, second, the hospital board wanted to bring hospital practice into compliance with the anticipated requirements of Bill 62, which proposed to set out guidelines on religious symbols in public places.[7] The board referenced the requirement that the state be neutral in relation to religion and also noted the particular vulnerability of its patients.[8]

Those who objected to the removal of the crucifix in the furor that ensued couched their protests in the language of culture and heritage—"this is our culture and heritage"—and not in terms of religion, which, though not entirely absent from discussions, took a decidedly marginal position to the defense of the symbol. Even when religion was mentioned, a core focus of the public debate was its cultural and heritage significance. Mention of religion was incidental. Advocates of keeping the crucifix effectively transubstantiated it from a religious symbol to a cultural artifact. The minister of Employment and Social Solidarity said, "It's not about religion. It's about the very important historical symbol for Quebecers."[9]

At issue is not what is "really religion" or "really culture or history." When religion is transformed into culture, it is not a matter of insisting that religion reveal its true nature. Rather, it is important to ask what this shift in the production of a particular set of symbols, practices, and techniques enables.[10] What are the consequences of such a shift? What is the work this configuration does on the ground? By constituting religion as culture or heritage, a different kind of imaginary about who "we" are is constructed in ways that then enable the exclusion, scrutiny, and regulation of what is designated as religion and the exemption of certain constituencies from it. As Sharkey and Green argue, religion is only one part of the story and contests over meaning are inherently political. Moreover, calling into question "our" culture or heritage is difficult: The challenger is immediately positioned on the margins, as an outsider who does not belong and is not one of "us" because culture is taken to be self-evident, as is also often the case with its frequent companion, "our values."

In the following sections, I'll examine three cases from three different contexts, using them as a prism to think through the ways in which religion and culture are constructed. This discussion picks up on the point made by Sharkey and Green in the introduction to this volume that "the terrain of religious freedom has never been easy or smooth." The cases I have chosen are not the only such cases in these jurisdictions, but they are all relatively recent, representing current debates within the context of contemporary diversity. First, I will examine the *Saguenay* case in which Alain Simoneau, an atheist from Quebec, Canada, challenged the constitutionality of the recitation of a prayer to begin municipal council meetings. Simoneau claimed that the recitation of prayer in town hall meetings violated multiple sections of the Quebec Charter of Human Rights and Freedoms, including those related to discrimination and religious freedom.[11] Second, I explore a case originating from the town of La Roche-Sur-Yon in the Pays de la Loire region in western France. In this case, the Vendée Federation of Free Thought challenged the legality of the presence of a nativity scene in the city hall and whether it violated Article 1 of the Law of 1905. Third, I consider the Supreme Court of the United States' 2014 *Town of Greece* decision in which Susan Galloway and Linda Stephens—a Jew and an atheist, respectively—challenged the constitutionality of the prayers recited at the beginning of town hall meetings in the United States. Galloway and Stephens claimed that the use of such prayer violated the First Amendment's Establishment Clause.

What impact does the shift from religion to culture have? Why does it matter that a prayer is transmuted into a practice that is framed as being universal and inclusive of shared values? Broadly, such a move contributes to exclusionary practices in diverse societies. It does this by fabricating an entrenched vision and version of a history that belongs only to a particular segment of society, which is in turn located at the apex of a hierarchy of citizenship and belonging. At a normative level, this translates into the language of core values. But it also has significance on another register: Symbols generate powerful emotional responses that vary from person to person; one person's comfort is another person's pain. Beyond the individual, symbols carry nationalist, colonial, and founding people's stories.[12] They also mark group boundaries, signaling both exclusion and inclusion.

A critical understanding of heritage and culture examines the circumstances under which they are produced, rather than seeing them as fixed entities or truths that stand above examination.[13] From this perspective, heritage and culture tell particular stories of who "we" are. Those stories emphasize "certain time periods, events, and narratives while obscuring others, and are connected to projects of identity formation and nation building."[14] These narratives carry a particular weight when they are reproduced in social institutions such as education or law. They shape reality.[15]

Western democracies are becoming increasingly diverse in religious and nonreligious ways, resulting in a concomitant pressure on human rights guarantees and democracy itself to deliver on its promises. This new diversity[16] requires a renegotiation of the sedimented privilege associated with majoritarian status. Much of the current conversation about freedom of religion or belief and its limits is taking place around minority religions. In the meantime, religions that have traditionally been majority religions, and indeed remain so at least nominally, are refashioning themselves as culture, heritage, and history. Thus, rather than being one among many whose beliefs and practices are subject to the same scrutiny, the move to culture embeds majoritarian religions in their social contexts as inextricably linked to nation, citizenship, and "shared values."[17]

A beginning assumption of this chapter is that every social context has a religious establishment. This premise may be especially difficult for American audiences, who are often deeply invested in the notion that there is no establishment in the United States. I take the position that everywhere there is establishment no matter what the constitutional position is (separation or not), and I argue that this shapes the interpretation of rights of religious minorities.[18] This is how, for example, crucifixes are possible in public-school classrooms and publicly funded hospitals, and Christian prayer in legislatures and council meetings can be imagined as universal and a matter of culture and heritage even when state and church are separated or when states are allegedly neutral. This claim may seem to be paradoxical, but the recognition of de facto establishment is not a justification of it; rather, it is a necessary beginning place for the move toward ensuring social inclusion and equality in diverse societies. Here I turn briefly to Zygmunt Bauman's observation that we have arrived at a place in history when the "'art of living with difference' has become an everyday problem."[19] Assimilation is shredded and "cultural relations are no longer vertical but horizontal: no culture can demand or be entitled to subservience, humility or submission on the part of any other simply on account of its own assumed superiority or 'progressiveness.'"[20] Nor, I would add, its foundational status, though this is a battle that is currently being fought, articulated as a defense of culture, justified by history and heritage. It is precisely this state of affairs, bolstered and perhaps created by human rights (which Bauman reduces to "the right to difference"), that is at the crux of religion's transformation to culture and heritage. It is the challenge by human rights to religious and cultural primacy that puts privilege to the test by pushing toward a model in which majoritarian religions are one among many.[21] The move from religion to culture is precisely because of this: The protection of religious freedom has created a horizontal relationship between religions.[22] No religion can legitimately claim superiority. The move to culture is a protective strategy, an attempt to reframe religion as culture and heritage. The defense of majoritarian religious symbols and practices is a dangerous game that threatens to undermine the credibility of liberal democracies by failing to give robust meaning to freedom of religion and promises of equality.

Law is often the site on which the tension between the new diversity and de facto establishment plays out. Religious minorities generally approach this terrain by asking for more space for their own religious practice, rather than challenging the dominance of majoritarian religion in so-called secular societies. Religious majorities are increasingly claiming pride of place under the guise of culture and heritage. This is so for a number of reasons, including the pervasive rhetoric of "people of faith" as a unifying mantra that acts, essentially, to create rules of membership that subvert any possibility of challenge. We see this, for example, in the deployment of the notion of "people of the Book" by Muslims faced with discrimination.[23] Thus, it is most likely to be the nonreligious who are most involved in challenges to majoritarian religions. A further complication is the claim by religious majorities to minority status, usually against a secular state or civil society. Christians, especially (but not always) conservative Christians, argue that their voices are not heard or welcome in the public sphere. This claim to religious persecution is often made simultaneously with the justification of religious practices and symbols as culture and heritage. In the remainder of this chapter, I will briefly consider three examples—again, from Canada, France, and the United States—that illustrate how challenges to majoritarian symbols and practices have ensued. As I will show, the dominant theme of defense of culture and heritage runs through all of them, despite their very different contexts. In this discussion, culture, heritage, and history work in tandem and for the same purpose and result—"it is part of our culture" references history and historical precedent (whether imagined or real) that in turn conjures a particular configuration of who "we" are and the authority to name and deploy that culture and heritage.

"Under the Guise of Culture": The City of Saguenay

In December 2006, Alain Simoneau asked the mayor of his municipality, the city of Saguenay, Quebec, to stop reciting prayers at the beginning of municipal council meetings. Not only did the mayor pray, he also made the sign of the cross and stated "in the name of the Father, the Son and the Holy Spirit."[24] Mayor Jean Tremblay refused Simoneau's request and continued to recite the prayer. In March 2007, the Mouvement Laïque Québécois (Quebec

Secular Movement), an atheist activist group in Quebec, filed a complaint on Simoneau's behalf with the Quebec Human Rights Commission.[25] Also at issue were a crucifix hanging in the council chambers as well as the presence of a Sacred Heart statue.

The Human Rights Commission focused on the prayer, ignoring the complaint about the crucifix and the statue. The commission affirmed the validity of the complaint, but as is its prerogative, decided not to proceed to the Human Rights Tribunal. The option to take that step was open to Simoneau and he decided to proceed. Between the decision of the commission and the tribunal hearing, the council of the city of Saguenay passed a bylaw that changed the wording of the prayer, their intention being to make it more neutral.[26]

Numerous witnesses were called at the 2011 tribunal hearing.[27] In its argument, the city of Saguenay claimed that the prayer and the artifacts were part of the heritage and culture of Saguenay and Quebec rather than religious symbols. The city also argued that the crucifix, statue, and prayer were representative of universal values and that the state had a duty to protect them. The tribunal rejected this position, finding that the prayer and artifacts had religious meaning and that Simoneau had been discriminated against: "The reciting of a prayer and the exhibiting of religious symbols in the state-controlled space constituted by the meetings of the municipal council, where representatives of the people discuss questions of public interest, also have a non-trivial exclusionary effect that substantially stigmatizes people who do not share those values."[28] The tribunal granted damages to Simoneau. The city appealed to the Court of Appeal of Quebec,[29] which found that the prayer and artifacts should be protected under a principle of benevolent neutrality.[30] The Court of Appeal cited with approval the *Lautsi* decision from Italy, mirroring it in tone and approach. In that case, the Grand Chamber of the European Court of Human Rights issued a decision in 2011 that, while largely based on the "margin of appreciation," ultimately allowed a crucifix to remain on the walls of an Italian classroom despite the complaint from an atheist mother. Much of the discussion in the case revolved around the crucifix as an important cultural symbol with religious roots.

The mayor, members of the public, and the Court of Appeal reproduced a construction of the crucifix as a crucial element of a shared history that is virtually uncontested and incontestable. Inextricably bound with identity, a *we* who is foundational, the crucifix and prayer became part of a story of nation and peoples. As a media statement by Mayor Tremblay illustrates: "For me, a Tremblay from Saguenay-Lac-St-Jean, a French-Canadian Catholic, a

Quebecer—for me, it's the basis of our culture here" and "If we let go of everything that distinguishes us, where will French-Canadians be in a few years?"[31]

The city argued that the religious artifacts and practice of prayer were part of tradition and culture. What constitutes tradition is not entirely clear, though. The evidence suggested that the crucifix had been commissioned in the early 1980s and placed in the chambers then. The crucifix was more than 2 feet high, 1 foot wide, and 5 inches thick. The Sacred Heart statue was placed in the front corner of the Chicoutimi town hall in the late 1970s and measured 2 feet high by 1 foot wide and 12 inches thick. It was placed more than 9 feet from the floor, occupying a prominent place in the space where municipal business is conducted. There was vague evidence about when the practice of prayer commenced.

The city of Saguenay not only argued on the basis of tradition but also emphasized the cultural rather than the religious nature of the crucifix and the statue, framing them as secular: "Indeed, things that were once closely linked to specific religious dogma have since become secularized. Given this new context, they cannot, in my view, be removed in the name of a draconian conception of State neutrality. What would be the point of such a result if these things, despite their original meaning, were merely passive witnesses to history? In short, the exercise would involve only drawbacks because it would add nothing more to the concept of neutrality."[32] A local sculptor had made the crucifix in the 1980s at the request of the council. The tribunal reviewed the evidence of the sculptor, Dallaire, who had been creating such works, which he described as works of art, for fifty years. Dallaire explained to the tribunal that "he did not put nails in the hands, which are instead open toward the room: 'Christ is speaking to the mayor and the councillors.' Mr. Dallaire believes that the crucifix was blessed at the time. Mr. Dallaire sculpted more crucifixes formerly, for schools and churches, when 'religion was stronger.' He said he never sculpted exactly the same Christ. He uses the same creative approach for all the crucifixes he sculpts."[33] Despite relying on the same evidence, the Court of Appeal interpreted it quite differently, concluding that "Dallaire testified that his sculpture did not have a religious purpose. Indeed, he explained that the work does not represent the dead Christ and does not show the character nailed to the cross."[34]

Part and parcel of the construction of the crucifix and the prayer as culture and heritage is a paradoxical mix of both its specificity—"our heritage and culture," which is foundational and thus unassailable—as well as its universal applicability.[35] Robert Yelle argues, "Universalism is a political strategy for the marginalization and replacement of competing systems designated as tribal, parochial or limited."[36] The claim to be universal has a uniquely paralyzing effect: The complainant is denied traction for the assertion that he is not included through the deployment of the fact of universalism, which can take the shape of values, ethical frameworks, or simply inclusivity.

Although the Court of Appeal concluded that the prayer and symbols were nonreligious and representative of universal values, the city's mayor clearly articulated his religious motivations. In speaking about the case when it was before the Human Rights Tribunal, Tremblay said to journalists: "I'm in this battle because I worship Christ. When I get to the hereafter, I'm going to be able to be a little proud. I'll be able to say to Him: 'I fought for You; I even went to trial for You.' There's no better argument. It's extraordinary. I'm in this fight because I worship Christ. I want to go to heaven and it is the most noble fight of my entire life."[37] Thus, although the practices and symbols were presented as culture and heritage for the purposes of law, it was clear that for the mayor they connected to a deeply held religious belief and practice. This was precisely the point that Simoneau was making—such symbols and practices link the state to religion in a manner that violated his rights (including "interfere[ing] in a discriminatory manner, on the ground of religion, in the freedom of conscience and religion of Mr. Simoneau"),[38] but they also send a message about the religious position of the state. The move from personal religious belief, such as that held by the mayor, and the erasure or minimization of religion is to claim that the symbols are both personal and universal, representative of values that are shared by everyone.

Universalization erects a protective shield around the symbols and practices in question: Even when challenged as being exclusionary, those symbols and practices are represented as being inclusive, effectively neutralizing the challenger. Implicated in this tension is a narrative of goodness—the challenged symbol represents the community, a time-honored tradition, and culture. It represents a consensus and social cohesion. It carries the mark of collective identity. The challenger is consequently marked as unreasonable, radical, or draconian, clearly outside of the so-called us. Traces of these marks of difference are woven through the cases and the public conversations that surrounded the case.

Ultimately, the matter was appealed to the Supreme Court of Canada,[39] which agreed with the tribunal and found that the recitation of the prayer violated Simoneau's rights protected under Section 3 (which includes freedom of conscience and religion) and Section 10 (the "equality" provisions of the charter, which provide protection from discrimination, including on the basis of religion) of the Quebec Charter of Human Rights and Freedoms. Though the court pointedly noted that the state cannot hide behind "the guise" of culture and heritage to justify privileging religion, it also preserved the possibility that some religious practices and symbols *could* be protected as culturally important. The court itself seemed to be caught between a narrative of diversity, including a vision of a multicultural Canada, and the establishment of Christian practice and symbols. The characterization of the prayer and symbols as culture captures the tension between these visions of who "we" are.

"Noël est fêté par tous les français": La Fédération de la Libre Pensée de Vendée

The town of La Roche-Sur-Yon is the capital of the Vendée department in the Pays de la Loire region in western France and home to a population of more than 53,000 people. In December 2012, the Vendée Federation of Free Thought complained about a nativity scene in La Roche-Sur-Yon's city hall, arguing that it was a violation of the law of 1905 and the Constitution of 1958, which guaranteed freedom of conscience and religious freedom but forbade religious symbols on public buildings. The president of the general council refused to prohibit the installation of a nativity scene in the Vendée town hall, which typically appeared at the beginning of December each year, when some citizens asked him to do so. The town's officials argued that the 1905 law, which had aimed to separate religion and state in France while limiting the church's power, did not support a demand that religious symbols be completely absent; that a Christmas nativity scene did not constitute a religious symbol but a traditional celebration that evolved from a "religious fact"; and that a strong religious tradition in Vendée justified tolerating the presence of a nativity scene as a symbol of a local specificity, which had never been challenged by opposition politicians.[40] The implication was that the presence of the crèche had the agreement of all.

The Administrative Tribunal of Nantes agreed with the federation and outlined the specifically religious nature of the nativity scene in its decision. The tribunal found that the scene represents the birth of Jesus Christ; that the coinciding of the construction of the display with preparations for a Christian festival and of a specifically religious symbol surpasses the simple traditional familial and popular representation of this period; and that the municipality had not successfully established that the display, which takes place at the same time each year, was analogous with a museum display (which is permissible). The tribunal considered the display religious, not culture or heritage.[41]

It was not the end of the matter, and in 2015 the Administrative Court of Appeal of Nantes issued a decision reversing that of the Administrative Tribunal. The Appeal Court reasoned that the display—made up of Mary, Joseph, and accompanying shepherds around the bed of Baby Jesus—was not of a religious nature because it was of a small and unostentatious size; that the scene did not contain other religious elements; and that it belonged to a tradition of the family Christmas celebration.[42] The nativity scene did not, therefore, enter into the realm of those things prohibited by the 1905 law, and it violated neither the principles of freedom of conscience nor the neutrality of the public service.

The case was appealed to the Conseil d'État, France's Administrative Supreme Court, with the federation reminding the Conseil d'État that "La République n'est ni chrétienne, ni juive, ni musulmane, ni athée! La République est laïque! C'est ce que vient de rappeler le Conseil d'État!" ("The republic is not Christian, Jewish, Muslim, or atheist. The republic is secular! This is the verdict of the Council of State!")[43] In November 2016, the Conseil d'État ruled on the *Vendée* case in addition to another case from the Paris Administrative Court of Appeal.[44] The Conseil d'État held that the Administrative Court of Appeal of Nantes had not taken into account all necessary elements, especially the local context, to determine the lawfulness of the display and so referred the case back to the Court of Appeal for reexamination. The Conseil held that the nativity scene could have religious meaning, but it could also simply be decoration marking the end-of-year celebration and could therefore have no religious significance. The Conseil highlighted the placement of the nativity scene as well as whether it could be construed as an act of proselytization or as conforming to the principle of the neutrality of public officials.

Denied religious meaning, the crèche shrunk to an inconsequential, innocuous size that could not possibly harm, even as it took on epic proportions in its significance to French identity. In their submission, the Departement de la Vendée argued that the crèche was not by nature a religious symbol in the sense of the 1905 law, that "Noël est fêté par tous les français" ("Christmas is celebrated by all French people"), and that religious displays that do not upset the public order and that coincide with local and popular traditions do not violate the 1905 law.[45] The municipality circumscribed the boundary of what it meant to be French, implying that anyone who did not join in the celebration was not truly French. The universal relevance of Christmas was taken as a matter of fact, rendering it beyond scrutiny except superficially and certainly not reducible to a mere religious symbol or practice. It was a matter of culture, historically embedded in French society, and a practice of everyone.

Both the court and the municipality identified collective belonging through the notion of the "*fait religieux*" (religious fact), which further embedded the crèche in French culture as a fact that could not be disputed, thereby rendering any effort to do so all the more heinous. The constitution of the crèche de Noël as a cultural symbol emphasized tradition by denying its religious symbolism while at the same time identifying the practice as a mere "fact" of France's Christian religious heritage. Asserting the religious fact erases diversity, both of other religious practices and of nonparticipation or nonreligion and constitutes the celebration of Christmas as a national activity in which all French can or should participate. On this point, the municipality of Vendée was adamant in its insistence, again, that "Christmas is celebrated by all French citizens."[46] Senator Bruno Retailleau positioned participation in this symbolic celebration par excellence as a social interaction capable of weaving strong familial bonds, forging national unity, and fostering social cohesion across humanity.[47]

Over the course of the various court processes, the public reaction to the decisions made local, national, and international news. After the initial tribunal decision, the former chair of the general council for the municipality declared that the elected officials would not apply the decision, which he described as unjust. He accused Libre Pensée of trying to do away with the "roots of our [French] culture," which he described as "an old Christian territory. The nativity is part of its heritage, beyond beliefs and sensibilities."[48] Using the same slippery-slope lament that the mayor of the city of Saguenay had used in Quebec, he declared, "If we give up on this symbol today, we'll have to give up the rest tomorrow."[49] In another comment along similar lines, he wondered if street decorations would also have to be removed: "Le respect de la laïcité n'est pas l'abandon de toutes nos traditions et la coupure avec nos racines culturelles. . . . Faudrait-il interdire les étoiles dans les guirlandes de Noël qui décorent nos rues, sous prétexte qu'il s'agit d'un symbole religieux?" ("Respecting laïcité[50] does not mean abandoning all our traditions and cutting off our cultural roots. . . . Must we ban [even] the stars from Christmas garlands that decorate our streets, under the pretext that they are religious symbols?")[51] These extensions, linked to our traditions and our roots produced a discourse of loss and threat to "us."

French authorities are willing to protect nativity scenes as sacred symbols of what it means to be French: There is no possibility of opting out, or of diversity, a position reinforced by language such as "everyone" and "no one," with those who might object being rendered both noncitizens and a threat. The state, entrusted with guarding *laïcité*, claims to remain committed to ensuring that the public sphere will be free of religious symbols even while preserving vertical, hierarchical relations in the crèche, which is us.

"Not to Divide, but to Unite": The Town of Greece

In 1999, the town of Greece in upstate New York began the practice of opening its town board meetings with a prayer that was intended to "place town board members in a solemn and deliberative frame of mind, invoke divine guidance in town affairs, and follow a tradition practiced by Congress and dozens of state legislatures."[52] Two members of the community, Susan Galloway and Linda Stephens, attended these board meetings and "objected that the prayers violated their religious or philosophical views."[53] Galloway told board members "that she found the prayers 'offensive,' 'intolerable,' and an affront to a 'diverse community.'"[54] Rather than open conversation about diversity and inclusion, Galloway and Stephens received an oppositional and defensive response that eventually propelled them to use the law as a vehicle for change.

At the District Court level, the prayer practice was found not to violate the Establishment Clause, which holds that "Congress shall make no law respecting an establishment of religion, or prohibiting the free exercise thereof." The court held that it was not demonstrated how the town's prayer practice established Christianity. The District Court had noted that the town opened the prayer program to everyone and that no creed had been excluded. However, records showed that from 1999 to 2007 all clergy who gave the invocations were Christian.[55] The Court of Appeals reversed the decision of the District Court, which concluded that a constellation of factors, including the limited promotion of the inclusive invitation to lead the invocation, its geographic limitation, the actions of the board members (bowing heads or making the sign of the cross), and the continuous use of Christian prayers would lead a "reasonable observer" to conclude that the town was affiliating itself with Christianity and was thus unconstitutionally establishing religion. The case was then brought before the Supreme Court of the United States,[56] which held in 2014 that "the town of Greece does not violate the First Amendment by opening its meetings with prayer that comports with our tradition and does not coerce participation by nonadherents. The judgment of the U.S. Court of Appeals for the Second Circuit is reversed."[57] Four of the justices were in dissent (Justices Breyer, Kagan, Ginsburg, and Sotomayor).

In this chapter, I have argued, again, that religion is being transformed into heritage and culture in law and public discourse in the face of challenges to majoritarian practices and symbols. These challenges are becoming more likely because of a new diversity that forces a critical engagement with the privilege that has attached to Christianity during the past centuries in many western democracies. *Town of Greece* is intriguing in that the prayer practice was given some measure of privilege as religion as well as culture, heritage, and history. Caroline Mala Corbin notes that "in earlier cases the Court downplayed the religious significance by claiming that the religious display was really about acknowledging our nation's history or celebrating a national holiday."[58] However, though religion as religion may have been permitted to have a slightly greater presence in *Town of Greece*, it was nonetheless accompanied by a recurring emphasis on the historical presence of Christianity, a Supreme Being, and prayer as a part of legislative ceremonies and a matter of heritage, as is illustrated by this statement from the judgment: "The prayer opportunity in this case must be evaluated against the backdrop of historical practice. As a practice that has long endured, legislative prayer has become part of our heritage and tradition, part of our expressive idiom, similar to the Pledge of Allegiance, inaugural prayer, or the recitation of 'God save the United States and this honorable Court' at the opening of this Court's sessions."[59] The court interpreted the constitutionality of "legislative prayer," which was established as an exception to the prohibition otherwise imposed by the Constitution and the case law, to mean that the town had no obligation to attempt a nonsectarian prayer. The possibility that prayer as a restatement of Christian hegemony might be seen as problematic was not something that the court took up in any serious way. In fact, it was seen as a positive good.[60] Yet, as Nancy Blyth Hersman argues, "The government actions in both *Marsh* and *Lynch v. Donnelly* should have been found to violate the establishment clause based on the *Lemon* test. However, the court appeared to be of the opinion that the governmental practices in those cases had been a part of our society for decades and the 'status quo' should be preserved."[61] These cases were subsequently used in *Town of Greece* (and other cases) to justify a blurry boundary between church and state based on historical "fact."[62] The flexible boundary was affirmed by Justice Anthony M. Kennedy who said, "It is not necessary to define the precise boundary of the Establishment Clause where history shows that the specific practice is permitted."[63]

A distinguishing feature of the legal rhetoric around religious practices that might at first blush seem to be a violation of the U.S. Constitution is the extraordinary emphasis put on history explicitly as history (rather than culture) and the weight it has to justify continuing practices of exclusion, such as Christian prayers at state functions. This straightjacket of history, sometimes referred to as the framers' intention, the intentions of the founding fathers, or the originalist position, has occupied an inordinate amount of scholarly and legal energy in the United States.[64] Further, as Caroline Mala Corbin points out, "Justice Scalia's view of the Establishment Clause, which is itself a reflection of his originalist theory of constitutional interpretation, reflects a certain privileged viewpoint. More particularly, both at a general (originalism) and a specific (the Establishment Clause allows state preference for Judeo-Christianity) level, it is one made possible by white/Christian privilege."[65] Moreover, as Winnifred Fallers Sullivan notes, there is a strong argument for the position that "religion was viewed as a privileged public good by *all* of the founders. The pro-religionists argue, then, that the only constitutional issue is the equal treatment of religions and of believers."[66] Although culture is not often part of the language used in the American context, history steps in to create a justificatory framework that works to preserve the privilege of Christianity in the same way that culture and history do in Canada and France (as well as in Italy, Germany, and elsewhere).

Despite the pervasiveness of the myth of the Christian nation, there was a tension evidenced in the *Town of Greece* decisions: While the *religious* nature of the prayers was to some extent admitted, their specifically *Christian* nature is not. To be sure, the courts acknowledged (and justify) their "sectarian" nature, but not the fact that the sectarian was explicitly Christian. Similarly, God was cloaked as a "higher power" and the purpose of prayer was about lending "gravity to the occasion and [to] reflect values long part of the Nation's heritage."[67] This may seem to be splitting hairs, but it is an effective tool for displacing the privilege given to one religion in a nation that is theoretically diverse and even multicultural.

What is especially intriguing is that the history in the specific instance of *Town of Greece* was relatively recent—the prayer practice had not been part of the council proceedings until 1999. As was the case with the symbols and prayers in the *Saguenay* and *Vendée* cases, the limited historical span of the practice is overlooked. Instead, the local practice is linked to a broader narrative of a Christian history and character of the nation that in turn recreates the local history as a truth. The factual length of time becomes irrelevant—an inconvenient truth that is swept aside in the grand narrative of who "we" are. Terence Ranger and Eric Hobsbawm explore this tenuous relationship between facts and tradition in their edited collection *The Invention of Tradition*.[68] In that volume, they examine the relationship between tradition and social cohesion and, in his chapter, Hobsbawm explicitly identifies the challenge of integrating heterogeneous masses and the solution of creating rituals and practices, which quickly become tradition identified with the nation. Although Hobsbawm mentions this specifically within the context of the United States, his argument may have relevance for the contexts I have explored here. I would add that potential loss of majoritarian status and its concomitant loss of power is another factor to be added into the mix. So, too, are racism, prejudice. and fear of the "other."

Conclusion

Increasingly, law and public discourse identify majoritarian religion in countries around the globe as culture, heritage, or history. This accelerating trend has no single cause, inspiration, or trajectory, but it is quite possibly part of broader social patterns that link to populism, Islamophobia, fear and anxiety related to social change, racism, and nationalism. The move to reconstruct the thing formerly known as religion as culture and heritage effectively takes it outside of religion-based human rights scrutiny. It creates a zone of exemption: By accepting the argument that, for example, prayer before a municipal council meeting or a nativity scene at a town hall are examples of heritage or culture and that they are somehow harmless, noncoercive, and universal, such practices and symbols are set apart from minority religious practices. Further, through their designation as heritage and culture, these symbols and practices become inextricably intertwined with national identities, which are monotone in their religious character. A potential worrisome consequence of this is an erosion of trust in law to bring about the promises of human rights protections, which in turn erodes democracy and the rule of law.

For example, in a recent decision by the Kentucky state government, public schools will now be able to teach a course on the Bible: "The bill's sponsor says students need to understand the role the Bible played in American history."[69] For those who might object, the governor of Kentucky, Matt Bevin, said, "The idea that we would not want this to be an option for people in school, that would be crazy. I don't know why every state would not embrace this, why we as a nation would not embrace this."[70] The notion that the Bible and Christianity are the foundation of human rights and constitutional documents is stated as fact by Representative D. J. Johnson (R-Owensboro) in the Kentucky legislature: "It really did set the foundation that our founding fathers used to develop documents like the Declaration of Independence, the Constitution, the Bill of Rights. . . . All of those came from principles from the Bible."[71] The folding in of everyone, who surely must appreciate this historical fact and its value, reproduces the universal impetus of Christianity identified by scholars like Jonathan Boyarin and Daniel Boyarin.[72] Governor Bevin, for example, claimed: "You could be an atheist, and you would appreciate there's a lot of wisdom in the Bible."[73] It is not clear whether the governor consulted atheists in coming to this conclusion, but appreciating biblical wisdom is not the same as approving its study in public schools. Moreover, such an approach colonizes the entirety of human rights as Christian territory, as though goodness is only accessible through this route.

The narrative of history and its importance is not woven only through decisions of courts but into the very fabric of American society. It is a story that has powerful resonance and which structures the "we" in a manner that is similar to that of the *laïcité*-crèche story in France or the neutrality-crucifix/prayer story in Canada. In both instances, the legal and public discussion erases the "other," who is folded into the narrative or is dismissed as unreasonable, too radical, or mentally unstable.

In societies that are increasingly characterized by all manner of diversity, including the aspects of religious/nonreligious diversity that I have described as the new diversity at the beginning of this chapter, there are potentially serious consequences for failing to renegotiate power and privilege. These include the risk of irreparably damaging the credibility of liberal democracies and their claims about human rights, equality, and universal access. Freedom of religion, for example, cannot be only freedom to be religious exactly like us. In addition, freedom of religion includes the freedom not to be religious at all, or to be a "none." The creation of divisive binaries undermines social inclusion and our ability to live well together with difference. "Our" culture and heritage flattens the rich diversity that creates histories and begs the questions of who defines the content of our culture and heritage and who gets to tell the story of who we are; and, finally, there is a potential that open, frank, and productive conversation about majoritarian culture, power, and inclusion will be shut down or subverted by simply converting Christianity to culture, heritage, and universal values. When people like Alain Simoneau or Susan Galloway say they don't feel included or they feel alienated, and they are met with the response that the practice of symbol is universal, it is akin to telling them that they are not part of the society in which they live.

The story of religion to culture does not belong solely to Christianity. In this chapter, I have focused on three examples that each have a majority Christian population or, put another way, in which Christianity has historically been the dominant religion. It is important to consider this context when examining the religion-to-culture project and to recognize that specific consequences flow from these particular contexts. However, this is not to say that the transformation of religion to culture belongs solely to what might broadly be described as western democracies with majoritarian Christian histories (and in persistent Christian majorities, despite increased diversity and decline of participation in institutional Christianity). For example, Jason Ānanda Josephson maps the creation of a secular Shinto in nineteenth-century Japan, which took a strikingly similar shape to the present-day configurations of religion to culture I discussed above.[74] In Josephson's work, the themes of citizenship and national identity play a key role: Secular Shinto, as it is described by Josephson, bears an uncanny resemblance to the universal Christianity that is folded into stories of "us" in contemporary cases about symbols and practices and their place in late modern societies. The dynamic between the nation and its religion requires a site-specific unpacking. At the same time, stepping back from those specifics suggests that the configuration of the boundaries of religion and culture is part of a complex social web.

Ultimately, the cases I have discussed in this chapter show how each society's unique histories and present circumstances have entangled religion within both the state and civil society. The presence of these entanglements should not deter us from seeking a fair interpretation of religious freedom; they should, instead, lead us to challenge the notion that those with resources can or should have a greater say in the contours of religious freedom and in the shape and interpretation of competing claims. Interpretations of religious freedom require an inclusive approach that recognizes the claims of marginalized groups, including religious, sexual, racial, and gender minorities, as Sharkey and Green suggest in their introduction to this volume. Finally, equitable interpretations of religious freedom also demand a more critical and complex review of histories and a bolder and more expansive understanding of who and what counts as "us."

CHAPTER 5

"Baptism of Ire"

Atheist Plaintiffs and Irreligious Freedom in Postwar America

Leigh E. Schmidt

Woven into modern constructions of religious liberty is an enduring conundrum: Does religious freedom include irreligious freedom? In his foundational essay, *A Letter Concerning Toleration* (1689), John Locke decidedly thought not. Arguing for sharp limits on the state's power to impose or suppress particular modes of worship, Locke concerned himself especially with accommodating different varieties of Protestant Christianity, but he did not end there. His principle of religious toleration was much more sweeping than that. "Neither *Pagan*, nor *Mahumetan*, nor *Jew* ought to be excluded from the Civil Rights of the Commonwealth, because of his Religion," he wrote. This was strong stuff—Locke's principle of religious liberty applied very widely indeed: Christians, Jews, Muslims, and pagans, the customary fourfold way of imagining the world's religious variety in the late seventeenth century—all were included under the umbrella of toleration. Alas, Locke soon ran up against a crucial limitation: atheists and unbelievers. "Those are not at all to be tolerated who *deny the Being of a God*," he declared. "Promises, Covenants, and Oaths, which are the Bonds of Humane Society, can have no hold upon an atheist. The taking away of God, though but even in thought, dissolves all. Besides also, those that by their Atheism undermine and destroy all Religion, can have no pretense of Religion whereupon to challenge the Privilege of a Toleration." Religious toleration did not include irreligious toleration; religious liberty was specifically for the religious, not the irreligious.[1]

The nineteenth-century American Protestant apologist Robert Baird echoed this same principle in his *Religion in America* (1844), a standard compendium on the nation's evangelical churches and its pervasively Christian character. "Rights of conscience are religious rights," Baird insisted, "that is, rights to entertain and utter religious opinions, and to enjoy public religious worship. Now this expression, even in its widest acceptation, cannot include irreligion; opinions contrary to the nature of religion, subversive of the reverence, love, and service due to God, of virtue, morality, and good manners. What rights of conscience can atheism, irreligion, and licentiousness pretend to?" Or, as a Minneapolis newspaper blithely editorialized in 1904: "We claim religious freedom for our strongest plank in [our] national foundations, but irreligious freedom is another matter entirely. Let a man believe what he likes. Let him believe, however." Another half century on, Richard Nixon drew the same line at irreligion when he offered John F. Kennedy an olive branch of toleration for his Roman Catholic faith in the 1960 presidential election: "There is only one way that I can visualize religion being a legitimate issue in an American political campaign. That would be if one of the candidates for the Presidency had *no* religious belief." The unacceptability of atheists in civil society long amounted to an intellectual, political, and cultural commonplace.[2]

Few rushed to defend the rights and liberties of unbelievers in the seventeenth and eighteenth centuries, but there were nonetheless inklings of more expansive views of toleration. The Virginia Statute for Religious Freedom (1786), the brainchild of Thomas Jefferson, had enjoined that religious opinions and beliefs should in no way diminish or enlarge a citizen's civil capacities. Jefferson later specified in his *Autobiography* that he expressly intended the bill to reach beyond the religious to the irreligious, that it comprehended within its mantle of protection "the Jew and the Gentile, the Christian and Mahometan, the Hindoo and infidel." John Adams, writing to his son John Quincy Adams in 1816, insisted that "Government has no Right to hurt a hair of the head of an Atheist for his Opinions," before admonishing: "Let him have a care of his Practices." As Adams's caveat suggested, even when toleration was extended to atheists and unbelievers, it was often done so with an abundance of caution: Could they be counted on as virtuous citizens? Could they be trusted as witnesses in courtrooms or as holders of public office? Could they be accorded the rights of free speech and assembly without their blasphemies subverting public order and morality? Was their freedom to express irreligious opinions—about God or the Bible or the Virgin Birth—the same as for those who conveyed more pious perspectives? Such questions were debated time and again in American public life from the early republic forward and were far from easily resolved.[3]

A progressive story line about the growing toleration of atheists and the advance of the secularist principle of equal citizenship for unbelievers would not be hard to plot. Locke's view of atheists as "wild beasts" to be excluded from civil society sounds entirely illiberal—all but inexplicable by the Jeffersonian standards of church-state separation that prevailed in the United States by the middle decades of the twentieth century. In a series of landmark decisions from *McCollum v. Board of Education* (1948) through *Abington v. Schempp* (1963), the U.S. Supreme Court, guided especially by the opinions of Justice Hugo Black, made the evenhanded treatment of believers and nonbelievers integral to its construal of the First Amendment. Even Justice Potter Stewart, the lone dissenter in the *Schempp* case that disallowed public schools from requiring Bible reading and the recitation of the Lord's Prayer, embraced Black's principle that the religious and the irreligious enjoyed the same rights and liberties: "What our Constitution indispensably protects," Stewart wrote, "is the freedom of each of us, be he Jew or Agnostic, Christian or Atheist, Buddhist or Freethinker, to believe or disbelieve, to worship or not worship, to pray or keep silent, according to his own conscience, uncoerced and unrestrained by government." How this leveled playing field was supposed to work in practice, however, remained much in dispute: How far did a Christian majority have to go to accommodate the objections of a nonbelieving minority? Would atheist protestations of the national motto, "In God We Trust," or the phrase "under God" in the Pledge of Allegiance need to be recognized? Would the principle of evenhanded neutrality have to be applied to military and prison chaplaincies, nativity scenes in public parks, prayers before municipal board meetings, and courtroom displays of the Ten Commandments? This much was nonetheless hard to dispute: Atheists and nonbelievers were on far firmer constitutional ground by 1965 than they had been in 1791, let alone in 1689.[4]

How much firmer, though? The terrain was obviously more shifting and treacherous than the panoramic view from Locke to Black suggests; the progressive story line was necessarily bleaker and more potholed. The cases that atheist and secularist plaintiffs pursued in the mid-twentieth century often came at considerable personal cost. Publicly vilified, many of them faced significant harassment, intimidation, and social dislocation. As freethinking activists for very strict constructions of church-state separation, they routinely ran afoul of religious sensibilities that wove together church, home, community, and school as the essential fabric of a God-blessed nation. Justice William O. Douglas, suspicious of the growing height of Black's wall of separation, worried in 1952 about how far the court might go to meet the objections of what he called the "fastidious atheist." What would become of "prayers in our legislative halls" or "the proclamations making Thanksgiving Day a holiday" or the invocations of God in courtroom oaths? "These and all other references to the Almighty that run through our laws, our public rituals, our ceremonies," Douglas warned, might fall prey to the persnickety secularist. "We are a religious people," he summarily concluded, "whose institutions presuppose a Supreme Being." No matter the judicial affirmations of neutrality—that the religious and irreligious enjoyed the same rights, liberties, and protections under the First Amendment—the fastidious atheist, even when victorious in the courtroom, often remained engulfed in hostility, discrimination, and intolerance in a nation that overwhelmingly presupposed God. The lived experience of these mid-century plaintiffs suggests how hard it was to uphold the equal liberty and citizenship of atheists even after the nation's highest court had weighed in on the matter. The how-far-freedom-has-come story is helpfully re-scripted through closer examination of what it was like to be one of these plaintiffs at the very time the principle of neutrality was ascendant. It was not that religious freedom was impossible for nontheists, but it certainly remained fugitive in the face of mundane practices of exclusion, dissociation, and prejudice.[5]

With the Supreme Court newly open to Establishment Clause challenges of Christianity's favored status, litigation grew increasingly pivotal to atheist activism from the mid-1940s on. "Sue the Bastards!" became the rallying cry of Madalyn Murray O'Hair and her organization, American Atheists, and that group created its own legal fund and in-house counsel to file "suit after suit" in the decades following O'Hair's initial salvo against the Baltimore public schools in 1959. O'Hair labeled these activities an exercise in "litigious education"; even when American Atheists lost, each court fight provided her organization an opportunity to lecture the public about the principle of strict church-state separation. Lifted up by the media as headline-grabbing provocateurs, atheist plaintiffs came to be seen as dauntless protagonists inside secularist ranks and godless militants beyond those circles. They became convenient Cold War emblems of the joined threats of secularism and communism to the nation's religious character. O'Hair was the most vociferous, litigious, and despised of this cohort, but none of these fastidious atheists got off easy. They lived with a certain vigilantism and bullying designed to intimidate anyone else who might come forward with a similar challenge to the nation's civic faith in God, prayer, the Bible, and Christmas. The more legal success they had, the more intense extralegal threats became. Lawrence Roth, a Jewish atheist plaintiff in the *Engel* school-prayer case, had his home picketed and he received death threats. A cross of gasoline-drenched rags was burned in his driveway by a group of teenagers who went unprosecuted.[6]

Arthur Cromwell, founder of a local Society of Freethinkers in Rochester, New York, was another among the high-profile petitioners who repeatedly challenged religious programs and activities in the public schools. Typical of the ire he provoked was a letter he received in 1951 about a threatened suit against a Christmas pageant at an area high school: "You had better get down on your knees and thank God that the people here in America allow you and others like you to live," this self-identified 100 percent American and Christian urged. "You ought to be shipped over to Russia where you belong. Thank God, your funds are running low and I hope they run so low that you and yours starve to death. That would be a better death than you deserve. I am sure God has no place in heaven for such a thing as you are. Wishing you all the tortures of Hell, and hoping you lose your mind and end up in the State Institution—and get the worst kind of treatment." Cromwell's compensation for all the antipathy he provoked as a devoted atheist was the modest celebrity it earned him in secularist circles. Journals like *Progressive World* and the *Bulletin* of the Freethinkers of America sang his praises, and he was lionized at the annual convention of the American Rationalist Federation in St. Louis, Missouri, in 1961, for having so long kept up the fight against religion in the public schools. Mostly, though, he was pictured as a godless crank and communist tool inimical to the nation's welfare.[7]

Cromwell would have remained primarily a local combatant but for his freethinking daughter Vashti McCollum, the successful litigant against a release-time program for religious instruction in Champaign, Illinois. The fact that McCollum's case wound its way to the Supreme Court—and that she prevailed—elevated the attention given her father's efforts, even as her own notoriety and consequence quickly surpassed his. The hate mail she received, pouring in from around the country, was as voluminous as it was venomous. One letter writer enclosed a newspaper clipping of her picture disfigured with devil's horns and a tail, along with the scrawled assurance: "God will find a way to overcome the devil's work." Another correspondent scribbled, "You are a disgrace to our nation . . . and should be driven out of this country at once";

still another accused the conventionally monogamous McCollum of loose sexuality and suggested a violent remedy: "You probably had your child before you married if you are married. What you need is someone to beat the hell out of you." The bullying of her son Jim, whose refusal to participate in the release-time program of religious instruction had triggered the whole case, became so intense that McCollum and her husband felt compelled to withdraw him from the Champaign schools. They sent him to live with his grandparents in Rochester, where he enrolled in a private school at a safe distance from the immediate conflict. McCollum lost her part-time job at the University of Illinois, and her husband's appointment was threatened as well. Although she won significant allies among civil liberties activists and humanistic Unitarians, she and her family were nonetheless ostracized, maligned, and menaced with an intensity that made her court victory look quite limited in effect. She successfully challenged one release-time program, but the community's majority continued to elevate religion above irreligion with only modest relief for the minority standing of McCollum's humanistic secularism.[8]

McCollum had the satisfaction of the Supreme Court's vindication, which launched her to some celebrity (she published a memoir, *One Woman's Fight*, and became a widely recognized standard-bearer in secularist circles). Most atheist plaintiffs, though, had far less to show for their contrarian showdowns with state and local officials. The story of Garry and Mary De Young, a pair of Delaware atheists, is worth dwelling on in that regard. Bit players compared to headliners like McCollum and O'Hair, the De Youngs were tenacious church-state separationists in the 1960s and 1970s. Their atheistic preoccupations and litigious predilections, Garry's especially, made a mess of their lives, and they left an archive that amply demonstrates the instability that was the consequence of their freethinking activism: twenty-five unprocessed boxes sitting in the Dolph Briscoe Center for American History at the University of Texas at Austin. The De Youngs were fastidious atheists, and certainly litigants like them were having their day in court, winning crucial victories about prayer and Bible reading in the public schools, about the rights of nontheists to hold offices of public trust as well as to claim a humanistic ground for conscientious objection. The principle of neutrality—that impartiality was to govern the state's treatment of believers and unbelievers, theists and nontheists—had come to enjoy (at least for a time) a constitutional consensus. Yet, so much went wrong for Mary and Garry De Young as they pursued their ardent secularism on the margins of communities from Delaware to Minnesota to Iowa to Texas to Kansas. The Supreme Court's eloquent opinions regarding the religious liberty and full equality of nonbelievers failed, time and again, to materialize at a local level where "microclimates" of hostility toward atheist activists like the De Youngs proved impossible to escape from one place to the next.[9]

The De Youngs wanted to get religion out of the Delaware public schools, much like the McCollums in Illinois, the Murrays in Maryland, and the Schempps in Pennsylvania. Garry, especially, had been raised for a life of fractious unbelief. His father, a poultry farmer in New Jersey, was a socialist who had left behind his Dutch Reformed faith and embraced the freethinking iconoclasm of Emanuel Haldeman-Julius, a prolific publisher of irreligious literature, based in Girard, Kansas. The family's finances, particularly during the Great Depression, had been precarious. Garry recalled his father renting out the family home and moving them all into one of his chicken coops, but he also remembered socialist luminaries like Norman Thomas and Scott Nearing visiting the small farm and picnicking with them. All told, he recollected a youth of painful peculiarity—on the outs with the wider community over religion, politics, and socioeconomic status. Finishing high school and unable to afford college, he enlisted in the United States Army, earned six bronze stars during World War II, and reenlisted thereafter. Shortly after the war, he learned of another social marker of marginality for his family: His father had a half-brother who was black. Having "an uncle of color" brought racial discrimination into sharp focus for De Young—an awareness that was only heightened when he decided he wanted to attend Delaware State College, which until 1947 had been known as the State College for Colored Students. Despite white segregationist objections, De Young managed to enroll there and became the school's first white graduate in 1956. His years at Delaware State in the mid-1950s effectively educated him in civil rights activism as he eagerly joined in protests to desegregate local restaurants and theaters. Fighting injustice and discrimination, he saw clearly, required direct involvement on his part, not simply "vicarious experiences" of outrage. "Brotherhood," he wrote at the head of one of his poems in 1964, "is really the act of keeping your head on the chopping block until every human being can walk in freedom and dignity."[10]

Mary De Young, a teacher in the Delaware public schools, was keenly aware—along with her husband—of the growing agitation over prayer and Bible reading in the classroom. The Supreme Court cases of 1962 and 1963 that had declared both practices unconstitutional seemed right on target to the De Youngs, both of whom were nonbelievers and were raising their children that way. The unison recitation of the Lord's Prayer and the reading of at least five verses from the King James Bible were required at the opening of each day in Delaware's public schools, and students were instructed to "assume a reverential attitude" when performing both. The state's attorney general, David Buckson, had been openly critical of the Supreme Court decisions against such practices and had no interest in enforcing the rulings. The De Youngs, along with a liberal Protestant family, had stepped forward with the backing of the American Civil Liberties Union (ACLU) to challenge the state's continued allowance of these ceremonies. The Third U.S. District Court sided with the plaintiffs and required compliance with the *Engel* and *Schempp* decisions. Much to Attorney General Buckson's chagrin, Delaware had been forced (in his view) "to ignore God" in its public schools and endorse this disturbing secularist trend in American public life. "I believe it is a religious country," Buckson told reporters, and he brought in Episcopal bishop James A. Pike to corroborate his stance in the case. Reciting the Lord's Prayer and reading the Bible, Pike explained on television with Buckson, were "nonsectarian" gestures, basic to what it meant to be part of a "Judeo-Christian culture." Atheist children who refused to participate in these schoolhouse devotions threatened the very fabric of that culture in much the same way that children of the Jehovah's Witnesses did when refusing to salute the flag and pledge allegiance to it. God and country were at stake in the hallowed rites of the nation's schoolchildren. And the atheists were worse: They wanted the revered practices banned; the Jehovah's Witnesses only sought exemptions from coerced uniformity.[11]

The De Youngs, in this initial battle, had been relatively careful in their public statements. They both rejected the atheist label and claimed the gentler one of agnostic. Garry emphasized that he thought knowledge of the Bible was an important feature of his children's cultural education and that he simply opposed compulsory devotional reading in the public schools; Mary, for her part, said she would keep performing these religious practices in her classroom as required until the three-judge panel ruled on their constitutionality. Those gestures did not help them much in swaying local opinion, which Buckson was effectively channeling. "If you don't like the way the school is run in the US," one man wrote Mary from Wilmington, "why don't you go to Russia? You can teach fine over there and you don't have to read the Bible there. That is the place for all your kind of people." Popular scorn, though, was only part of the price the De Youngs paid for their litigiousness. Mary, untenured, lost her teaching job (few parents were willing to expose their second graders to her unbelief, and the Middletown school board made no bones about wanting to get rid of her for taking part in this lawsuit). Garry, having refashioned himself in his late thirties as a poet of the open road, had already been patching jobs together in haphazard ways—raising bees, selling encyclopedias, and hawking his self-published verse. His latest collection of poems, journalists noted with lurid glee, was called *Sex, Church, and the Jungle*. Garry lacked, to say the least, anything like job security. "Me and my family," he wrote later, "were reduced to destitution as a result of the black-listing and job loss resulting from this lawsuit." Despite their legal vindication, the case had damaged the De Youngs financially and exhausted them emotionally. They were keenly aware now of being a family of outsiders in Middletown, an unwanted minority at odds with most of their neighbors.[12]

Within the year, the De Youngs left Delaware for a fresh start in Minnesota, first moving to Cass Lake and then to Duluth where Mary got a job as a caseworker in the county welfare department. Garry remained as eccentric and underemployed as ever, prone to exaggerating his educational and artistic accomplishments, picking up odd jobs now and again, and then opening a freethought bookshop in a converted storefront in the family's Duluth home in 1967. He stocked his shelves with a range of anticlerical literature from Voltaire to Robert Ingersoll to the Little Blue Books of Emanuel Haldeman-Julius, while also continuing to vend his own poetry. Inside the store, he kept "a large plywood sign with a black inscription reading 'Help Stamp Out Atheists,'" which someone had deposited on his lawn and which De Young saved as indicative of "typical Christian tactics" to intimidate him. Since leaving Delaware, he had become all the more aggressive in his irreligious posture; he delighted in the atheist mantle and had picked up some of O'Hair's flair for the staging of conflict. A thoroughgoing secularist, he was ready to object to everything from Sunday closing laws to the phrase "under God" in the Pledge of Allegiance.[13]

Undeterred by the opposition they had faced in Delaware, the De Youngs complained in late 1967 about elements of "sectarian religious indoctrination" that they detected in Duluth's public schools. They saw this as particularly evident in the routine of a lunchtime grace and the annual Christmas programming. Their protest had the desired effect: The daily blessing, broadcast over the high school's public address system, was suspended, and their children's elementary school dropped a number of religious hymns from its holiday celebration. To say the least, the couple's complaint proved controversial, and their challenge bred far more hostility than it did understanding. Their children were taunted and harassed; Garry's bookshop and the family's car were vandalized; a county commissioner speculated on a television news program that Mary, as an atheist, was unqualified to be a caseworker and should be fired; the city slapped housing code violations on the family's residence; they were deluged with hate mail; and the police warned them of bomb threats to their home. It was, as one newspaper headline declared, a "baptism of ire." Garry was understandably furious and raved now against the prejudice that he and his family faced as atheists: "I do not consider the religious community as anything but my enemy. I have been personally subjected to the rankest and vilest forms of discriminatory practice at the hands of religionists. . . . Frankly, there is nothing to discuss. Just get the superstition out of the schools." Cooler heads urged careful review of the church-state issues—say, how religious ideas and symbols might be studied in public schools as part of history, social studies, and the arts. But neither De Young nor his exasperated critics could muster that kind of dispassion as the controversy roiled the community. "He makes life so miserable for himself and his family," the pastor of First Lutheran Church lamented. "If there is no God, why should he fight so hard against him?" For his part, De Young had come to see such confrontations as a fundamental test of his secularist commitments. "The more you get knocked down," he explained, "the more of a responsibility it becomes."[14]

The family, ostracized in Duluth, felt compelled to relocate again, this time to St. Paul, where Garry finally gave up on the notion that he would make a living as a poet and got a job with the Minnesota Highway Department, writing brochures and news releases. With the events in Duluth and Middletown weighing on him, Garry had come to see fighting discrimination against atheists, more than emulating Walt Whitman, as his defining purpose—a cause that he increasingly couched in the language of civil rights activism. By 1971, he had incorporated the Church of Philosophical Materialism "to minister to the needs of Atheists" along with the Minnesota Institute of Philosophy, a correspondence school that awarded PhDs and that better pedigreed rationalists disdained as a diploma mill. (The institute awarded O'Hair a PhD in 1972 that seemed honorary at best.) Already notorious in the state as an atheist meddler, De Young continued to call attention to prejudices—large and small—against nonbelievers. All the routine habits of civic theism—from invocations at city council meetings to the ritual opening of court sessions, "God save this honorable court"—attracted his indignation. When the master of a local Masonic lodge publicly reiterated the group's ban on atheists, along with the senile and insane, De Young denounced the statement as slanderous. So toxic had De Young's reputation become that even the Minnesota chapter of the ACLU wanted to avoid association with him when he tried to join the fight against the use of state taxes to aid parochial schools. "We don't want any Atheists as part of this," De Young recalled being told when he volunteered to help. "We definitely don't want you."[15]

Meanwhile, his job at the Highway Department started to unravel. The first year or two went smoothly enough, but in the spring of 1971 he got involved in a civil rights case concerning the firing of an African American colleague. De Young saw the maneuvering that had gone into eliminating the man's job as rife with racial discrimination and protested to state officials. From then on, De Young reported that the work environment turned increasingly hostile: His writing was nitpicked, and his pieces rejected; his looks—his beard, long hair, yellow socks, and sandals—were criticized. Predictably, it was music at a Christmas party that provided the final flashpoint. He found the religious playlist offensive—as if the office holiday party was only for Christians, not Jews, Muslims, or secularists. When De Young interrupted the Christmas music with a recording of a recent pop song by the band Think called "Things Get a Little Easier Once You Understand," his Roman Catholic supervisor saw the gesture as insubordinate and perverse. (The song highlights the generation gap, but it is not overtly atheistic; De Young described it as having a "Humanist thrust" and intended his playing of it as "a symbolic expression of dissent.") His boss was already scornful of De Young's moonlighting as an organizer of an atheist institute, and this latest jab at Christmas cemented his view of De Young as a disruptive propagandist. (De Young pointed out that his boss had no problem allowing the Little Sisters of the Poor to solicit funds on state premises, while counting De Young's expression of his minority religious opinions as proselytizing.) The conflict between De Young and his supervisor rapidly devolved from there. It ended in De Young's firing and an extended lawsuit over workplace discrimination. A little more than two years later, in January 1974, De Young briefly prevailed. With the Minnesota Human Rights Commission on his side, the Highway Department was ordered to pay him $12,200 in back wages for firing him largely because he was an outspoken atheist. On appeal, however, the Minnesota Supreme Court upheld De Young's firing—that it had been on performance grounds, not because he was an argumentative secularist.[16]

The mess at the Highway Department almost destroyed the couple's marriage. After years of enduring her husband's fitful employment and his unending battles, Mary had filed for divorce. Somehow, though, the De Youngs persevered. They decided to put the combined wreckage of Garry's dismissal, the resulting legal quagmire, and their own marital breakdown behind them by moving again, this time to Mercedes, Texas, where they spent three years. They kept up their old freethinking habits. They continued to publish a journal called the *Crucible*, which they presented as the official publication of their atheistic ministry, the Church of Philosophical Materialism. They marked their opposition to Christian prayers at city council meetings, to blue laws, and to the distribution of Gideon Bibles in the public schools. There were some visible slights in Mercedes, but none with the drama of Middletown, Duluth, or St. Paul. Mary was hastily replaced by a Baptist minister on a local committee when her atheism became manifest in a column she wrote for the town's newspaper. "Humiliation in Mercedes" was the headline the couple gave to the piece in the *Crucible* recounting her removal. Likewise, Garry's claim that he helped the new mayor in his election campaign earned a quick public denial and distancing: "I believe in God. I love God. I fear God. I am not an atheist," the mayor pledged to an inquiring journalist. But these were tiny dustups compared to the controversies the couple had provoked elsewhere. They had a little more freedom for their irreligion in Mercedes, Texas, but their neighbors were certainly not rushing to be associated with them. By now, the De Youngs were accustomed to a life of tenuous connection and vagrant movement from one place to the next.[17]

In March 1978, they moved to Hull, Iowa, drawn there by cheap housing afforded by an aged subscriber to their secularist mission. They were living primarily on a monthly disability pension of $447 from the Veterans Administration and, as ever, needed whatever financial help they could get. Hull, however, was an inauspicious place for an atheist family to land. In the northwest corner of the state, with a strong Dutch Reformed heritage, it was a small community in which Protestant folkways securely prevailed. Prayer and Bible reading were still commonplace in the public schools there, and Mary immediately wrote a letter to the superintendent questioning the constitutionality of those practices. Knowing the negative outcome of any court fight, Hull school officials relented and stopped the classroom religious exercises. Soon the De Youngs were in the news again: "Atheists, Christians feud in Hull," proclaimed a headline in the *Des Moines Register*. "I don't know why [Garry] De Young would want to come here and disturb the peace and tranquility of a God-fearing people," Hull's mayor told a reporter. "He's like a fish out of water. He doesn't belong in this area."

The couple's fifteen-year-old son, Charles Darwin De Young, then a freshman in high school, took much of the heat in this latest disturbance. Taunted on the school bus as a "Dirty Atheist" and provoked into misbehavior, he was suspended from the bus and stopped going to school. The bus driver admitted that Charles and his younger brother, Frank, had been "harassed a lot," so much so that the driver had once admonished the other kids: "If you're really Christians, then what's with this hateful attitude towards these people?" The De Youngs resorted to homeschooling the two boys and filed a protest with the Iowa Civil Rights Commission, claiming that their older son's treatment by the school district was a form of religious discrimination. They got nowhere with their latest complaint, and Garry increasingly saw his "second-class citizenship" in evidence in every bureaucratic encounter he had in Hull: no response to his request for a deed, a new zoning law that prevented him from processing his berries into preserves, the foot-dragging of the Rural Water Association to avoid providing him with service, school personnel who were indifferent to his sons' educational fate. He found it almost impossible, he said, "to survive in Northwest Iowa when holding views at variance with the majority of the local population." One schoolteacher finally decided she wanted to be helpful to these misfits, writing the De Youngs in June 1980: "Since you are not comfortable living here, I am willing to stick my neck out and help you move to more suitable surroundings." It was not long before the De Youngs gave up on Hull and relocated to Spencer, Iowa, before landing in Stanwood, Washington.[18]

Late in life, in the 1990s, the De Youngs were trying to keep the creditors at bay through a tree nursery in Stark, Kansas. The children were all long grown, so the couple no longer had to do battle with the public schools on their behalf. Garry embraced the nineteenth-century moniker of "The Village Atheist," emblematic of his lifetime of forlorn nonconformity at odds with local religious norms. He created some letterhead with that designation and suggested he was going to start a new publication under that title. But his health was poor, and his frame of mind was increasingly bitter and conspiratorial. The idea never materialized. His old dream of sustaining an atheist church and university had run aground years ago. He felt forgotten and marginal, cheated of his due for his decades of sacrifice for the secularist cause. In 1993, at age 70, he managed one last manifesto of atheistic grievance, *Religion: The Disease*. It bemoaned the exclusion of atheists by the Boy Scouts as well as by organizations like the Veterans of Foreign Wars and the American Legion, but it took particular aim at a beekeeper's association in Oklahoma that had refused him a program spot unless he refrained from commenting on religion. He had suffered through religious invocations and benedictions at a national convention of beekeepers in Kansas City and felt the imperative to remind those in the trade of the warfare between science and religion. The Religious Right, in De Young's view, would substitute creationism for evolutionary science anywhere they could, even in the honey industry. The self-published book had no circulation; it was a last rant of an angry old man whose rage at everything from Bill Clinton's philandering to Rush Limbaugh's bombast had become boundless. When an editor of a free-thought journal asked him for a review copy, De Young felt too strapped for resources to send one. "Please keep in mind that I have been on the very front line in fighting these Atheist battles in the most difficult forum of all, the courts!" he explained. "It has not been easy at all, the stresses of these lawsuits resulting in six bypasses and financial ruin." His gloom did not seem overblown; rather, it was a realistic assessment of how much his fastidious atheism had cost him and his family.[19]

What had the ascendant principle of neutrality been worth to the De Youngs over the course of their highly litigious lives? With the *Engel* and *Schempp* decisions on their side, they pursued successful challenges to religious practices in the public schools of Middletown, Duluth, and Hull. When it came to prayer, Bible reading, and Christmas programs in the public schools, a nonbelieving minority was able to compel the believing majority to recognize its secularist demands. Those were substantial victories. Yet, when those wins are seen against the wider backdrop of the hardships the De Youngs faced, they look rather wan. Garry and Mary both lost jobs in large part because of their godless stands; their children endured considerable grief as troublemaking atheists and suffered from the financial insecurity of their parents; and public officials treated the family as nuisances, if not pariahs. They were forced into a marginal, vagrant existence, often with quite meager resources for sustaining themselves. Garry was, to be sure, a disagreeable soul who only got more acerbic and litigious as the years went by; he was often his own worst enemy. He had an enormous chip on his shoulder; privation and ill-health only made it bigger; he launched protest runs for public office that looked delusional; he could not understand why elite PhD programs would not admit him; he was, by the end of his life, an ill-tempered curmudgeon as much as a principled activist.[20] Whatever Garry's flaws, though, much of his irascibility grew out of a bitter realization: The playing field remained, for all his work, quite slanted against overt nonbelievers. The winning cases of plaintiffs such as Vashti McCollum and Lawrence Roth were important vindications, but the promise of equal rights and liberties for atheists had proven very hard to realize in practice. Affirmations of neutrality—that the state was to ensure that the irreligious enjoyed the same freedoms and protections as the religious—sounded impressive in the abstract, but they were far muddier in application. The lived experience of exacting atheists like the De Youngs made the breadth of that gap quite apparent. They were often still treated like Locke's "wild beasts," dangers to civil society who had to be contained. Toleration of them was grudging at best.

"What is freedom of religion?" the freethinker Miriam Allen deFord had asked in 1947 in the pages of *Progressive World*, a secularist monthly favored by the De Youngs and other atheist activists of the era. The American system still seemed, in deFord's view, governed by the old Lockean premise: "You choose the manner in which you worship a god, and the style in which you address him, but worship some sort of god you must." Freedom of religion, she suggested, meant little without corresponding liberty for those who wanted freedom from religion. The close entwining of faith and citizenship that deFord lamented was only heightened as the Cold War intensified, but she also wrote at the front edge of the Supreme Court's sustained reconsideration of Jefferson's wall of separation. In 1947, Justice Hugo Black vigorously asserted his views on the importance of closely monitoring violations of the Establishment Clause in his majority opinion in *Everson v. Board of Education*. All citizens—whether "Catholics, Lutherans, Mohammedans, Baptists, Jews, Methodists, Nonbelievers, Presbyterians, or the members of any other faith," in Black's compendious listing—were to share equally in the rights and liberties of the First Amendment. The state should be studiously "neutral in its relations" with "religious believers and nonbelievers," he argued. Plaintiffs like Vashti McCollum, Lawrence Roth, Madalyn Murray O'Hair, and Edward Schempp depended on that proposition as did the De Youngs, but their trust in how far Black's reasoning would reach was only partially rewarded.[21]

Secularists won some, but they lost more as the suits piled up in the long wake of the Supreme Court's reappraisal of the Establishment Clause. The wins that nonbelievers chalked up were generally of two types. First, there were those that built on the *Engel* decision, banning prayer from the public schools. A case in Chandler, Arizona, in 1981, for example, successfully challenged prayers at high school commencements—a position that was then confirmed in *Lee v. Weisman*, which the Supreme Court decided in 1992. Second, there were those that built on the *Torcaso v. Watkins* decision of 1961 overruling Maryland's constitutional requirement of a declared belief in God for those holding offices of public trust. (The state had tried to prevent Roy Torcaso, an atheistic freethinker, from becoming a notary public but lost the case at the Supreme Court, thanks again to the reasoning of Justice Hugo Black.) Hence, South Carolina, despite the efforts of the governor and other state officials, failed to maintain a religious test and prevent an atheistic mathematics professor, Herb Silverman, from becoming a notary public in the 1990s. The areas in which freethinking plaintiffs consistently lost were more numerous: challenges to tax exemptions for church property; to prayers opening city council meetings and sessions of Congress; and to ceremonial and formulaic theistic expressions, such as "In God We Trust" on currency. Some issues, such as the public display of religious imagery at Christmas, ended up split. Expressly religious banners came down in a case in Escondido, California, in 1987; a nativity scene, taken as a cultural representation of the family, remained in place in the capitol rotunda in Texas in 1980. In *Lynch v. Donnelly* (1984), in a 5–4 decision, the Supreme Court gave that cultural reading of crèche symbolism its imprimatur and rejected a stricter secularist view of the Establishment Clause. After four-plus decades of litigation, fastidious atheists were left well short of the clarity they sought in their legal campaigns for thorough disestablishment.[22]

Employment discrimination cases, like the ones that the De Youngs lost, were another type that often did not go well. The potential snares for atheists in the workplace were on full display in math teacher Bruce Hunter's long-running battle with the Dallas Independent School District in the 1970s. Hunter had been teaching in the district for well over a decade and had become a recognized leader of several successful math and science programs at Bryan Adams High School. When a Canadian evangelist was invited to speak at the school in October 1970, ostensibly about the prevention of drug abuse, several teachers objected to his "revival-type preaching." Hunter took the lead in an effort to pass a resolution against combining Christian evangelism with school assembly programs. The proposed resolution was tabled for fear of sparking a community backlash against the teachers involved, but word got out to the news media all the same. Hunter was singled out as the one pushing for removing "sectarian religious viewpoints" from the Dallas schools, and this occasioned the principal to warn him: "I have gotten parents and students coming to me asking me to kick you out."[23]

That initial controversy died down, but rumors lingered that Hunter was an atheist. The next flashpoint came in 1972 when a student asked him what he thought of the "under God" phrase in the Pledge of Allegiance, and Hunter admitted he was opposed to it, which caused the gossip to intensify and cemented his reputation as "the Atheist teacher." At that point, some parents began requesting that their children be transferred out of his classes, and the principal obliged their qualms. The situation gradually worsened from there. By 1974, the principal had joined arms with the PTA to force Hunter's transfer to another high school, where he was demoted to teaching remedial math classes and where the new principal saw it as his mission to bring people to Christ, openly promoting evangelical groups such as Young Life and the Fellowship of Christian Athletes in school assemblies. The new principal perceived Hunter's objections to his efforts to cultivate a positive Christian ethos at the school as insubordinate, as failing to be a team player. How could Hunter object to a program promoting Christian service and warning of the moral dangers of "godlessness"—adultery, drunkenness, dishonesty, and drugs? Meanwhile, parents were again requesting transfers, and some of his students had begun calling him out as an "Atheist queer" and "Atheist weirdo," among other choice expressions. The principal found cause to place Hunter on probation in 1975 and then to terminate him in 1976. Filing suit against the district for religious discrimination, Hunter sought reinstatement and back pay but lost in the District Court and on appeal to the Fifth Circuit, both of which upheld the school district's actions. The court accepted the performance rationales the principal had cited and dismissed religion as a motivating factor in his firing. Hunter had clearly found no relief from his quandary through claiming Title VII protections against employment discrimination or through invoking Black's principle of neutrality. The Supreme Court's constitutional readings of the Establishment Clause failed to guide the practices of school administrators, to protect Hunter from censure and termination, or to place nonbelief on anything like equal footing with belief in the Dallas public schools.[24]

The situation has not gotten much clearer since plaintiffs like Hunter and the De Youngs waged their battles. Justices William Rehnquist and Antonin Scalia, hoping to whittle down Black's church-state legacy, launched sharp attacks on what Scalia termed "the supposed principle of neutrality between religion and irreligion." Forcefully calling into question the wall-of-separation views that the court had advanced in the mid-twentieth century, Scalia defended a common-ground monotheism as the nation's shared inheritance—one that the state had long endorsed and should not abandon. As he wrote in a 2005 dissent supporting the display of the Ten Commandments in Kentucky courtrooms, "With respect to public acknowledgment of religious belief, it is entirely clear from our Nation's historical practices that the Establishment Clause permits . . . the disregard of devout atheists." Both the nation's religious history and its original political framing were, Scalia argued, on the side of the God-affirming against the God-denying. On this counter-reading, the challenges posed by fastidious atheists—from Vashti McCollum to more recent agitators like Michael Newdow—simply do not need to be taken seriously. The nation's "ceremonial deism" is a given of the American polity. The very pursuit of neutrality, so the counter-argument goes, is little more than a subterfuge that masks secularist hostility toward religion. Seen as a belated innovation in First Amendment jurisprudence, the principle should be set aside as an aggressive assault on the country's religious underpinnings.[25]

Much of the contemporary landscape for atheist plaintiffs would remain quite familiar to the freethinking activists of the postwar era. Recent conflicts over the Pledge of Allegiance and the Boy Scouts would be all too familiar, so would questions about the treatment of atheists in the military, including the question of recognizing nontheistic chaplains. With three sons following his footsteps into the military, it had always rankled Garry De Young that their dog tags did not specify their religious identity as atheist and that there were no atheist chaplains to provide them support. "There ARE Atheists in foxholes," he insisted, but they hardly dared to "open their yaps" about it. Familiar, too, would be the old fights over religion in the public schools. The case of Jessica Ahlquist, a sixteen-year-old high school student in Rhode Island, makes that plain. In 2011, she challenged a religious display on the wall of her school's auditorium—an eight-foot-high prayer banner that invoked "Our Heavenly Father" for moral strength and character. Placed in the auditorium in 1963, it was intended as a local reproach to the Supreme Court's blanket rulings removing prayer and Bible reading from the public schools. Though baptized Catholic, Ahlquist had come to see herself as a committed atheist and found the prayer exclusionary: "It seemed like it was saying, every time I saw it, 'You don't belong here.'" With the support of the ACLU, Ahlquist filed a lawsuit to have the exhibited prayer taken down. Much as had been the case with the McCollums and the De Youngs, that legal challenge immediately made Ahlquist the object of hate-filled threats as a scourge to God and country. When a federal judge decided the case in Ahlquist's favor in January 2012, her own state representative denounced her on talk radio as "an evil little thing." It all sounded so strangely overheated and yet also utterly familiar. Ahlquist had become a fastidious atheist. Arthur Cromwell, Vashti McCollum, Lawrence

Roth, Madalyn Murray O'Hair, Edward Schempp, Garry and Mary De Young, Bruce Hunter—any of them could have written this latest schoolhouse script. Ahlquist prevailed but not without her own baptism of ire. In theory, over the last several decades, atheists had been accorded equal rights, liberties, and protections; they were officially tolerable. In practice, irreligious freedom proved fraught and fractional in a nation resolutely under God.[26]

CHAPTER 6

The Heads or Tails of Cow Protection in India

Religious Freedom and Secular Agriculture

Cassie Adcock

When we survey the global politics of religion, what do we see? Tracts of unruly religion awaiting the cultivation of religious freedom, boundaries demarcating religious communities, lines of conflict; is it the terrain of religious freedom that we see, or the product of surveying itself?[1]

A cautionary tale from colonial history serves to remind us that "map is not territory."[2] In India under British rule, surveying and mapping were core procedures of colonial government. But the boundaries plotted on official maps often charted the surveyor's imagination rather than life on the ground. Some "villages had a life only on the sheets of a map, or in signboards hung on trees." The British could not conceive the countryside without the village, and so they drew their lines even across forest and pastoral landscapes that knew no such fixed borders. Colonial maps were not just inaccurate or incomplete. Through force of repetition and the accumulated weight of bureaucratic practice, colonial surveyors' portrait of "village India" gained traction. In time, Indian nationalists, too, rallied for "village India." Decades after independence, Indians are still reckoning with the costs of this impoverished political ideal.[3]

How should we regard the terrain of religious freedom in India? Not as a newly cultivated field but as a heavily trafficked path, a rut carved in the Indian landscape by generations of people with misleading maps.

This essay considers religious freedom in India from the vantage point of the "sacred cow," icon of village India, icon of Hinduism. In India today, a divisive politics has taken hold around the cow. Can religious freedom offer a way out?

The Indian Politics of Cow Protection

The cow may be a famously gentle animal, but, in India today, violence committed in her name has reached alarming proportions. Since September 2015, when a Hindu mob assaulted and killed Mohammad Akhlaq in Dadri, Uttar Pradesh, on the alleged suspicion that he had beef in his possession, "mob-lynchings" by self-styled "cow-protectors" (*gau-rakshak*) have occurred with disturbing regularity. From Junaid Khan, a passenger on a Delhi-Mathura train in Uttar Pradesh, to fifty-five-year-old Pehlu Khan, members of vulnerable groups, young and old, have been brutally murdered by Hindu assailants. Cow protectionist violence follows the tightening of laws against cattle slaughter and beef possession. It takes the form of vigilantism: Hindu perpetrators file complaints against their victims with the police and broadcast videos of their assaults on social media. As human rights organizations and the Supreme Court of India have noted with concern, cow vigilantes have been emboldened by the attitude of the ruling government. Prominent government officials have expressed support for the cow protectors and have characterized their victims as deserving of punishment. The surviving victims of cow protectionists' assaults, far from finding legal redress against vigilante violence, have often been charged with violating anti-slaughter laws.

Cow protection (*gau-rakshā*) is typically attributed to Hindu reverence for the "sacred cow." It has figured in Indian politics since the late nineteenth century, when India was subject to British colonial rule. Since then, the politics of cow protection has been characterized by predominantly Hindu efforts to prevent cattle slaughter by law or by force, and by Hindu violence against vulnerable groups, including Muslims and historically oppressed, or "backward," castes. Since Indian independence in 1947, Hindu nationalist political parties have championed the cause of cow protection; the Hindu nationalist Bharatiya Janata Party (BJP) has been in power since May 2014.

Disregarding India's culturally plural demographics, Hindu nationalism identifies the Indian nation as Hindu. Hindu nationalists aim to rally Indians to a Hindu political identity by mobilizing hatred and fear of non-Hindus, especially Muslims. Hindu nationalists deploy an encompassing definition of "Hindu-ness" (*Hindutva*) that includes Indians of many castes and communities—including those who are religiously Sikh or Jain—but emphatically excludes Muslims and Christians.[4] Hindu nationalists portray Indian Muslims as anti-nationals with foreign loyalties, whose patriotism is inherently in question. Hindu nationalist activists have been regularly implicated in organized violence against Muslims, including, in 1992, the destruction of the Babri Masjid mosque in Ayodhya, Uttar Pradesh, and the anti-Muslim riots that followed; and, in 2002, an anti-Muslim pogrom in Gujarat that left at least 2,000 Muslims dead and displaced thousands more.[5] Hindu nationalist violence thrives on a stereotyped image of Muslims as bloodthirsty and of Hindus as the gentle victims of Muslim atrocity. Throughout its long history, the discourse of cow protection, too, has regularly conflated all Muslims with the figure of the "butcher."[6] Hindu nationalists and cow protectionists regularly portray Indian Muslims as a threat to the national interest.[7]

In the light of these circumstances—and with Hindu nationalist politicians asserting that cow slaughter in India must be ended out of deference to Hindu religious feelings—it seems natural, if not necessary, to address cow protection as a failure of religious freedom: an imposition of Hindu religious dictates on others, a failure to accommodate India's "religiously plural society."[8] Many critics of cow protection in India and the United States advocate a more vigorous pursuit of religious freedom for the sake of minority rights. South Asianist scholarship, too, describes a shift in the politics of cow protection after Indian independence that would seem to support a response rooted in religious freedom. Scholars describe a change in cow protectionist politics when British colonial rule ended and the independent, democratic Republic of India was established. The British colonial state never failed to insist that cow protectionists' demands for anti-slaughter legislation must be recognized as religious in nature and balanced against the religious rights of Indian Muslims—specifically, Muslims' right to sacrifice a cow in celebration of the Islamic holiday of Bakra Eid. But in 1958, the Supreme Court of the new Republic of India overturned colonial policy: It dismissed the idea that Muslims held a religious right to sacrifice cattle, and it allowed the slaughter of (specifically, *female*) cows to be totally prohibited.[9] The court's decision has appeared to many observers to be a patent example of Hindu religious bias, a betrayal of the republic's secular promise, and a deplorable departure from colonial-era protections for minority religious rights.[10]

In this essay, I argue that a critical response couched in terms of religious freedom is far from a fail-safe solution to the politics of cow protection in India. To address cow protection as a religion problem does not prevent, and may foster and facilitate, a sectarian divide between majority and minority religious communities. That it may foster sectarian conflict is evidenced in contemporary India, where opposition to the politics of cow protection transects and belies the picture of conflicting majority and minority religions on which religious freedom advocacy depends. To obscure this nonsectarian story of cow protection risks adding fuel to the Hindu nationalist fire, which aims to reduce all Indian politics and history to conflict between Muslim and Hindu. To address cow protection as a religion problem also obscures how the cow protectionist cause has advanced under the banner of the secular. Historical evidence shows many decades of collusion or collaboration between cow protectionist institutions and the state, beginning at the start of the twentieth century, in the name of scientific animal husbandry. This partnership between cow protection and the state was perfectly compatible with a firm adherence to religious freedom; indeed, the positing of a firm distinction between "secular" husbandry and "religious" cow protection may have allowed it to go largely unremarked.[11] To address cow protection as a religion problem does not prevent, and may facilitate, sectarian conflict centered on the cow.

Cow protection's association with animal husbandry is not the first example of a majority tradition—a tradition dominant in numbers or influence—traveling under the sign of the secular. But it is an example with a difference. Scholarship on religious freedom, religion, and law has remarked on how intangibles like spirituality, morality, or culture can function as bridge concepts, enabling spokespeople for majority traditions to "engineer a win-win situation by darting back and forth across the secular divide."[12] The politics of cow protection in India is distinctive, however, inasmuch as it incorporates the solidly material breeding of bovine bodies—a sphere of concern that falls indisputably within the authoritative sphere of science.

My argument unfolds in four parts. The first discusses what it means to address cow protection as a "religion problem," and how we might do otherwise. Through a brief and selective review of recent literature on secularism and religious freedom, I indicate how my analysis of cow protectionist politics builds on existing scholarship and how it carries us onto new ground. The second measures accounts of cow protection provided by the U.S. Department of State's Office of International Religious Freedom (IRF) and the independent advisory body, the U.S. Commission on International Religious Freedom (USCIRF), against contemporary Indian politics surrounding cattle slaughter and beef eating.[13] This section demonstrates that a political focus on religious freedom tends unnecessarily to single out Muslims as the primary victims and opponents of cow protection, portraying the controversy in the stark terms of Hindu-Muslim religious difference.[14]

The third part of my argument turns to critics of cow protection in India who insist—not unlike American advocates of religious freedom—that cow protection is inherently a "religion problem" and should be addressed as such. They make their point in response to the legal rationale for anti-slaughter laws in postcolonial India: Legislation restricting cattle slaughter does not refer to moral reasons of Hindu sentiment; rather, it cites the material imperatives of agricultural development and animal husbandry. Critics find this secular rationale disingenuous. But, I contend, the indeterminacy of concerns with cattle in India—when are they secular, and when religious?—means that any political strategy of unmasking religious motives rests on shaky ground. Finally, my argument turns to the colonial prehistory of cow protection's legal basis in animal husbandry to expand on this point: In the case of cow protection, religious freedom and secular agriculture are not discrete alternatives, they are two sides of the same coin.

This part of my argument also draws on my research to counter the notion that colonial policy on cow protection marked an ideal in which strict adherence to religious freedom secured minority protections. This notion is implied in the way religious freedom critiques posit a contrast between the colonial policy on cow protection, which championed Muslims' religious right to cow sacrifice, and the postcolonial policy laid down by the Indian Supreme Court in 1958, which denied that cow sacrifice was an essential religious practice for Indian Muslims. But, my research shows, the Supreme Court's 1958 ruling was based on decades of quiet alliance between cow protectionists and the colonial state in the name of animal husbandry that lent legitimacy to cow protection's claims to serve the material interests of all Indians. During the colonial period and today, a policy of religious freedom—in which cow protection is defined in narrowly religious terms—has enabled Muslims to be singled out as a religious minority, separable and separate from the national interest, while national interest was defined in Hindu majoritarian terms.

The Politics of Religion

On its face, the politics of religious freedom is premised on the assumption that religious beliefs and practices, religious conflicts, and religious communities can be easily identified, and that the challenge lies in defending the rights of religious minorities against those of the religious majority or in balancing the religious rights of one group against other legal and moral imperatives, such as the religious rights of others, public health, or morality.

But as critical scholarship on religion and secularism teaches us, there is, and can be, no stable definition of religion that stands outside history or politics.[15] The insight that religion is a modern category originating in Europe, and not a universal feature of human life, has been productive for thinking about the histories of the colonial world and the politics of secularism everywhere. Secular states cannot stand apart from the politics of religion to make neutral determinations about religious rights or freedoms; they inevitably intervene in that politics when they determine what counts as religion and what does not. Secular governance is characterized not by the separation of the state from religion, as is generally supposed, but by contested efforts to define or demarcate the religious from the secular. It is the contestation, debate, or questioning around how the line between religious and secular is to be drawn in each instance that is most characteristic of secular politics.[16] The pursuit of religious freedom is entangled in this definitional dilemma.[17]

Recent scholarship suggests that because religious freedom prioritizes *religious* rights and equality, it may make religion more rather than less determinative of political identity, and more rather than less a focal point for political conflict.[18] The case of cow protection supports this conclusion. It also seems to support the contention that religious freedom tends to favor the religious majority.[19] Scholars have remarked that majority traditions are able to travel sometimes under the flag of religion, sometimes under the flag of the secular, and thus to secure their own advantage at the expense of minorities. Majority traditions may be identified with national culture rather than with religion, obviating the need to balance majority preferences against minority rights.[20] In national and international legal instruments governing religious liberty from Egypt to the European Union, this outcome is often achieved by means of the limiting principle of "public order." The political imperative to preserve public order provides a mechanism by which national majorities can gain preference in disputes over religious rights, when majority concerns are identified with "national culture" or "public morality" rather than religion.[21] In the case of cow slaughter, too, the legal predominance of Hindu majoritarian values has been secured, in part, by means of cow protection's ability to tack across the religious-secular divide.

Authoritative determinations of what counts as religion and what does not can appear to be a matter of semantics or vocabulary choice more than anything else. In the United States, ministry or "chaplaincy" is finding a place in public institutions from hospitals and prisons to the U.S. military, dodging First Amendment restrictions by adopting an "intentionally and deliberately secularizing language" that speaks of spirituality rather than religion.[22] From the United States to Asia, spirituality serves "a kind of global bridge function," enabling connections and borrowings across distant conceptual universes under the rubric of the modern, the universal, and the secular.[23] The secular status of the new American chaplaincy has been further secured by medicalizing spirituality (as empirically grounded) and naturalizing it (as a universal aspect of the biological human). Both processes date back at least a century in the United States: What looks like mere semantics carries the weight of history as well as scientific expertise.[24]

The secular status of cow protection in Indian law follows a similar pattern, as we will see; it is also based on the authority of expert opinion. Still, against the backdrop of this scholarship, certain contrasting features in cow protection stand out. It is striking that cow protection has been able to secure secular status in Indian law by reference to the thoroughly material and scientific domain of animal husbandry or breed improvement, rather than to less tangible concepts like culture or spirituality. This difference is not easily chalked up to a supposed difference between Protestant Christian and Hindu religiosities—the one arguably interior, focused on the belief, faith, or psychology of the human individual; the other, arguably, concerned with material substance and embodied practice as much as with the inner person. Nor is it easily ascribed to majority rule, because cow protection became connected to animal husbandry under British government, through collaboration with the colonial state. In this respect, the case of cow protection charts new territory for reflections on secularism and religious freedom.

My research pursues what is obscured when cow protection is framed in religious terms.[25] The classic scholarship on colonial cow protection focuses on violence against Muslims or, to a lesser degree, treats violence against low castes. It addresses the question of just how readily the Hindu religious significance of the cow was translated into Hindu communal identification and mobilization. Although the question in this scholarship is ultimately political—how and when did Hindu religious identity take shape and become the basis of Hindu nationalist political action?—it is premised on a framing of cow protectionist concern as religious in the first instance.[26] But Hindus' regard for the so-called sacred cow is a slippery affair. Today, cow-revering Hindus most commonly explain their attitude by referring to the special value of cattle in material terms: The cow, male and female, is said to be a uniquely "useful" animal.[27] Since the nineteenth century, Hindu proponents of cow protection have often argued for cattle preservation on economic grounds and have abjured religious reasoning. In framing cow protection as a religious matter, then, scholars have disregarded the predominant emphasis in the discourse of cow protection from the nineteenth through the twenty-first centuries. My research expands on this observation to flesh out cow protectionists' concerns with material cattle from the 1880s through the 1960s.

If "religion" in South Asia must be understood to be a political category originating in modern Europe, then we must attend closely to the politics that have governed, and continue to govern, the translations of South Asian practices and concerns into the language of religion over the past two centuries and more.[28] What comes under the spotlight when religious freedom is invoked in India, and what falls into shadow?

Religious Freedom on the Global Stage

The professed aim of religious freedom in international policy is to diminish religious discrimination and interreligious violence, and the U.S. religious freedom reports treat the freedom and equality of religious minorities with special concern. But scholars have observed that in the very act of seeking out cases of religious discrimination that demand remedy, an international policy of religious freedom has a tendency to single out individuals and groups as religious groups, to portray social conflict as religious or sectarian in origin, and to allow other forms of group affiliation and other causes of social conflict to drop out of sight. In short, the politics of religious freedom, which aims to diminish sectarian conflict, runs the risk of strengthening sectarian identification and diminishing the very "possibility of crosscutting, nonsectarian forms of politics."[29] This observation rings true in the U.S. religious freedom reports' account of cow protection.

The U.S. religious freedom reports stress cow protection's negative impact on the Muslim religious minority in India. In keeping with their mandate to uphold religious freedom, the reports stress that most victims of cow protectionist violence have been Muslims, the largest religious minority in India. In addition to fostering anti-Muslim discrimination, they observe, India's anti-slaughter laws prevent Indian Muslims from freely practicing their religion. The reports describe legal prohibitions on cattle slaughter as a violation of Muslims' right to sacrifice a cow on the occasion of the Islamic holy day,

Eid al-Adha. It is true that before independence, the British colonial policy of religious neutrality claimed to balance Hindus' religious demand that cattle lives be preserved against Muslims' religious right to cow sacrifice. In the first decades after independence, Muslim groups presented the strongest legal challenge to India's anti-slaughter legislation.[30] But the politics of religious freedom can exert a subtle pressure to portray religious teachings as unanimous and clear-cut. The U.S. religious freedom reports are more accurate when they say that "many Muslims believe" or "Muslims complain" that sacrifice is essential to their religion: South Asian Muslims have long disagreed about whether the sacrifice of a cow, rather than another animal, such as a goat, is religiously obligatory. Although they aim to reduce sectarian conflict in India, the U.S. religious freedom reports paint an exaggerated picture of conflicting Muslim and Hindu religious imperatives (to kill cows; not to kill cows).

Most Muslim victims of cow protectionist violence since 2015 have not been interrupted in celebration of their religion but in everyday pursuits, commonly in pursuit of their livelihoods.[31] Many have been accused of illegally slaughtering or smuggling cattle. Pehlu Khan, who was accused of "cattle smuggling," was a small-scale dairy farmer returning home with two newly purchased dairy cows and their calves.[32] Others have been assaulted for allegedly eating beef. Young Junaid Khan was taunted and called a "beef-eater" before he was stabbed to death. At issue is not Muslim religious practice but hateful stereotypes of Indian Muslims. As one journalist put it, quoting a prominent Indian lawyer and commentator, "At the heart of the problem is that some Hindus view Muslims, the country's largest minority, as simple 'cow killers, beef eaters and in that sense, not worthy of protection.'"[33] In defining cow protection by reference to a supposed Hindu religious interdiction against cow-killing and a putative religious imperative of Islam, the U.S. religious freedom reports confuse the issue and lend support to cow vigilantes' account of their actions.

Not only Muslims but also a great number of Hindus in India eat beef, and are oppressed by the politics of cow protection. In the southern state of Kerala, Hindus as well as Muslims and Christians consider beef to be "part of Kerala's food culture." Throughout India, many members of the most historically disadvantaged groups, including those who identify as "Dalit," eat beef, by necessity or by choice.[34] Although religious and cultural separatism remains an important strand in Dalit politics, and many Dalits reject Hindu domination by converting to Buddhism or other religions, most are officially classed as Hindus in the Republic of India. For many Dalits, beef is a matter of active preference and cultural pride. University students in Hyderabad, Telangana, in south India have been pressing for beef to be given equal place with other nonvegetarian meats on campus menus for years. The dominant, upper-caste Hindu understanding that is virulently defended and violently imposed by Hindu nationalists and champions of cow protection arranges castes and communities in a food hierarchy that puts beef, and beef eaters, at the bottom.[35] By pressing to bring beef eating into the open, Dalit activists seek to "democratize the public sphere" and erase the stigma meted out to themselves and others.[36] Since 2017, Dalit and Dalit-bahujan alliances of so-called low-caste groups have organized "beef festivals" to protest government efforts to criminalize cattle slaughter,[37] and they have mobilized to protest cow vigilantes' violent assaults on Dalits and other "backward" castes and marginalized groups.

Dalits, including Hindu Dalits, have borne the brunt of cow vigilantes' intimidation and violence alongside Muslims, as they have been brutally assaulted on suspicion of slaughtering cows or consuming beef. In July 2016, members of a Dalit family in Una, Gujarat, who were skinning a dead cow they had just bought, were accused of killing the animal; cow vigilantes stripped them, bound them, and beat them brutally, then promulgated video of the assault on social media. Dalits in the state of Gujarat organized a ten-day march to protest the attack and the ruling BJP government's indifference to growing atrocities, while Dalits of Surendranagar, whose occupation it was to collect dead cattle, dumped cow carcasses outside the district collector's office and suspended work. Many Indians—Muslim and Hindu, from many regional, cultural, and caste backgrounds—are harmed by the criminalization of beef eating and by vigilante violence.

Although cow protection is not reducible to Hindu-Muslim conflict, Hindu nationalists work hard to ensure that cow killing and beef eating are identified as Muslim (or Christian) practices—and that Hinduism (or "Hinduness") is identified with unbending opposition to both.[38] Hindu vigilantes reportedly taunted their Dalit victims at Una by calling them "Muslims."[39] Members of another Dalit community in Telangana, who were attacked by cow vigilantes as they prepared to slaughter a cow on a festival occasion, were reportedly abused in similar fashion: "They asked us: 'Are you Muslims to eat cow meat?'"[40] Hindu nationalists deride as "unHindu" any Indians who are ready to accept beef eating. When the chief minister of Karnataka rolled back restrictions on cattle slaughter in the state to its 1964 levels, reversing the legislation pushed through by the BJP in 2010, a prominent Hindu nationalist official called the minister's Hindu identity into question. To the extent that it emphasizes Hindu-Muslim religious difference, glossing over the differences among Hindus and the shared experiences of Hindus and non-Hindus in the face of cow protectionist aggression, the appeal to religious freedom reinforces this sectarian politics of Hindu nationalism.

Yet crosscutting political alliances exist. Protests against cow vigilante violence have cut across the lines of religious difference. In the wake of the killing of young Junaid, NotInMyName protests against mob lynching drew members of all religions and all castes in cities across India. Protests against anti-beef laws have also drawn from members of all religions and castes. Whatever their own food preferences, many Indians oppose both anti-slaughter and anti-beef laws as illegitimate interference with citizens' right to choose their own food. Not only those directly engaged in slaughter-related trades in hides, leather, or meat are adversely affected by the economic impact of cow protection, but all who earn their livelihoods with the aid of cattle are affected. Prohibitions on slaughter have made it difficult for farmers across India to refresh their work animals; farmers suffer further losses from growing numbers of marauding stray cattle that threaten their fields. Indian agriculturalists have come out in force to protest restrictions on the cattle trade imposed by law and by vigilante violence, which have added to the already severe agricultural crisis in India.[41] The accounts of the Indian politics of cow protection that are provided in the U.S. religious freedom reports give no hint of this nonsectarian story of cow protection's victims, or its opponents.

The U.S. religious freedom reports are not wrong when they state that India's Muslim religious minority has been a special target of cow vigilante violence. But by omitting key facets of the controversy surrounding cow protection—the politics of beef eating; the dependence of many Indians on India's cattle-slaughter economy[42]—the U.S. religious freedom reports give the false impression of a Hindu community in India that is united in its abhorrence of cow slaughter. This portrait of Hindu India is not only exaggerated or lacking in sufficient nuance; rather, it is patently false and it is foundational to the Hindu nationalist politics of cow protection. By framing the politics of cow protection in religious terms, this appeal to religious freedom puts excessive emphasis on a supposed religious conflict between Hindus and Muslims around the cow-slaughter issue. It reinforces the very sectarian division that it seeks to undermine.

Religion and Secularism in India

From the legislative angle, too, the U.S. religious freedom reports posit a more direct connection between Hindu religion and cow protection than is warranted. They link India's legislation restricting cattle slaughter directly to Hindu religious sentiment, describing it as a naked imposition of Hindu religious scruples on India's non-Hindu citizens.[43] It is true that in recent years, Hindu nationalists have loudly advocated cow protection as a matter of Hindu faith that all minorities must "respect." But neither the Constitution of India nor the Supreme Court decision of 1958 advocate restrictions on cattle slaughter for overtly religious reasons; both couch the imperative to preserve cattle from slaughter within the imperatives of scientific agriculture. Article 48 reads as follows: "Organisation of agriculture and animal husbandry. The State shall endeavour to organise agriculture and animal husbandry on modern and scientific lines and shall, in particular, take steps for preserving and improving the breeds, and prohibiting the slaughter, of cows and calves and other milch and draught cattle." Article 48 of the Constitution is only a "directive"; it does not dictate state policy. The Supreme Court ruling of 1958 determined that the directive to prohibit slaughter is not independent but is entirely subordinate to the needs of scientific agriculture and animal husbandry.[44] So the law does not articulate a Hindu religious rationale for prohibiting slaughter.[45] This point of clarification carries important ramifications, which I explore further in the next section on the Role of Expertise.

The U.S. religious freedom reports' account of cow protection is dangerously oversimplified in certain respects, and yet we must acknowledge that the reports' overall assessment is shared by scholars and by Indian critics. A prominent scholar of Indian secularism once remarked, the "legal bans on cow slaughter . . . must be viewed primarily as attempts to impose the taboos of one religion upon all citizens. They are certainly contrary to the spirit of the secular state."[46] Shraddha Chigateri, an important critical voice in the controversy around cow slaughter, argues similarly that the ostensibly neutral, secular framing of anti-slaughter jurisprudence in India "is predicated on a fundamental constitutive elision of the religious aspects of cow slaughter. This elision both masks the prioritising of dominant-caste Hindu identity in the regulation of cow slaughter and it glosses over religious differences over the sacredness of the cow. . . . Such a move is at the expense of the even-handed recognition of all religious sensibilities, and strikes at the heart of

Indian secularism."[47] Chigateri's critical move is to demand the unmasking of the religious motives behind anti-slaughter legislation, and, having brought them into the open, to demand revision of the Constitution's Article 48. She argues that only by debating cow slaughter openly as a Hindu religious concern will it be possible to engage seriously in the political work of secularism, that is, "accommodating diverging and opposing beliefs and practices in the context of a religiously plural society" with a view to "equal respect of all religions."[48]

But is a politics of religious freedom capable of addressing the "contested ethical claims, and diverse cultural practices" with respect to slaughter, beef consumption, or assessments of animal value that inform India's social hierarchy of food? The long history of upper-caste Hindu encompassment of Dalits by means of their religious classification as "Hindu" demonstrates how the language of religion masks the ethical and cultural pluralism within the nominal community of "Hindus," even as it imputes an exaggerated, false difference between homogenized categories of "Hindu" and "Muslim."

Finally, we may recall the ambivalence of the Hindu "sacred cow," which renders the strategy of unmasking especially circular and bootless. The revelation that pretensions to concern with the agricultural utility of cattle mask Hindu religious sentiment is quickly reversed, when Hindus cite the particular usefulness of cattle as the basis for their religious sentiment. Where does secular agriculture end and religious valuation begin? The logic of political secularism directs us to scientific expertise to settle the arbitrary valuations of religious belief on the solid ground of objective, scientific fact.[49] But does this course settle the issue, or do we find ourselves circling back, once again, to the politics of religion?

The Role of Expertise

In the name of religious neutrality, the British colonial state in India held firm to the policy that today's champions of religious freedom advocate. From the 1880s through independence, British colonial officials steadfastly held to their understanding of cow protection as rooted in Hindu religious sentiment. Colonial officials consistently rejected cow protectionists' demands for legislation restricting slaughter, and they sought to balance a Hindu religious prohibition on cow killing against what colonial courts determined was a Muslim religious right to sacrifice cattle.

The Supreme Court ruling of 1958 overturned this policy and laid the groundwork for the anti-slaughter laws on the books today.[50] How did the secular rationale of Article 48 of the constitution produce this legal result? Critics have cried foul play. The court carefully weighed the material advantages and disadvantages to be gained from allowing or disallowing bovine slaughter, both for the country as a whole and for discrete sections of the population, including minorities. It noted butchers' and leatherworkers' needs for livelihood, as well as the needs of the poor for beef as a cheap protein. The court concluded that a total prohibition on cattle slaughter was unconstitutional. The slaughter of cattle that were not useful or were no longer useful could not be banned. But the court made an exception that critics have found baffling: It allowed an exception for female cows. It ruled that the slaughter of buffaloes and male cattle could be prohibited only during their useful years, but the slaughter of female cows could be prohibited absolutely. Here, the Supreme Court seemed to depart from its meticulously secular reasoning—indeed, it seemed to abandon reasoning altogether, baldly to impose a Hindu religious scruple on all citizens. In the words of one scholar of Indian secularism, "Why was not the same criterion of usefulness applied to the slaughter of cows?"[51] Critics have concluded that the court's secular reasoning was mere pretense, religious motives masquerading as agriculture and economics.

But the Supreme Court did not abandon secular reasoning in its 1958 ruling on female cows; to the contrary, its decision on this point was based on the recommendations of experts — specifically, the recommendations of the 1955 *Report of the Expert Committee on the Prevention of Slaughter of Cattle in India*.[52] This report, in turn, was based on scientific expertise that extended back decades, well into the period of British colonial rule. Like the colonial statements that preceded it, the 1955 *Report of the Expert Committee* consistently portrayed cow protectionist opposition to cattle slaughter as religious in nature and, moreover, as fundamentally opposed to the rational, scientific husbandry of India's cattle resources.

The Expert Committee's report is not easily dismissed as pretense, or unmasked as Hindu pseudoscience. It is premised on evidence and argumentation that accumulated during the colonial period, and it repeatedly reaffirmed the colonial state's secularist position on cow protection. In designating cow protectionists' appeals for state action to restrict cattle slaughter as religious in nature, the colonial state held a balance between Hindu and Muslim religious dictates. However, it also articulated a contrast between cow protectionists' irrational, sentimental concern with preserving cattle lives at all costs and the colonial state's purportedly rational, scientific, and economic concern with improving cattle resources. The *Report of the Royal Commission on Agriculture*, issued in 1928, exemplified this position: It described India's cattle to be in a deplorable condition and attributed the degeneration of the breeds to Hindus' religious scruple against culling.[53] The Hindu religious prohibition against killing even weak or useless animals, the *Report* concluded, had resulted in a "vicious circle." As work animals became increasingly weak and inefficient, Indian cultivators were obliged to keep more animals; as meager feed resources were stretched to feed more cattle, their quality degenerated still further. The *Report* described a clear solution: Scientific animal husbandry, organized by the expertise of the colonial state, would gradually improve the strength, efficiency, and productivity of Indian cattle.

Before we take the 1928 *Report*'s assessment as bare fact, we must remember that the Royal Commission's entire endeavor was designed above all to serve a polemical purpose. The *Report* reasserted the authority of British colonial rule in India as good government—as government that used science to bring development or "improvement" to India[54]—in an effort to silence nationalists' complaints that colonial policies had reduced Indians to poverty.

The *Report of the Royal Commission on Agriculture* also repeated, in 1928, what was by then a well-established official position against Indians' complaints about cattle. Increasingly, after 1912, colonial officials blamed India's cattle problems on Indians' supposed lack of initiative: Indians did not adjust to lost pasture grounds by sowing cattle feed alongside their cash crops, Indian cultivators did not compensate for the skyrocketing costs of cattle by breeding their own work animals, and Indians failed to organize a modern dairy industry in India. Moreover, they contended, Indians' cattle-breeding practices and putative aversion to culling brought degeneration rather than improvement. Where the colonial state's promises of improvement had patently not been realized, the *Report* cited Indian impediments in the way: Indian culture, Hindu religion, the sacred cow.

In 1955, the *Report of the Expert Committee* repeated the colonial state's expert, scientific, "secular" position against "religious" cow protection on all of these points. The *Report* affirmed the secularist position that a total prohibition on cattle slaughter would worsen a "vicious circle." It affirmed that the solution to this vicious circle was to improve the quality of Indian cattle through scientific breeding. It repeated colonial experts' statements about the need to develop the Indian dairy industry. The 1955 *Report* also echoed colonial officials and experts when it identified a problem in the cities, what came to be described in official literature and in the literature of cow protection as the need for urban "salvage." The salvage problem was the unstated justification for the Supreme Court's decision, in 1958, that a total prohibition on the slaughter of female cows was reasonable on purely secular grounds.

The Expert Committee on the Prevention of Slaughter of Cattle in India was formed specifically to consider the problem of how to prevent the premature destruction of good-quality cows who were brought into the cities to provide urban populations with fresh milk. Because it was far too expensive to maintain such animals during the dry period between their lactations, urban dairymen sold them for slaughter. This practice was said to be a problem of national proportions. The "milch animals and their progeny" that made their way to urban dairies were said to be "the best milking (and breeding) stock the country possesses."[55] Their destruction meant the loss of the "most valuable breeding material, the basic stock needed for improving the country's cattle wealth."[56] The 1955 *Report of the Expert Committee* argued that "salvage" of these cows was urgently needed in order to advance the objective of improving the productivity, value, and efficiency of India's cattle through scientific breeding.

The 1955 *Report* echoed decades of statements by British colonial government agencies and officials at the highest level in identifying the problem of "salvage." W. Smith, who was appointed "Imperial Dairy Expert" for India in 1920, advocated the urgent importance of salvage for scientific breeding work as early as 1913, and repeated the refrain in 1922 and again in his evidence before the Royal Commission on Agriculture in 1928.[57] Smith's warning was taken up by the incoming viceroy, Lord Linlithgow, after 1936. Linlithgow had chaired the Royal Commission's inquiry, and he immediately directed the Imperial Council of Agricultural Research to turn its attention to the improvement of cattle breeds in India. The Imperial Council of Agricultural Research in 1937 and 1940 stressed the "urgency and importance of the matter" of urban salvage and the "importance of taking steps to obviate the premature slaughter of prime milch cows when they go dry in cities" as the basis for sound breeding policy.[58]

In 1955, the *Report of the Expert Committee* cited these imperial precedents, and it observed that immediate action was needed until full development of the dairy industry (and the removal of milch animals outside the cities) could be achieved. It observed that urban dairymen were under extreme pressure to sell good, dry cattle for slaughter, and that economic compulsion regularly forced them to do so. It advocated that legislation prohibiting the slaughter of useful animals be made fully effective.[59] The 1955 *Report of the Expert Committee* did not depart from the secular rationale of economic development and scientific animal husbandry, but it did advocate that the slaughter of female cows be more effectively prevented through legislation. The Supreme Court decision of 1958 cited this *Report* when it observed that already stringent municipal regulations against the slaughter of useful animals were insufficient and ruled that female cows required extra protection, which might extend to a total prohibition on their slaughter at the state level.[60]

When the 1958 Supreme Court made its ruling about the need to preserve the lives of female cows, it did not depart from secular reasoning or baldly impose a Hindu religious scruple on all Indian citizens. The 1955 *Report of the Expert Committee*, on which that decision rested, echoed the British colonial government's avowedly secular, scientific critique of cow protection's Hindu religious demand that cattle lives be preserved at all costs. Thus, it is no simple matter to unmask the Hindu religious bias of the Supreme Court's 1958 ruling. The constitution's appeal to the scientific organization of animal husbandry is not so easily swept aside; it has deep roots. Cow protectionists and colonial experts had marched in step to the tune of breed improvement for decades before independence. Religious freedom and scientific agriculture were two sides of the same coin.

Let us now observe the contours of the colonial policy on cow protection. Colonial policy defined cow protection as a matter of a Hindu religious prohibition against cattle killing. But in the colonial period, as today, both Hindus and Muslims participated in the slaughter economy. The colonial conception of the determining force of belief in the Hindu sacred cow in conjunction with the understanding of Muslims' sacrificial practices as essential to their religious freedom yielded a split account of slaughter practices. Hindu dairymen and Hindu farmers were described to sell the spent cattle in their possession despite their religious principles, out of economic compunction. Indian Muslims, by contrast, were described as committed to cattle killing as a matter of religious principle. Yet India's butchers were predominantly Muslim, so slaughter was as much a concern for many Indian Muslims as was sacrifice. Both Hindus and Muslims included beef in their diet, whether from preference or economic necessity. Like the U.S. religious freedom reports, the colonial policy on cow protection singled out Muslims as a religious group, exaggerated the difference between Hindus and Muslims, and depicted an intractable sectarian difference over cow killing. Many cow protectionists did the same.

The colonial state's identification of cow protection as fundamentally religious did not prevent state experts and officials from endorsing it. Colonial officials of the highest rank openly advocated Hindu cow protection as a solution to the problem of urban salvage, and they extended support to cow protectionist activities and institutions. In 1936, Viceroy Linlithgow very publicly enlisted cow protectionists in his campaign to improve India's cattle through deliberate breeding. In one of his first public acts, he presented several dry cows to a cow protectionist cattle shelter, or *gaushala*, in Delhi, while urging the Indian public to follow his example.[61] Throughout the 1940s, the Imperial Council for Agricultural Research and the government of India actively encouraged urban salvage schemes as urgently important to the scientific and economic progress of the country, and they enlisted cow protectionist organizations and institutions to design and to implement those schemes.

The colonial state maintained a principled distance from the religious politics of cow protection. But, at the same time, the colonial state lent active support to the work of cow protection in the name of animal husbandry. By relying on cow protectionist institutions and personnel for state initiatives for breed improvement, the colonial state gave the imprimatur of the supposedly neutral colonial state to the central claim of cow protection: that preventing cow slaughter was not a sectional Hindu concern, but rather was in the material interest of the country as a whole, serving the food needs of all castes and communities.[62]

Conclusion

Where can we find a secure boundary between a "religious" approach to cow slaughter and a "secular" one? Perhaps the most authoritative secularist approach to the issue has been that articulated by the colonial state, which held to its avowed principle of religious freedom and never ceased to declaim the Hindu religious basis of cow protectionist appeals.[63] Yet that secularist approach was combined with practical and institutional support for the work of cow protectionist organizations and institutions, including their work to preserve cattle from slaughter. Moreover, that secularist approach reproduced a sectarian divide between Hindus and Muslims, inasmuch as it focused not on actions (participation in the slaughter economy, beef consumption) but on the conflicting Hindu and Islamic religious principles that presumably lay behind those actions. It served to marginalize Muslims, representing their religious beliefs as an obstacle to the best material interests of the country. For these reasons, a political strategy that depends on unmasking the religious motives behind cow protectionists' veneer of science, agriculture, and economy rests on shaky ground. A political strategy that consists of reasserting the value of religious freedom is similarly uncertain: The evidence of contemporary initiatives for international religious freedom based in the United States and the evidence of colonial history both indicate that a policy of religious freedom is as likely to entrench a sectarian divide between Hindu and Muslim in India as to dissolve it.

As this book was going to press in 2021, the United States Commission on International Religious Freedom downgraded India's religious freedom ranking, opening a door for possible diplomatic sanctions.[64] The politics of cow protection has been joined by a list of state violations of Indians' most fundamental rights: These include the imposition of a military lockdown in the Muslim-majority state of Jammu and Kashmir and the abrogation of the constitutional rights of its citizens;[65] the enactment of a law (the Citizenship Amendment Act, or CAA) that puts Indian Muslims' citizenship rights in question; and, in the wake of this legislation, the repressive and discriminatory actions and violence shown by Indian government and police toward peaceful anti-CAA protesters, Muslims, and students. Any pressure on India's Hindu nationalist government to remedy this baleful list of abuses must be celebrated. Still, it is possible, even urgent, to ask whether a policy framed by religious freedom is the best option.

There are alternatives. The United Nations has expressed concern about the trend of state action in India by recalling India's commitments to basic rights, without foregrounding religious rights. The UN invoked India's international commitments by citing "India's obligations under the International Covenant on Civil and Political Rights and the Convention for the Elimination of Racial Discrimination . . . which prohibit discrimination based on racial, ethnic or religious grounds."[66] In doing so, it addressed the Indian government's violations of the rights of India's Muslim citizens by referencing broad principles of nondiscrimination, without giving special emphasis to religious freedom.[67] Remarking that the CAA is "fundamentally discriminatory," the United Nations stressed its violation of "the commitment to equality before the law enshrined in India's constitution." And within India, too, protests have not given undue emphasis to religious rights. Despite government efforts to portray opposition to the CAA as Muslim, criminal, and anti-national by definition, anti-CAA protesters in India have bridged the lines of Hindu-Muslim difference.[68] Appealing to their foundational rights as Indians, protesters have been reciting the Constitution of India, and the principles of justice, liberty, equality, and fraternity enshrined therein.

CHAPTER 7

Bad Faith

Religious Fraud and Religious Freedom in the "Mighty I AM" Case

William Schultz

"Occasionally," wrote the journalist Westbrook Pegler in October 1939, law enforcement "has to burst up a flock for the sake of the lambs, which is fine commentary on religious freedom, but that's the way it goes, nevertheless."[1] Pegler reached this pithy conclusion after speaking with a pair of law enforcement officers about the government's response to the "Mighty I AM" movement. Largely forgotten today, at its peak I AM was one of the largest of the alternative religious movements that flourished in the United States in the 1920s and 1930s.[2] Its leaders claimed more than a million adherents; while that number was certainly exaggerated, more objective observers nonetheless estimated that tens of thousands of Americans responded to the I AM message. Thousands of people packed into venues like the Shrine Auditorium in Los Angeles and the Metropolitan Opera House in Philadelphia to hear the movement's leaders, the married couple Guy and Edna Ballard, channel the voices of "Ascended Masters." Attendees joined the Ballards in shouting demands at these cosmic powers, demanding health and wealth for themselves and annihilation for their enemies. I AM generated tremendous enthusiasm—and an equal amount of anxiety. According to one critic, the movement was a case of "mass hypnosis," which threatened to bring about a "psychic dictatorship in America." These anxieties culminated in a high-profile trial of the I AM leaders for mail fraud. Years of trials and convoluted rulings followed, concluding with a conviction that was thrown out by the United States Supreme Court.[3]

More than a sideshow, the controversy that surrounded the I AM movement illuminates an important truth about American religious freedom: In the United States, religious freedom is inseparable from financial practices. For religious communities, money is anything but mundane; the ways they collect and spend money are often inseparable from their belief system. It is not surprising, then, that many of the cases that contributed to the jurisprudence of American religious freedom involved questions of money. *Cantwell v. Connecticut* (1940), for instance, which incorporated the First Amendment's free exercise clause (i.e., making it applicable to states), concerned whether Jehovah's Witnesses needed to seek a government license before soliciting funds. *Everson v. Board of Education* (1947), which incorporated the establishment clause of the First Amendment, concerned the use of public money to reimburse parents who sent their children to Catholic schools. *Walz v. Tax Commission of the City of New York* (1970) addressed the exemption of churches from property taxes. More recently, *Burwell v. Hobby Lobby* (2014) dealt with the rights of closely held corporations. Indeed, questions of fundraising and taxation have often forced the courts to decide whether new religious movements were "really" religious. When, for instance, the Internal Revenue Service withdrew the Church of Scientology's tax-exempt status in 1958, it justified its decision by claiming that Scientology was not a religion but a "business, a profit-making organization, run by [L. Ron] Hubbard for his personal enrichment."[4] And when, in 1977, the Tax Commission of the City of New York rejected the Unification Church's request for a property tax exemption, its decision noted that, "although the applicant association does in certain respects bespeak of a religious association, it is in our opinion so threaded with political motives that it requires us to deny its application."[5]

The economic realm is thus an essential part of the history of American religious freedom. As the introduction to this volume makes clear, in recent years scholars have done exemplary work explaining the social and political forces that have shaped religious freedom. They have been particularly sensitive to the ways in which religious freedom interacts with categories of identification like race and ethnicity.[6] Financial practices, however, are often absent from these accounts. Thus, there is a golden opportunity to link the scholarship on religious freedom with another flourishing subfield: studies of religion and capitalism. Scholars from different disciplines have produced a series of important works examining the interplay between capitalism and American religion, with an emphasis on the links between corporations and evangelical Christianity.[7] Bringing together these subfields can provide a new perspective on the formation of American religious freedom, drawing our attention to how this concept influences and is influenced by economic factors.

The study of religious fraud provides an ideal way to bridge these subfields. Charges of religious fraud often involve both a financial aspect and a religious freedom aspect. Here, scholars of religion in the United States might look to recent work on religion in the Caribbean. Diana Paton and Danielle Boaz have examined how governments in Caribbean nations regulated the category of folk religious practices, often termed "*obeah*," by defining *obeah* as a form of fraud. Some work on this subject in the United States is already underway; LaShawn Harris has delved into the world of New York City's "occult consultants," many of them African American women, who made a living by promising clients supernatural help, while Charles McCrary has explored proscriptions on fortune telling in the United States at the turn of the twentieth century.[8] The I AM controversy fits nicely within this expanding literature. It speaks to the long American tradition of what might be called religious muckraking: efforts by investigative journalists and crusading politicians to expose and prosecute fraudulent religious leaders in the name of protecting American consumers. These efforts were particularly intense in the first half of the twentieth century as part of a broader campaign against "rackets" in American society, whether those rackets were criminal syndicates, corrupt labor unions, or "cults." This chapter examines the sudden rise and gradual decline of the I AM movement in order to understand how the interplay of faith, fraud, and finances shaped religious freedom in the United States.

Mystical Racketeers

"Racket" was a keyword in the first half of the twentieth century, at least in the United States. The term's strength lay in its flexibility. "Racket" and the associated term "racketeering" could be applied to almost any sort of illegal or semi-legal activity. As the labor economist Harry Millis noted in 1945, "The expression 'racket' is used so loosely as to include a great variety of things one does not like—graft, violence, monopolistic extractions, etc."[9] The historians Andrew Cohen and David Witwer have shown how the concept of racketeering was most often applied (usually by conservative, anti-union forces) to corruption within labor unions.[10] Yet "rackets" could also be found in government, in the corporate world, and in religion.

Some of the earliest muckraking journalists turned their attention to the "religious racket." Upton Sinclair, best known for exposing the squalor of the meat-packing industry in his novel *The Jungle*, assailed religion in equally harsh terms, condemning it as "a Source of Income and a Shield to Privilege." Sinclair's *The Profits of Religion* (1918) recast the history of religion as an extended story of fraud, perpetuated on humanity by a priestly caste of exploiters.[11] Every religion was simply "a mighty fortress of Graft"—no exceptions. Sinclair attacked mainstream religions, pointing out how Manhattan's Trinity Church, bastion of the city's Episcopalian establishment, used its vast real estate holdings to construct shabby tenements. He was equally scornful of less-established faiths; a chapter of *The Profits of Religion* dedicated to "The Church of the Quacks" profiled (and ridiculed) figures like "Newo Newi New," the San Francisco "bishop" indicted on charges of mail fraud, and "Dr. Otoman Prince of Adusht Ha'nish," a grocer-turned-yogi from Illinois. Throughout the book, Sinclair reiterated his claim that religion existed solely to defraud the religious and enrich their leaders.

Spiritualism proved a particularly inviting target for crusading journalists.[12] Many of these muckrakers were entertainers who used their knowledge of stagecraft to expose mediums who used these same tricks of the trade to defraud customers. Escape artist Harry Houdini dedicated the latter part of his career to exposing mediums, as chronicled in his book *A Magician Among the Spirits*.[13] Equally indefatigable in his pursuit of fraud was Julien Proskauer, president of the Society of American Magicians, whose book *Spook Crooks!* targeted (as the subtitle put it) "the prophet-eers who conduct our wickedest industry."[14] Proskauer documented the techniques used by these "spook crooks," ranging from invisible ink to concealed radios to magnetic chalk. Most of the chapters ended with the victim (often an attractive young woman) going mad or committing suicide as a result of the fraud. Beyond this human cost, Proskauer estimated that spiritual frauds conned millions of Americans out of millions each year.

But more mainstream religions were not spared from charges of racketeering. Journalists exposed many semi-legal tactics, often involving tax exemptions, which religious leaders used to fill their treasuries. The *New Republic* excoriated several orders of Catholic monks who engaged in an elaborate shell game to lease tax-free property to the United States Wheat Corporation; this, the magazine charged, was a perfect example of the "foundation racket."[15] The *Nation* condemned New York City churches and synagogues for realizing gargantuan profits through the sale of real estate in downtown Manhattan.[16]

The *Christian Century* was particularly unsparing in its attacks on "religious rackets," even calling for an end to religious tax exemptions as a way to stop this abuse—though it should be noted that the *Century* framed this move as a check on the growing power of the Catholic Church in the United States.[17]

Crusades against religious corruption often drew the government into the fray. In *Spook Crooks!*, for instance, Julien Proskauer recounted how the Society of American Magicians had collaborated with the New York City police to clear the city of "clairvoyants." Investigations of "phony" religions were a staple of state legislative committees. In California, a subcommittee of the state assembly enlisted a Los Angeles woman to apply for ordination with the Oakland-based "Universal Church of the Master." After sending the church $30.20, the woman received an "official-looking certificate of ordination," empowering her to "legally marry, bury or baptize"—a fact that the subcommittee cited as proof that the state's "diploma mills" were out of control and required legislative oversight.[18] In New York, a joint committee of the state legislature spent several months investigating "charity rackets," ultimately drawing up a bill that would give the state greater control over fundraising.[19] Sometimes the power of the federal government was mobilized as well. When a reporter for the *Cleveland Press* launched an investigation into the city's storefront missions, her stories led the Office of Price Administration to file charges against several of these storefront ministers for the improper use of food and gasoline rations.[20]

What defined these "rackets" was that they were too transactional. According to their critics, they facilitated exchanges between sacred and profane that were obvious to the point of crass.[21] Julien Proskauer's *Spook Crooks!* drew a clear line between true and false spiritualists: "Genuine spiritualists," Proskauer wrote, "never recommend oil stocks, investments, or charge exorbitant fees," suggesting that religious frauds were defined by their hunger for financial gain.[22] The journalist Richard Mathison made a similar point in the introduction to *Faiths, Cults and Sects of America* (later republished with the revealing new title *God Is a Millionaire*): "Legitimate denominations and sincere clergymen cannot—and will not—compete with the show biz trickery which is rampant today. They won't try to draw helpless unfortunates with alluring ads such as: 'What Christ told me about cancer!' 'I visited a flying saucer and found the prophet!' or 'Jesus will return in 1959 (100% biblical proof guaranteed!)'"[23] Yet this dividing line, easily drawn in theory, proved harder to draw in practice. The I AM movement was one case in which that line appeared particularly blurry.

The "Mighty I AM" Presence

Alternative religious movements, or cults, as they were usually called at the time, flourished in the United States in the 1920s and 1930s. The journalist Charles Ferguson, writing in 1931, observed that "the land is overrun with messiahs."[24] Ferguson's *The New Books of Revelations* cataloged these movements. Some had been founded decades earlier, among them Theosophy, the Unity School of Christianity, and the Dukhobors. Others, like Moral Rearmament and the Foursquare Gospel Church, were relatively recent creations. Ferguson noted that, despite their variety, all these movements promised their followers prosperity and happiness in the here and now. Moreover, he wrote, these movements offered easy and painless solutions: "They will solve any problem over night, and the results are practically guaranteed."[25]

I AM certainly fit this description. Its founders, Guy and Edna Ballard, were a married couple with an abiding interest in the occult. Edna Ballard had once worked as a medium, while Guy Ballard was a mining engineer possessed by the desire to find a gold mine. On a prospecting trip to California's Mt. Shasta in 1930, Guy Ballard had a life-changing experience. He claimed to have met a mysterious figure who identified himself as "Saint Germain."[26] Saint Germain demonstrated his ability to produce gold from thin air. He then took Ballard on a journey through time and space, which included visits to ancient Egypt, to the Amazon, and to the lost continent of Atlantis, as well as to a mysterious lodge buried beneath the Royal Teton mountain, where Ballard witnessed rooms filled with gold and jewels. Ballard also learned that he, his wife Edna, and his son Donald had lived many previous lives. Guy Ballard, for instance, had been an Egyptian priest, an Incan engineer, and a (female) French singer. During these travels, Saint Germain discoursed upon the nature of reality and the fate of humankind.

That, at least, was what Ballard claimed in his 1934 book *Unveiled Mysteries*. Published under the pseudonym Godfre Ray King, *Unveiled Mysteries* became the foundational text of the I AM movement. It was later joined on the I AM bookshelf by several other sacred texts: *The Magic Presence*, also by Godfre Ray King; *The "I AM" Adorations and Affirmations* by Chanera, a pseudonym for Edna Ballard; and *The "I AM" Discourses*, putatively by Saint Germain himself. The originality of these works was open to dispute. Gerald Bryan, a vocal critic of the movement, marshaled convincing evidence that the Ballards borrowed much of their system from older occult texts. Ballard's account of meeting Saint Germain resembled mystic experiences recounted in the books *A Dweller on Two Planets* (1894) and *The Brother of the Third Degree* (1894), both of which involved the transmission of knowledge from a long-lost civilization by way of a supernatural intermediary. Other I AM teachings resembled those found in *Life and Teaching of the Masters of the Far East* (1927), whose author, Baird Spalding, had once lived with the Ballards.[27]

I AM's theology was, depending on one's perspective, either extremely intricate or extremely muddled. As recounted by Ballard, it was less a series of precepts than a set of overlapping concepts. Terms like energy, harmony, unity, love, and tranquility recurred throughout the I AM texts. If the movement had a central principle, it was that expressed by Saint Germain in the first chapter of *Unveiled Mysteries*: "What you think and feel you bring into form; where your thought is there you are, for you are your consciousness; and what you meditate on, you become."[28] There was, Saint Germain told Ballard, no limit to what human beings could achieve once they grasped this "Great Law of Magnetic Attraction." Saint Germain demonstrated as much through his various wondrous accomplishments: He not only possessed the power to travel through time and space but also to become invisible, precipitate matter from thin air, and communicate telepathically. His powers distinguished him as an "Ascended Master"—another theosophical concept borrowed and repurposed by the Ballards. According to *Unveiled Mysteries*, "The Ascended Master is an individual who by Self-Conscious effort has generated enough Love and Power within himself to snap the chains of all human limitation, and so he stands free and worthy to be trusted with the use of forces, beyond those of human experience."[29] Beginning with Saint Germain, the I AM pantheon gradually expanded to include more and more of these Ascended Masters. Their names testified to the movement's eclecticism: Arcturus, Angel Deva of the Jade Temple, Archangel Michael, Hercules, Quan Yin, and Ray-O-Light.[30]

The central promise of the I AM texts was comfort. In *Unveiled Mysteries*, Saint Germain's first act on meeting Guy Ballard is to provide him a cup of creamy liquid to drink—indeed, nearly every encounter between the two featured a different sort of drink, all of them described as impossibly delicious. Similarly, every meal that takes place in the I AM texts is recounted in great detail, as when Saint Germain provides Guy Ballard and his friends with a dinner of vegetable cake, honey loaf ("all agreed it was the most perfect thing we had ever eaten"), ice cream ("refreshingly cool, not ice cold"), angel food cake ("much more delicious than anything we know of in the outer world"), and a creamy liquid ("as we drank it, a force rushed through our bodies like

Living Light").[31] Comfort shaded into opulence when Ballard described the lodges occupied by I AM initiates. One such lodge, for instance, had walls of gold, polished onyx, and blue and rose granite that were inlaid with gold, crystal, and diamonds. "The whole atmosphere was one of magnificence and beauty," Ballard wrote. "Words utterly fail to convey that which my eyes beheld and my feelings experienced."[32] Moreover, every person who appeared in the I AM texts is uniformly described as tall, beautiful, and in perfect health.

Such elaborate promises of health, wealth, and happiness proved alluring to a nation in the depths of the Great Depression. The Ballards held their first meetings in Chicago in 1934, followed by a successful series of meetings that same year in Philadelphia.[33] Within a few years, the Ballards were regularly lecturing to tens of thousands of people during their multiday "seminars." One journalist described the trappings of these events: "At the back of the stage is a great American flag; there is an illumined chart of the 'I AM' being, and on each side of the platform, are large portraits of Saint Germain and Jesus, with bright flood-lights beating down on them."[34] I AM study groups and reading rooms sprung up in many cities; these groups pored over I AM's sacred texts, especially Guy Ballard's *Unveiled Mysteries*. I AM merchandise proliferated. When the journalist Westbrook Pegler attended an I AM meeting in Cleveland, he noted some of the prices: Booklets sold for $1.60; pictures ranged from $1.20 to $15.00; and $2.50 would get you a "hand-colored etching of Jesus—drawn from life as he stood conversing with the tall master from Venus on a mountain in California." Phonograph records and books sold for $5.00.[35] *The Voice of the I AM*, the movement's official publication, advertised other merchandise, ranging from Saint Germain bookmarks ($0.50) to a Victrola record of Edna Ballard playing "Silent Night" on her harp ($3.00).[36]

If comfort was one pole of the I AM theology, best expressed in the movement's writings, these mass meetings expressed the other pole: conflict. The universe of I AM was defined by struggle. Evil was relentless, good was besieged, and the apocalypse was imminent. Individuals, the movement, and the nation itself were under constant attack from beings "carnate and discarnate." I AM meetings devoted time to casting out hundreds of thousands of these malign entities; at one Philadelphia meeting, the Ballards claimed to have cast out 400,000 entities from the city. Sinister "black magicians" posed another threat. At I AM meetings, the Ballards gave periodic updates on how many black magicians had been rooted out and destroyed by Saint Germain. As war approached in the late 1930s, evil entities and black magicians gave way to more corporeal enemies. At one point, the Ballards announced that a cosmic entity known as "K-17" had destroyed several German submarines bound for the Panama Canal.[37]

America had a critical role to play in this war-torn cosmology. According to Ballard, the Ascended Master Saint Germain had guided the drafting of the Declaration of Independence and had lent aid to George Washington and Abraham Lincoln.[38] That, however, was only the beginning of what (according to the Ballards) was destined be a long and fruitful relationship between the Ascended Masters and the United States. Saint Germain (again, according to Ballard in *Unveiled Mysteries*) proclaimed: "America is the Way Shower among the nations, bearing the 'Light' that heralds the incoming Golden Age."[39] *The Magic Presence* found Saint Germain returning to this theme: "America Is the 'Grail'—'The Cup' for this earth, that carries the Light of the Cosmic Christ which shall illumine the earth, and set it in Divine Order, by the power of the 'Mighty I AM Presence.'"[40] Reflecting this belief, I AM meetings typically featured an American flag on stage and were interspersed with performances of patriotic songs. *The Voice of the I AM* regularly featured patriotic exhortations; its July 1937 issue celebrated Independence Day by declaring: "America we love you! America we love you! America we love you!"[41]

As the movement grew larger, its critics grew louder. Pegler heaped scorn on the Ballards and their followers. His first story on the movement began: "It seems impossible that in all history the human race has produced any more humiliating rebuke to its claims of reason and dignity than a certain congregation of about 1,000 Americans who have been gathering afternoons and evenings lately in Cleveland to take part in a religious cult known as The Great I AM."[42] *The Rosicrucian Digest*, published by Supreme Order of the Rosicrucian Council, had little patience with their competition in the field of mysticism. A *Rosicrucian Digest* article titled "The Great Master Hoax" never mentioned the Ballards by name, but it was not hard to guess to whom they were referring when they denounced "the claims and pretensions of some of the so-called mystical, spiritual, metaphysical, occult, and 'secret' societies" as "preposterous," "inane," "fraudulent," and "insidiously destructive."[43]

The movement's most persistent critic was Gerald B. Bryan. Bryan, an attorney with an interest in the occult, had briefly associated with the Ballards, only to break with them after concluding that they were perverting the worthy cause of mysticism. Bryan attacked I AM in a series of pamphlets published throughout the 1930s, which, in 1940, he gathered into a book titled *Psychic Dictatorship in America*. Bryan ridiculed the vulgarity of the I AM dramaturgy and the shallowness of its message. He also delighted in pointing out contradictions in the movement's "sacred texts." Nonetheless, he regarded I AM not as a clownish sideshow but as a threat to personal liberty. "Probably in no other movement," he wrote, "has there ever been such an attempt at widespread interference with the personal lives of its members in this cult of the Mighty I AM."[44] The Ballards did indeed impose stern proscriptions on their followers, forbidding them from indulging in meat, liquor, tobacco, and sex (except for the purpose of procreation).[45]

Moreover, many critics regarded I AM's super-patriotism as embryonic fascism. Bryan's *Psychic Dictatorship in America* classified I AM with other "American fascist organizations" like the Knights of the White Camellia, the Crusading White Shirts, and the Defenders of the Christian Faith.[46] The vehemence with which the Ballards called on followers to pray for the "release"—that is, death—of their enemies seemed to lend credence to these fears, as did allegations that I AM's inner circle secretly prayed for the destruction of Franklin and Eleanor Roosevelt. As Gerald Bryan charged, quoting an unnamed source, the Ballards would yell the names of the Roosevelts and then chant: "Blast! Blast! Blast! their carcasses from the face of the earth forever!"[47] Such allegations proved deeply unsettling to Americans already made anxious by unrest at home and by rising fascism abroad.[48]

Faith on Trial

Charges of fascism and mass hypnotism could be shrugged off, at least by the movement's leadership. Harder to avoid were the charges of fraud that dogged Guy Ballard. These allegations dated back to Ballard's days as a gold prospector, prior to his revelations from Saint Germain and the formation of the I AM movement. In October 1938, Ballard was served with a summons while leading an I AM meeting at Chicago's Civic Opera House. The charge was filed by a Chicago woman who accused Ballard of swindling her out of $6,755 between 1924 and 1926; the money, she said, went to finance Ballard's plan to drain a California lake and collect the gold supposedly lining the lake bed.[49] Ballard was so infuriated by this charge that he "promised to send the cows, pigs, and sheep which have been slaughtered in the stockyards, to haunt the people of Chicago" for daring to affront him.[50]

Guy Ballard never had a chance to contest these charges. He died of cardiac disease in December 1939, triggering an escalating series of disasters for his movement. The Ballards had long claimed that "Ascension," the final step to salvation in their cosmology, would involve being taken bodily into the next life. To die and leave a physical corpse indicated that one had been condemned to reincarnation.[51] The Ballards later hedged this point. *The Voice of the I AM*, the movement's official magazine, announced a new dispensation as of 1938: One could, in fact, ascend while leaving behind a physical body. This left open the possibility that physical death did not mean one had failed to ascend.[52] Still, for death to take the movement's leader, a man who had long boasted of his supernatural vitality, was humiliating. Only a few months after Guy Ballard's death, his son Donald became embroiled in a nasty divorce suit with his wife Marjorie. In response to Marjorie's demand for $500 per month in alimony, Donald claimed poverty, saying he had no salary and lived entirely off an allowance provided by his mother. The subsequent investigation shed light on I AM's opaque finances; it was revealed, for instance, that Donald and Marjorie had received $11,000 from Donald's parents between 1936 and 1937, which was later cited as evidence that the Ballards were using their followers' "love gifts" to fund lavish lifestyles.[53]

Then came a still more serious blow: In July 1940, a federal grand jury indicted Edna and Donald Ballard, as well as twenty-two other I AM leaders, on eighteen counts of mail fraud. The charges boiled down to a single allegation: I AM was not a religion but a scam. As proof, the indictment pointed to the (now-cremated) corpse of Guy Ballard. I AM had claimed that its founder "had attained a supernatural state of self-immortality," and yet, the indictment charged, Ballard "did in fact die on December 29, 1939."[54] The indictment charged the Ballards with falsely claiming healing powers; with promising their followers that they "had the power to bring forth from a supernatural state, money, riches, and other material needs necessary to mankind"; and, generally, with claiming that the teachings of I AM were "absolutely essential to the salvation of mankind."[55]

The fact that the Ballards had received money from their followers was essential to the charge of fraud. The indictment explained every element of I AM's belief system in terms of how it helped the movement scam its devotees. It charged I AM's leaders with teaching that "the power to conquer 'disease, death, old age, poverty, and misery' could be transmitted to others willing to part with money or other valuables." I AM's apocalypticism was explained as a tactic to convince followers to withdraw their money from the bank and give it to I AM as a "love gift." The claim that Saint Germain had physically posed for a portrait by Charles Sindelar went from outlandish to criminal once the Ballards taught that purchasing a copy of the painting "was desirable if one would hope to achieve salvation."[56] To reinforce this point, government attorneys Norman Neukom and William Fleet Palmer, on announcing the indictment, made sure to mention that the movement had collected almost $3,000,000 since it was founded in 1930.[57]

The trial opened in Los Angeles in December 1940. The presiding judge, Leon R. Yankwich of the United States District Court, did his best to keep the issue of religion out of the trial, saying he would confine the case "strictly to mail fraud."[58] Yankwich began the trial by reading the First Amendment aloud, then reminding jurors that religious freedom could not serve as a cloak for breaking the law. His pleas had little effect. Though the government ostensibly agreed that this was "just another mail fraud case," they repeatedly sought to bring religion into the case. They highlighted I AM's most outlandish beliefs, with the implication that such beliefs could not possibly be sincerely held—and thus must have been created solely to defraud. A good deal of their evidence consisted of reading to the jury from I AM discourses, especially *Unveiled Mysteries*. Government attorneys read Guy Ballard's account of taming a panther through love, and about how the three Ballards attended an assembly hosted by the "Brotherhood of the Royal Teton," at which they conversed with a dozen visitors from Venus.[59] The jury heard about the claim that the mysterious presence K-17 had destroyed German submarines and about how the Ballards preached the healing qualities of the color blue.[60] One witness recounted that Guy Ballard promised her she could heal her husband's blindness by visualizing a ray of light passing through his head. This same witness said she was instructed to look for sparkles in the atmosphere, which "the ascended masters used in the books to deliver diamond necklaces and money, even food and clothing and automobiles."[61] This claim provoked laughter in the courtroom, which was likely the government attorney's intent.

Money was the key factor in the testimony of all the government witnesses. Several testified about how much money the movement took in, with one saying that love gifts "averaged well over $1,000 a day during classes" and that Ballard regularly "received checks in the mail which totaled from $1,500 to $2,000."[62] The jury learned about Edna Ballard's fantastic jewelry, which Guy Ballard allegedly justified by saying that "a body was healed every time a student gave [his wife] a jewel."[63] They also heard of how Edna Ballard supposedly told an I AM leader to suggest to a student that he cash in his life insurance on account of the coming world-ending cataclysm.[64] Evidence was even introduced as to the size of allowance Donald Ballard received from his parents.[65] The aim was to depict the movement, or at least its leaders, as money-mad, driven not by sincere belief but by a hunger for profit.

The defense countered these claims by arguing that I AM was no different from any other faith. When cross-examining a government witness, for instance, defense attorney Charles Carr forced her to admit that the "various classes and meetings of the I AM services were conducted much the same as in 'the good old Methodist Church.'"[66] The defense attorneys sought to couch seemingly outlandish I AM claims in language that would be more familiar to a Christian audience. One government witness had testified that the Ballards claimed one could "precipitate" material goods out of thin air; a defense witness challenged this claim, explaining that "precipitation did not mean one can decree an automobile and have a car out of the heavens, but rather one can decree a car, visualize it, and call on one's Mighty I AM presence for it."[67] Other witnesses said that the Ballards had never claimed otherworldly healing powers but had simply told followers to heal themselves by calling on their own "Mighty I AM" presence.[68] The culmination of this argument came in testimony from Edna Ballard herself, who, in her explication of the movement's ideas, explained that "I AM" was simply another name for God.[69] The defense also emphasized that I AM, far from being a fringe movement, attracted people from all walks of life. In a single day of testimony, the defense "produced a sea captain, a contractor, a former oil company executive, a woman lawyer and two housewives."[70]

Both the government and the defense cases posed an implicit question: Did the Ballards deliver on their promises? The government aimed to show that people who joined I AM were swindled. They received nothing for their money, despite the Ballards' promises. One government witness complained that I AM had failed to heal her kidney and bladder trouble.[71] Another complained that she never could precipitate an automobile out of thin air.[72] One witness even blamed the I AM movement for failing to protect her from a nasty stumble in which she sprained her ankle and broke her glasses. Judge Yankwich greeted this claim with some incredulity: "You blame that on the I AM presence?" he asked. To which the witness replied: "I do, because they didn't make good. I asked them to protect me and they didn't do it."[73] Her claim encapsulated the government's case: The Ballards had failed to "make good."

The defense responded with a series of testimonials from satisfied I AM devotees. These witnesses credited I AM with turning their lives around. One I AM leader enthused that, since joining the movement, "I am a better man physically, mentally, and spiritually, and—I am happy!" One witness, a Latvian immigrant, testified that he had once been a communist plotting to overthrow the U.S. government, but that on joining I AM he had become a law-abiding citizen.[74] A doctor claimed that reading I AM books had healed his encephalitis, and a dentist testified that I AM teaching had increased his skill at treating patients.[75] "We do not expect to convert you gentlemen of the jury," defense attorney Charles Carr said before the defense opened its case, but one could be forgiven for thinking that was their goal—if not to convert the jury, then at least to convince them that reasonable people could be converted for understandable reasons.[76]

The jury was unable to reach a verdict, in part because it was unclear what, exactly, the jury was being asked to decide, and what evidence the jurors were supposed to use in deciding it. Judge Yankwich repeatedly struck material from the record as irrelevant to the charges of mail fraud. After the government rested its case, Judge Yankwich ordered the jury to ignore anything dealing with sexual abstinence, K-17, and cataclysms.[77] Just before the case went to the jury, Yankwich struck out still more material, including everything related to "visions of Jesus Christ; the rays of light by which the late Guy W. Ballard received many of his dictations from the ascended masters, and supernatural events occurring at Mt. Shasta."[78] The jury, without much to work with, spent several days without reaching a decision. At one point, the jurors requested that Judge Yankwich explain to them how they were supposed to interpret claims regarding the supernatural; Yankwich responded that the "government is not challenging the verity of any one's belief in the supernatural," which did little to clarify matters. Ultimately, the jury could not decide. It acquitted three defendants and split on the remaining six, Edna and Donald Ballard among them.[79]

A second trial was held in the court of federal judge J. F. T. O'Connor.[80] The cast was the same, but the outcome was different: Though four of the defendants were acquitted, Edna and Donald Ballard were convicted of fraud and conspiracy to commit fraud. They were fined a total of $8,400 and sentenced to probation.[81] The case then wound its way through a labyrinth of court decisions until it reached the United States Supreme Court, which, in May 1944, upheld the Ballards' conviction in a complicated ruling. Five justices upheld the conviction but left open the possibility for the Ballards to appeal on different legal grounds; writing for the majority, Justice William Douglas also asserted that the Ballards should not be judged on the truth or falsity of their religious beliefs, as "heresy trials are foreign to our Constitution." Three justices said that the conviction should be upheld and that the Ballards should not be allowed to appeal the decision on any grounds. Standing alone was Justice Robert Jackson, whose dissenting opinion declared that the initial indictment was an unconstitutional violation of religious freedom.[82]

Jackson's eloquent defense of freedom of conscience concluded: "I would dismiss the indictment and have done with this business of judicially examining other people's faiths."[83] But it also contained a line that suggested that *United States v. Ballard* was inseparable from the question of consumer fraud. "If the members of the sect get comfort from the celestial guidance of their 'Saint Germain,' however doubtful it seems to me," Jackson wrote, "it is hard to say that they do not get what they pay for."[84]

The conviction of Edna and Donald Ballard was ultimately thrown out—though not on the grounds of religious freedom, but rather because the California jury that had convicted the Ballards had not included any women. By that point, however, I AM had already begun a slow but steady decline. When religious historian Charles Braden investigated the movement in the mid-1940s, he found most of its adherents hostile to outsiders and embittered by a sense that their leaders had been unfairly persecuted.[85] But while the movement weakened, it never went extinct. As of 1975, the writer David Stupple was able to find at least one I AM temple or reading room in every large western city. He attributed the movement's persistence to its decentralized nature, with each local temple run by a dedicated trustee; this was a far cry from the "authoritarian cult" that had so terrified people in the 1930s.[86] The historian Robert Ellwood, visiting an I AM temple in the late 1980s, described the building as a "modest house set well back from the street in a suburban city in the American Southwest," though its interior, with its gold-trimmed walls and its vivid portraits of the Ballards and of Saint Germain, managed to capture something of "the glory days of the thirties"—those glory days when I AM seemed poised to remake American religion.[87]

Strange Bedfellows

In their hour of need, the Ballards found sympathy from an unexpected source: the liberal Protestant journal *The Christian Century*.[88] Charles Braden, writing in the *Century*, criticized I AM's beliefs but nonetheless suggested that Christians could learn from the "tremendous sense of urgency and a high degree of commitment" displayed by members of the I AM movement and similar "cults."[89] And when the Ballards were indicted, an editorial in the *Century* warned that "if the police are going after all who have accepted gifts on the promise of spiritual benefits of a nature incredible to the unbelieving, or even health and healing, they have started something!"[90] The *Century* suggested that the charges levied against I AM, taken to their logical conclusion, might give government officials the authority to judge the validity and efficacy of religious claims.

In the decades following the I AM controversy, there would be many similar cases of "fringe" and "mainstream" religions coming together to defend the right of religious institutions to control their finances. One such case involved the Worldwide Church of God (WCG), an apocalyptic, Adventist-influenced faith founded by Herbert W. Armstrong.[91] Following charges that Armstrong and one of his aides had pilfered millions of dollars from the church, the state of California took the drastic step of placing the entire church in receivership.[92] The state's decision aroused furious protest, not only from the Worldwide Church of God but also from a broad cross section of American religion. The National Council of Churches, the Synagogue Council of America, the Lutheran Church in America, the United Methodist Church, and the National Association of Evangelicals filed an amicus brief on behalf of the Worldwide Church of God, warning that "when the technicalities of statutes designed to regulate ordinary corporate activities are used and abused as instrumentalities to destroy a religious association which may be in governmental disfavor at a particular time, the result is a threat to the security of all religions."[93] A similar dynamic was visible in the case of another marginalized religion, the Unification Church of the Reverend Sun Myung Moon. When the federal government charged Moon with tax fraud in the early 1980s, he received support from religious leaders ranging from Jerry Falwell of the Moral Majority to Joseph Lowery of the Southern Christian Leadership Conference.[94] The unusual nature of this alliance was evident at a hearing held by a subcommittee of the Senate Judiciary Committee in June 1984. At this hearing, dedicated to "the State of Religious Liberty in America Today" and chaired by Senator Orrin Hatch (R-UT), Moon himself appeared to condemn the government's case against him: "From the very beginning, this was not a tax case," he told the subcommittee. "It has been an invasion by the Government into the internal affairs of religion." Appearing on the witness stand immediately before Moon was a Christian minister who declared: "The IRS is now a terrorist organization, they have become so strong that they can jail religious leaders for legitimate practices."[95] Opposing the government in disputes over financial practices served as a rallying point for religious figures who had little else in common.

Other religious communities sought to defend their financial practices from state intervention by creating organizations for self-regulation. One example of this strategy was the Evangelical Council for Financial Accountability, founded by a coalition of evangelical Christian ministries in the late 1970s. These ministries were responding to proposed legislation, put forward in the wake of several high-profile financial scandals among religious groups, which would have tightened the regulation of charitable donations.[96] This shift toward self-regulation reflected a broader change in the American treatment of fraud: a move away from the principle of *caveat venditor* ("seller beware") and back toward that of *caveat emptor* ("buyer beware"), which had prevailed prior to the 1930s.[97]

Increasingly, then, religious freedom in the United States became entangled with resistance to taxation and regulation—indeed, with resistance to state power in general. Religious leaders pushed back against any attempt by the government to intervene in the exchange of money and services between religious organizations and their donors. The days in which the law could, as Westbrook Pegler put it, "burst up a flock for the sake of the lambs" seemed to be coming to an end. The I AM case was an important step in this direction; the scrutiny that the government applied to the movement's beliefs suggested (at least to religious leaders) the dangers inherent in empowering state officials to protect "lambs" from religious fraud.

PART III

The (Mis)application of Religious Freedom

CHAPTER 8

The Historian's Pickaxe

Uncovering the Racist Origins of the Religious Right

Randall Balmer

The Religious Right's most cherished and durable myth is its myth of origins. According to this well-rehearsed narrative, articulated by Jerry Falwell, Pat Robertson, and countless others, after nearly half a century of electoral quiescence evangelical leaders were shaken out of their political complacency by the United States Supreme Court's *Roe v. Wade* decision of January 22, 1973. Falwell even recounted (albeit fourteen years later) his horror at reading the news in the January 23, 1973, edition of the *Lynchburg News*. "The Supreme Court had just made a decision by a seven-to-two margin that would legalize the killing of millions of unborn children," Falwell wrote. "I sat there staring at the *Roe v. Wade* story growing more and more fearful of the consequences of the Supreme Court's act and wondering why so few voices had been raised against it." The myth of origins has Falwell and other evangelical leaders emerging like mollusks out of their apolitical stupor to fight the moral outrage of legalized abortion. Some even went so far as to invoke the moniker "new abolitionists" in an effort to ally themselves with their antebellum evangelical predecessors who sought to eradicate the scourge of slavery.[1]

In casting their political movement as a defense of the fetus, and therefore as a defense of evangelicals' putative religious beliefs, the Religious Right anticipated arguments used to great effect in subsequent legal cases, including *Burwell v. Hobby Lobby* (2014) and *Masterpiece Cakeshop v. Colorado Civil Rights Commission* (2018). Central to those arguments was the posture, adopted by the Religious Right in the late 1970s, that the convictions of these believers were somehow under attack. The rhetoric of victimization, though counterintuitive (given the numbers and the influence of evangelicals throughout American history), has emerged as a central strategy for the Religious Right, even though the supposed origins of the movement—opposition to abortion—are fictional. An examination of the real origins of the Religious Right, moreover, reveals the ways in which the notion of religious freedom has been construed, misconstrued, and weaponized by evangelical leaders since the late 1970s.

* * *

I was a student at an evangelical college and seminary for most of the 1970s, so I had some personal recollections of the era during which the Religious Right emerged as a political force. As a pastor's son, I had spent my entire life in the cocoon of what I would later identify as the evangelical subculture, the interlocking network of congregations and denominations, Bible camps and Bible institutes, mission societies and publishing houses. So when I learned, retroactively, that *Roe v. Wade* had been the catalyst for evangelicals moving into politics, I raised an eyebrow. That's not how I remembered it, not at all. But I was far removed from that world by the early 1980s, immersed in graduate school and the study of American colonial history, so I paid it little mind. Besides, if preachers like Falwell and Robertson and a host of others said it was abortion that drew them into politics, who was I to dispute them?

In November 1990, however, for reasons that I still cannot discern, I was invited to a small conference in Washington, D.C. Not knowing what to expect, I almost begged off at the last minute, but I decided to attend. I soon found myself in a conference room with the likes of Richard Land, Donald Wildmon, Ralph Reed, Carl F. H. Henry, and Ed Dobson, as well as Paul Weyrich, the architect of the Religious Right. I quickly picked up that this gathering was meant to be a ten-year celebration of the election of Ronald Reagan as well as a retrospective—again, celebratory—of the Religious Right. Having refused to celebrate the election of Ronald Reagan for the previous decade, I was in no mood to begin then, but, having made the trip to Washington, I saw no harm in listening in on the conversation.

In the initial session, someone made passing reference to the standard narrative that the *Roe v. Wade* decision of 1973 had served as the catalyst for the Religious Right. I tuned in. Weyrich forcefully disputed that assumption, recounting that ever since Barry Goldwater's run for the presidency in 1964, he had been trying to enlist evangelicals in conservative political causes, but it was the tax exemption for religious schools that finally caught the attention of evangelical leaders. Abortion, he said, had nothing to do with it. That comment, apparently, got others thinking. "The Religious New Right did not start because of a concern about abortion," Ed Dobson, formerly Jerry Falwell's lieutenant, added. "I sat in the non-smoke-filled back room with the Moral Majority, and I frankly do not remember abortion being mentioned as a reason why we ought to do something." During the ensuing break in the proceedings, I pulled Weyrich aside to be certain I had heard him correctly, that *Roe v. Wade* did not precipitate the Religious Right. He was emphatic. Abortion, he repeated, had nothing whatsoever to do with the rise of the Religious Right.[2]

Thus began my decades-long quest to ascertain the true origins of the Religious Right. It was a journey that took me to denominational records, magazine sources, the archives at such institutions as Liberty University; Bob Jones University; the presidential libraries of Gerald Ford, Ronald Reagan, and Jimmy Carter; and the American Heritage Center in Laramie, Wyoming, the improbable location of Paul Weyrich's papers.

* * *

The initial step was to dispel what I call the abortion myth, the fiction that the Religious Right emerged directly from *Roe v. Wade*. Indeed, the abortion myth collapses quickly in the face of historical scrutiny. In 1970, the United Methodist Church General Conference called on state legislatures to repeal laws restricting abortion, and, in 1972, at the same gathering that Jimmy Carter addressed as governor of Georgia, the Methodists acknowledged "the sanctity of unborn human life" but also declared that "we are equally bound to respect the sacredness of the life and well-being of the mother, for whom devastating damage may result from unacceptable pregnancy." Meeting in St. Louis, Missouri, during the summer of 1971, the messengers (delegates) to the Southern Baptist Convention passed a resolution that stated, "We call upon Southern Baptists to work for legislation that will allow the possibility of abortion under such conditions as rape, incest, clear evidence of severe fetal deformity, and carefully ascertained evidence of the likelihood of damage to the emotional, mental, and physical health of the mother." The Southern Baptist Convention, hardly a redoubt of liberalism, reaffirmed that position in 1974, the year after the *Roe* decision, and again in 1976.[3]

When the *Roe* decision was handed down, W. A. Criswell, former president of the Southern Baptist Convention and pastor of First Baptist Church in Dallas, Texas, expressed his satisfaction with the ruling. "I have always felt that it was only after a child was born and had a life separate from its mother that it became an individual person," one of the most famous fundamentalists of the twentieth century declared, "and it has always, therefore, seemed to me that what is best for the mother and for the future should be allowed."[4]

While a few evangelical voices, including *Christianity Today* magazine, mildly criticized the ruling, the overwhelming response on the part of evangelicals was silence, even approval; Baptists, in particular, applauded the decision as an appropriate articulation of the line of division between church and state, between personal morality and state regulation of individual behavior. "Religious liberty, human equality and justice are advanced by the Supreme Court abortion decision," W. Barry Garrett of *Baptist Press* wrote. Floyd Robertson of the National Association of Evangelicals disagreed with the *Roe* decision, but he believed that legal redress should not be a priority for evangelicals. "The abortion issue should also remind evangelicals that the church must never rely on the state to support its mission or enforce its moral standards," he wrote in the summer 1973 issue of the organization's newsletter, *United Evangelical Action*. "The church and state must be separate. The actions and conduct of Christians transcend the secular community for which the state is responsible."[5]

The real origins of the Religious Right, it turns out, are rather more prosaic and less high-minded. In May 1969, a group of African American parents in Holmes County, Mississippi, filed suit to prevent three new whites-only academies from securing tax exemption from the Internal Revenue Service (IRS); each of the schools had been founded to evade desegregation of the public schools. In Holmes County, the number of white students enrolled in the public schools had dropped from 771 to 28 during the first year of desegregation; the following year, that number fell to zero. The court case, known as *Green v. Kennedy*, won a temporary injunction against the "segregation academies" in January 1970, and, later that year, Richard Nixon ordered the IRS to enact a new policy that would deny tax exemptions to segregated schools. In July 1970, the IRS announced that, in accordance with the provisions of the Civil Rights Act of 1964, which forbade racial segregation and discrimination, it would no longer grant tax-exempt status to private schools with racially discriminatory policies. Such institutions were not—by definition—charitable organizations, and therefore they had no claims to tax-exempt status; similarly, donations to such organizations would no longer qualify as tax-deductible contributions. On November 30, 1970, the IRS sent letters of inquiry to the schools in question in an effort to ascertain whether they discriminated on the basis of race. Bob Jones University, a fundamentalist school in Greenville, South Carolina, responded that it did not admit African Americans.[6]

Meanwhile, the *Green v. Kennedy* suit was joined with a similar suit to become *Green v. Connally*. On June 30, 1971, the United States District Court for the District of Columbia issued its ruling in the *Green v. Connally* case: "Under the Internal Revenue Code, properly construed, racially discriminatory private schools are not entitled to the Federal tax exemption provided for charitable, educational institutions, and persons making gifts to such schools are not entitled to the deductions provided in case of gifts to charitable, educational institutions."[7]

Paul Weyrich saw his opening. Ever since Goldwater's campaign, Weyrich had been trying to organize evangelicals politically. Their numbers alone, he reasoned, would constitute a formidable voting bloc, and he aspired to marshal them behind conservative causes. "The new political philosophy must be defined by us in moral terms, packaged in non-religious language, and propagated throughout the country by our new coalition," Weyrich wrote in spelling out his vision. "When political power is achieved, the moral majority will have the opportunity to re-create this great nation." Weyrich believed that the political possibilities of such a coalition were unlimited. "The leadership, moral philosophy, and workable vehicle are at hand just waiting to be blended and activated," he wrote. "If the moral majority acts, results could well exceed our wildest dreams."[8]

But Weyrich's dreams, still a hypothetical coalition that he already referred to as "moral majority" (lowercase letters), needed a catalyst—not simply an event or issue that would ignite all the indignation that had been accumulating but also a standard around which to rally. For nearly two decades, Weyrich, by his own account, had tried various issues to pique evangelical interest in his scheme, including pornography, school prayer, the proposed Equal Rights Amendment to the Constitution, and abortion. "I was trying to get these people interested in those issues and I utterly failed," Weyrich recalled in 1990. "What changed their mind was Jimmy Carter's intervention against the Christian schools, trying to deny them tax-exempt status on the basis of so-called de facto segregation."[9]

Because the *Green v. Connally* ruling was "applicable to all private schools in the United States at all levels of education," Bob Jones University stood directly in the IRS crosshairs. Founded in Florida by arch-fundamentalist Bob Jones in 1926, the school had been located for a time in Cleveland, Tennessee, before moving to South Carolina in 1947. In response to *Green v. Connally*, Bob Jones University admitted a married black man, a worker in the school's radio station, as a part-time student. He dropped out a month later. Out of fears of racial mixing, the school maintained its restrictions against admitting unmarried African Americans until 1975. Even then, however, the school stipulated that interracial dating would be grounds for expulsion, and the school also promised that any students who "espouse, promote, or encourage others to violate the University's dating rules and regulations will be expelled."[10]

The Internal Revenue Service pursued its case against Bob Jones University and on April 16, 1975, notified the school of the proposed revocation of its tax-exempt status. On January 19, 1976, the IRS officially revoked Bob Jones University's tax-exempt status, effective retroactively to 1971, when the school had first been formally notified of the IRS policy. As Bob Jones University sued to retain its tax exemption, Weyrich pressed his case. Evangelical leaders, especially those whose schools were affected by the ruling, were angry, construing the decision as government intrusion in religious matters. Weyrich used the *Green v. Connally* case to rally evangelicals against the government. When "the Internal Revenue Service tried to deny tax exemption to private schools," Weyrich said in an interview with *Conservative Digest*, that "more than any single act brought the fundamentalists and evangelicals into the political process."[11]

Inadvertently, during the Carter administration, the Internal Revenue Service poured fuel on the embers of evangelical resentment. Although there is no evidence to suggest that the Carter White House participated in drafting the regulations, and Carter himself was unaware of them, Jerome Kurtz, the IRS commissioner, on August 22, 1978, proposed that schools founded or expanded at the time of desegregation of public schools in their locality meet a quota of minority students or certify that they operated "in good faith on a racially non-discriminatory basis." The regulations, in effect, shifted the burden of proof from the Internal Revenue Service to the schools. A number of evangelicals interpreted the IRS proposals as an unwarranted violation of the sanctity of their subculture, a network of alternative institutions they had constructed as a shelter from "worldliness" in the decades following the Scopes Trial of 1925. Evangelicals flooded the IRS with letters of protest, more than 125,000 in all. The proposed regulations "kicked a sleeping dog," Richard Viguerie, one of the founders of the New Right, said. "It was the episode that ignited the religious right's involvement in real politics." When *Conservative Digest* cataloged evangelical discontent with Carter in August 1979, the IRS regulations headed the list. Abortion was not mentioned.[12]

Although the Internal Revenue Service backed away from many of the proposals, the fires of resentment flared. "To impose student and faculty quotas on private schools is a treacherous intervention into a Constitutionally protected activity," John Ashbrook, Republican member of Congress from Ohio, wrote to Carter. "Its arbitrary formula for student and staff recruitment will place Federal bureaucrats at the helm of policy formation for private schools." Ashbrook's House colleague, Robert Dornan of California, warned that Americans "are sick and tired of unelected bureaucrats engaging in social engineering at the expense of our cherished liberties." Weyrich encouraged Robert Billings, an evangelical, to form an organization called Christian School Action as a vehicle for building on evangelical discontent, an organization Weyrich came to regard as a "tremendous asset" to his hopes for politicizing conservative evangelicals. Billings, who had earlier founded the National Christian Action Coalition to thwart what he characterized as "an attempt by the IRS to control private schools," quickly mobilized evangelical ministers. Billings later declared, "Jerome Kurtz has done more to bring Christians together than any man since the Apostle Paul." Even Anita Bryant, who had been goaded into activism by her opposition to gay rights, recognized the centrality of the school issue. "I believe the day of the comfortable Christian is over," Bryant declared. "Maybe it hasn't reached everybody in the rural areas, but it's a battle in the cities to keep them from taking over and reaching private and religious schools."[13]

In ramping up for political activism, evangelicals portrayed themselves as defending what they considered the sanctity of the evangelical subculture from outside interference. Weyrich astutely picked up on those fears. "What caused the movement to surface was the federal government's moves against Christian schools," Weyrich reiterated in 1990. "This absolutely shattered the Christian community's notions that Christians could isolate themselves inside their own institutions and teach what they pleased." For agitated evangelicals, Weyrich's conservative gospel of less government suddenly struck a responsive chord. "It wasn't the abortion issue; that wasn't sufficient," Weyrich recalled. "It was the recognition that isolation simply would no longer work in this society."[14]

Leaders of the Religious Right in later years would seek to portray their politicization as a direct response to the *Roe v. Wade* ruling of 1973, but Weyrich and other organizers of the Religious Right have been emphatic in dismissing this abortion myth. *Green v. Connally*, not *Roe v. Wade*, served as the catalyst. Although many evangelicals certainly felt troubled by abortion and viewed it as part of the broader problem of promiscuity in American society, most of them regarded it as a "Catholic issue" in the realm of politics until the late 1970s. (Falwell acknowledged as much when he preached against abortion for the first time on February 26, 1978, from his pulpit at Thomas Road Baptist Church.) Evangelical leaders, prodded by Weyrich, chose to interpret the IRS ruling against segregationist schools as an assault on the integrity and the sanctity of the evangelical subculture, ignoring the fact that exemption from taxes is itself a form of public subsidy. And that is what prompted them to action and to organize into a political movement. "What caused the movement to surface," Weyrich reiterated, "was the federal government's moves against Christian schools," which, he added, "enraged the Christian community."[15]

More recently, another conservative activist, Grover Norquist, has confirmed that the *Roe v. Wade* decision did not factor into the rise of the Religious Right. "The religious right did not get started in 1962 with prayer in school," Norquist told Dan Gilgoff, of *U.S. News & World Report*, in June 2009. "And it didn't get started in '73 with *Roe v. Wade*. It started in '77 or '78 with the Carter administration's attack on Christian schools and radio stations. That's where all of the organization flowed out of. It was complete self-defense."[16]

The actions of the Internal Revenue Service especially affected Bob Jones University, goading those associated with the school into political activism. Elmer L. Rumminger, longtime administrator at the university who became politically active in 1980, remembered that the IRS case "alerted the Christian school community about what could happen with government interference" in the affairs of evangelical institutions. "That was really the major issue that got us all involved to begin with—at least it was for me." What about abortion? "No, no, that wasn't the issue," he said emphatically. "This wasn't an anti-abortion movement per se. That was one of the issues we were interested in. I'm sure some people pointed to *Roe v. Wade*, but that's not what got us going. For me it was government intrusion into private education."[17]

* * *

The IRS pursuit of Bob Jones University and other schools may have captured the attention of evangelical leaders, but Weyrich was clever enough to realize that the political mobilization of evangelical and fundamentalist leaders represented only half of the equation. Unless these leaders could enlist rank-and-file evangelicals, Weyrich's dream of a politically conservative coalition of evangelicals would remain unfulfilled. And here is where abortion finally figures into the narrative.

In the 1978 midterm elections, the Democratic Party suffered a net loss of three seats in the Senate and fifteen seats in the House of Representatives. Though not unexpected for the party in power—Republicans suffered far greater losses in the previous midterm-election year of 1974, the year of Nixon's resignation—those reading the election returns could see that abortion had the potential to emerge as a political issue.

In Iowa, for example, polls and pundits expected that the incumbent Democratic senator, Richard C. "Dick" Clark, would coast easily to reelection; no poll heading into the November balloting indicated that Clark held a lead of fewer than 10 percentage points. Six years earlier, Clark had walked across the state to call attention to his grassroots, upstart challenge to Jack Miller, the two-term Republican incumbent, and Clark prevailed with 55 percent of the vote. He remained a popular figure in the state. Pro-life activists, however, had targeted Clark, and, on the final weekend of Clark's reelection campaign, opponents of abortion (predominantly Roman Catholics) distributed approximately 300,000 pamphlets in church parking lots. Two days later, in an election with very low turnout, Roger Jepsen, the Republican pro-life challenger, defeated Clark. An Election Day survey by the *Des Moines Register* indicated that about 25,000 Iowans voted for Jepsen because of his stand on abortion. "I personally believe that the abortion issue was the central issue," Clark told Bruce Morton of *CBS News*. The senator's campaign manager agreed. "It comes right down to those leaflets they put out," he said.[18]

Christianity Today noted Clark's unexpected defeat, and the magazine also credited pro-lifers for the Republican trifecta in Minnesota, where Republican candidates who opposed abortion captured both Senate seats (one for the unexpired term of Walter Mondale) and the office of governor. "Anti-abortionists figured in the collapse of Minnesota's liberal Democratic-Farmer-Labor Party," the magazine reported, adding that the campaign of Albert Quie, the governor-elect and ally of Charles Colson, "distributed 250,000 leaflets to churchgoers throughout the state on the Sunday before election day."[19]

None of this was lost on Paul Weyrich. Earlier that year, Weyrich, head of the Committee for the Survival of a Free Congress, had received a check in the amount of twenty-five dollars from Georgia G. Glassman, of Gravity, Iowa. "Please make Good use of the proceeds," she wrote, "as soon as we hear that a good Republican, a Lawyer I hope, has announced his candidacy for the U.S. Senate, we Republicans will try to 'Hang Sen. Dick Clark on a telephone pole!'"[20]

Weyrich could barely contain his delight with the 1978 election returns, especially the Senate elections in Iowa and in New Hampshire, where Gordon Humphrey had ousted Thomas J. McIntyre, another Democratic incumbent. "The election of Roger Jepsen and Gordon Humphrey to the U.S. Senate is true cause for celebration, especially in view of the fact that two of the most liberal senators went down to defeat," Weyrich wrote. Even more notable, however, was how it happened: with the support of politically conservative evangelicals. Weyrich immediately set about fortifying the nascent coalition. On December 5, just a month after the election, Weyrich brought Humphrey, the senator-elect from New Hampshire, and his wife to a gathering of evangelical activists. The following day, Robert Billings penned an exultant letter to Weyrich, praising him for his "wise remarks" and congratulating him on the "smashing success" of an evening. "Paul, we did something that no-one has done in years—we brought together the three main factions of the fundamentalist community," Billings wrote. "I believe something was started last night that will pull together many of our 'fringe' Christian friends." Billings concluded his handwritten letter: "Thank you for your important part. God bless you![21]

The 1978 election had provided the opening that Weyrich had been seeking. The previous year, Weyrich had appealed to the head of the Republican National Committee to court evangelical and fundamentalist voters, but the appeal fell on deaf ears; the chair of the committee "didn't understand what I was talking about," Weyrich said. "It was so foreign to him that it didn't make any sense." Undeterred, Weyrich resolved to "go out and elect some improbable people in the '78 elections." Although Weyrich highlighted the school issue, the defeat of Dick Clark in Iowa and the triple win for prolife Republicans in Minnesota suggested that abortion might very well be the issue that would galvanize grassroots evangelicals and fundamentalists into a cohesive political movement. Recall Robert Billings's letter to Weyrich a month after the midterm elections: "Paul, we did something that no-one has done in years—we brought together the three main factions of the fundamentalist community."[22]

Weyrich's approach to politicizing the evangelical community proceeded on two tracks: the mobilizing of evangelical leaders on the one hand, and the energizing of grassroots evangelicals on the other. Weyrich had already secured the activism of evangelical leaders over what he characterized as overreach on the part of the IRS over racial segregation in evangelical institutions. But Weyrich was also savvy enough to recognize that an overt appeal to racism would be a tough sell at the grassroots level. He brilliantly executed what Vivien A. Schmidt describes as "discursive institutionalism," where a "coordinative discourse" devises policy and strategy among the leadership and a "communicative discourse" conveys something different to a more general public. In this case, the coordinative discourse centered on the defense of segregated institutions and the communicative discourse emphasized opposition to abortion, an issue more likely to inflame popular passions.[23]

In persuading evangelicals that abortion was a moral issue that demanded their political activism, Weyrich received help from an unlikely source, Francis A. Schaeffer, a Presbyterian minister. Schaeffer, considered by many the intellectual godfather of the Religious Right, began to weigh in about the pervasiveness of what he called "secular humanism" in American society. He lamented the loss of "basically a Christian consensus" and said that "we now live in a secularized society."[24]

By the late 1970s, Schaeffer was beginning to cite abortion as one consequence of a troubling cultural shift away from the mores of evangelical Christianity and toward the reviled "secular humanism." Schaeffer viewed abortion as the inevitable prelude to infanticide and euthanasia, and he wanted to sound the alarm. When Schaeffer visited Fulton J. Sheen, the famous Roman Catholic bishop, in the late 1970s, Sheen applauded Schaeffer for his attempts to engage Protestants on the abortion issue. "The problem is," Sheen said, "that abortion is perceived as a Catholic issue. I want you to help me change that." Schaeffer did so through his writings and lectures, but he also teamed with C. Everett Koop, a pediatric surgeon, to produce a series of five films, collectively titled *Whatever Happened to the Human Race?* These films, produced by Billy Zeoli, Gerald Ford's religious adviser, financed in part by Richard DeVos of Amway, and directed by Schaeffer's son, Frank, found a wide audience among evangelicals when they appeared early in 1979. Although Francis Schaeffer died in 1983, and Frank Schaeffer now claims that his father was appalled at the machinations of Religious Right leaders, the films, together with a companion book by the same title, served to introduce abortion to evangelicals as a moral concern. "By the end of the *Whatever Happened to the Human Race?* tour," Frank Schaeffer recalled, "we were calling for civil disobedience, the takeover of the Republican Party, and even hinting at overthrowing our 'unjust pro-abortion government.'" Years later,

Robert Maddox, Jimmy Carter's liaison for religious affairs, recounted his only encounter with Schaeffer, who was visiting the office of Alonzo McDonald, an evangelical who served as Carter's deputy chief of staff. "I think you've caused a great damage here with this abortion stuff," Maddox said. Schaeffer's quiet response, according to Maddox: "Could be."[25]

Weyrich's prescience about expanding abortion from a preponderantly "Catholic issue" into an evangelical preoccupation was nothing short of brilliant. His success in blaming Carter for the IRS action against Christian schools may also have been brilliant, but it also was mendacious because Carter bore no responsibility for that. After years of warnings, the Internal Revenue Service finally rescinded the tax exemption of Bob Jones University on January 19, 1976, because of its persistent racist policies. That date, January 19, 1976, was a notable one for Jimmy Carter—but not because he was in any way responsible for the action against Bob Jones University. Carter won the Iowa precinct caucuses on January 19, 1976, his first major step toward capturing the Democratic presidential nomination. He took office as president a year and a day later. Weyrich and the Religious Right, however, persuaded many evangelicals that Carter, not Gerald Ford who was then president, was somehow responsible for this unconscionable "assault" on Christian schools. In Weyrich's words, "Jimmy Carter's intervention against the Christian schools, trying to deny them tax-exempt status on the basis of so-called de facto segregation" prompted preachers like Jerry Falwell to mobilize against him.[26]

* * *

For politically conservative evangelicals in the late 1970s, Jimmy Carter's refusal to seek a constitutional amendment banning abortion came to be seen as an unpardonable sin, despite his long-standing opposition to abortion and the efforts of his administration to limit the incidence of abortion. Carter, in fact, had a longer and more consistent record of opposing abortion than did Ronald Reagan, who as governor of California had signed into law the most liberal abortion bill in the nation.

The 1980 presidential election would test the mettle of this new coalition crafted by the hands of Weyrich, Falwell, Billings, and others. The nascent Religious Right courted several candidates in advance of the 1980 Republican primaries, including Philip Crane, member of Congress from Illinois, and John Connally, the former governor of Texas and former secretary of the treasury. The meeting with Connally was going smoothly until one of the preachers asked Connally's views on secular humanism. No one, apparently, had briefed the former governor that the term "secular humanism" was Religious Right code language for everything amiss in America. "Well, I don't know much about it," Connally declared, "but it sounds good to me!"[27]

The leaders of the Religious Right settled on Reagan. And the rest, as they say, is history.

CHAPTER 9

Female Genital Cutting in Michigan

How Advocates of the Dawoodi Bohra Distorted Religious Freedom to Control Women's Sexual Conduct

Kristina Arriaga

The relationship between women's rights and religious freedom is fraught with difficulties. In many religious traditions, for instance, the position of authority belongs only to men. Further, some communities invoke religious beliefs to justify practices that are harmful and discriminatory against girls and women, such as limiting their education; dictating the way they dress; or dealing with marriages, divorces, and inheritance. The family laws on which those practices are based and which are often detrimental for women are rooted in religion.

These realities have led some observers to conclude that religious freedom is conceptually adversarial to women. However, such a perception is based on a misunderstanding of the nature of religious freedom. Religious freedom does not protect religious traditions; religious freedom is a human right that "empowers human beings to find their various ways within, without or beyond those traditions."[1] Robust religious freedom protections can, in short, afford space for everyone—including girls and women—to advocate for their right to live according to their deeply held convictions.

When religious freedom arguments are falsely manipulated to justify protecting harmful practices for girls and women, such as female genital mutilation/cutting (FGM/C), the fabric of women's rights and religious freedom is weakened. Regrettably, such is the dialectic that has been taking place in the United States since 2017 when a U.S. federal court in Michigan heard the first FGM/C case in the nation. This dialectic was further exacerbated by the lack of medical research on the clitoris—the part of the anatomy most often altered when girls and women are subjected to this practice.

Today, more than 500,000 girls, in the United States alone, are at risk of being forced to undergo FGM/C because their families come from regions and cultures where the operations routinely occur as an expected rite of girls' entry into womanhood. It is estimated that more than 200 million worldwide have undergone the procedure. Although often associated with Islam and presumed to be practiced only in certain countries, there is evidence that many religious communities worldwide have excised girls, including some strict Christian sects in the United States as late as the 1980s.

This essay considers the details of the first FGM/C case in the United States as it relates to the Bohra Ismaili community involved in the case and to larger debates about FGM/C on the global stage. It rejects claims to recognizing FGM/C as a practice deserving the protections of religious freedom law while examining the implications of this practice for women and girls and for rights bearing upon matters of health, sexuality, and children's agency.

This essay takes as its point of departure *United States v. Nagarwala*, a 2017 case before a federal court in Detroit, which involves a doctor who had allegedly cut the genitals of dozens of girls. The doctor, a woman named Jumana Nagarwala, justified the practice on the grounds of the religious culture of the Dawoodi Bohra Ismaili community, whose members belong to a sect that historically developed in South Asia as an offshoot of Shi'i Islam. Instead of addressing the implications of invoking religious freedom protections to justify FGM/C, as many observers expected, the court dismissed most of the charges against the doctor on complex legal technicalities. Meanwhile, the religious community involved made two powerful but false claims to the public. First, it claimed that religious freedom protects the community's practice. Second, it declared that the practice did not consist of FGM/C. The community's assertions were amplified by a Harvard Law School constitutional law expert, Alan Dershowitz, who lent the claims legal and cultural legitimacy. These public claims remained largely unchallenged, muddling public perception not only regarding the practice itself but whether religious freedom laws actually protected FGM/C.

Had the case been heard on its merits, because it was a federal prosecution, the Religious Freedom Restoration Act (RFRA) would have applied. A robust discussion of RFRA would have most likely debunked claims that the community and its attorneys made to the public, and would have probably resulted in the rejection of religious freedom protections as a legal basis for permitting FGM/C. Namely, RFRA states: "Government may substantially burden a person's exercise of religion only if it demonstrates that application of the burden to the person (1) is in furtherance of a compelling governmental interest; and (2) is the least restrictive means of furthering that compelling governmental interest."[2]

It is of note that, in American law, "the right to a religious exemption belongs to a religious believer because of his religious beliefs, whatever they might be."[3] "The right does not belong to a religious group . . . nor does it belong to an individual by virtue of his membership in the group."[4] In short, RFRA protects people, not belief systems. Under RFRA, the court could have clearly and definitively addressed several issues central to the public debate.

The first matter the court would have been expected to address would not have been whether the practice itself was religious but whether the practitioners believed it was religious. Religious freedom protections do not allow judges to put a limit on the number of gods a religion can claim or to decide whether Jesus Christ is the son of God or whether one interpretation of the Bible is better than another one. What matters to the court, as stated earlier, is that the believer believes it is religious. As a result, "Small sects, minority groups within sects, and even idiosyncratic religious believers are as protected as large sects. One doesn't need a note from one's priest to prevail in a religious exemption case."[5] In very broad strokes, a practice is considered religious as long as the beliefs are sincere.[6]

However, determining that a practice is born of a sincerely held religious belief does not automatically mean that the practice is protected by religious freedom laws. In this case, for instance, under RFRA, the court would have had to ask, does the state have a compelling interest in restricting FGM/C, a practice that an individual and a community sincerely believe is religious? The short answer should have been a resounding yes. In this case, the state would have had a compelling interest to protect minors from serious and long-lasting harm.

At this point, the prosecution could have made the case that there is extensive medical evidence that the community's description of its FGM/C practice was aspirational but not, in fact, reflected in the lived experience of girls and women subjected to the genital cutting. In short, the compelling state-interest argument should have prevailed, thereby refuting the claim that religious freedom protected individuals in the community who engaged in the practice. Similarly, as documented in this essay, international human rights jurisprudence is clear on this matter. Religious freedom (articulated internationally as "freedom of religion or belief," or FoRB), does not protect FGM/C.[7]

As former vice chair (from 2016 to 2019) on the U.S. Commission on International Religious Freedom (USCIRF) and as a religious freedom advocate in the United States for more than twenty years, I contend in this study that the claim that religious freedom protects the rights of this particular community to perform FGM/C is a dangerous publicity stunt that has put girls and women at risk worldwide and has distorted the vital right that is freedom of religion or belief. The views expressed here are my own, yet I ground them in a close reading of the case in its local American context and in the light of the international relevance it may have for women and FoRB.

The Background to the Michigan Case

On April 10, 2019, in a letter to Congress,[8] Solicitor General Noel Francisco announced that the U.S. Department of Justice (DOJ) decided to forgo pursuing the first federal female mutilation/cutting (FGM/C)[9] case[10] against a Michigan doctor who allegedly performed the ritual cutting on as many as a hundred girls over the course of twelve years.[11] The physician, Dr. Jumana Nagarwala, and the girls she cut belong to a prosperous South Asian Shiite Muslim sect called the Dawoodi Bohra, some of whose members refer to the clitoris as a sinful lump of flesh.[12] The cutting, *khatna* or *khafdz*,[13] is considered by the Bohra, and other communities, a religious observance to prevent girls from becoming promiscuous.[14]

The DOJ's decision to drop the case, which had been ongoing since 2017, came after U.S. District Judge Bernard Friedman ruled that Congress did not have the authority to criminalize FGM/C under the commerce clause of the U.S. Constitution.[15] Therefore, the statute could not be used by DOJ to prosecute FGM/C cases. The judge also stated that the power to outlaw FGM/C pertained to individual states.[16] The DOJ agreed with the district judge that the statute, as worded, was unconstitutional and proposed Congress amend the statute.[17]

Technically, the judge's decision only applies to the Eastern district of Michigan where the case was heard. However, the impact of his ruling regarding the federal statute and, therefore, his refusal to deal with the serious, substantive issues associated with FGM/C, will have effects outside his courtroom. A leading advocacy group against FGM/C, Equality Now, summarized the potential dangers in this manner: "[DOJ] is placing thousands of girls at risk and is sending a damaging message to law enforcement, the courts . . . both in the U.S. and across the international community."[18]

It is, therefore, critical that the U.S. Congress and each state legislature that has not adopted anti-FGM/C laws address the issue. Three significant interrelated factors contribute to the urgency. First, migration patterns have brought many FGM/C-practicing communities, not only the Dawoodi Bohra but also immigrants from Egypt, Somalia, Sudan, and other countries where the procedure is common, to North America, Europe, and Australia. In the United States alone, the U.S. Citizenship and Immigration Services (USCIS) agency estimates that more than 500,000 girls from various FGM/C-practicing countries have undergone the procedure or may be subjected to it.[19] A confusing, technical ruling like this one may be interpreted by these communities as tacit approval. Second, the Dawoodi Bohra claims the practice does not constitute an extraneous act of excision, and instead conflates its specific ritual cutting practice with male circumcision. Since Muslims, Jews, and other communities have historically practiced male circumcision as a religious routine, the Bohras claim their cutting has a similar religious status and thereby warrants protection on grounds of religious freedom.[20] Third, the Dawoodi Bohra is a prosperous, secretive, tightly knit, and politically connected community determined to use its influence to continue this practice.

As will be discussed later in this essay, in 2018 the community's legal teams were already successful in overturning a highly publicized first-time FGM/C case conviction in Australia and a few months later persuading the prime minister of India to side with the community on FGM/C practices. In the United States, the defense hired Alan Dershowitz, the retired Harvard Law School constitutional expert, to advise the legal team.[21] If this community prevails in convincing the court of public opinion or any U.S. court that FGM/C is a benign practice with religious legitimacy, then members of other FGM/C-practicing communities worldwide may use the same arguments to continue the practice.

In order to identify the complexities of the case, this essay will survey the practice of FGM/C from a global perspective. It will also assess FGM/C's origins, review international and U.S. jurisprudence on FGM/C, and consider specific characteristics of the Dawoodi Bohra community's ritual cutting practice, as well as some of the outstanding traits of the Dawoodi Bohra FGM/C cases in Australia and India.

What Is FGM/C?

Numerous medical journals[22] and the World Health Organization (WHO) characterize FGM/C as a harmful practice, all forms of which carry health complications and have absolutely no health benefits.[23] According to the WHO, FGM/C includes "all procedures that involve partial or total removal of the external female genitalia, or other injury to the female genital organs for non-medical reasons."[24] Although there are multiple reasons given to perform FGM/C, all forms affect parts of the body that are central to most women's orgasm,[25] in order to curtail and/or control women's enjoyment of sex and, in some cases, enhance male pleasure.[26] As will be explored later in this essay, contrary to some of the claims by the Dawoodi Bohra who support the practice, there is no benign form of FGM/C.

The WHO classifies FGM/C into four major types, which are summarized as follows:

Type I: Clitoridectomy: a partial or total removal of the clitoris and of the prepuce.
Type II: Excision: a partial or total removal of the clitoris and the labia minora.
Type III: Infibulation: the narrowing of the vaginal opening through the creation of a "covering seal by cutting and a-positioning the labia minora and/or the labia majora . . . with or without excision of the clitoris."[27]
Type IV: All other harmful procedures to the female genitalia for nonmedical purposes (pricking, piercing, incising, scraping, and cauterizing).[28]

UNICEF estimates that today more than 200 million girls and women in more than 30 countries have been subjected to FGM/C.[29] However, researchers have found it difficult to gather empirical data on the practice. A 2017 study on the Dawoodi Bohra, for example, stated that because of "the very private nature of the procedure" and the inability of researchers to "find large populations of 'cut' women willing to participate in studies . . . most data in this field continues to be drawn from case studies and small samples."[30]

The same study points out that most often numbers cited are largely restricted to sub-Saharan Africa[31] and cites UNICEF's assertion that in "Indonesia alone, half of the girls under the age of 14 [have] gone through FGC."[32]

There is also evidence of FGM/C in South America, Asia, "Oman, Yemen, United Arab Emirates, Pakistan, Iraq, Iran, Malaysia, Singapore, Thailand, Sri Lanka, Maldives, Brunei, Russia (Dagestan) and Bangladesh."[33] In Iraq, to cite yet another understudied region, the Germany-based Association for Crisis Assistance and Development Co-operation has documented the widespread practice of FGM/C among the Kurdish population.[34]

Further, the WHO's current categorizations do not include detailed descriptions of all forms of FGM/C, as the procedure may also vary greatly from country to country. For example, in parts of Congo and Tanzania, FGM/C involves lengthening "the labia minora and/or clitoris over a period of about 2 to 3 weeks."[35] The process "is usually initiated by an old woman designated for this task, who puts sticks of a special type in place to hold the stretched genital parts so that they do not revert back to their original size."[36] The girl has to stretch her genitalia every day, adding up to four sticks.[37]

The age at which girls undergo this procedure is generally reported as between infancy and 15.[38] However, the WHO states that ages vary greatly and depend on the community. In sum, girls undergo the procedure as babies, during childhood or adolescence, before getting married, or while in labor.[39]

Physical and Psychological Consequences of FGM/C

Although there is a dearth of hospital-based studies on the impact of FGM/C on physical and psychological health,[40] the WHO estimates the health consequences for girls who undergo FGM/C are often significant.[41] Depending on the severity of the cutting, medical complications occur either immediately or later in a woman's life, and they can become chronic.[42]

Many of the complications associated with FGM/C are directly associated with the skill and medical knowledge of the traditional cutters who perform the procedure. Most of these cutters do not have any formal medical training and use instruments such as razor blades, tin lids, thorns, knives, stones, scissors, and glass.[43] In some countries, cutters use other equally crude methods, such as cauterization (Ethiopia) or bare fingernails on babies (Gambia).[44] Because of the practitioners' lack of knowledge of the human anatomy, there is also great variation in the performance of these procedures.[45] In addition, cutters generally do not use any protocols to prevent infections, which can spread if the same instruments are used on multiple girls. In Uganda in 2018, for instance, a cutter revealed she used the same knife on seven girls. The first one had HIV/AIDS. As a result, the other six contracted it, and all seven girls died.[46]

Depending on the cutter, the type of FGM/C performed, and whether the girls resist, the WHO estimates that most procedures take 15 or 20 minutes.[47] Afterward, the wound is "dabbed with anything from alcohol or lemon juice to ash, herb mixtures, porridge, or cow dung, and the girl's legs may have to be bound together until healing is completed."[48]

In a few countries, the practice has been medicalized or pseudo-medicalized.[49] That is, families take their daughters to health-care professionals who use sterilized surgical tools, anesthesia, and antiseptics in hopes of reducing complications.[50] Alternatively, families ask medical professionals to administer medications such as painkillers while cutting is still done with the traditional cutter.[51] The term "medicalization" is also used when a woman undergoes re-infibulation, the closure of the external genitalia of a woman who have been de-infibulated so that she can engage in sexual intercourse or deliver a baby.[52] In countries where health care is lacking, FGM/C is sometimes performed by community health-care workers with little or no training. However, because those workers often use antiseptics, anesthesia, or surgical tools, it may appear to families that the process has been properly medicalized. This type of pseudo-medicalization also makes it a challenge to be able to gather data on medicalized procedures.[53]

For all cutting, medicalized or not, the first complication is severe pain. The clitoris and surrounding tissue comprise a complex web of nerves and vessels that are extremely sensitive.[54] Cutting the nerve ends of this sensitive area causes extreme pain.[55] In addition, excessive bleeding can result if an artery or a blood vessel is cut during the procedure.[56] Overall, Type III FGM/C appears to carry the greatest risk of death, with up to 50 percent of women experiencing some form of complication. However, this number may be much higher than that because it is estimated that only 15–20 percent of those who experience complications seek medical attention.[57] In 2018, in a highly publicized incident of FGM/C, two sisters in Somalia died when they bled to death.[58] In places like Uganda, after Type III FGM/C is performed on a day selected by the village elders, as many as fifty girls ages nine to eleven are made to wash in cold water and form a line, and undergo the procedure. Then the girls, blood gushing, are carried to a resting place where some die. If they survive, it will be two weeks until they can walk again.[59]

Life-long risks of infections, including HIV and Hepatitis B, are prevalent and even endemic in countries where women undergo Type III FGM/C.[60] This happens because the vaginal opening is narrowed to allow only the passage of urine or blood and to increase the man's sexual pleasure.[61] As a result, penetration is often difficult and painful and sometimes causes lesions and bleeding, which facilitate the transmission of infections such as HIV.[62] In addition, to avoid vaginal penetration and pain, some of these women resort to anal sex, which increases the likelihood of tears and HIV transmission.[63]

FGM/C also increases the likelihood of chronic painful periods, lesions in neighboring organs,[64] reduced fertility,[65] chronic urinary tract infections, and complications during childbirth.[66] A collaborative study of international doctors documented that women who have undergone the most severe type of FMG/C have a 30 percent higher probability of having to deliver a baby by C-section and higher than 70 percent chance of hemorrhaging.[67] For those who have undergone FGM/C and are able to get pregnant, they are at an increased risk of Caesarean sections, difficult labors, tears and lacerations while delivering, prolonged labor, and extended hospital stays.[68] Their newborns have a higher probability of needing resuscitation.[69]

It is not surprising that many women who have undergone any kind of FGM/C report experiencing pain during intercourse.[70] Notably, women who have undergone infibulation experience an excruciating procedure on their wedding night as the bridegroom must reopen the infibulation and prevent it from healing shut.[71]

The WHO reports there is also evidence that FGM/C inflicts multiple layers of psychological trauma.[72] After all, "genital mutilation is commonly performed when girls are young and uninformed and is often preceded by acts of deception, intimidation, coercion, and violence by parents, relatives, and friends that the girl has trusted."[73] The effects of FGM/C "include anxiety and phobic behavior, with recurrent flashbacks of the pain and trauma of the procedure, especially during intercourse."[74] Although there are not enough studies to assess the entire gamut of psychological trauma or to develop techniques to deal with these issues,[75] a small pilot study conducted in 2005 in Senegal showed women who had undergone FGM/C exhibited significantly higher rates of PTSD (30.4 percent) and other psychiatric symptoms (47.9 percent) than those women who had not. The PTSD was also accompanied by memory problems.[76]

The Origin of FGM/C

The origin of FGM/C is unclear, but historical records indicate that it precedes both Islam and Christianity. In the fifth century BCE, for instance, Herodotus reported its existence in ancient Egypt, documenting the practice among the Phoenicians, Hittites, and Ethiopians.[77] A Greek papyrus in the British Museum dated 163 BCE confirms Herodotus's claim.[78] In the first century BCE, Strabo, a Greek philosopher, recorded that the Falasha Jews of Ethiopia practiced excision on their girls.[79] In the second and the sixth centuries CE, two doctors who worked in Alexandria and Rome, respectively, left fairly precise instructions on how to perform the procedure.[80] In Rome, genital cutting was performed on boy and girl slaves to prevent them from engaging in sexual activity.[81]

In developed countries, the practice can be traced to a nineteenth-century medical journal, *The Lancet*, which reported in 1825 that the surgery was performed on a 14-year-old in Berlin, in 1822. The doctor pronounced that she had discontinued "self-pollution but the intellectual faculties of the patient began to develop and her education could be commenced,"[82] allowing her to begin to "'talk, read, reckon, execute several kinds of needlework and a few easy pieces in the piano forte.'"[83] Also in the nineteenth century, there is evidence of multiple clitoral excisions performed in France and England. Doctors justified the procedure as a treatment for illnesses they considered sexual deviations, like masturbation, as well as for diseases they erroneously believed masturbation caused, such as hysteria and insanity.[84] In 1894, a doctor in the United States reported curing a 14-year-old girl of "'nervousness and pallor' by 'liberating the clitoris.'"[85] American physicians who adopted the practice also used it to treat "suspected Lesbian inclinations."[86] In 1947, there is evidence that some Christian clinics removed the clitoris as a "cure" for masturbation.[87] As late as the 1960s, some physicians in Australia and the United States endorsed FGM/C as a treatment for excessive masturbation.[88] In April 2019, as a result of the publicity surrounding the Michigan case, an American white woman from a strict Christian background revealed to Thompson Reuters news service that she had been cut in the early 1980s, when she was five years old.[89]

One proposed theory is that members of some societies rationalized genital cutting by asserting that the foreskin represents the feminine part of the male and the clitoris the masculine part of the female and that both needed excision to confirm gender distinction.[90] Specifically, in Egyptian Pharaonic mythology, it was believed that human beings were created androgynous and that circumcision for both sexes helped define the femininity and masculinity of each human being.[91] Those who were not circumcised would have their "natures compete during intercourse."[92] Members of many African societies have advanced similar arguments. The Dogon and Bambara of Mali, for instance, believe all humans are born with two souls of a different sex. To ensure balance, each person has to transform into one or the other. The men remove the prepuce and the women the clitoris.[93]

In the Middle East, FGM/C is often called a *sunna* practice, which means that it complies with customs that prevailed when the Prophet Mohammed was alive and leading the Muslim community.[94] "Those who practice it view it as a way to rid women of 'dirty surpluses that if left would hide the demon.'"[95] Although there is no mention of FGM/C in the Koran[96] some Muslims rely on the *hadith*, records of the sayings and traditions of Mohammed, which contains narratives in which the prophet is said to have discussed FGM/C.[97] They also rely upon commentaries of the Koran, the *tafsir*, which discuss the practice.

One commonly invoked narrative is a conversation between a woman who excised slaves and the Prophet Mohammed.[98] The woman, whose name is Um-Habibah, asked the Prophet if she should continue with her practice. "'Yes, it is allowed. Come close so I can teach you. If you cut, do not overdo it, because it brings radiance to the face and it is more pleasant to the husband.'"[99]

Another narrative includes the biblical story of Abraham and Sarah. In the Koranic version of the story, since Sarah was unable to get pregnant, she gave her slave Hagar to Abraham. However, after Hagar gets pregnant, Sarah becomes jealous and decides to cut off three parts of Hagar. In the end, she excises Hagar's clitoris, as the ninth-century Koran commentator, al-Tabari, explained:[100]

> Sarah said to Abraham, "You may take pleasure in Hagar, for I have permitted it." So he had intercourse with Hagar and she gave birth to Ishmael. Then he had intercourse with Sarah, and she gave birth to Isaac. When Isaac grew up, he and Ishmael fought. Sarah became angry and jealous towards Ishmael's mother and sent her away. Then she called her back and took her in. But later she became angry and sent her away again, and brought her back yet again. She swore to cut something off of her, and said to herself, "I shall cut off her nose, I shall cut off her ear—but no, that would deform her. I will circumcise her instead." So she did that, and Hagar took a piece of cloth to wipe the blood away. For that reason women have been circumcised and have taken pieces of cloth down to today. Sarah said, "She will not live in the same town with me." God told Abraham to go to Mecca, where there was no House at the time. He took Hagar and her son to Mecca and put them there."[101]

Some Muslim advocates of FGM/C rely on fatwas, meaning religious legal opinions,[102] to justify the practice. For instance, in the Shiite tradition, many cite the fourth caliph of Prophet Mohammed, who called the practice on women a "meritorious act."[103] In 1981, the Grand Sheik of Al-Azhar, Sheik Shaltout, said the Prophet approved of the practice, adding that the teachings of the Prophet should not be secondary to the teachings of doctors.[104] As recently as 2017, in the United States, a prominent Virginia Imam, Shaker Elsayed, advocated for "the cutting of 'the tip of the sexually sensitive part of the girl so that she is not hypersexually active.' . . . He also warned that 'in societies where circumcision of girls is completely prohibited, hypersexuality takes over the entire society and a woman is not satisfied with one person or two or three.'"[105]

However, those who oppose the practice argue that FGM/C is not commonly performed in the birthplace of Islam, Saudi Arabia.[106] Further, in 2006, an Egyptian conference of Muslim scholars from around the world "declared female circumcision to be contrary to Islam and an attack on women, and called today for those who practice it to be punished," issuing fatwas against FGM/C.[107]

Recently, other religious leaders, such as Pope Francis[108] and a leading elder of the Church of Jesus Christ of Latter-day Saints (LDS), have made statements against FGM/C.[109] Significantly, however, more than half of women in four out of fourteen countries where the data is available still believe FGM/C is a religious obligation.[110] The WHO concludes that because not all Muslims practice FGM/C and members from other religions do practice it, FGM/C is "thus a cultural rather than a religious practice."[111]

The conclusion the WHO reaches seems to assume that what defines a practice as religious or not is whether all members of the same religious group subscribe to the same practice. However, in countries where there is religious diversity, like the United States, intra-religious disagreement does not automatically mean a particular claim is not religious. For instance, in a friend-of-the-court brief filed by Islamic Law Scholars[112] for the Supreme Court case *Holt v. Hobbs*, the scholars explain that Muslims "take an array of approaches to hadith." The scholars go on to point out that this "kind of diversity is unsurprising; . . . Jews disagree not only about what is kosher, but about whether the kosher laws should be followed at all. That Reform Jews exist, however, does not impeach the sincerity of the Orthodox (or vice versa). Catholics may believe in transubstantiation; Reform Christians (like Presbyterians) may deny it. This inculpates no one; this is ordinary religious pluralism and nothing more."[113]

Therefore, if the Dawoodi Bohra claim in court that their cutting practice is religious, the fact that many other Muslim groups disavow the practice does not automatically reduce the Dawoodi Bohra's claim to a cultural, rather than a religious, one. However, even if the court accepts that the practice is religious or of a religious nature, it does not automatically mean the practice is protected by religious freedom. This is because in U.S. jurisprudence it is clear that if the state has a compelling interest, such as protecting children from harm, the state can take measures to reject a religious freedom claim. The seminal case, as it pertains to children's health, dates back to 1944 in which the Supreme Court, in *Prince v. Massachusetts*, ruled: "The right to practice religion freely does not include liberty to expose the community or child to communicable disease, or the latter to ill health or death."[114] The question of harm, therefore, will be central to the litigation in Michigan and will be addressed later in this essay.

Jurisprudence on FGM/C

International and U.S. jurisprudence has made FGM/C illegal. In 2014, the UN General Assembly adopted a resolution calling for a worldwide ban; it was adopted by consensus by all members.[115] Several countries have also criminalized the practice.[116]

The WHO lists a number of conventions and declarations that provide for the promotion and protection of the health of the child and the woman, some of which specifically provide for the elimination of FGM. These are as follows:

The Universal Declaration of Human Rights (1948) proclaims the right of all human beings to live in conditions that enable them to enjoy good health and health care.

The International Covenant on Civil and Political Rights and the International Covenant on Economic, Social and Cultural Rights (1966) condemn discrimination on the grounds of sex and recognize the universal right of all persons to the highest attainable standard of physical and mental health.

The Convention on the Elimination of All Forms of Discrimination Against Women (1979) can be interpreted as obliging states to take action against female genital mutilation which is:

- to take all appropriate measures, including legislation, to modify or abolish existing laws, regulations, customs and practices that constitute discrimination against women (Art. 2.f)

- to modify the social and cultural patterns of conduct of men and women, with a view to achieving the elimination of prejudices, and customary and all other practices that are based on the idea of the inferiority or superiority of either of the sexes or on stereotypes for men and women (Art. 5.a).

The Convention on the Rights of the Child (1990) protects the right to equality irrespective of sex (Art. 2), to freedom from all forms of mental and physical violence and maltreatment (Art.19.1), and to the highest attainable levels of health.

The Vienna Declaration and the Programme of Action of the World Conference on Human Rights (1993) expanded the international human rights agenda to include gender-based violations, which include female genital mutilation.

The Declaration on the Elimination of Violence Against Women (1993) states that violence against women must be understood to include physical and psychological violence occurring within the family, including female genital mutilation and other traditional practices harmful to women.

The Programme of Action of the International Conference on Population and Development (ICPD, 1994) included a recommendation on female genital cutting, which commits governments and communities to "urgently take steps to stop the practice of female genital mutilation and to protect women and girls from all such similar unnecessary and dangerous practices."

The Platform for Action of the Fourth World Conference on Women (1995) included a section on the girl-child and urged governments, international organizations, and nongovernmental groups to develop policies and programs to eliminate all forms of discrimination against the girl-child, including female genital mutilation.[117]

Before the DOJ's April 2019 letter was sent to Congress, one could have assumed that the 1996 statute made FGM/C illegal.[118] Further, in 2013, an amendment was added to make it a crime to transport a girl to another country to perform the procedure.[119] However, given the DOJ's interpretation of the statute, it is now unclear if those federal laws can be used to prosecute FGM/C practitioners.

State laws are now even more significant. Before this case, anti-FGM/C advocates had already stated that the divide between federal and state legislation was significant; therefore, state-specific legislation was needed to strengthen prosecutions against FGM/C practitioners.[120] According to AHA Foundation senior director Amanda Parker, "This is largely because prosecutors often defer to state laws when charging a crime, rather than abiding by federal legislation."[121] Therefore, "in states that solely follow the federal law[,] . . . FGM typically gets categorized as child abuse, assault or other charges, which frequently results in lesser sentences."[122] As of 2020, thirty-eight states have laws that criminalize the procedure.[123]

The Dawoodi Bohras' Ritual Cutting Practice

Before addressing the specific FGM/C cases in the United States, Australia, and India, it is important to understand characteristics of the Dawoodi Bohra community and where its practice of FGM/C originates. The Dawoodi Bohras "are a sub-sect of Ismaili Shia Islam, who trace their roots back to the Fatimid dynasty of Yemen in the 11th century. They believe that the religious or spiritual leader of the community is the Da'i al-Mutlaq, referred to with the title of 'Syedna.'"[124] The word *Bohra* comes from the Gujarati word *vehru* or "trade."[125] Generally, the Bohra are described as "a well-integrated trader community with a high literacy rate," with a large number of Bohra women pursuing postgraduate and doctoral studies.[126] There are an estimated one to two million Bohra around the world.[127] Approximately half of the Bohra community lives in India and Pakistan while the rest lives in the United States, United Kingdom, Australia, and other countries.[128] The Bohra community has a mix of "Yemeni, Egyptian, Indian, and African elements, and thus differs from other Shia Muslims."[129] They also follow the *Da'im al-Islam*, a work of Isma'ili jurisprudence, which, significantly, endorses the practice of FGM/C.[130]

The community is tightly controlled by its religious head, the Syedna. It is mandatory for all in the community to obey the Syedna and obtain permission for everyday endeavors, as well as for family issues. Disobedience can result in punishments "like not being allowed to pray in the mosque, bury a parent, being forcefully divorced, being forcefully disowned by families, physical harm, and sabotage of businesses and careers."[131]

The cutting in this community is generally performed by women who have religious standing, called *mullanis*, in the summer of the seventh year when the girl is considered innocent (*nadan*) and not capable of understanding what is being done to her (*nasamaj*).[132] Those who defend the practice in the Dawoodi Bohra community insist their cutting is a "harmless religious ritual" that is centuries old, likening it to routine circumcisions performed on males. They even call "for the abolition of female genital mutilation."[133]

The differentiation between the Dawoodi Bohra's cutting practice and other forms of FMG/C has been publicly defended in the United States by Alan Dershowitz, who was hired to advise the Dawoodi Bohra defense team by Dawat-e-Hadiyah, an international organization representing the Shia Muslim sect.[134] In a press interview, Dershowitz stated: "I am categorically opposed to female genital mutilation and I agreed to consult with this group in order to help end it. . . . If that happens, it will be a win-win. It will help protect young girls and it will help protect religious rights."[135] In addition, in a letter to the editor of the *Wall Street Journal*, responding to an op-ed piece[136] written by the author of this essay, Dershowitz said: "I have never advocated a pricking of the clitoris, but rather a benign, sterilized, symbolic pinprick in the hood covering the clitoris, which is much like the foreskin of the penis."[137] Dershowitz treads an extremely dangerous line in contending that the Dawoodi Bohra's cutting practice is anything other than FGM/C.

Dershowitz makes two assertions: that the foreskin of the penis and the clitoral hood are analogous and that the Dawoodi Bohra's practice consists of a symbolic, minimally invasive pinprick of the clitoral hood, somewhat similar to male circumcision. He syllogizes that because male circumcision is protected by religious freedom, the Dawoodi Bohra's practice should also be protected by religious freedom. The syllogism is problematic because the two premises do not seem to be based on evidence, thus rendering his conclusion fallacious. The additional conflation of FMG/C and male circumcision will be addressed later in this essay.

The first questionable premise is Dershowitz's assertion that the clitoral hood is "much like the foreskin of the penis." Medical experts have not reached the same categorical conclusion. In fact, a 2002 study by the Boston University School of Medicine stated, "Although the erogenous function of [the clitoris] has been known since antiquity, remarkably, the detail of its highly vascular anatomical structure is still in dispute."[138] This study goes on to describe the clitoral hood as "formed in part by the fusion of the upper part of the two labia minora,"[139] which in no way indicates that the hood is equivalent to the male foreskin.

A 2005 study on clitoral anatomy in the *Journal of Urology* states that the "typical textbook descriptions of the clitoris lack detail and include inaccuracies."[140] In lamenting the lack of accuracy about the anatomical depictions of the clitoris, the study goes on to add: "To a major extent its study has been dominated by social factors."[141] In 2011, another medical journal, *ISRN Obstetrics and Gynecology*, issued revisions on terms used by medical professionals to describe the clitoris and its functions.[142] It was not until 2017 that Odile Fillod, a French engineer working on biomedical and gender issues, created the first life-size model of the clitoris to dispel inaccuracies about this part of women's anatomy.[143] The first inaccuracy Fillod addressed was the very size of the clitoris, which in many medical dictionaries is described as "pea-sized."[144] In reality, the clitoris may be approximately 10 centimeters long.[145] Further, although the clitoris plays a central role in women's sexual pleasure, this may not be its only function. Scientists are now investigating its role in women's immune systems.[146] In short, Dershowitz's anatomical comparison does not seem founded in medical research.

Dershowitz also claims he is advocating for a benign, sterilized, symbolic pinprick to the hood of the clitoris. His assertion is clearly aspirational, given the experiences of Dawoodi Bohra women who actually underwent the procedure. Notably, in the Michigan case in which Dershowitz is advising the defense, the girls who were allegedly cut relate a very different procedure than the kind Dershowitz is describing. Both girls, whose names are withheld because they are minors, told the investigators they had been brought to Michigan for a special "girls' trip."[147] It was not until they arrived in Michigan that the girls were told they would see a doctor because "their tummies hurt"[148] and "to get the germs out."[149] One girl said the doctor took off her underwear and "'pinched' her on the 'place [where] she goes pee.'" She had to wear a pad and "was told not to talk about the procedure."[150] The second girl told a similar story, adding that she could "barely walk and felt the pain all the way down to her ankle."[151] A medical examination revealed that both girls had had two parts of their anatomy altered: the labia minora and the clitoral hood.[152]

The girls' account resonates with other Dawoodi Bohra women who have come forward to describe both the deceit before the practice as well as the excruciating pain. Massoma Ranalvi, from India, says that when she was seven years old, she "was told to lie down on the floor and spread her legs. . . . Holding her grandmother's hand, Ranalvi, still not understanding what was going on, did as she was told—while another woman removed her pants and underwear. . . . Ranalvi then recalls an excruciating, sharp pain between her legs."[153] "This woman pulls my pants down, holds my legs and does something which is extremely painful down [there]."[154] Not until she was in her thirties was this memory revisited, after reading about FGM/C in certain African countries.[155]

FGM/C survivor Maryum Saifee, a highly educated, successful, articulate diplomat for the U.S. government, wrote about her experience for *The Guardian* in 2016:

> I was sitting in an anthropology seminar at the University of Texas, cramming for a final, only half-listening to a fellow classmate describe her research project. "Female genital mutilation. . . . As she spoke, goosebumps began to form and I sat paralysed in my seat. Memories I had suppressed since childhood came flooding to the foreground.[156]
>
> I was seven years old. My parents had sent my brother and me to visit family in India for two months. On a humid mid-summer afternoon, my dad's sister decided to throw a party for my brother. . . . At the party, she pulled me aside, wielding a jumbo-sized Toblerone. She said that if I stayed on my best behaviour, I wouldn't have to share it with anyone, including my brother. I was overjoyed.
>
> My aunt was a doctor. So when she led me downstairs to her clinic and instructed me to lie flat on my back on her operating table, I didn't think to question her authority. With no anesthetic and very little warning, she performed the ritualized cut. . . . I blocked out the memory until the day when I discovered what happened to me had an acronym that could be found in the glossary of a medical anthropology textbook.
>
> When I confronted my parents, they were stunned. My aunt had carried out the ritual without their consent. . . . As I have engaged with friends and family members who support the ritual, some will argue that it is not technically mutilation. They even go as far as asserting that "mutilation is what is done in Africa," as though our community practices a more civilised, humane version.

Although no representative data on FGM/C exists for the Dawoodi Bohra communities in India or worldwide,[157] a 2017 study by Mariya Taher corroborated the results of another study by Sahiyo, a nonprofit founded by Dawoodi Bohra women.[158]

> In 2015–16, Sahiyo surveyed 309 women in the Dawoodi Bohra community. In the survey, over 98 percent of women described experiencing pain immediately after FGC [sic].[159]
>
> When asked about their mental state right after the procedure, the most common emotions were fear (51%), anger (21%), and sadness (15%). Twenty-nine percent of respondents did not remember what they were feeling following the procedure. Three percent felt happy and 8% were ambivalent. Other responses included: Confusion, shame, numbness, humiliation, despair, mistrust or betrayal, normal, and traumatized.[160]
>
> "Thirty-five percent of respondents reported that FGC had affected their sex life," of which "ninety-four participants (87%) indicated that their sexual life had been impacted negatively [and] eight participants (7%) responded that their sexual life [had] been positively affected."[161] Another 23 percent of respondents "reported that their sex life had not been disturbed [and] 32 percent of respondents were unsure if FGC had any impact on their sex life."[162]
>
> Participants were also "asked to depict how they felt about the practice of FGC continuing. . . . Three hundred and twenty-eight participants (85%) reported not being okay with FGC [sic] continuing. Only 28 participants or 7% reported being okay with the practice continuing."[163]

The Sahiyo study is a good start, but much research remains to be done. For example, the FGM/C Dawoodi Bohra case in Australia illustrates how difficult it is to prove the practice has taken place. In 2012, after a nineteen-day trial, a jury took only one day to find a Dawoodi Bohra former nurse, Kubra Magennis, guilty of cutting the genitals of two sisters who were then ages six and seven. The mother of the girls and the head cleric for the community were also found guilty. The head cleric was named as an accessory for directing members to cut the girls and then to lie about the practice.[164]

However, upon appeal in 2018, the court was presented with evidence that the tip of the clitoris of each girl was still visible.[165] The court thought this was enough evidence that the practice had been largely symbolic. This conclusion was in spite of a child protection specialist at a children's hospital arguing that there might be "no long-term evidence of cutting and nicking in the form of visible scarring due to excellent blood supply to that area of the body."[166] Notably, between the 2012 decision and the 2018 reversal, the Syedna stated:

"The act has to happen! If it is a man, . . . it can be openly done, but if it is a woman then it must be done discreetly, but the act has to be done."[167]

The question of what really happened in Australia remains unresolved. While the younger of the sisters, Caroline, described that she was "hurting" after the procedure,[168] the nurse said she only "touched" the genitals as part of the ceremony.[169] Given the obligation to obey the Syedna, and his 2016 admonition that the "act has to be done," one wonders about the veracity of the nurse's statement.

India

The case in India is particularly problematic; it is also emblematic of the power of the Syedna. In spite of more than 86,000 women presenting a petition to the ministers of Women and Child Development, Law, and Health, asking India to ban FGM/C,[170] the response came shortly thereafter: "At present there is no official data or study which supports the existence of FGM in India."[171]

In July 2018, after a public uproar, a lower court referred the case to the Indian Supreme Court, stating that the practice of female genital cutting results in "serious violations of basic fundamental rights of the victims who in these cases are minors."[172] It added, "FGM is performed 'illegally upon girls (between five years and before she attains puberty)' and is against the 'UN Convention on the Rights of the Child, UN Universal Declaration of Human Rights of which is [sic] India is a signatory,' . . . [and] caused 'permanent disfiguration to the body of a girl child.'"[173]

In September 2018, Prime Minister Narendra Modi met with the spiritual head of the Dawoodi Bohra community, and within days the Indian government "in a complete volte-face . . . threw its weight behind the Dawoodi Bohra . . . [saying] the matter should be referred to a constitution bench to decide on the issue of religious right and freedom."[174]

Both in India and in the United States, lawyers for the Dawoodi Bohra have equated FGM/C with male circumcision in an effort to extend religious protections for male circumcision to the Dawoodi Bohra practice of FGM/C. However, as stated earlier in this essay, the two procedures differ in significant ways and, therefore, deserve to be treated differently by the law. Several medical entities, including the WHO, have stated that FGM/C has absolutely no medical benefits. In contrast, the WHO and "the U.S. Centers for Disease

Control and Prevention have noted the benefits [of male circumcision] include prevention of urinary tract infections, penile cancer and the transmission of some sexually transmitted infections, including HIV."[175] Significantly, the WHO also conducted three randomized, controlled trials, which prove "circumcised men have a significantly lower risk of becoming infected with the human immunodeficiency virus (HIV)."[176] The American Academy of Pediatrics has stated that the benefits of circumcision for newborns outweighs the risks, although it has stopped short of recommending universal male circumcision for all newborns.[177]

In addition, the nature of the procedures causes FGM/C to leave physical and psychological scars[178] that male circumcision typically does not. Again, the foreskin of the penis and the clitoral hood are incomparable anatomically. The clitoris consists of numerous nerves and muscles that are extremely sensitive, thus making FGM/C far more invasive and traumatic than male circumcision.[179] It is simply impossible to equate cutting the foreskin with cutting the clitoral hood without acknowledging critical differences between the two.[180]

Correlating male circumcision and FGM/C is also flawed in that FGM/C is often performed to curb or eliminate women's sexual enjoyment, sometimes for the enhanced enjoyment of males.[181] Both procedures can have positive effects for men, but for women FGM/C carries primarily harmful consequences. As the anti-FGM/C advocacy conference Women Deliver stated, "It reflects deep-rooted inequality between the sexes and constitutes an extreme form of discrimination against women."[182]

Because of its acceptance as a sound medical practice, male circumcision is vastly more prevalent than FGM/C. The WHO estimates that approximately one-third of the global male population over age fifteen has been circumcised.[183] Those who advocate for FGM/C are eager to elevate its legal status to that of male circumcision, but to do so would be premature and defy prevailing medical expertise.

It is important to note, however, that Dershowitz is not alone in advocating for a medicalized intervention in lieu of traditional FGM/C. In 2010, the American Academy of Pediatrics argued that some forms of FGM/C are "harmless" and doctors dealing with immigrant populations, in recognition of their cultural practices, should be allowed to "prick" or "nick" girls' clitoral skin.[184] In Australia, the Royal Australian and New Zealand College of Obstetrics and Gynecologists also considered taking measures in order to prevent more severe forms of FGM/C.[185]

Conclusion

Evidence indicates that the Dawoodi Bohra ritual cutting is FGM/C, a harmful practice that has no medical benefits and that is meant to control women's sexual conduct. Therefore, even if the Dawoodi Bohra FGM/C practice is rooted in a sincerely held religious belief system and even if the community claims it is minimal in its actual implementation, numerous international human rights instruments[186] identify FGM/C as a form of violence against women[187] and state that freedom of religion or belief (FoRB) does not protect FGM/C.[188]

If the legal team for the Dawoodi Bohra continues to succeed either with technical arguments or by persuading any U.S. court or the court of public opinion that FGM/C is a protected religious practice, it will reverberate throughout FGM/C-practicing communities, human rights advocacy, FoRB developments, and the world.

In the end, a multidisciplinary approach is needed to end this practice. Arsalan Suleman, the former acting U.S. special envoy to the Organization of Islamic Cooperation (OIC), makes a compelling argument when he states: "Ending the practice of female genital mutilation/cutting (FGM/C) requires a comprehensive approach that includes education, advocacy, coalition building, and law enforcement. . . . While law enforcement is an important tool to combat the practice, education and community-based advocacy will likely prove most influential in ending FGM/C."[189]

To conclude, the FGM/C Michigan case, which inspired this study, has implications that reverberate globally for girls and women. It suggests that medical science needs to advance to understand the role that the clitoris plays in women's health to demonstrate, unequivocally, that the practice is harmful. It also suggests that the manipulation of religious freedom laws to justify a harmful practice against females is detrimental not only to girls and women but to the vital right that is freedom of religion or belief, not only in the United States but worldwide.

CHAPTER 10

The U.S. Supreme Court and the Future of Religious Freedom in the United States

Joshua Matz

In 2018 and 2019, the United States Supreme Court decided three landmark cases on the meaning of religious freedom. In the first case, *Trump v. Hawaii*, it upheld a governmental policy issued by President Donald J. Trump, who had repeatedly, publicly, and unabashedly proclaimed his intent to subordinate adherents of a single faith.[1] In the second case, *Masterpiece Cakeshop Ltd. v. Colorado Civil Rights Commission*, it ruled against a state commission on the grounds that two of its seven members had made statements disrespecting a religious objector seeking an exemption from civil rights laws.[2] In the final case, *Dunn v. Ray*, it allowed Alabama to execute an inmate who could have brought a Christian chaplain to the execution chamber, but who was barred from inviting a Muslim imam.[3] These decisions all recognized the principle that government may not act on the basis of anti-religious animus. But the court applied the principle inconsistently, in ways that track an emerging social and legal schism over religious freedom.

As the introduction to this volume recounts, "the terrain of religious freedom has never been easy or smooth."[4] In the United States, with its pronounced lawyerly streak, the resulting conflicts have long sparked judicial controversy.[5] Yet even as measured against that unstable baseline, the Supreme Court under Chief Justice John G. Roberts Jr. has presided over the rapid, startling erosion of legal principles that structured First Amendment law for many decades. The result has been a dramatic unsettling of the doctrines that govern religious freedom—often accompanied by bold calls for an even more radical revolution in the jurisprudence of religion.[6]

Increasingly, "religious liberty" as articulated by conservative objectors (and their allies on the bench) appears threatening to the civil rights, social equality, and religious freedom of many other Americans. At the same time, the very justices who profess a fierce commitment to religious freedom have failed to thwart high-salience official acts motivated by animus toward minority religions. This has prompted criticism that the court unevenly protects religious liberty—as well as worries that legal debates over "religious liberty" will be reduced to little more than yet another battleground for warring, partisan factions in American life.

* * *

First consider *Trump v. Hawaii* (2018), which involved a challenge to the third iteration of President Trump's "travel ban."

Trump first announced the "travel ban" policy—commonly referred to as a "Muslim ban"—on January 27, 2017, just a week after he was inaugurated.[7] The initial version of this policy banned for ninety days the entry of nationals from seven Muslim-majority countries: Iran, Iraq, Libya, Somalia, Sudan, Syria, and Yemen.[8] It also contained language ensuring that Christians would be given priority for entry as refugees into the United States; Trump subsequently explained to the media that this was designed "to help" the Christians in Syria.[9]

Trump's abrupt announcement of the first travel ban order came as a surprise, including to many officials charged with implementing it, and sparked pandemonium nationwide.[10] People who had permission to enter the United States when their flights took off were unexpectedly detained and denied entry when their flights landed. Massive protests erupted at international airports and near courthouses. Government lawyers struggled to defend the policy at emergency midnight hearings before outraged federal judges, several of whom entered injunctions blocking Trump's order. Over the chaotic days that followed, it was unclear whether the travel ban policy applied to lawful permanent residents, what the Trump administration would do with detained travelers, and whether Trump would stand by the policy notwithstanding its disastrous rollout.

On January 28, one of Trump's key advisers candidly explained that the travel ban was meant to effectuate Trump's campaign promise to ban Muslims from entering the United States: "When [Trump] first announced it, he said, 'Muslim ban.' He called me up. He said, 'Put a commission together. Show me the right way to do it legally.'"[11]

Looking back on the period from 2016 through 2018, this statement was just one of *many* public indications that the travel ban policy—in each of its iterations—existed primarily to harm and demean Muslims.[12] Throughout his presidential campaign in 2016 and again after taking office in January 2017, Trump had widely broadcast his belief that Muslims were dangerous and unwelcome. He had also advocated a government-run database to record and track Muslims in the United States. These statements were consistent with his campaign promise to ban Muslim migrants, which remained on his campaign website for several months after inauguration day. And even after his associates changed the website, Trump's advisers pointedly connected the travel ban with the president's continuing anti-Muslim statements—which included retweeting anti-Muslim hate videos and promoting a fictional account of U.S. soldiers executing Muslims with bullets dipped in pig's blood. The result was a clear and quite unusual record that linked a specific presidential order to motives prohibited by the Constitution. While Trump could not ban all Muslim immigration, he could (and did) forge a policy in that same spirit of exclusion.

Apart from Trump's many direct admissions of illicit intent, perhaps the clearest evidence of his anti-Muslim animus was the glaring absence of any *other* objective that the travel ban policy actually achieved. Nobody with relevant experience seriously believed that the travel ban policy, in any of its iterations, was an anti-terror measure. To the contrary, experts widely agreed that Trump's order imposed arbitrary restrictions and made America *less* safe.[13]

On February 9, 2017, the United States Court of Appeals for the Ninth Circuit—based in California—upheld an injunction against the first travel ban policy.[14] On March 6, 2017, Trump responded by issuing a second version of the policy, which differed from the first version in a number of minor and largely immaterial respects (but which cured several of the most ostentatious constitutional flaws in the first order, including its religious preferences regarding refugees).[15] One of the president's senior advisers explained that this second order would have "the same basic policy outcome" as the first one, observing that it contained only "very technical" variations.[16] The White House press secretary later stated that, in issuing this revised order, Trump "continue[d] to deliver on . . . his most significant campaign promises."[17]

Shortly after Trump issued the second travel ban order—and as he continued making statements linking this order to anti-Muslim sentiments—the state of Hawaii filed suit. It alleged that Trump's policy violated the Establishment Clause, which prohibits official action motivated by animus toward any religion. Hawaii's claim was compelling. Although the second travel ban order did not explicitly mention Muslims, Trump had used his bully pulpit to generate a broad public understanding that his order targeted Muslims for stigma and exclusion. It would have been absurd, even dangerous, to pretend that those statements never occurred, and to insist that Trump's order be judged in a manner whereby its deliberately constructed social meaning was disregarded.

After several months of hard-fought litigation, Hawaii won its case: The Ninth Circuit Court of Appeals again invalidated Trump's policy, though this time it sidestepped the constitutional issues by holding that Trump had violated applicable immigration statutes.[18] Around the same time, the United States Court of Appeals for the Fourth Circuit—based in Virginia—reached the constitutional question and held that the second version of the travel ban did, in fact, offend the Establishment Clause.[19]

Trump responded with defiance: On September 24, 2017, he issued a third travel ban.[20] This proclamation applied to six Muslim-majority countries, as well as to a few Venezuelan government officials and North Korea (which was already subject to a separate order restricting entry). Once again, Hawaii and other plaintiffs nationwide filed suit—and, once again, they prevailed in the lower federal courts.[21]

On appeal, the United States Supreme Court disagreed and sided with Trump in a decision announced on June 26, 2018. Writing for a bare conservative majority, Chief Justice Roberts asserted that deference to the president on matters of immigration and national security required the court to narrow its field of vision. In his telling, Trump's policy had to be upheld if there was *any* rational basis apart from anti-Muslim animus that might be said to justify it. Put differently, the chief justice held that Trump was free to act with an anti-Muslim motive in crafting immigration policy—and to admit his bigoted motives on TV and Twitter—so long as government lawyers could subsequently gin up a half-decent pretext. The chief justice divined this standard of review from a hodge-podge of precedents involving presidential control over migration and foreign policy. Applying his extremely lenient standard, Roberts easily upheld the travel ban.[22]

Although many justices wrote separately in *Hawaii*, two opinions stand out. The first is a concurrence by now retired Justice Anthony M. Kennedy. Kennedy had devoted his career to an extraordinarily robust conception of the judicial role in protecting fundamental rights. He had written many of the court's leading precedents on religious freedom. But here, faced with one of the most open and notorious assaults on religious liberty in modern American history, he blinked. He then beseeched the president to follow the Constitution despite judicial inaction.

"There are numerous instances," Kennedy wrote, "in which the statements and actions of Government officials are not subject to judicial scrutiny or intervention."[23] But, he added, "that does not mean those officials are free to disregard the Constitution and the rights it proclaims and protects."[24] In Kennedy's telling, "the very fact that an official may have broad discretion, discretion free from judicial scrutiny, makes it all the more imperative for him or her to adhere to the Constitution and to its meaning and its promise."[25] Kennedy thus concluded by pleading with Trump to respect the First Amendment: "It is an urgent necessity that officials adhere to these constitutional guarantees and mandates in all their actions, even in the sphere of foreign affairs. An anxious world must know that our Government remains committed always to the liberties the Constitution seeks to preserve and protect, so that freedom extends outward, and lasts."[26]

These are noble words. They evoke the finest aspects of our legal tradition. It is unfortunate that they were written to excuse judicial inaction, rather than to justify judicial vindication of religious liberty.

The shortfalls of Kennedy's concurrence loom large in contrast to Justice Sonia Sotomayor's extraordinary dissent. Invoking common ground with Roberts and Kennedy, she emphasized that "the United States of America is a nation built upon the promise of religious liberty."[27] But, unlike the majority, Sotomayor insisted that the court actually enforce this promise. As she demonstrated in simple, vivid terms, the majority had utterly failed to grasp "the pain and suffering the Proclamation inflicts upon countless families and individuals, many of whom are United States citizens."[28] Even worse, Sotomayor observed, the majority replicated the basic error of *Korematsu v. United States* (1944), the ignominious opinion that upheld Japanese-American internment.[29] There, too, the court had uncritically accepted "the Government's misguided invitation to sanction a discriminatory policy motivated by animosity toward a disfavored group, all in the name of a superficial claim of national security."[30] The *Hawaii* majority thus forgot a vital lesson: Official policies motivated by animus corrupt our society and debase our national principles.

It is not clear if religious freedom in America can ever truly recover from *Hawaii*. This is the kind of decision that might forever change how a religious community views itself in relation to the American legal system. By upholding Trump's travel ban, the court revealed that it may, in critical circumstances, leave historically vulnerable religious groups defenseless against official policies arising from animus. Although the sphere of judicial abdication may technically be confined to immigration and national security, that supposed limitation will provide cold comfort to many Muslims, Jews, Sikhs, Hindus, and other groups. And understandably so. America's beacon of religious freedom burns less brightly in *Hawaii*'s shadow.

* * *

Hawaii's failings are magnified when that ruling is contrasted with the court's decision in *Masterpiece Cakeshop Ltd. v. Colorado Civil Rights Commission* (2018). There, seven justices reversed a decision by the Colorado Supreme Court, which had rejected a Christian baker's argument that Colorado could not require him to serve a same-sex couple.

As presented to the court, *Masterpiece* involved a potentially sweeping assault on civil rights laws. The baker, Jack C. Phillips, argued that Colorado could not enforce its anti-discrimination law without offending the Free Speech Clause and Free Exercise Clause of the First Amendment. If accepted, these arguments would have blasted a gaping hole in civil rights statutes. Americans everywhere would have a newfound constitutional right to discriminate.[31]

In its broadest formulation, Phillips's free speech claim was especially troubling. Describing the creation of a customized wedding cake as "speech," he insisted that market participants—including corporations—are constitutionally entitled to opt out of commercial transactions that require them to express messages with which they disagree. That is true, he argued, even when those transactions are required by anti-discrimination laws protecting gays and lesbians (and potentially others). In defining which commercial dealings are covered by this claim, Phillips highlighted bespoke services; his reasoning, however, pointed to a much larger universe of marketplace interactions and had few obvious limiting principles.[32]

Phillips's free exercise arguments were equally subversive. Pursuant to settled precedent, laws pass muster under the Free Exercise Clause if they are neutral toward religion and generally applicable.[33] Phillips argued that Colorado's civil rights law failed this test because the state had allowed bakers to refuse to make cakes expressing religious opposition to gay rights. In his view, it was discriminatory to require him to create a cake for same-sex couples, while allowing other bakers to refuse to create cakes for Christians who wished to condemn same-sex couples. But this argument omitted a key fact. Colorado had allowed bakers to refuse to create anti-gay cakes only because that refusal had nothing to do with religion. The bakers would have refused similar requests from *any* person, religious or secular. Phillips's charge of hypocrisy thus lacked merit: Under Colorado law, religious people (and all others) cannot refuse to serve gay people by virtue of their sexual orientation; gay people (and all others) cannot refuse to serve religious people by virtue of their religious identity; and merchants cannot refuse service to religious or gay people unless they would refuse the same request from all others. This is the basic plan of modern anti-discrimination law. In treating this plan as antireligious, Phillips advanced arguments that would imperil many civil rights statutes while uniquely advantaging religious market participants.[34]

At bottom, Phillips's constitutional argument departed from Americans' long-standing national commitment to equal treatment in commerce as an exceedingly compelling interest. It separated the faithful from all others for purposes of civil rights law. And it invited many to see religion as a constitutionally privileged force opposing tolerance. If this position had been accepted by the court, religious freedom may have become synonymous with a lived experience of unequal treatment, dignitary harm, and concrete disadvantage. In Phillips's preferred world, gays, women, Jews, Republicans, veterans, and many others could have found themselves researching who would serve people like them before leaving their homes. Mutual understanding and compromise might then recede, even as acrimony and polarization sank deeper roots.

Fortunately, the court largely avoided Phillips's most radical arguments. Writing for an ideologically diverse majority, and in an obvious effort to compromise, Justice Kennedy instead based his holding on the unusual facts of the case. He emphasized that when Phillips appeared before the Colorado Civil Rights Commission, one of the commissioners described "freedom of religion" as "one of the most despicable pieces of rhetoric that people can use . . . to hurt others."[35] To support this point, that commissioner had invoked slavery.[36] Another commissioner said, "If a businessman wants to do business in the state and he's got an issue with the—the law's impacting his personal belief system, he needs to look at being able to compromise."[37]

In Kennedy's view, these statements revealed "elements of a clear and impermissible hostility" that deprived Phillips of "neutral and respectful consideration of his claims."[38] Kennedy reasoned that these statements disparaged Phillips's Christian faith in two respects: "by describing it as despicable, and also by characterizing it as merely rhetorical—something insubstantial and even insincere."[39] Invoking a legal principle that *should* have doomed the travel ban (but did not), Kennedy warned that the government "cannot act in a manner that passes judgment upon or presupposes the illegitimacy of religious beliefs and practices."[40] On this basis, he reversed the commission's decision and returned Phillips's case to Colorado.

As Kennedy would hasten to observe, there are differences between *Masterpiece* and *Hawaii*. Most notably, *Hawaii* raised separation-of-powers and national security questions absent in *Masterpiece*.

Still, the contrast is remarkable. In *Masterpiece*, the court found intolerable animus where two of seven commissioners made statements that might be seen as disrespectful of Phillips's faith. It reached that result without a shred of proof that those statements affected the commission's unanimous determination that Phillips unlawfully denied service based on sexual orientation. And it reversed the commission's decision on the theory that nobody should be subjected to official process tainted by the specter of hostility to his or her faith.

Hawaii displayed none of these concerns. There, a single official issued a single policy, which he repeatedly and explicitly linked to his own anti-Muslim statements. The life-shattering harm inflicted by this policy vastly exceeded the liability confronting Phillips. The broader damage to religious freedom in America was all but incalculable. And yet, without ever denying that anti-Muslim animus guided Trump's hand, the court upheld his travel ban on the basis that this policy may conceivably owe some tiny part of its existence to motives other than bigotry.

It is therefore jarring to read *Hawaii* and *Masterpiece* together. For all the formal distinctions in play, it is hard to avoid the sense that basic principles of religious liberty were applied inconsistently. The court's decisions thus cast the future of religious freedom and equality in the United States into doubt—at least for some minority religious groups.

Two especially notable developments in the year following *Hawaii* and *Masterpiece* amplified that sense of dissonance.

The first occurred on February 7, 2019, when the Supreme Court sent Domineque Ray to his death in an Alabama prison. Ray was a Muslim. His prison facility regularly allowed Christian chaplains to accompany inmates to the execution chamber, but it refused Ray's request to have an imam attend him in the last moments of his life. The Court of Appeals for the Eleventh Circuit, based in Georgia, stayed the execution to investigate this policy. As that court noted, there was strong reason to believe that the policy violated the Establishment Clause principle that "one religious denomination cannot be officially preferred over another."[41]

In a decision that stunned most observers, the Supreme Court, split five to four, reversed the Court of Appeals.[42] The only reason it gave was that Ray should have filed his lawsuit sooner (rather than in the days immediately preceding his execution). As Justice Elena Kagan pointed out in dissent, that simply was not true: "There is no reason Ray should have known . . . that his imam would be granted less access than the Christian chaplain to the execution chamber."[43]

Justice Kagan then emphasized, in commendably direct terms, the nature of the constitutional error at issue: "A Christian prisoner may have a minister of his own faith accompany him into the execution chamber to say his last rites. But if an inmate practices a different religion—whether Islam, Judaism, or any other—he may not die with a minister of his own faith by his side. That treatment goes against the Establishment Clause's core principle of denominational neutrality."[44] Whatever views one might hold on the death penalty, this is surely the wrong way to administer it. A nation that claims to value religious liberty should not sentence a man to die under circumstances that deny his faith while privileging another.

It is likely that the majority in Ray's case focused less on religious freedom and more on quashing opposition to capital punishment. In 2015, Justice Samuel Alito decried a "guerrilla war against the death penalty."[45] Since then, he and his conservative colleagues have evinced a desire to uphold the death penalty at every turn, and to treat challenges as tainted with bad faith.[46] Indeed, in an opinion issued months after Ray's execution—*Bucklew v. Precythe* (2019)—the conservative majority made a point of reaffirming its ruling against Ray.[47]

Regardless of its motives, the court's willingness to consciously blow past a clear Establishment Clause violation is a disturbing sign. That is doubly true when this case is considered alongside *Hawaii*. Remarking upon both decisions, the *New York Times* bluntly asked, "Is Religious Freedom for Christians Only?"[48] Together, *Hawaii* and *Ray* suggest an alarming unwillingness to prioritize the rights of Muslims and other minorities—at least in cases of perceived conflict with conservative policy priorities, such as effectuating the death penalty system or allowing the president broad latitude to exclude migrants.

A second key development in religious freedom occurred shortly before the court allowed Ray's execution. In January 2019, the Trump administration's Department of Health and Human Services (HHS) formally authorized

South Carolina to provide federal funds to a foster care agency that refuses to serve Jews, Muslims, atheists, and others.[49] The agency claimed that its Christian faith prohibited it from placing children with anyone other than heterosexual Protestant Christians. Like South Carolina, HHS took the position that it was required to grant an exemption in order to respect statutory principles of religious freedom.[50] On this view, the government must provide taxpayer funds to self-described religious entities that refuse, on religious grounds, to serve people because of their religion.

The decision by HHS carried forward the increasingly unbounded conception of religious freedom that had led to *Masterpiece*. In this new world order, championed by conservative groups and embraced by the Trump administration, civil rights laws and nondiscrimination clauses in government contracts must fall if they burden any religious practice. That is true, apparently, even of asserted religious practices that require formal sectarian discrimination against other religions. "No Jews Allowed" may thus become the future of religious freedom.

Whereas some have hinted that *Masterpiece* was fundamentally a case about the balance between religious accommodation and lesbian, gay, bisexual, and transgender (LGBT) rights, HHS's decision under Trump exemplified a flaw in that outlook. *Masterpiece* was merely the first step in a larger constitutional agenda to authorize expanded discrimination throughout American life, as long as it is based on religious belief. The consequences of that effort, if it succeeds, will be far-reaching and radical. For many minority groups, including religious minorities, they will also be destructive.

In practice, there is a terrible irony to these "religious freedom" arguments. In case after case—including *Masterpiece* itself—conservative religious objectors have argued that the existence and application of civil rights laws is motivated by anti-religious animus. That is true even where there is no evidence of anything but a secular commitment to ensuring equality for historically disadvantaged groups. Here, but nowhere else, conservative lawyers and justices are comfortable making sweeping claims about governmental motives and statutory purpose. And, perversely, those claims often amount to an assertion that support for LGBT equality—or the equality of other religions—can be readily equated with invidious hostility to religion. The indefensible premise of such analysis is that refusing service to certain groups is so inherently a part of religious identity that anybody who seeks to prevent such discrimination must hate religious people. In this respect, and in violation of anti-establishment principles, legal efforts to immunize discrimination in the name of "religious freedom" rest on avowedly *theological* premises that are actually quite offensive toward most religious adherents.

* * *

The Supreme Court's conception of religious freedom has never been a model of clarity or consistency. Recently, though, the court has charted an especially unnerving course. Referring to *Masterpiece, Hawaii, and Dunn*, Dahlia Lithwick puts the point sharply: "For a court that cannot bear the thought of a religious baker forced to frost a cake in violation of his spiritual convictions to be wholly unaffected at the prospect of a man given last rites by a member of another faith borders on staggering. The court that had no problem with a transparently anti-Muslim immigration ban, promised and performed as an anti-religious measure, looks more and more like it has two standards for protecting religious liberty."[51]

It would be wrong and unfair to suggest that the court never protects the rights of Muslims. In 2015, for example, in *Holt v. Hobbs*, it issued an important opinion unanimously protecting the free exercise rights of a Muslim inmate who wished to maintain religiously required facial hair.[52] That same year, in *Equal Employment Opportunity Commission v. Abercrombie & Fitch, Inc.* (2015), the court sided with a hijab-wearing Muslim job applicant whose application had been rejected based on perceived inability to comply with a store's "Look Policy."[53] But there is no denying that the court has given the nation's religious minorities reason to doubt that it will shield them steadfastly from official animus and sectarian discrimination.

At the same time, the court has bent over backward and sideways to discern discrimination against religious conservatives, claiming that it violates their rights to comply with certain civil rights laws. The court has extended this logic, moreover, to commercial settings in which it has never previously applied—a development with extraordinary implications for how religious freedom is experienced throughout American life. And the court has taken a narrow view of the societal interests that might justify requiring conservative religious objectors to adhere to neutral, generally applicable rules. If this trend persists, the greatest threat to religious freedom for many Americans may be the religious freedom of their fellow citizens.

We thus stand at a crossroads. The future of religious freedom in the United States is both uncertain and hotly contested. The Supreme Court's rulings in *Hawaii*, *Masterpiece*, and *Ray* reflect societal tumult—and suggest trouble on the horizon. Particularly if the court continues to display pronounced sympathy for the claims of conservative religious objectors, while denying or diminishing claims that sound in a more progressive register, debates over religious freedom may collapse into the broader partisan chasm that runs through American life. We can but hope that the court steps more wisely in the years ahead, striking a balance that guards against religious animus without allowing objectors to undermine religious freedom for all.

NOTES

Introduction

1. Winnifred Fallers Sullivan, *The Impossibility of Religious Freedom* (Princeton, NJ: Princeton University Press, 2005); Peter Gottschalk, *American Heretics: Catholics, Jews, Muslims, and the History of Religious Intolerance* (New York: St. Martin's Press, 2013).

2. David Sehat, *The Myth of American Religious Freedom* (Oxford: Oxford University Press, 2015); Finbarr Curtis, *The Production of American Religious Freedom* (New York: New York University Press, 2016).

3. Elizabeth Shakman Hurd, *Beyond Religious Freedom: The New Global Politics of Religion* (Princeton, NJ: Princeton University Press, 2015); Winnifred Fallers Sullivan, Elizabeth Shakman Hurd, Saba Mahmood, and Peter G. Danchin, *Politics of Religious Freedom* (Chicago: University of Chicago Press, 2015); Anna Su, *Exporting Freedom: Religious Liberty and American Power* (Cambridge, MA: Harvard University Press, 2016); Melani McAlister, *The Kingdom of God Has No Borders: A Global History of American Evangelicals* (New York: Oxford University Press, 2018); Jolyon Baraka Thomas, *Faking Liberties: Religious Freedom in American-Occupied Japan* (Chicago: University of Chicago Press, 2019).

4. John Witte Jr., *Religion and Human Rights: An Introduction* (Oxford: Oxford University Press, 2011); Heiner Bielefeldt, Nazila Ghanea, and Michael Weiner, *Freedom of Religion or Belief: An International Law Commentary* (Oxford: Oxford University Press, 2016).

5. Brian J. Grim and Roger Finke, *The Price of Freedom Denied* (New York: Cambridge University Press, 2011); Jonathan Fox, *The Unfree Exercise of Religion: A World Survey of Discrimination Against Religious Minorities* (Cambridge: Cambridge University Press, 2016).

6. W. Cole Durham Jr. and Donlu D. Thayer, eds., *Religion, Pluralism, and Reconciling Difference* (New York: Routledge, 2019).

7. Nelson Tebbe, *Religious Freedom in an Egalitarian Age* (Cambridge, MA: Harvard University Press, 2017).

8. Jolyon Thomas, conversation with Heather J. Sharkey, Philadelphia, Pennsylvania, December 11, 2017.

9. Tom Gjelten, "The Debate Grows over What Religious Freedom Means," *National Public Radio*, May 22, 2019.

10. Thomas Scott-Railton, "A Legal Sanctuary: How the Religious Freedom Restoration Act Could Protect Sanctuary Churches," *Yale Law Journal* 128, no. 2 (2018): 408.

11. Amanda Brennan, "Playing Outside the Joints: Where the Religious Freedom Restoration Act Meets Title VII," *American University Law Review* 68, no. 2 (2018): 569–619, see 569.

12. Daniel Philpott and Timothy Samuel Shah, "In Defense of Religious Freedom: New Critics of a Beleaguered Human Right," *Journal of Law and Religion* 31, no. 3 (2016): 394–95.

13. Timothy Samuel Shah, *Religious Freedom: Why Now? Defending an Embattled Human Right* (Princeton, NJ: Witherspoon Institute, 2012); Steven Waldman, *Sacred Liberty: America's Long, Bloody, and Ongoing Struggle for Religious Freedom* (New York: HarperOne, 2019), 11.

14. Amnesty International, "Up to One Million Detained in China's Mass 'Re-Education' Drive," accessed June 8, 2019, www.amnesty.org/en/latest/news/2018/09/china-up-to-one-million-detained.

15. Anthony Ware and Costas Laoutides, *Myanmar's 'Rohingya' Conflict* (New York: Oxford University Press, 2019).

16. Leslie Kendrick and Micah Schwartzman, "The Etiquette of Animus," *Harvard Law Review* 132, no. 133 (2018): 133–70.

17. Waldman, *Sacred Liberty*, 309.

18. Joshua Matz, "Amicus Brief in Support of State of Hawaii in the Trump Travel Ban Case," Annual Conference, "States of Religious Freedom," University of Pennsylvania, May 4, 2018.

19. Heather J. Sharkey, "Muslim Apostasy, Christian Conversion, and Religious Freedom in Egypt: A Study of American Missionaries, Western Imperialism, and Human Rights Agendas," in *Proselytization Revisited: Rights, Free Markets, and Culture Wars*, ed. Rosalind I. J. Hackett (London: Equinox, 2008), 139–66, see, esp., 146–47.

20. Thomas Jefferson to Mssrs. Nehemian Dodge, Ephraim Robbins, and Stephen S. Nelson, a Committee of the Danbury Baptist Association in the State of Connecticut, Jan. 1, 1802. In *The Life and Writings of Thomas Jefferson*, ed. Adrienne Koch (New York: Modern Library, 1998), 307.

21. See, e.g., Chris Eisgruber and Lawrence Sager, "The Vulnerability of Conscience: The Constitutional Basis for Protecting Religious Conduct," *University of Chicago Law Review* 61, no. 4 (1994): 1245–1315; Martha Nussbaum, "Liberty of Conscience: The Attack on Equal Respect," *Journal of Human Development* 8, no. 3 (2007): 337–57.

22. Consider World Vision. From the early 1950s, this evangelical parachurch organization often cooperated with U.S. government authorities abroad (for example, by liaising with personnel on U.S. military bases in Korea as it worked among Korean orphans), although it drew its funding wholly from private donors. David P. King, *God's Internationalists: World Vision and the Age of Evangelical Humanitarianism* (Philadelphia: University of Pennsylvania Press, 2019).

23. Edward Queen, "History, Hysteria, and Hype: Government Contracting with Faith-Based Social Services Agencies," *Religions* 8, no. 22 (2017): 1–29.

24. Ibid.

25. Rebecca Sager, "Faith-Based Initiatives," *The Oxford Companion to American Politics* (Oxford: Oxford University Press, 2012), 355–57.

26. Justin Vaïsse, "Veiled Meaning: The French Law Banning Religious Symbols in Public Schools," Brookings Institution, U.S.-France Analysis Series, March 1, 2004, accessed May 6, 2020, www.brookings.edu/articles/veiled-meaning-the-french-law-banning-religious-symbols-in-public-schools.

27. Joan Wallach Scott, *The Politics of the Veil* (Princeton, NJ: Princeton University Press, 2007); Jason A. Springs, "Tentacles of the Leviathan? Nationalism, Islamophobia, and the Insufficiency-Yet-Indispensability of Human Rights for Religious Freedom in Contemporary Europe," *Journal of the American Academy of Religion* 84, no. 4 (2016): 903–36.

28. For these examples, see John C. Domino, *Civil Rights and Liberties in the 21st Century*, 3rd ed. (London: Routledge, 2009), 91.

29. For arguments that support expansive exemptions to religious minorities from otherwise binding laws, see, e.g., Nussbaum, "Liberty of Conscience"; Michael McConnell, "Religious Participation in Public Programs: Religious Freedom at a Crossroads," *University of Chicago Law Review* 59, no. 1 (1992): 115–94. For more restrictive views on exemptions, see Eisgruber and Sager, "The Vulnerability of Conscience"; and Amy Gutmann, "Children, Paternalism, and Education: A Liberal Argument," *Philosophy & Public Affairs* 9, no. 4 (1980): 338–58.

30. Tyler Pager, "'Monkey, Rat, and Pig DNA': How Misinformation Is Driving the Measles Outbreak Among Ultra-Orthodox Jews," *New York Times*, April 9, 2019.

31. Azhar Hussein, Syed Ali, Madiha Ahmed, and Sheharyar Hussain, "The Anti-Vaccination Movement: A Regression in Modern Medicine," *Cureus* 10, no. 7 (2018), e2919. doi:10.7759/cureus.2919; Anne Applebaum, "Italians Decided to Fight a Conspiracy Theory: Here's What Happened Next," *Washington Post*, August 8, 2019.

32. National Vaccine Information Center, "Frequently Asked Questions About Vaccine Exemption Information," accessed August 11, 2019, www.nvic.org/faqs/vaccine-exemptions.aspx.

33. Danielle Ziri, "Between Anti-Vaxxers and Anti-Semitism: N.Y.C.'s Orthodox Jews' War Against Measles," *Haaretz*, April 18, 2019; Alfred Lubrano, "Anti-Vaccine Parents Are Often White, College-Educated, 'Whole Foods Moms,'" *Philadelphia Inquirer*, April 10, 2019.

34. Senol Bicer et al., "At What Age Range Should Children Be Circumcised?," *Iranian Red Crescent Medical Journal* 17, no. 3 (2015), e26258. doi: 10.5812/ircmj.26258.

35. Mattha Busby and Agencies, "Danish Parliament to Consider Becoming First Country to Ban Circumcision of Boys," *The Independent*, June 3, 2018; Cnaan Liphshiz, "Danish Lawmakers to Mull Circumcision Ban, Sparking Protest," *The Times of Israel*, September 7, 2020.

36. See Gutmann, "Children, Paternalism, and Education."

37. Busby, "Danish Parliament."

38. James G. Dwyer, "Parents' Religion and Children's Welfare: Debunking the Doctrine of Parents' Rights," *California Law Review* 82, no. 6 (1994): 1371–1447, see 1382.

39. For a fascinating discussion on the precursors to this case and their implications—and on the lengths to which courts and schools were ready to go to enforce the pledge, and parents and children to resist it—see Jennifer Jacobs Henderson, "Conditional Liberty: The Flag Salute Before Gobitis and Barnette," *Journal of Church and State* 47, no. 4 (2005): 747–67.

40. Tisa Wenger, *We Have a Religion: The 1920s Pueblo Indian Dance Controversy and American Religious Freedom* (Chapel Hill: University of North Carolina Press, 2009).

41. Tisa Wenger, *Religious Freedom: The Contested History of an American Ideal* (Chapel Hill: University of North Carolina Press, 2017).

42. Suzan Shown Harjo, "Keynote Lecture: The American Indian Religious Freedom Act: Looking Back and Looking Forward," *Wicazo Sa Review* 19, no. 2 (2004): 143–51, see, esp., 149.

43. Michael Corbett, Julia Corbett-Hemeyer, and J. Matthew Wilson, *Politics and Religion in the United States*, 2nd ed. (New York: Routledge, 2014), 166.

44. Lori G. Beaman, "Aboriginal Spirituality and the Legal Construction of Freedom of Religion," *Journal of Church and State* 44, no. 1 (2002): 125–49.

45. National Oceanic and Atmospheric Administration, Office for Coastal Management, "American Indian Religious Freedom Act," accessed May 7, 2020, https://coast.noaa.gov/data/Documents/OceanLawSearch/Summary%20of%20Law%20-%20American%20Indian%20Religious%20Freedom%20Act.pdf.

46. Andrew Woolford, *This Benevolent Experiment: Indigenous Boarding Schools, Genocide, and Redress in Canada and the United States* (Lincoln: University of Nebraska Press, 2015). For

parallels in Australia, see, for example, Regina Ganter, *The Conquest for Aboriginal Souls: European Missionary Agendas in Australia* (Canberra: ANU Press, 2018).

47. Anna Su, "Varieties of Burden in Religious Accommodations," *Journal of Law and Religion* 34, no. 1 (2009): 1–22.

48. *Ktunaxa Nation v. British Columbia (Forests, Lands, and Natural Resource Operations)*, November 2, 2017, accessed June 7, 2019, https://scc-csc.lexum.com/scc-csc/scc-csc/en/item/16816/index.do.

49. "Skiers v. the Religious Rights of Canada's Indigenous Peoples," *Economist*, November 24, 2016.

50. Sean Fine, "Top Court Declares Blow to Indigenous Peoples," *Globe and Mail*, November 3, 2017; Su, "Varieties of Burden in Religious Accommodations," 9–10.

51. Eleanor Ainge Roy, "New Zealand River Granted Same Legal Rights as Human Being," *Guardian*, March 16, 2017.

52. Anupam Trivedi and Kamal Jagati, "Uttarakhand HC Declares Ganga, Yamuna Living Entities, Gives Them Legal Rights," *Hindustan Times*, March 22, 2017; "Supreme Court Stays Uttarakhand High Court's Order Declaring Ganga and Yamuna 'Living Entities,'" *Times of India*, July 7, 2017; "India's Ganges and Yamuna Rivers Are 'Not Living Entities,' *BBC News*, July 7, 2017.

53. For instances of the interpenetration of environmental and religious liberty concerns, see, e.g., Amanda J. Baugh, *God and the Green Divide: Religious Environmentalism in Black and White* (Oakland: University of California Press, 2017); and, to cite a non-U.S.-centered example, Laura Wickström, "Secular and Religious Environmentalism in Contemporary Turkey," *Approaching Religion* 4, no. 2 (2014): 125–40.

54. Seattle Times Staff, "5 Things to Know About Hobby Lobby's Owners," *Seattle Times*, July 2, 2014.

55. Elizabeth Pollman, "Corporate Law and Theory in *Hobby Lobby*," in *The Rise of Corporate Religious Liberty*, ed. Micah Schwartzman, Chad Flanders, and Zöe Robinson (Oxford: Oxford University Press, 2016), 149–71, 163. At the same time, the court based its decision on statutory grounds (as an interpretation of the Religious Freedom Restoration Act [RFRA]) and not on purely constitutional grounds.

56. Greg Urban, ed., *Corporations and Citizenship* (Philadelphia: University of Pennsylvania Press, 2014).

57. Godfre Ray King, *Unveiled Mysteries* (Chicago: Saint Germain Press, 1935), 6.

58. Candida R. Moss and Joel S. Baden, *Bible Nation: The United States of Hobby Lobby* (Princeton, NJ: Princeton University Press, 2019); Seattle Times Staff, "5 Things to Know About Hobby Lobby's Owners."

59. Conrad Hackett and Brian J. Grim, "The Global Religious Landscape," Pew Research Center, December 2012, accessed August 19, 2019, www.pewforum.org/2012/12/18/global-religious-landscape-exec.

60. Michael Lipka and Claire Gecewicz, "More Americans Now Say They're Spiritual but Not Religious," Pew Research Center, September 6, 2017, accessed August 11, 2019, www.pewresearch.org/fact-tank/2017/09/06/more-americans-now-say-theyre-spiritual-but-not-religious.

61. Jürgen Habermas, *Postmetaphysical Thinking II* (Cambridge: Polity, 2017), 214.

62. Charles Taylor, *A Secular Age* (Cambridge, MA: Belknap Press, 2007).

63. The singer-songwriter Bob Dylan showed this kind of awareness, admitting that he "never could learn to drink that blood and call it wine"! Bob Dylan, "Tight Connection to My Heart (Has Anybody Seen My Love)," *Lyrics* (New York: Columbia Records, 1985).

64. Jeffrey Edward Green, "Reassessing Max Weber's Thesis of the Disenchantment of the World," *Philosophy & Theology* 17, nos. 1–2 (2005): 51–83.

65. Taylor, *A Secular Age*, 25.

66. Coleman Barks, trans., *The Essential Rumi*, new expanded ed. (San Francisco: HarperCollins, 2004), 32.

67. Hussein Ali Agrama, *Questioning Secularism: Islam, Sovereignty, and the Rule of Law in Modern Egypt* (Chicago: University of Chicago Press, 2012); Saba Mahmood, *Religious Difference in a Secular Age: A Minority Report* (Princeton, NJ: Princeton University Press, 2016); Talal Asad, *Formations of the Secular: Christianity, Islam, Modernity* (Stanford, CA: Stanford University Press, 2003).

68. Michael Lipka, "A Closer Look at America's Rapidly Growing Religious 'Nones,'" Pew Research Center, May 13, 2015, accessed August 11, 2019, https://www.pewresearch.org/fact-tank/2015/05/13/a-closer-look-at-americas-rapidly-growing-religious-nones/.

69. Peter Gottschalk, "The Equality Paradigm in *Warner v. Boca Raton*: Winnifred Sullivan and *The Impossibility of Religious Freedom*," in *The Social Equality of Religion or Belief*, ed. Alan Carling (London: Palgrave Macmillan, 2016), 80–91.

70. Nathan Schneider, "An Interview with Winnifred Fallers Sullivan," *The Immanent Frame*, August 11, 2009, accessed August 5, 2019, https://tif.ssrc.org/2009/08/11/religion-takes-the-stand.

71. Sullivan, *The Impossibility of Religious Freedom*, 7–8, 138.

72. Philpott and Shah, "In Defense of Religious Freedom," 381.

73. Alan Carling, ed., *The Social Equality of Religion or Belief* (London: Palgrave Macmillan, 2016), 1–48.

74. Brent Nongbri, *Before Religion: A History of a Modern Concept* (New Haven, CT: Yale University Press, 2013), 2–4.

75. Kevin Schilbrack, "What *Isn't* Religion?," *Journal of Religion* 93, no. 3 (2013): 291–318.

76. Ronald Dworkin, *Religion Without God* (Cambridge, MA: Harvard University Press, 2013).

77. Martin Riesebrodt, *The Promise of Salvation: A Theory of Religion* (Chicago: University of Chicago Press, 2010), 21.

78. Mary Ellen Konieczny, Loren D. Lybarger, and Kelly H. Chong, "Theory as a Tool in the Social Scientific Study of Religion and Martin Riesebrodt's *The Promise of Salvation*," *Journal for the Scientific Study of Religion* 51, no. 3 (2012): 397–411.

79. Meredith B. McGuire, *Lived Religion: Faith and Practice in Everyday Life* (New York: Oxford University Press, 2008).

80. Nega Sahgal et al., *Being Christian in Western Europe*, Pew Research Center, Section 5: "Attitudes Towards Spirituality and Religion," May 29, 2018 (Washington, DC: Pew Research Center, 2018), 119.

81. Becka A. Alper, "From the Solidly Secular to Sunday Stalwarts, a Look at Our New Religious Typology," Pew Research Center, August 29, 2018, accessed August 11, 2019, www.pewresearch.org/fact-tank/2018/08/29/religious-typology-overview.

82. Michel Winock, *La France et les juifs de 1789 à nos jours* (Paris: Éditions du Seuil, 2004), 27.

83. Heather J. Sharkey, *A History of Muslims, Christians, and Jews in the Middle East* (Cambridge: Cambridge University Press, 2017).

84. See, e.g., Lawrence Sager, "Why Churches (and, Possibly, the Tarpon Bay Women's Blue Water Fishing Club) Can Discriminate," in Schwartzman et al., *The Rise of Corporate Religious Liberty*, 77–101.

85. Waldman, *Sacred Liberty*, 25–27.

86. Robert Wuthnow, *America and the Challenges of Religious Diversity* (Princeton, NJ: Princeton University Press, 2005).

87. Elizabeth M. Geffen, "Industrial Development and Social Crisis, 1841-1854," in *Philadelphia: A 300-Year History*, ed. Russell F. Weigley (New York: W. W. Norton, 1982), 307–62.

88. John E. Buschman, "The Upper Class and Blacks in the Philadelphia Anti-Catholic Riots of 1844: Exploring Two Gaps in the Social History," *Records of the American Catholic Historical Society of Philadelphia* 99, nos. 1-4 (1988): 1–16.

89. Waldman, *Sacred Liberty*, 154.

90. Heiner Bielefeldt, "Misperceptions of Freedom of Religion or Belief," *Human Rights Quarterly* 35, no. 1 (2013): 33–68, see 37.

91. Douglas Laycock, "The Campaign Against Religious Liberty," in Schwartzman et al., *The Rise of Corporate Religious Liberty*, 231–55, see 255.

92. Quoted in Denise Spellberg, "Benjamin Franklin and Islam," in *American and Muslim Worlds Before 1900*, ed. John Ghazvinian and Arthur Mitchell Fraas (London: Bloomsbury, 2020), 9.

Chapter 1

1. Pew Research Center, "Global Restrictions on Religion," December 17, 2009, accessed February 6, 2017, www.pewforum.org/2009/12/17/global-restrictions-on-religion; Pew Research Center, "Rising Tide of Restrictions on Religion," September 20, 2012, accessed February 6, 2017, www.pewforum.org/2012/09/20/rising-tide-of-restrictions-on-religion-findings; Pew Research Center, "Arab Spring Adds to Global Restrictions on Religion," June 20, 2013, accessed November 30, 2020, www.pewforum.org/2013/06/20/arab-spring-restrictions-on-religion-findings; Pew Research Center, "Latest Trends in Religious Restrictions and Hostilities," February 26, 2015, accessed February 6, 2017, www.pewforum.org/2015/02/26/regions-and-countries; Pew Research Center, "Trends in Global Restrictions on Religion," June 23, 2016, accessed February 6, 2017, www.pewforum.org/2016/06/23/trends-in-global-restrictions-on-religion; Pew Research Center, "Global Restrictions on Religion Rise Modestly in 2015, Reversing Downward Trend," April 11, 2017, accessed June 13, 2017, www.pewforum.org/2017/04/11/global-restrictions-on-religion-rise-modestly-in-2015-reversing-downward-trend.

2. On recent tensions between religious freedom and norms of sexuality and marriage, see Paul Marshall, "Western Christians' Responses to Denials of Religious Freedom," in *Under Caesar's Sword: How Christians Respond to Persecution*, ed. Daniel Philpott and Timothy Samuel Shah (Cambridge: Cambridge University Press, 2018), 428–55, esp. 428–42.

3. *West Virginia State Board of Education v. Barnette*, 319 U.S. 624 (1943).

4. For skeptics who think that religion deserves a status of its own in law, see Brian Leiter, *Why Tolerate Religion?* (Princeton, NJ: Princeton University Press, 2012); Winnifred Fallers Sullivan, *The Impossibility of Religious Freedom* (Princeton, NJ: Princeton University Press, 2005), 155–59; and Micah Schwartzman, "What If Religion Is Not Special?" *University of Chicago Law Review* 79, no. 4 (2012): 1351–1427.

5. Talal Asad, "Anthropological Conceptions of Religion: Reflections on Geertz," *Man* 18, no. 2, (1983): 251; Elizabeth Shakman Hurd, *Beyond Religious Freedom: The New Global Politics of Religious Freedom* (Princeton, NJ: Princeton University Press, 2015), 6; William Cavanaugh, *The Myth of Religious Violence: Secular Ideology and the Roots of Modern Conflict* (Oxford: Oxford University Press, 2009), 9.

6. Christopher Hitchens, *God Is Not Great: How Religion Poisons Everything* (New York: McClelland, 2007); Richard Dawkins, *The God Delusion* (New York: Houghton Mifflin, 2006); Daniel C. Dennett, *Breaking the Spell: Religion as a Natural Phenomenon* (New York: Penguin, 2006); Sam Harris, *The End of Faith: Religion, Terror and the Future of Reason* (New York: W. W. Norton, 2004).

7. Most (but not all) of the pieces in the following collection take this view: Winnifred Fallers Sullivan, Elizabeth Shakman Hurd, Saba Mahmood, and Peter G. Danchin, eds., *Politics of Religious Freedom* (Chicago: University of Chicago Press, 2015). See also Hurd, *Beyond Religious Freedom*; Saba Mahmood, *Religious Difference in a Secular Age: A Minority Report* (Princeton, NJ: Princeton University Press, 2015); and Talal Asad, "Thinking About Religion, Belief, and Politics," in *The Cambridge Companion to Religious Studies*, ed. Robert A. Orsi (Cambridge: Cambridge University Press, 2012), 36–57. To be clear, I am describing their view here. I do not mean to imply that all of the world's Muslims think alike about religious freedom, only that the critique I am describing takes issue with what it sees as a Western prescription (and imposition) of norms on Muslims. For a critique of these works, see Daniel Philpott and Timothy Samuel Shah, "In Defense of Religious Freedom: New Critics of a Beleaguered Human Right," *Journal of Law and Religion* 31, no. 3 (2017): 380–95.

8. See, for instance, the Muslim perspective of Abdullah Saeed and Hassan Saeed, *Freedom of Religion, Apostasy and Islam* (Aldershot, UK: Ashgate, 2004); and David Novak, *In Defense of Religious Liberty* (Wilmington, DE: ISI Books, 2009), and the Jewish perspective of David Novak. Arguably the most well-known Christian argument for religious freedom is the declaration of the Second Vatican Council, *Dignitatis Humanae*, of 1965, which makes the case for religious freedom on the grounds of natural reason and the Bible.

9. Jonathan Fox reports that 158 state constitutions, 91.9 percent of those that he looks at, contain religious freedom clauses. See his *Political Secularism, Religion, and the State: A Time Series Analysis of Worldwide Data* (Cambridge: Cambridge University Press, 2015), 220–21. A less positive but still significant result comes from the Pew Research Center, which shows that 74 percent of 147 countries had explicit provisions for religious freedom in their constitutions. See Pew Research Center, "Global Uptick in Government Restrictions on Religion in 2016," 68, June 21, 2018, accessed December 12, 2018, www.pewforum.org/2018/06/21/global-uptick-in-government-restrictions-on-religion-in-2016.

10. For a compelling dignitarian account of human rights, see Thomas Williams, *Who Is My Neighbor? Personalism and the Foundations of Human Rights* (Washington, DC: Catholic University of America Press, 2005).

11. Martin Riesebrodt, *The Promise of Salvation: A Theory of Religion*, trans. Steven Rendall (Chicago: University of Chicago Press, 2010), xi.

12. See, for instance, several of the pieces in, and the general thesis of, Sullivan et al., *Politics of Religious Freedom*.

13. In addition to Martin Riesebrodt and Christian Smith, who are about to be discussed, see Kevin Shilbrack, *Philosophy and the Study of Religions* (Malden, MA: Wiley Blackwell, 2014); Kathleen Brady, *The Distinctiveness of Religion in American Law; Rethinking Religion Clause Jurisprudence* (Cambridge: Cambridge University Press, 2015); and William P. Alston, "Religion," *Encyclopedia of Philosophy*, vol. 7 (New York: Macmillan, 1972).

14. Riesebrodt, *The Promise of Salvation*.

15. Christian Smith, *Religion: What It Is, How It Works, and Why It Matters* (Princeton, NJ: Princeton University Press, 2017).

16. Ibid., 22.

17. Ibid., 26.

18. Smith compiles a remarkable list of more than one hundred of these practices (*Religion*, 29).

19. Smith, *Religion*, 23–25. Smith points out that these same religions contain diverse beliefs about the nature of superhuman powers.

20. Smith, *Religion*, 30, 44–46. Consistent with Smith's arguments, I take issue with those scholars who hold that Protestantism uniquely stresses beliefs relative to outward rituals. These are represented in note 7. Within Christianity, Catholicism, from which Protestantism broke away, is highly creedal, even more so than most Protestant churches. Both Judaism and Islam contain propositions that call for assent, though they vary from school to school. As Smith argues, though, even non-Abrahamic religions contain premises, sometimes articulated, sometimes implicit, that describe the identity and nature of superhuman powers and any number of other matters.

21. See, for instance, David Miller, *On Nationality* (Oxford: Oxford University Press, 1997); Anthony D. Smith, *Theories of Nationalism* (London: Duckworth, 1971), 171, 175; and Yael Tamir, *Liberal Nationalism* (Princeton, NJ: Princeton University Press, 1993).

22. Relevant here is Max Weber's concept of charisma, which he defines as "a certain quality of an individual personality by virtue of which he is set apart from ordinary men and treated as endowed with supernatural, superhuman, or at least specifically exceptional powers or qualities. These are such as are not accessible to the ordinary person, but are regarded as of divine origin or as exemplary, and on the basis of them the individual concerned is treated as a leader." Quoted in Max Weber, *The Theory of Social and Economic Organization*, ed. and intro. Talcott Parsons (New York: Macmillan, 1947), 358–59. Indeed, groups of people can invest certain individuals with superhuman qualities and, insofar as they do, they are doing something religion-like. My argument is that nationalism can sometimes take a religious (or at least a quasi-religious) form, though neither nations nor nationalism are intrinsically religious.

23. For an excellent introduction to work on religious nationalism, including an annotated bibliography of relevant works, see Atalia Omer and Jason A. Springs, *Religious Nationalism: A Reference Handbook* (Santa Barbara, CA: ABC-CLIO, 2013).

24. Riesebrodt, *The Promise of Salvation*, 21–45.

25. These questions are similar to what Michael J. Perry has called "limit questions." See his *The Idea of Human Rights: Four Inquiries* (Oxford: Oxford University Press, 1998), 15.

26. Smith, *Religion*, 24.

27. Riesebrodt, *The Promise of Salvation*, 84–89.

28. Riesebrodt makes the point.

29. See Elif Batuman, "The Sanctuary," *New Yorker*, December 19 and 29, 2011, accessed December 13, 2018, www.newyorker.com/magazine/2011/12/19/the-sanctuary. Batuman reports the view of Klaus Schmidt, Göbekli Tepe's discoverer and chief interpreter, that the site was one of worship. It is unclear, though, who or what was being worshipped.

30. Tertullian and Lactantius frequently use the word *religion* as something that could denote several different religions. See Tertullian, *Apology and De Spectaculis. Minucius Felix: Octavius*, trans. T. R. Glover and Gerald H. Rendall, Loeb Classical Library edition (Cambridge, MA: Harvard University Press, 1931); Lactantius, *Divine Institutes*, trans. Anthony Bowen and Peter Garnsey (Liverpool: Liverpool University Press, 2004). Thomas Aquinas, "Question 81: Of Religion," in *Summa Theologica*, vol. 3, trans. Fathers of the English Dominican Province (Notre Dame, IN: Ave Maria Press), 1522–28.

31. Riesebrodt, *The Promise of Salvation*, 26–30.

32. Brian J. Grim and Roger Finke, *The Price of Freedom Denied: Religious Persecution and Conflict in the Twenty-First Century* (Cambridge: Cambridge University Press, 2011), 203–4.

33. "'Nones' on the Rise: One-In-Five Adults Have No Religious Affiliation," Pew Forum on Religion and Public Life, accessed June 20, 2013, www.pewforum.org/Unaffiliated/nones-on-the-rise.aspx.

34. Aristotle, *Nicomachean Ethics*, trans. Robert C. Bartlett and Susan D. Collins (Chicago: University of Chicago Press, 2011), Book 1, 1–25.

35. On basic goods, see John Finnis, *Natural Law and Natural Rights* (Oxford: Oxford University Press, 1980), 59–99; John Finnis, *Aquinas* (Oxford: Oxford University Press, 1998), 79–86; and Germain Grisez, *Christian Moral Principles* (Chicago: Franciscan Herald Press, 1983), 115–40. For a general survey of goods theories, see Sabina Alkire, *Valuing Freedoms: Sen's Capability Approach and Poverty Reduction* (Oxford: Oxford University Press, 2002). On pages 78–84, she presents a table with thirty-nine lists of "dimensions of human development" that theorists have proposed, variously terming them goods, needs, values, concerns, life domains, and the like. My own view is influenced by the approach pioneered by Grisez and Finnis, whose thought is rooted in the thought of Thomas Aquinas. While Aquinas was a theologian, their theory of basic goods is based entirely on natural reason and does not require theological premises. As Alkire shows, goods are not foreign to contemporary political thought and are central in the thought of prominent theorists such as John Rawls, Martha Nussbaum, and Amartya Sen. Which goods are the right ones to include, how goods relate to a larger view of the human person, and related questions are the kinds of questions that demand a more extended inquiry.

One other important point: While basic goods are final ends in the sense of being opposed to instrumental goods, they are not to be confused with a "summum bonum," or a single final end that is decisive for human life. The summum bonum is, of course, associated with religion and is the kind of good that religious people pursue in the light of their tradition. Here, by contrast, religion is presented as a natural good, meaning that it is grasped through reason alone. It is one of several natural goods, all of which are equally basic, that is, enjoying the status of (natural) final ends.

36. Finnis and Grisez both argue that religion is a basic good. Others who belong to their school of thought also make this case. See Christopher Tollefsen, "Religious Liberty, Human Dignity, and Human Goods," in *Homo Religiosus? Exploring the Roots of Religion and Religious Freedom in Human Experience*, ed. Timothy Samuel Shah and Jack Friedman (Cambridge: Cambridge University Press, 2018), 230–42; and Joseph Boyle, "The Place of Religion in the Practical Reasoning of Individuals and Groups," *American Journal of Jurisprudence* 43 (1998), 1–24.

37. Justin L. Barrett, *Why Would Anyone Believe in God?* (Lanham, MD: AltaMira Press, 2004); Jesse Bering, *The Belief Instinct: The Psychology of Souls, Destiny, and the Meaning of Life* (New York: W. W. Norton, 2011).

38. Another possibility is that a person practices a religion without believing in superhuman powers. Consider, for instance, the Jew who celebrates Jewish holidays, partakes in a Seder meal annually, and so on, but does not believe in God. Is this person still practicing the basic good of religion? I argue, yes. Smith, following Riesebrodt, distinguishes between religion and religiousness, the latter term meaning the subjective features of practitioners in religion. Religion, by contrast, is a complex of practices, socially shared and extended across time, that exist apart from the subjective experience of any one of its practitioners. So, while the Jew in my example does not believe in God, she participates in the Jewish faith, which is ever a religion. See Smith, *Religion*, p. 47, and Riesebrodt, *The Promise of Salvation*, p. 76.

39. Here I am not proving the existence of God or other superhuman powers nor am I decisively refuting atheism. I am only expressing skepticism that atheism has been proved at the expense of the other alternatives. A central problem with atheism, in my view, is its materialism, which is, in turn, self-refuting.

40. See John Finnis, Joseph Boyle, and Germain Grisez, *Nuclear Deterrence, Morality, and Realism* (Oxford: Oxford University Press, 1987), 251–60.

41. This fact further complicates the claim of some scholars (such as those listed in note 7 and discussed in note 20) that Protestantism ushered in a religion of interiority, a claim closely related to the argument that Protestantism is uniquely a religion of "belief." In these scholars' view, Protestantism's combination of belief, interiority, and devaluation of outward rituals proved critical for the development of religious freedom. While it is true that Protestant reformers criticized the Catholic Church for empty ritual, the claim about interiority is problematic. The entire Catholic tradition, like every religion, modern or premodern, has stressed sincerity of heart or some other version of interior commitment, while the vast majority of Protestant churches teach the importance of outward action, including good works and worship. The main source of the claim about Protestant interiority, on whom other scholars rely, is Talal Asad. See his "Modern Power and the Reconfiguration of Religious Traditions: Interview with Saba Mahmood," *Stanford Electronic Humanities Review* 5, no. 1, February 27, 1996. For a critique of the claim about Protestantism, interiority, and religious freedom, see Philpott and Shah, "In Defense of Religious Freedom."

42. Lactantius, *Divine Institutes*, ed. Alexander Roberts, Sir James Donaldson, and Arthur Cleveland Coxe (publisher and date n.a.), 246.

43. Kyai Haji Abdurrahman Wahid, "Foreword: God Needs No Defense," in *Silenced: How Apostasy and Blasphemy Codes Are Choking Freedom Worldwide*, ed. Paul Marshall and Nina Shea (Oxford: Oxford University Press, 2011), xx.

44. A thorough discussion of the many legal, practical, and institutional dimensions of religious freedom can be found in Jonathan Fox, *The Unfree Exercise of Religion: A World Survey of Discrimination against Religious Minorities* (Cambridge, UK: Cambridge University Press, 2016), 11–32.

45. I underscore the point. There are large literatures exploring how religious freedom is to be balanced against competing rights and goods. Much of U.S. constitutional case law on the religion clauses of the First Amendment is about this problem, and there is no shortage of such issues on the global scale. I do not accept, however, that the difficulty of finding stable "bright lines" yields the conclusion that religious freedom, or religion itself, is "impossible," as Winnifred Fallers Sullivan concludes, or that these concepts have no identifiable or stable meaning. Any number of goods, values, and principles are not absolute in their application and are subject to balancing against other goods, values, and principles, yet their coherence is not questioned for the fact that they are thus subject. That something has fuzzy boundaries does not mean that it doesn't exist. See Sullivan, *The Impossibility of Religious Freedom*, and my critique of this work in Daniel Philpott, *Religious Freedom in Islam: The Fate of a Universal Human Right in the Muslim World Today* (Oxford: Oxford University Press, 2019), 30–36.

Chapter 2

1. The present article summarizes reflections which in a much more detailed form have appeared in Chapter 1 of Heiner Bielefeldt and Michael Wiener, Religious Freedom Under Scrutiny (University of Pennsylvania Press 2020). I would like to express my gratitude to Penn Press for permission to draw on the book when composing the present article.

2. James Griffin, *On Human Rights* (Oxford: Oxford University Press, 2008), 2.

3. See, e.g., the formulation in Article 18 of the UDHR: "Everyone has the right to freedom of thought, conscience and religion; this right includes freedom to change his religion or belief, and freedom, either alone or in community with others and in public or private, to manifest his religion or belief in teaching, practice, worship and observance."

4. The original title of the panel for which I prepared the draft version of this essay was "Can Religious Freedom Be Universal?" I generally prefer the wording "freedom of religion or belief," which itself is shorthand for "freedom of thought, conscience, religion or belief." It is worth emphasizing that the term "belief" also covers nonreligious forms of existential conviction and related practice.

5. See Heather J. Sharkey and Jeffrey E. Green, "Introduction," in this volume, page 23.

6. For a critical analysis, see, e.g., Makau Mutua, "Savages, Victims, and Saviors: The Metaphor of Human Rights," in *Harvard International Law Journal* 42 (2001): 201–45.

7. See also Jürgen Habermas, "The Concept of Human Dignity and the Realistic Utopia of Human Rights," *Metaphilosophy* 41, no. 4 (2010): 464–80.

8. Within the confines of this essay, I cannot tackle the issue of borderline cases, in which the potential of responsible agency may appear questionable. However, the axiomatic status of the ascription of human dignity requires that even such cases must be covered by respect for human dignity. See Suzanne Cahill, *Dementia and Human Rights* (Bristol: Policy Press, 2018).

9. The sentence culminates in the admonition that all human beings "should act towards one another in a spirit of brotherhood." The obvious androcentric bias may be one of the reasons for the (understandable!) lack of popularity of the whole sentence.

10. See Jeremy Waldron, *Dignity, Rank, and Rights*, ed. Meir Dan-Cohen, with comments by Wai Chee Dimock, Don Herzog, and Michael Rosen, repr. ed. (Oxford: Oxford University Press, 2015), 33: "So that is my hypothesis: The modern notion of *human* dignity involves an upwards equalization of rank, so that we now try to accord to every human being something of the dignity, rank, and expectation of respect that was formerly accorded to nobility" (emphasis in the original).

11. See Heiner Bielefeldt, *Auslaufmodell Menschenwürde? Warum sie in Frage steht und warum wir sie verteidigen müssen* (Freiburg: Herder, 2011).

12. Michael Ignatieff, *Human Rights as Politics and Idolatry*, ed. Amy Gutmann, with commentary by K. Anthony Appiah, David A. Hollinger, Thomas W. Laqueur, and Diane F. Orentlicher (Princeton, NJ: Princeton University Press, 2001), 57.

13. The Convention on the Rights of Persons with Disabilities (CRPD) was adopted by the UN General Assembly on December 9, 2006.

14. See Heiner Bielefeldt, "Historical and Philosophical Foundations of Human Rights," in *International Protection of Human Rights: A Textbook*, ed. Martin Scheinin and Catarina Krause (Turku: Abo Akademi University, 2009), 3–18.

15. See Cassie Adcock, "The Heads or Tails of Cow Protection in India: Religious Freedom and Secular Agriculture," in this volume.

16. Winnifred Fallers Sullivan, *The Impossibility of Religious Freedom* (Princeton, NJ: Princeton University Press, 2005).

17. Ibid, 151.

18. Ibid, 154.

19. See Heiner Bielefeldt, "Misperceptions of Freedom of Religion or Belief," in *Human Rights Quarterly* 35 (2013): 33–68.

20. See Paul M. Taylor, *Freedom of Religion: UN and European Human Rights Law and Practice* (Cambridge: Cambridge University Press 2005), 203–8.

21. See Malcolm D. Evans, "Historical Analysis of Freedom of Religion or Belief as a Technique for Resolving Religious Conflict," in *Facilitating Freedom of Religion or Belief: A Deskbook*, ed. Tore Lindholm, W. Cole Durham Jr., and Bahia G. Tahzib-Lie (Leiden: Martinus Nijhoff, 2004), 1-17.

22. Ignatieff, *Human Rights as Politics and Idolatry*, 53.

23. This reflection draws on John Rawls, who, in his *Political Liberalism* (New York: Columbia University Press, 2005), proposes a distinction between the legally binding concept of "political justice," on the one hand, and a multiplicity of "comprehensive doctrines," on the other. This differentiation is supposed to facilitate a broad endorsement of the guiding idea of political justice within a pluralistic society, which is characterized by a rich diversity of religious or nonreligious worldviews, philosophies, etc. Rawls's main point is that the guiding idea of political justice is *inherently limited* in its scope by having its focus on basic normative issues of fair coexistence and cooperation. Only on the understanding of such inherent limitedness can the idea of political justice claim a practical priority over the various existing worldviews ("comprehensive doctrines"). Whereas the idea of political justice claims a clear priority at the level of politics and law, the various comprehensive doctrines may exceed the realm of political justice. Rawls's purpose is the facilitation of an "overlapping consensus," which accommodates a broad variety of religions, philosophies, and worldviews, the holders of which may nonetheless be able to endorse the main principles of political justice that normally govern societal coexistence and cooperation.

24. See my report on "recognition issues" produced in my then capacity as UN special rapporteur on freedom of religion or belief, UN Doc. A/HRC/19/60 (December 22, 2011).

25. Human Rights Committee, General Comment no. 22, UN Doc. A/48/40, vol. I, annex VI, paragraph. 2. It should be noted in passing that the Human Rights Committee brings together experts from all regions, thus not reflecting a particular regional (e.g., Western) viewpoint.

26. Human Rights Committee, General Comment no. 22, UN Doc. A/48/40, vol. I, annex VI, paragraph. 2.

27. See Article 14 of the Convention on the Rights of the Child. For an interpretation of children's and parental rights in this respect, see Heiner Bielefeldt, Nazila Ghanea, and Michael Wiener, *Freedom of Religion or Belief: An International Law Commentary* (Oxford: Oxford University Press, 2016), 415–38 and 204–22.

28. Here is the wording of Article 18, paragraph 3, of the ICCPR: "Freedom to manifest one's religion or belief may be subject only to such limitations as are prescribed by law and are necessary to protect public safety, order, health, or morals or the fundamental rights and freedoms of others."

29. See Nazila Ghanea and Thiago Alves Pinto, eds., *Limitations to Freedom of Religion or Belief in Theory and Practice.* Special Issue of *Religion and Human Rights* 15 (2020).

30. See, e.g., Ronan McCrea, "Religion, Law and State in Contemporary Europe: Key Trends and Dilemmas," in *Belief, Law and Politics: What Future for a Secular Europe?*, ed. Marie Claire Foblet et al. (London: Ashgate 2014), 91–98, at 92: "The individualised view of religious freedom . . . is most consistent with a Protestant vision of religion as primarily a matter of the individual's belief and conscience." Jolyon Baraka Thomas, in this volume, likewise points out that certain "Protestant" assumptions have been influential in the U.S. practice of promoting religious freedom.

31. For details, see Bielefeldt et al., *Freedom of Religion or Belief*, 92–305.

32. Article 18 UDHR and Article 18, paragraph 1, of the ICCPR.

33. Peter G. Danchin, "Religious Freedom in the Panopticon of Enlightenment Rationality," in *Politics of Religious Freedom*, ed. Winnifred Fallers Sullivan, Elizabeth Shakman Hurd, Saba Mahmood, Peter G. Danchin (Chicago: University of Chicago Press, 2015), 240–52, at 251.

34. It should be noted that while the criteria for entering a community remain diverse, FoRB does prescribe the freedom to leave and abandon a community; FoRB can merely recognize noncoercive religiosity. For details, see Bielefeldt et al., *Freedom of Religion or Belief*, 75–91.

35. Talal Asad, *Formations of the Secular: Christianity, Islam, Modernity* (Stanford, CA: Stanford University Press, 2003), 147.

36. Elizabeth Shakman Hurd, "Believing in Religious Freedom," in *Politics of Religious Freedom*, ed. Winnifred Fallers Sullivan, Elizabeth Shakman Hurd, Saba Mahmood, and Peter G. Danchin (Chicago: University of Chicago Press, 2015), 45–56, at 52.

37. Ibid.

38. See Bielefeldt et al., *Freedom of Religion or Belief*, 70–72.

39. See Hurd, "Believing in Religious Freedom," 52: "Contemporary international religious freedom advocacy both presupposes and produces the neoliberal religious subject of the religious economies model: a rational, voluntary religious actor who seeks out the religious options that suit her best."

Chapter 3

1. The Wissahickon was home to the religious recluse Johannes Kelpius and his followers, and remnants of their simple hermitage can still be found in the park today near Hermit Lane.

2. Wendy Brown, *Regulating Aversion: Tolerance in the Age of Identity and Empire* (Princeton, NJ: Princeton University Press, 2006).

3. Elizabeth Shakman Hurd, *Beyond Religious Freedom: The New Global Politics of Religion* (Princeton, NJ: Princeton University Press, 2015); Anna Su, *Exporting Freedom: Religious Liberty and American Power* (Cambridge, MA: Harvard University Press, 2016); Tisa Wenger, *Religious Freedom: The Contested History of an American Ideal* (Chapel Hill: University of North Carolina Press, 2017).

4. Spurred in part by Winnifred Fallers Sullivan's pioneering *The Impossibility of Religious Freedom* (Princeton, NJ: Princeton University Press, 2005), a robust critical literature on religious freedom has emerged in the last several years. Building on recent trends in religious studies theory, this literature has generally adopted a constructivist approach to religion that eschews the notion of religious freedom as a perennial or universal *principle*, showing instead how the discursively constructed and hotly contested concept of religious freedom has historically performed—and continues to perform—powerful political work in both domestic and foreign policy. See, e.g., Winnifred Fallers Sullivan, Elizabeth Shakman Hurd, Saba Mahmood, and Peter Danchin, eds., *The Politics of Religious Freedom* (Chicago: University of Chicago Press, 2015), and Finbarr Curtis, *The Production of American Religious Freedom* (New York: New York University Press, 2016), as well as the books by Hurd, Su, and Wenger cited in note 3. Notably, however, few of the authors writing in this vein have extended the same constructivist approach to the word *freedom* (see Charles McCrary's review essay, "New Directions in the Study of American Religious Freedom," *Symposia* 8 [2017]: 33–42). One point of my essay is to extend the constructivist critique to both of the operative terms, holding in mind that understandings of freedom in the United States have always been shaped and constrained by prevailing conceptions of racial hierarchy and associated notions of "civilization."

5. Nicolas Howe, *Landscapes of the Secular: Law, Religion, and American Sacred Space* (Chicago: University of Chicago Press, 2016); Chad Seales, *The Secular Spectacle: Performing Religion in a Southern Town* (Oxford: Oxford University Press, 2013).

6. Finbarr Curtis, *The Production of American Religious Freedom* (New York: New York University Press, 2016).

7. Constructivist critics and normative practitioners often talk past one another on this point. The constructivists are skeptical that any definition of religion will be capacious enough to perform true emancipatory work, recognizing that stakeholders will often define or interpret "religion" and "freedom" in ways that privilege some types of religion over others. The sharpest critiques (e.g., Hurd, *Beyond Religious Freedom*) suggest that asking people to define themselves in terms of religious identity for the sake of securing religious liberty often has the unfortunate outcome of ossifying religious difference. Meanwhile, practitioner literature often suggests that if policy makers adopt a sufficiently capacious definition of religion (usually premised on the notion that religion is a human universal and that humans, as a species, are naturally religious), then freedom of religion or belief (FoRB) can be reasonably protected. See, for example, Timothy Samuel Shah, *Religious Freedom: Why Now? Defending an Embattled Human Right* (Princeton, NJ: Witherspoon Institute, 2012). The two parties talk past one another because the practitioners assume that religion is a universal genus of which there are many species, while the constructivists reject that assumption based on the premise that religions are discursively constructed. A constructivist critique of the UN Universal Declaration of Human Rights (1948) or the International Covenant on Civil and Political Rights (1966) would suggest that these documents tend to privilege notions of religion *as belief* even when they include explicit acknowledgments of the right to unbelief. Moreover, although they may adopt language protecting individual freedom of conscience, these documents generally privilege notions of religions as communities that are formally recognized by states. These tendencies raise problems for traditions that implicitly value practice over explicit attestations of belief (as in Shintō); they also raise problems for marginal movements that remain illegible to political, legal, or academic authorities as "religion." For meditations on these differing perspectives, see the three essays by Elizabeth Shakman Hurd, Ed Brown, and me collected by Helge Årsheim under the title "The Politics of Religious Freedom" at www.tf.uio.no/english/research/projects/goba/project-hub/blog/plurel.

8. Winnifred Fallers Sullivan addresses these questions in *The Impossibility of Religious Freedom*.

9. Kevin Schilbrack, "Religions: Are There Any?" *Journal of the American Academy of Religion* 78, no. 4 (2011): 1112–38.

10. John Breen, "'Conventional Wisdom' and the Politics of Shinto in Postwar Japan." *Politics and Religion* 4, no. 1 (2010): 68–82.

11. The debates about the propriety of teaching yoga in U.S. public schools have hinged on the question of whether yoga is essentially related to, or derived from, Hinduism. When people have answered this question in the affirmative, public schools that offer instruction in postural yoga have risked running afoul of the establishment clause. But when stakeholders have answered this question in the negative, religious groups like the Hindu America Foundation have taken offense at the sullying of their religious tradition and have claimed to be substantially burdened. Candy Gunther Brown, *Debating Yoga and Mindfulness in Public Schools: Reforming Secular Education or Reestablishing Religion?* (Chapel Hill: University of North Carolina Press, 2019).

12. On religious freedom and corporate conscience, see Curtis, *Production*, esp. 147–66. I address the religious freedom and labor debates in more detail below.

13. Michael Lambek, "Recognizing Religion: Disciplinary Traditions, Epistemology, and History," *Numen* 61, nos. 2–3 (2014): 145–65.

14. Mike Hulme, *Why We Disagree About Climate Change: Understanding Controversy, Inaction, and Opportunity* (Cambridge: Cambridge University Press, 2009), esp. 1–34.

15. Ibid., 3–4.

16. Kimberley Anh Thomas and Benjamin P. Warner, "Weaponizing Vulnerability to Climate Change," *Global Environmental Change* 57, no. 101928 (2019): 1–11.

17. Henri Lefebvre, *The Production of Space*, trans. Donald Nicholson-Smith (Malden, MA: Blackwell, 1991 [1974]).

18. Wenger, *Religious Freedom*.

19. Hurd, *Beyond Religious Freedom*.

20. One recent strain of scholarship on religious freedom adopts a declensionist narrative that suggests that the perennial American "principle" of religious freedom was attenuated through a drastic mid-twentieth-century shift in Supreme Court jurisprudence (see, e.g., Steven D. Smith, *The Rise and Decline of American Religious Freedom* [Cambridge, MA: Harvard University Press, 2014]) or that it has been periodically distorted across U.S. history by Protestant "moral majoritarians" (see, e.g., David Sehat, *The Myth of American Religious Freedom* [Oxford and New York: Oxford University Press, 2011]). Normative political philosophical research has also rendered religious freedom as a universal principle that has been unfairly "deconstructed" by critics (see, e.g., Daniel Philpott and Timothy Samuel Shah, "In Defense of Religious Freedom: New Critics of a Beleaguered Human Right," *Journal of Law and Religion* 31, no. 3 [2016]: 380–95). Yet as Wenger (*Religious Freedom*) persuasively demonstrates, throughout the history of the United States Americans have always unevenly applied the contested ideal of religious freedom.

21. I write "Hawai`i" and "Hawai`ian" unless citing sources that do not include the *`okina* (glottal stop).

22. U.S. House of Representatives, "*Labor Problems in Hawaii: Hearings Before the Committee on Immigration and Naturalization*, H.R., 67th Cong., 1st Sess. on H.J. 158 (A Joint Resolution Providing for an Emergency Remedy for the Acute Labor Shortage in Hawaii) and H.J. 171 (A Joint Resolution Providing for Immigration to Meet the Emergency Caused by an Acute Labor Shortage in the Territory of Hawaii), Serial 7, Part I. Washington, DC: U.S. Government Printing Office, 1921.

23. U.S. House of Representatives, *Labor Problems*, 215.

24. See Alexander Rocklin's *The Regulation of Religion and the Making of Hinduism in Colonial Trinidad* (Chapel Hill: University of North Carolina Press, 2019) for a similar set of dynamics involving "Hinduism" in British colonial Trinidad.

25. For more on these disputes, see Noriko Asato, *Teaching Mikadoism: The Attack on Japanese Language Schools in Hawaii, California, and Washington* (Honolulu: University of Hawai`i Press, 2006).

26. Vaughan MacCaughey, "Some Outstanding Educational Problems in Hawaii," *School and Society* 9 (1919): 101–2.

27. Anonymous editorial in *Nippu jiji* (*Japan-Hawai`i Times*), "Nihonjin rōdō renmei naru," December 5, 1919, 1.

28. Victor Weingarten, *Raising Cane: A Brief History of Labor in Hawaii* (Honolulu: International Longshoremen and Warehousemen's Union, 1946), 25.

29. Noriko Shimada, "Social, Cultural, and Spiritual Struggles of the Japanese in Hawai`i: The Case of Okumura Takie and Imamura Yemyō and Americanization," in *Hawaii at the*

Crossroads of the U.S. and Japan Before the Pacific War, ed. Jon Thares Davidann (Honolulu: University of Hawai`i Press, 2008), 154.

30. P. P. Claxton et al., *A Survey of Education in Hawaii* (Washington, DC: Government Printing Office, 1920), 131.

31. Ibid., 133.

32. Ibid., 134.

33. Mariko Takagi-Kitayama, "In the Strong Wind of the Americanization Movement." In *Hawaii at the Crossroads of the U.S. and Japan Before the Pacific War*, ed. Jon Thares Davidann (Honolulu: University of Hawai`i Press, 2008), 221–22.

34. Charles J. McCarthy [as McCarty], "Calls Jap Ascendancy Dangerous to Hawaii: Ex-Governor Declares That Efforts to Solve Pressing Problems are Handicapped at Washington." *Los Angeles Times*, November 6, 1921.

35. All Japanese names in the main text are given in Japanese order, with the surname first.

36. Takagi-Kitayama, "Strong Wind," 223–25.

37. Yoshiko Imaizumi, *Sacred Space in the Modern City: The Fractured Pasts of Meiji Shrine, 1912–1958* (Leiden: Brill, 2013).

38. Akiko Takenaka, *Yasukuni Shrine: History, Memory, and Japan's Unending Postwar* (Honolulu: University of Hawai`i Press, 2015), 51–73.

39. Frank Capra, dir., *Know Your Enemy: Japan* (U.S. Office of War Information, 1945), and Anonymous, dir., *Our Job in Japan* (U.S. Office of War Information, 1945). Geisel's script was also the basis for a 48-minute feature film titled *Design for Death* that won the Academy Award for best documentary in 1947 and was widely screened in 1948 despite negative reviews from critics. Copies of *Design for Death* are either exceedingly rare or no longer extant, although the script is available in the Dr. Seuss Collection at the University of California, San Diego.

40. Jolyon Baraka Thomas, *Faking Liberties: Religious Freedom in American-Occupied Japan* (Chicago: University of Chicago Press, 2019), 160–64.

41. Ibid., 167–94.

42. Ibid., 141–65.

43. It is true that religious freedom entered Japan because of American intervention, but it did not happen during the Occupation. Religious freedom initially came to Japan as part of America's forceful "gunboat diplomacy" in the mid-nineteenth century. Thereafter, Japanese clerics and policy wonks worked assiduously to figure out what religious freedom meant and who deserved it. See Jason Ānanda Josephson, *The Invention of Religion in Japan* (Chicago: University of Chicago Press, 2012), and Hans Martin Krämer, *Shimaji Mokurai and the Re-conception of Religion and the Secular in Modern Japan* (Honolulu: University of Hawai`i Press, 2015).

44. Benjamin Dorman, "SCAP's Scapegoat? The Authorities, New Religions, and a Postwar Taboo," *Japanese Journal of Religious Studies* 31, no. 1 (2004): 105–40.

45. Thomas, *Faking Liberties*, 190–93.

46. Franklin Delano Roosevelt, "The Four Freedoms," www.fdrlibrary.marist.edu/_resources/images/sign/fdr_30.pdf.

47. Samuel Moyn, *The Last Utopia: Human Rights in History* (Cambridge, MA: Harvard University Press, 2010).

48. For a history of the position of religious freedom in the universal declaration, see Linde Lindkvist, *Religious Freedom and the Universal Declaration of Human Rights* (Cambridge: Cambridge University Press, 2017).

49. Kitaura Keitarō, *Zukai kenpō* (Nara: Nara Nichinichi Shinbunsha, 1947), 71.

50. Minobe Tatsukichi, *Shin kenpō gairon* (Tokyo: Yūhikaku, 1947), 102–11.

51. Thomas, *Faking Liberties*, 210–15.

52. Meiji-era (1868–1912) reforms in the area of religion had begun the process of establishing a religion-secular divide at the center of Japanese politics (in addition to Josephson's *The Invention of Religion in Japan*, see Trent Maxey, *The "Greatest Problem": Religion and State Formation in Meiji Japan* [Cambridge, MA: Harvard University Press, 2014]), but Occupation policies reinforced the religion/not-religion binary and strengthened the notion of religious affiliation as exclusivist and private.

53. Thomas, *Faking Liberties*, 167–69, 178–80.

54. Duncan Ryūken Williams, *American Sutra: A Story of Faith and Freedom During World War II* (Cambridge, MA: Harvard University Press, 2019).

Chapter 4

I would like to acknowledge the ongoing financial support of my research through my Canada Research Chair in Religious Diversity and Social Change. Heather Sharkey and Jeffrey E. Green offered invaluable comments and I offer my thanks for their kind patience. I am also grateful to Cory Steele for his editorial and research assistance.

1. Justin Huggler, "German State Orders All Government Buildings to Display Cross to Reflect 'Cultural Identity,'" *Telegraph*, April 25, 2018, www.telegraph.co.uk/news/2018/04/25/german-state-orders-government-buildings-display-crucifix-reflect.

2. Ibid.

3. Ibid.

4. "Germany: Catholic Cardinal Rebukes Bavaria for Ordering Crosses in State Buildings," *Deutsche Welle*, April 30, 2018, http://p.dw.com/p/2wsqK.

5. "Deutsche gegen Kreuz-Pflicht in Behörden," *Bild am Sonntag*, April 28, 2018, www.bild.de/politik/inland/umfrage/deutsche-wollen-keine-kreuz-pflicht-55543370.bild.html.

6. *Mouvement laïque québécois v. Saguenay (City)*, 2015 SCC 16, [2015] 2 S.C.R. 3. Hereafter, *Saguenay*.

7. Bill 62, known as "An Act to foster adherence to State religious neutrality and, in particular, to provide a framework for requests for accommodations on religious grounds in certain bodies," became law on October 18, 2017. Immediately after the bill became law, it was challenged on the basis of its violation of the equality guarantees of both the Quebec and Canadian Charters of Rights and Freedoms. The Superior Court of Quebec suspended the face-covering law until proper guidelines had been developed to address requests for accommodation.

8. The hospital's statement justifying the removal of the crucifix noted the following:

> Since our primary mission is to provide health care and services, we must first and foremost respect the rights of our patients, who are somehow captive to the institution. In this regard, the Commission on Human Rights and Freedoms has a clear position: [The] presence in a public institution of a religious symbol, such as a crucifix or a cross, does not raise a particular problem from the point of view of the Charter, unless that symbol acquires a coercive character because of the context in which it is inscribed. Thus, when the clientele of the institution is vulnerable, because it is captive, young or influential, such as in a school, for example, exposure to a religious symbol, such as a cross hanging on the wall, may be incompatible with the rights and freedoms of the person.

"Le CHU de Québec-Université Laval est victime d'une menace importante," *CHU de Québec-Université Laval*, February 28, 2017, www.chudequebec.ca/actualites/le-chu-de-quebec-universite-laval-est-victime-d%E2%80%99un.aspx.

9. CTV Montreal, "Quebec City Hospital Resurrects Crucifix Following Threats, Complaints," *CTV News Montreal*, March 2, 2017, https://montreal.ctvnews.ca/quebec-city-hospital-resurrects-crucifix-following-threats-complaints-1.3306370.

10. Christian Joppke writes about the "culturalizing" of religion and argues that the privileging of Christianity is "light" compared to that of Islam. I make the opposite argument. However, we agree on the following: "If the state wants to associate itself with religion, it can do so only by transforming religion into culture." Christian Joppke, "Culturalizing Religion in Western Europe: Patterns and Puzzles," *Social Compass* 65, no. 2 (2018): 236.

11. *Simoneau v. Tremblay*, [2011] QCTDP 1, at paras. 1–2. Hereafter, *Saguenay Tribunal.*

12. Ole Riis and Linda Woodhead, *A Sociology of Religious Emotion* (Oxford: Oxford University Press, 2012).

13. See Emma Waterton and Steve Watson, "Framing Theory: Towards a Critical Imagination in Heritage Studies," *International Journal of Heritage Studies* 19, no. 6 (2013): 546–61; and Avi Astor, Marian Burchardt, and Mar Griera, "The Politics of Religious Heritage: Framing Claims to Religion as Culture in Spain," *Journal for the Scientific Study of Religion* 56, no. 1 (2017): 126–42.

14. Astor, Burchardt, and Griera, "The Politics of Religious Heritage," 128.

15. Anthony G. Amsterdam and Jerome Bruner, *Minding the Law* (Cambridge, MA: Harvard University Press, 2002).

16. The "new diversity" includes "a dramatic increase in numbers of people who self-describe as nonreligious; increasing presence through migration of minority religious groups who are not Christian; declining presence and influence of traditionally majoritarian Christian religions; and a recognition of the impact of colonialism on indigenous peoples with a concomitant recognition of indigenous spiritualities." Lori G. Beaman, Lori G. Beaman, "Freedom of Religion and the New Diversity: Case Studies from Canada," in *The Routledge History of Human Rights*, ed. J.H. Quataert and L. Wildenthal (London: Routledge, 2020), 418. See also Lori G. Beaman, "Recognize the New Religious Diversity," *Canadian Diversity* 14, no. 4 (2017): 17–19.

17. Catholicism and Protestantism have been side by side since the constitutional beginning of Canada as a nation in 1867. The Constitution Act, 1867, recognized both Roman Catholic and Protestant interests, guaranteeing that Roman Catholic and Protestant schools would be funded in the provinces in which they were in the minority. To be sure, there are also linguistic aspects to this division, but this was not always the case and it was religion that formed the basis of the guarantee. This is just one example of the ways in which both Protestantism and Catholicism form part of the social fabric of Canada. Lori G. Beaman, "Is Religious Freedom Impossible in Canada?" *Law, Culture, and the Humanities* 8, no. 2 (2010): 272.

18. Lori G. Beaman and Winnifred F. Sullivan, "Neighbo(u)rly Misreadings and Misconstruals: A Cross-Border Conversation," in *Varieties of Religious Establishment*, ed. Winnifred F. Sullivan and Lori G. Beaman (Farnham: Ashgate, 2013), 1–11.

19. Zygmunt Bauman, *Culture in a Liquid Modern World* (Malden, MA: Polity Press, 2011), 36.

20. Ibid., 37.

21. See Peter Beyer, "Regional Differences and Continuities at the Intersection of Culture and Religion: A Case Study of Immigrant and Second-Generation Young Adults in Canada," in *Religion in the Public Sphere: Canadian Case Studies*, ed. Solange Lefebvre and Lori G. Beaman (Toronto: University of Toronto Press, 2014), 66–96; and Peter Beyer, "Sensing

Religion, Observing Religion, Reconstructing Religion: Contingency and Pluralization in Post-Westphalian Context," *Social Compass* 63, no. 2 (2016): 234–50, for one version of this transformation in Canada.

22. For critical discussions on the notion of religious freedom, see Winnifred Fallers Sullivan, Elizabeth Shakman Hurd, Saba Mahmood, and Peter G. Danchin, *Politics of Religious Freedom* (Chicago, IL: University of Chicago Press, 2015); Elizabeth Shakman Hurd, *Beyond Religious Freedom: The New Global Politics of Religion* (Princeton, NJ: Princeton University Press, 2015); Joshua T. Mauldin, "Contesting Religious Freedom: Impossibility, Normativity, and Justice," *Oxford Journal of Law and Religion* 5, no. 3 (2016): 1–25; and Daniel Philpott and Timothy Samuel Shah, "In Defense of Religious Freedom: New Critics of a Beleaguered Human Right," *Journal of Law and Religion* 31, no. 3 (2016): 380–95.

23. "People of the book" is a term used most commonly to refer to Muslims, Christians, and Jews. See David Lyle Jeffrey, *People of the Book: Christian Identity and Literary Culture* (Grand Rapids, MI: William B. Eerdmans, 1996); and Karen Armstrong, *A History of God: The 4,000-Year Quest of Judaism, Christianity and Islam* (New York: Ballantine Books, 1993), 159.

24. The prayer being recited when the complaint was filed read: "O God, eternal and almighty, from Whom all power and wisdom flow, we are assembled here in Your presence to ensure the good of our city and its prosperity. We beseech You to grant us the enlightenment and energy necessary for our deliberations to promote the honour and glory of Your holy name and the spiritual and material happiness of our city. Amen." *Saguenay Tribunal*, at para. 27.

25. Commission des droits de la personne et des droits de la jeunesse (or the "CDPDJ").

26. The more "neutral" prayer read as follows: "Almighty God, we thank You for the many favours that You have granted Saguenay and its citizens, including freedom, opportunities for development and peace. Guide us in our deliberations as members of the municipal council and help us to be well aware of our duties and responsibilities. Grant us the wisdom, knowledge and understanding that will enable us to preserve the advantages that our city enjoys, so that everyone can benefit from them and we can make wise decisions. Amen." *Saguenay Tribunal*, at para. 28.

27. *Simoneau v. Tremblay*, [2011] QCTDP 1.

28. *Saguenay Tribunal*, at para. 251.

29. *Saguenay (Ville de) c. Mouvement laïque Québécois*, 2013 QCCA 936. Hereafter, *Saguenay CA*.

30. For a discussion of various state approaches to religion, including benevolent neutrality, see W. Cole Durham Jr., "State Reactions to Minority Religions: A Legal Overview," in *State Responses to Minority Religions*, ed. David M. Kirkham (Surrey: Ashgate, 2013), 3–13.

31. Canadian Press, "Quebec Appeals Court Will Hear Bid By Mayor Who Wants Prayer Before Council," *iPolitics*, March 29, 2011, www.ipolitics.ca/2011/03/29/quebec-appeals-court-will-hear-bid-by-mayor-who-wants-prayer-before-council/.

32. *Saguenay CA*, at para. 70.

33. *Saguenay Tribunal*, at paras. 114–15.

34. *Saguenay CA*, at para. 122.

35. In this regard, *Saguenay* resonates with the Italian case of *Lautsi*, which also included a claim to universality: "Moreover, with the benefit of hindsight, it is easy to identify in the constant central core of Christian faith, despite the inquisition, despite anti-Semitism and despite the crusades, the principles of human dignity, tolerance and freedom, including religious freedom, and therefore, in the last analysis, the foundations of the secular State." See *Lautsi v. Italy* [Eur. Ct. H. R. 2012] E.H.R.R. 3.

36. Robert Yelle, *The Language of Disenchantment: Protestant Literalism and Colonial Discourse in British India* (Oxford: Oxford University Press, 2013), 161.

37. *Saguenay Tribunal*, at para. 88.

38. Ibid., at para. 1.

39. *Mouvement laïque québécois v. Saguenay (City)*, 2015 SCC 16, [2015] 2 S.C.R. 3. Hereafter *Saguenay SCC*.

40. Tribunal Administratif de Nantes, November 14, 2014, Fédération de Vendée de la Libre Pensée, no. 1211647 [*Crèche AC*] at 2.

41. *Crèche AC*, at 2. Original French: "Une crèche de Noël ne constitue pas un emblème religieux mais un emblème d'une fête traditionnelle issue d'un fait religieux; l'existence d'un particularisme local, issu d'une forte tradition religieuse en Vendée, permet de tolérer la présence d'une crèche de Noël comme un symbole d'une situation locale spécifique qui n'a d'ailleurs jamais été remise en cause par les élus de l'opposition."

42. La cour administrative d'appel de Nantes, October 13, 2015, no. 14NT03400 [*Crèche CA*]. Original French: "Que toutefois, compte tenu de sa faible taille, de sa situation non ostentatoire et de l'absence de tout autre élément religieux, elle s'inscrit dans le cadre d'une tradition relative à la préparation de la fête familiale de Noël et ne revêt pas la nature d'un '*signe ou emblème religieux.*'"

43. Fédération nationale de la libre pensée, "Crèches chrétiennes dans les bâtiments de la République," *Fédération nationale de la libre pensée*, November 9, 2016, www.fnlp.fr/2017/10/17/creches-chretiennes-dans-les-batiments-de-la-republique-prieres-de-rue-dans-la-manche/.

44. Ibid. In 2012, the Fédération départementale des libres penseurs de Seine-et-Marne asked the mayor of Melun not to install a Christmas crèche at City Hall during the month of December. The crèche was erected despite the request of the Libre Penseurs. The matter was brought before the Administrative Court of Melun and later the Administrative Court of Appeal of Paris (Cour administrative d'appel de Paris, 1ère chambre, October 8, 2015, no. 15PA00814, Inédit au recueil Lebon). The Paris court had ruled nativity scenes could not be displayed in public places under any circumstances. The Conseil d'État overruled the decision of the Court of Appeal of Paris (Conseil d'État, November 9, 2016, no. 395122, Publié au recueil Lebon).

45. *Crèche CA*, at 2.

46. Original quote in French: "Noël est fêté par tous les français." See *Crèche CA*.

47. Original quote in French: "Réalité sociale également, avec cette fête du rassemblement par excellence où se tisse, dans l'unité des familles, l'unité nationale et la grande unité de la grande famille humaine." Bruno Retailleau, "Crèche de Vendée: Oui au principe de laïcité, non au principe d'absurdité," *Le Figaro*, December 3, 2014, www.lefigaro.fr/vox/societe/2014/12/03/31003-20141203ARTFIG00415-creche-de-vendee-oui-au-principe-de-laicite-non-au-principe-d-absurdite.php.

48. *OuestFrance.fr*, "Laïcité: Pas de crèche de Noël au conseil général de Vendée," *Ouest-France.fr*, December 5, 2014, www.ouest-france.fr/une-creche-au-conseil-general-de-vendee-le-tribunal-dit-non-3018928.

49. Philippe de Villiers, l'ancien président du conseil général, critique avec virulence le jugement du tribunal administratif de Nantes interdisant l'installation de la crèche dans le hall. À l'origine de cette initiative, il appelle 'les élus du département à ne pas appliquer cette décision inique. À ne pas plier devant la Libre Pensée, qui n'est pas une pensée libre, et qui prône l'éradication de toutes les racines de notre culture. La France est une vieille terre chrétienne. La crèche fait partie de son patrimoine, par-delà les croyances et les sensibilités. Pourquoi ne pas interdire les cloches? Je récuse ce laïcisme

totalitaire, qui est une forme de terreur moderne aux conséquences incalculables. Si on cède aujourd'hui sur ce symbole, alors il faudra céder sur le reste demain.'

English translation: "Philippe de Villiers, the former president of the general council, harshly criticizes the judgment of the Nantes administrative court prohibiting the installation of the crèche in the hall. At the origin of this initiative, he calls on 'elected officials of the department [to] not to apply this unjust decision. To not bow to Free Thought, which is not free thought, and which advocates the eradication of all the origins of our culture. France is an old Christian land. The crèche is part of its heritage, beyond beliefs and sensibilities. Why not ban the bells? I object to this totalitarian secularism, which is a form of modern terror with incalculable consequences. If we yield this symbol today, then we will have to relinquish the rest tomorrow.'"

OuestFrance.fr, "Laïcité: Pas de crèche de Noël au conseil général de Vendée," *OuestFrance.fr*, December 5, 2014, www.ouest-france.fr/une-creche-au-conseil-general-de-vendee-le-tribunal-dit-non-3018928.

50. For debates about translating *laïcité* as secularism, see Solange Lefebvre, "Between Law and Public Opinion: The Case of Québec," in *Religion and Diversity in Canada*, ed. Lori G. Beaman and Peter Beyer (Leiden: Brill, 2008), 175–98.

51. "Pas de crèche de Noël au conseil général de Vendée."

52. *Town of Greece v. Galloway, 572 U.S. 565 (2014)*, 2. Hereafter, *Town of Greece SC*.

53. *Town of Greece SC*, 3.

54. *Town of Greece SC*, 3.

55. In 2008, following the complaints of Galloway and Stephens, four prayers were offered by non-Christian clergy. This, of course, begs the question of the very format of the process and the meaning of prayer as a practice in a public forum such as a town board meeting.

56. Numerous Supreme Court of the United States decisions can be used to illustrate the configuration of religion and culture. *Lynch v. Donnelly*, 465 U.S. 668 (1984), a case involving the public display of a crèche in Pawtucket, Rhode Island, would have been the obvious choice. In *Lynch*, the court used the language of tradition and culture to justify the celebration of public holidays that have religious aspects (*Lynch*, O'Connor concurring, p. 691). Another obvious choice is that of *Van Orden v. Perry*, 545 U.S. 677 (2005), in which the court ruled that a monument inscribed with the Ten Commandments that was displayed on the grounds of the Texas state capitol did not violate the Establishment Clause of the First Amendment. For the purposes of this chapter, I have chosen to focus on *Town of Greece*, as this decision provides for a more nuanced examination of the power of history and heritage as well as another vantage point from which to see a different configuration of religion and culture.

57. *Town of Greece SC*, p. 24.

58. Caroline Mala Corbin, "Intentional Discrimination in Establishment Clause Jurisprudence," *Alabama Law Review* 67, no. 1 (2015): 306.

59. *Town of Greece SC*, Opinion of Kennedy, J., p. 19. "Justice Kennedy conceded that the historical tradition of legislative prayer upheld in Marsh had some substantive limits. The purpose of the legislative prayer was ceremonial—to solemnize the legislative deliberations and inspire legislators to work together for the common good. Prayers that disparaged non-adherents or attempted to proselytize or preach conversion exceeded the permissible scope of

these invocations. Even where individual prayers ignored these constraints, however, the Constitution would not be violated. There must be a pattern of disparaging or proselytizing prayers over time to support a viable Establishment Clause claim. No such pattern had been demonstrated by plaintiffs in this case." Alan Brownstein, "Constitutional Myopia: The Supreme Court's Blindness to Religious Liberty and Religious Equality Values in Town of Greece v. Galloway," *Loyola of Los Angeles Law Review* 48, no. 2 (2014): 380.

60. Paul Horwitz, "The Religious Geography of Town of Greece v. Galloway," *Supreme Court Review* 2014, no. 1 (2014): 262.

61. Nancy Blyth Hersman, "Lynch v. Donnelly: Has the Lemon Test Soured?" *Loyola of Los Angeles Law Review* 19, no. 1 (1986): 174–75.

62. "*Marsh* stands for the proposition that it is not necessary to define the precise boundary of the Establishment Clause where history shows that the specific practice is permitted. Any test the Court adopts must acknowledge a practice that was accepted by the Framers and has withstood the critical scrutiny of time and political change." *Town of Greece SC*, Opinion of the Court, p. 8.

63. *Town of Greece SC*, Opinion of the Court, p. 8.

64. "Law and religion scholarship should ease up on its obsession with Founding-era history or abstract theory, stripped in both cases of geographical context, and take more account of the role played by space and place in American religious pluralism." Horwitz, "The Religious Geography," 295.

65. Caroline Mala Corbin, "Justice Scalia, the Establishment Clause, and Christian Privilege," *First Amendment Law Review* 15, no. 2 (2017): 191–92.

66. Winnifred Fallers Sullivan, *Paying the Words Extra: Religious Discourse in the Supreme Court of the United States* (Cambridge, MA: Harvard University Press, 1994), 164.

67. *Town of Greece SC*, Opinion of the Court, p. 14.

68. Eric Hobsbawm and Terence Ranger, *The Invention of Tradition* (Cambridge: Cambridge University Press, 1983).

69. Lawrence Smith, "Gov. Matt Bevin Publicly Signs Bill Allowing Kentucky's Public Schools to Teach the Bible," *WDRB.com*, June 28, 2017, www.wdrb.com/story/35761799/gov-matt-bevin-publicly-signs-bill-allowing-kentuckys-public-schools-to-teach-the-bible.

70. Ibid.

71. Ibid.

72. Boyarin and Boyarin argue: "The genius of Christianity is its concern for all the peoples of the world; the genius of Judaism is its ability to leave other people alone. And the evils of the two systems are the precise obverse of these genii. The genies all too easily become demons. Christian universalism, even at its most liberal and benevolent, has been a powerful force for coercive discourses of sameness, denying, as we have seen, the rights of Jews, women, and others to retain their difference." Daniel Boyarin and Jonathan Boyarin, "Diaspora: Generation and the Ground of Jewish Identity," *Critical Inquiry* 19, no. 4 (1993): 707.

73. Smith, "Gov. Matt Bevin."

74. Jason Ānanda Josephson, *The Invention of Religion in Japan* (Chicago, IL: University of Chicago Press, 2012).

Chapter 5

1. John Locke, *A Letter Concerning Toleration and Other Writings*, ed. Mark Goldie (Indianapolis, IN: Liberty Fund, 2010), 52–53, 58–59. The Latin edition of Locke's letter had appeared in 1685, the more renowned English translation in 1689. Locke's intolerance of atheists was widely shared at the outset of the Enlightenment. By the late eighteenth century, though, figures such as

Jefferson and Joseph Priestley had rejected Locke's blanket exclusion of atheists from toleration. For a comprehensive account, see John Marshall, *John Locke, Toleration and Early Enlightenment Culture* (Cambridge: Cambridge University Press, 2006), esp. 256–63, 694–706.

2. Robert Baird, *Religion in America: Or, An Account of the Origin, Progress, Relation to the State, and Present Condition of the Evangelical Churches in the United States* (New York: Harper and Brothers, 1844), 125; "Freedom of Unbelief Denied," *Truth Seeker*, April 23, 1904, 260. Nixon's gesture is discussed in Robert Bendiner, "Our Right Not to Believe," *Saturday Evening Post*, February 10, 1962, 10.

3. Thomas Jefferson, *The Autobiography of Thomas Jefferson, 1743–1790*, ed. Paul Leicester Ford (Philadelphia: University of Pennsylvania Press, 2005), 71; John Adams to John Quincy Adams in James H. Hutson, ed., *The Founders on Religion* (Princeton, NJ: Princeton University Press, 2005), 20.

4. Locke's description of atheists as "the most dangerous sorts of wild beasts" comes from an earlier essay of his on toleration. See Locke, *Letter and Other Writings*, 132. For Stewart's dissenting opinion, see *School District of Abington Township, Pennsylvania v. Schempp*, 374 U.S. 203 (1963).

5. For Douglas's worries over Black's wall, see *Zorach v. Clauson*, 343 U.S. 306 (1952).

6. For a twenty-five-year retrospective on all the suits that O'Hair and American Atheists had filed, see "Sue the Bastards!" *American Atheist* 30 (June 1988): 11–15. For the hate and harassment directed at the *Engel*, *Schempp*, and *Murray* plaintiffs, including the cross-burning episode, see Bruce J. Dierenfield, *The Battle over School Prayer: How Engel v. Vitale Changed America* (Lawrence: University Press of Kansas, 2007), 138–43, 163, 167–68, and also Stephen D. Solomon, *Ellery's Protest: How One Young Man Defied Tradition and Sparked the Battle over School Prayer* (Ann Arbor: University of Michigan Press, 2007), 204–6, 222–26. For the broader divisions and predicaments the prayer and Bible-reading decisions created, especially among ecumenical Protestants, see Sarah Barringer Gordon, *The Spirit of the Law: Religious Voices and the Constitution in Modern America* (Cambridge, MA: Belknap Press, 2010), 84–93. For a full biographical examination of O'Hair, including her sundry lawsuits, see Bryan F. Le Beau, *The Atheist: Madalyn Murray O'Hair* (New York: New York University Press, 2003).

7. G. M. C. to Arthur Cromwell, December 13, 1951, Edwin H. Wilson Papers of the American Humanist Association, 1913–89, box 25, f. 21, Special Collections Research Center, Southern Illinois University, Carbondale.

8. Dannel McCollum, *The Lord Was Not on Trial: The Inside Story of the Supreme Court's Precedent-Setting McCollum Ruling* (Silver Springs, MD: Americans for Religious Liberty, 2008), 29, 49–50, 70, 101, 105, 155–56; Vashti Cromwell McCollum, *One Woman's Fight* (New York: Doubleday, 1951), 72, 82–83, 97–102, 155–59, 185–87. For the defaced picture of her, see scrapbooked newspaper clippings, box 1, Dannel Angus McCollum Papers, Illinois History and Lincoln Collections, University of Illinois Library, Urbana, Illinois.

9. For discussion of the "microclimates" of religious freedom, including highly localized forms of harassment, see Heather J. Sharkey and Jeffrey E. Green, "Introduction," in this volume.

10. Garry De Young, *Quest for Justice: Systematic Discrimination in Iowa* (Hull, IA: De Young Press, 1984), 6–12; Garry De Young, *Everybody Knows My Name* (Centreville, MD: Tidewater Publishing, 1964), 19.

11. "Buckson Hits Trend to Ignore God," "Buckson Beliefs Put God in U.S. Picture," "Bible Case Goes from Court to TV," newspaper clippings, Mary and Garry De Young Papers, box 4zd499, Dolph Briscoe Center for American History, University of Texas at Austin. The unprocessed papers are still in the original shipping boxes and are a jumble of litigation files, secularist

periodicals and pamphlets, newspaper clippings, varied correspondence, and curricular materials for the Minnesota Institute of Philosophy. On the way the De Youngs were raising their large family to be "Good without God," see Mary De Young, "I Am Raising Nine Children as Atheists," box 4zd499, De Young Papers. For a description of daily religious ceremonies in the schools, see "Plaintiffs' Proposed Findings of Fact," box 4zd499, De Young Papers. Many of the newspaper clippings were reproduced in Garry de Young, *Garry's Scrapbook: The Thoughts and Actions of a Civil Rights Activist* (Spencer, IA: De Young Press, 1987). This volume is exceedingly scarce, however. A copy is available at the Wisconsin Historical Society, but it is not in the collection at the Briscoe Center.

12. "Two in Bible-Reading Suits Say They Aren't Atheists," "Agnostic Poet Fights Bible Reading in Delaware School," "Middletown Fires Teacher in Bible-Reading Protest," "Board Fires Teacher for Bible Protest," newspaper clippings; John Jones to Mary De Young, undated; box 4zd499, De Young Papers; De Young, *Garry's Scrapbook*, unpaginated; De Young, *Quest for Justice*, 13–14. The De Youngs had their share of liberal supporters, and many expressed outrage over Mary's firing and the blatant disregard it showed for her rights as a nonbeliever. See, for example, "For the Sake of Fair Play," newspaper clipping, box 4zd499, De Young Papers. The God-loving, God-fearing side—safely in the majority—also found ample expression, of course. See "Keep Our Heritage," "They Lived Better," and "An Earnest Plea," newspaper clippings, box 4zd499, De Young Papers.

13. "De Young Proud of Atheist Title," "Atheist Raps Panel on School Religion," newspaper clippings, box 4zd499, De Young Papers.

14. "Atheist Raps Panel," "Religious Controversy Continues," "Charges Filed Against Priley by De Young," "Atheism Missionary Gets Baptism of Ire," newspaper clippings, box 4zd499, De Young Papers; De Young, *Quest for Justice*, 14–15.

15. "Declaration," December 5, 1971; "Appeal to Minnesota Supreme Court: Petitioner's Brief," 9; "Portrait of an Atheist," October 1971, box 4zd499, De Young Papers. On De Young's conferral of O'Hair's PhD, see "Woman Who Won Fight Against School Prayer Joins Institute," *Minneapolis Star*, August 26, 1972, box 4zd499, De Young Papers. De Young worked off and on with O'Hair from the early 1960s through the mid-1970s, but the relationship fell apart as O'Hair consolidated power over American Atheists at the expense of various allies, including De Young who came to see her as wholly self-aggrandizing. For signs of his growing alienation from O'Hair, see Garry De Young to Ann Robertson, June 19, 1977, box 4zd498, De Young Papers; "Editorial," *Crucible*, June/July 1977, 5. O'Hair interviewed De Young for four episodes of her atheist radio program in 1973. She included transcripts of these in her collection called *The Atheist World* (Austin, TX: American Atheist Press, 1991), 239–69.

16. "Appeal to Minnesota Supreme Court: Petitioner's Brief," 1–2, 11–12, 19–20, 28–29.

17. De Young, *Quest for Justice*, 17; Garry De Young to Ann Robertson, May 10, 1977, box 4zd498; "Humiliation in Mercedes," *Crucible* (October–December 1977): 14–15, box 4zd502, De Young Papers; "Atheist Tie Hints Resented in Mercedes," *Valley Morning Star* (Harlingen, TX), July 2, 1976, 25.

18. De Young, *Quest for Justice*, 17–21; "Atheists, Christians Feud in Hull," *Des Moines Register*, June 8, 1980; "Pair Fight Bias Against Atheists," *Des Moines Tribune*, August 24, 1978, box 4zd499; "Supreme Court Ruling on Prayer Unpopular in Boyden-Hull," *Sheldon Sun*, September 16, 1978; "State Agency Report Critical of De Young," *Sheldon Sun*, August 2, 1980, box4zd509, De Young Papers. In the 1980s, Garry worked on a book called *The Meaning of Christianity*, which his own De Young Press published in 1982 and reprinted in 1989. It represented

an extended pause in his battle with Christianity: He now associated the genuine message of Jesus with love, compassion, and the fight against injustice. While he did not see many true Christians among American churchgoers, he now argued that real Christianity promoted a universal humanitarianism that aligned with his own efforts battling discrimination. His new affection for the social gospel (and also for Christian Science) lasted several years, but that fondness faded away in the last decade or so of his life as he returned to his unadorned atheism.

19. Garry De Young, *Religion: The Disease* (Stark, KS: De Young Press, 1993), 1, 4, 8–9; Garry De Young to Bonnie Lange, July 14, 1993, box 4zd499. For letters (and the letterhead) promoting his idea for a new publication called *The Village Atheist*, see Garry De Young to Jesse Ventura, May 10, 2000; Garry De Young to Delma Goff, May 10, 2000, box 4zd500, De Young Papers. These letters coincided with his seventy-seventh birthday and fifty-third wedding anniversary; he died two years later. I did not know about the De Young archive when working on my book on "village atheists," but Garry De Young fits the profile exceptionally well. In many ways, his career serves as an apt coda to that research. See Leigh Eric Schmidt, *Village Atheists: How America's Unbelievers Made Their Way in a Godly Nation* (Princeton, NJ: Princeton University Press, 2016). Some of the legal and cultural framing around "irreligious freedom" in this essay is explored in more detail there, especially in relation to the prosecution of blasphemy and obscenity.

20. Garry was often in a rage about one thing or another—from the Federal Reserve to the Educational Testing Service. His surviving correspondence, especially in the last decade or so of his life, frequently sounds irrational and desperate, frantic to vindicate his learning and accomplishment. For example, he hated the scholarly freethinker Gordon Stein for having disrespected the Minnesota Institute of Philosophy in the pages of the *American Rationalist*. He celebrated Stein's death in 1997, labeled him a degenerate, and then bragged about being the founder of a fantasized Atheist Law School. See Garry De Young to Editor of *American Rationalist*, January 29, 1997, box 4zd514, De Young Papers. But he also had saner moments. A letter to his son Frank in 1996, who was facing a hard recovery after fighting in Operation Desert Storm, is filled with compassion and understanding, even of Frank's expressed interest in becoming a Roman Catholic. "Neither Mom nor I would ever have any objections should you want to study to become a Roman Catholic, or to even enter the priesthood. That would be your own personal decision and as always, we would stand squarely behind you." See Garry De Young to Frank De Young, October 26, 1996, box 4zd514, De Young Papers.

21. Miriam Allen deFord, "What Is Freedom of Religion?" *Progressive World* 1 (March 1947): 24–25; *Everson v. Board of Education*, 330 U.S. 1 (1947).

22. "Sue the Bastards!" 11–15; "Atheist Wins Rights in South Carolina," *American Atheist Newsletter* 36 (June 1997): 12.

23. "Atheist Teacher Fights Firing," *American Atheist* 21 (May 1979): 6–12.

24. Ibid. Workplace discrimination has remained a major area of activist concern among secularists. For one report, see Margaret Downey, "Discrimination Against Atheists: The Facts," *Free Inquiry* 24 (June/July 2004): 41–43. See also Ryan T. Cragun, Barry Kosmin, Ariela Keysar, Joseph H. Hammer, and Michael Nielsen, "On the Receiving End: Discrimination Toward the Non-Religious in the United States," *Journal of Contemporary Religion* 27 (2012): 116–17. For a case in which an atheist did successfully appeal her firing based on religious discrimination, see *Young v. Southwestern Savings and Loan Association*, 509 F.2d 140 (5th Cir. 1975).

25. *McCreary County v. American Civil Liberties Union of Ky.*, 545 U.S. 844 (2005); *Elk Grove Unified School District v. Newdow*, 542 U.S. 1 (2004). For a defense of the neutrality principle against its critics, see Andrew Koppelman, *Defending American Religious Neutrality*

(Cambridge, MA: Harvard University Press, 2013). For a comprehensive overview of the legal terrain facing secularists and atheists, see Nelson Tebbe, "Nonbelievers," *Virginia Law Review* 97 (2011): 1112–80. The terrain beneath the neutrality versus hostility argument remains shifting, and the principle of neutrality can certainly be put to use for conservative purposes on religious freedom questions. In the famed *Masterpiece Cakeshop* case (2018), state hostility on the part of the Colorado Civil Rights Commission toward the religious conscience claims of the baker was used to let stand the denial of services to a gay couple seeking a wedding cake. The state had failed at neutrality in treating the baker's religious objections with hostility. In other words, the state need not worry about neutrality in relation to devout atheists, but it must be keenly aware of it in relation to evangelical Protestants and their views on LGBT issues. See Leslie Kendrick and Micah Schwartzman, "The Etiquette of Animus," *Harvard Law Review* 132 (2018): 133–70, and Heather J. Sharkey and Jeffrey E. Green, "Introduction," in this volume.

26. Garry De Young to Ann Robertson, July 25, 1977, October 8, 1977, box 4zd498, De Young Papers; Abby Goodnough, "Student Faces Town's Wrath in Protest Against a Prayer," *New York Times*, January 27, 2012, A11–12.

Chapter 6

1. An earlier version of this chapter appeared as "Cow Protection and Minority Rights in India: Reassessing Religious Freedom," *Asian Affairs* 49, no. 2 (June 2018): 340–54. My thanks to Taylor & Francis for allowing me to develop it further here. This chapter has benefited from the feedback of several groups of colleagues. I am grateful to Jeffrey Green and Heather Sharkey for their helpful editorial suggestions; to the Andrea Mitchell Center faculty workshop, "States of Religious Freedom," particularly for helpful comments by Heather Sharkey, Donovan Schaefer, and Lisa Mitchell; to the participants at the Religious Freedom in South Asia conference at the Wilson Center, Dina Siddiqi, Mridu Rai, Ali Riaz, Farahnaz Ispahani, Neil Devotta, Christina Fink, and Raza Rumi, and, above all, to Neeti Nair for organizing that thought-provoking, public-facing conversation.

2. Jonathan Z. Smith describes the "imperialist" quality of mapping, which, through its selection of "relevant" details, appears to make charted territory and populations hyper-visible, even as it renders certain relationships or identities politically invisible. "Map Is Not Territory," ch. 13, in *Map Is Not Territory* (Leiden: E. J. Brill, 1978), 289–309. Whereas Smith characterizes the intellectual labor characteristic of religion as so much "map-making," my use of the metaphor treats religion, instead, as a cartographic category, a concept that shapes and delimits our understanding of global politics. My thanks to Michael Kessler for lending a hand in difficult times with a copy.

3. I draw this example from Neeladri Bhattacharya, "How Villages Were Found," ch. 2, in *The Great Agrarian Conquest: The Colonial Reshaping of a Rural World* (Ranikhet: Permanent Black, 2018), 64–108, 91.

4. This does not mean that those ostensibly included under the umbrella of Hindutva wish to identify as Hindu or to subscribe to Hindu nationalist views—as this essay will explain.

5. Howard Spodek, "In the Hindutva Laboratory: Pogroms and Politics in Gujarat, 2002," *Modern Asian Studies* 44, no. 2 (2010): 349–99. In 2020, many see the grim history of Gujarat, 2002 repeating itself in the anti-Muslim violence in Delhi.

6. Parvis Ghassem-Fachandi has documented how Hindu nationalists deployed the Islamophobic stereotypes of Muslims as cow-killers and beef-eaters to provoke and legitimize anti-Muslim violence in Gujarat in 2002. Parvis Ghassem-Fachandi, *Pogrom in Gujarat: Hindu*

Nationalism and Anti-Muslim Violence in India (Princeton, NJ: Princeton University Press, 2012), 123–54. For historical examples of cow protectionist discourse, see Pt. Jagatnarayan, *Atha Gau Vinti* (Mumbai: 1905), 4, 8; Alarama, *Bhajana-Goraksha* (Allahabad: 1892), transliterated the English word *butcher* into Hindi for maximum impact.

7. On the contemporary politics of the cow in India, see Cassie Adcock and Radhika Govindrajan, "Bovine Politics in South Asia: Rethinking Religion, Law, & Ethics," and essays by Sahana Ghosh, James Staples, Kathryn C. Hardy, Aarti Sethi, and Shaheed Tayob in *South Asia: Journal of South Asian Studies* 42, no. 6 (2019). Pradeep Chibber and Nirvikar Jassal provide a useful overview in "India in 2017: The BJP, Economic Reform, and Contentious Politics," *Asian Survey* 58, no. 1 (2018): 86–99.

8. The phrase is Chigateri's. Shraddha Chigateri, "Negotiating the Sacred Cow: Cow Slaughter and the Regulation of Difference in India," in *Democracy, Religious Pluralism, and the Liberal Dilemma of Accommodation*, ed. Monica Mukherjee (New York: Springer, 2011): 17–149, 156.

9. The court allowed state governments, not the federal government, to prohibit slaughter of female cows.

10. This is particularly clear in the United States Commission on International Religious Freedom (USCIRF) reports for 2016 and 2017 (see note 13). For scholarship, see Chigateri, "Negotiating"; Ian Copland, "What to Do About Cows? Princely Versus British Approaches to a South Asian Dilemma," *Bulletin of the School of Oriental and African Studies* 68, no. 1 (2005): 59–76; and Donald Eugene Smith, *India as a Secular State* (Princeton, NJ: Princeton University Press, 1963). Rohit De has challenged this perspective on the 1958 ruling, using the Supreme Court's case files in *A People's Constitution: The Everyday Life of Law in the Indian Republic* (Princeton, NJ: Princeton University Press, 2018).

11. At least, it has escaped mention by historians of colonial India. In the postcolonial period, state officials' support for cow protection is well recognized. Cow protection's connection to state-led animal husbandry outside the legislative arena is less remarked upon, but see Deryck O. Lodrick, *Sacred Cows, Sacred Places: Origins and Survivals of Animal Homes in India* (Berkeley: University of California Press, 1981).

12. Winnifred Fallers Sullivan, *A Ministry of Presence: Chaplaincy, Spiritual Care, and the Law* (Chicago: University of Chicago Press, 2014), 171.

13. There are significant differences between IRF and USCIRF and the reports they produce, but it is not my purpose to assess their respective merits. I refer to the reports issued between 2015 and 2018—collectively, the "U.S. religious freedom reports." IRF reports can be found at www.state.gov/j/drl/rls/irf. USCIRF reports can be found at www.uscirf.gov/reports-briefs; I also include the USCIRF special report, I. K. Cheema, *Constitutional and Legal Challenges Faced by Religious Minorities in India* (Washington DC: U.S. Commission on International Religious Freedom, 2017), www.uscirf.gov/sites/default/files/Constitutional%20and%20Legal%20Challenges%20Faced%20by%20Religious%20Minorities%20in%20India.pdf.

14. The politics of cow protection centers on an exaggerated, putative conflict between Hindus and Muslims, specifically. Other issues are more usually mobilized to foreground a supposed conflict with Christians in contemporary India: for example, religious conversion. Nathaniel Roberts, *To Be Cared For: The Power of Conversion and Foreignness of Belonging in an Indian Slum* (Oakland: University of California Press, 2016); Chad Bauman, *Pentecostals, Proselytization, and Anti-Christian Violence in Contemporary India* (New York: Oxford University Press, 2015). Debates over conversion are far from limited to Indian Christians, however. Laura

Dudley Jenkins, *Religious Freedom and Mass Conversion in India* (Philadelphia: University of Pennsylvania Press, 2019); Goldie Osurie, *Religious Freedom in India: Sovereignty and (Anti) Conversion* (Routledge, 2012); C. S. Adcock, *The Limits of Tolerance: Indian Secularism and the Politics of Religious Freedom* (New York: Oxford University Press, 2013).

15. On this point, Talal Asad's genealogy of religion as an anthropological category found an echo in Winnifred Sullivan's critical reflection on First Amendment jurisprudence in the United States. Talal Asad, *Genealogies of Religion: Discipline and Reasons of Power in Christianity and Islam* (Baltimore: Johns Hopkins University Press, 1993), and Talal Asad, *Formations of the Secular: Christianity, Islam, Modernity* (Stanford, CA: Stanford University Press, 2003); Winnifred Fallers Sullivan, *Impossibility of Religious Freedom* (Princeton, NJ: Princeton University Press, 2005).

16. The reference to "questioning" comes from Hussein Ali Agrama, *Questioning Secularism: Islam, Sovereignty, and the Rule of Law in Modern Egypt* (Chicago: University of Chicago Press, 2012).

17. Scholars are reexamining the varied and unpredictable histories and politics of religious freedom around the world in the light of these insights. This literature has been collected in Winnifred Fallers Sullivan, Elizabeth Shakman Hurd, Saba Mahmood, and Peter G. Danchin, eds., *Politics of Religious Freedom* (Chicago: University of Chicago Press, 2015); "Symposium: Re-Thinking Religious Freedom," ed. Winnifred Fallers Sullivan and Elizabeth Shakman Hurd, *Journal of Law and Religion* 29, no. 3 (2014): 355–509; "Politics of Religious Freedom: Contested Genealogies," ed. Saba Mahmood and Peter Danchin, *South Atlantic Quarterly* 113, no. 1 (Winter 2014): 1-159.

18. Benjamin Schonthal, *Buddhism, Politics and the Limits of Law: The Pyrrhic Constitutionalism of Sri Lanka* (New York: Cambridge University Press, 2016); Markus Dressler, *Writing Religion: The Making of Turkish Alevi Islam* (Oxford: Oxford University Press, 2013). Mahmood argues that this is characteristic of political secularism more broadly. Precisely because secular states make equality in religion their central value, Mahmood suggests, national majorities and minorities come to be identified more and more in religious terms. Saba Mahmood, *Religious Difference in a Secular Age: A Minority Report* (Princeton, NJ: Princeton University Press, 2016), 3, 5, 10.

19. See Sullivan, *Impossibility*, for an early example of this argument.

20. Markus Dressler, "The Religio-Secular Continuum: Reflections on the Religious Dimensions of Turkish Secularism," in Winnifred Fallers Sullivan, Robert A. Yelle, and Mateo Taussig-Rubbo, eds., *After Secular Law* (Stanford, CA: Stanford University Press, 2011), 221–41; for a comparable example, see Jason Ānanda Josephson, *The Invention of Religion in Japan* (Chicago: University of Chicago Press, 2012).

21. Saba Mahmood and Peter G. Danchin, "Immunity or Regulation? Antinomies of Religious Freedom." *South Atlantic Quarterly* 113, no. 1 (Winter 2014): 129–59; Agrama, *Questioning*.

22. Sullivan, *Ministry*, 45.

23. Sullivan, *Ministry*; Peter van der Veer, *The Modern Spirit of Asia: The Spiritual and the Secular in China and India* (Princeton, NJ: Princeton University Press, 2014), 44.

24. Sullivan, *Ministry*; John Lardas Modern, *Secularism in Antebellum America: With Reference to Ghosts, Protestant Subcultures, Machines, and their Metaphors: Featuring Discussions of Mass Media,* Moby-Dick, *Spirituality, Phrenology, Anthropology, Sing Sing State Penitentiary, and Sex with the New Motive Power* (Chicago: University of Chicago Press, 2011); Christopher G. White, *Unsettled Minds: Psychology and the American Search for Spiritual Assurance, 1830–1940* (Berkeley: University of California Press, 2009); Ann Taves, *Fits, Trances, and Visions:*

Experiencing Religion and Explaining Experience from Wesley to James (Princeton, NJ: Princeton University Press, 1999).

25. I am particularly grateful for support from the National Endowment for the Humanities, which funded my American Institute of Indian Studies fellowship for research in India.

26. Sandria B. Freitag, *Collective Action and Community: Public Arenas and the Emergence of Communalism in North India* (Berkeley: University of California Press, 1989); John R. McLane, *Indian Nationalism and the Early Congress* (Princeton, NJ: Princeton University Press, 1977); Gyanendra Pandey, "Rallying Around the Cow: Sectarian Strife in the Bhojpur Region, c. 1888–1917," in *Subaltern Studies: Writings on South Asian History and Society*, vol. 2, ed. Ranajit Guha (New Delhi: Oxford University Press, 1983), 60–129; Anand A. Yang, "Sacred Symbol and Sacred Space in Rural India: Community Mobilization in the 'Anti-Cow Killing' Riot of 1893," *Comparative Studies in Society and History* 22, no. 4 (1980): 576–96.

27. The question of how or to what degree Indian cattle are "useful" is itself a matter for debate, as will become clear from the discussion below. For example: Are all cattle useful by definition? Or are individual animals useful so long as they can be profitably maintained by their owners for agricultural work or milk production?

28. To the extent that they disregard the variegated histories of translation that inflect the politics of religious freedom, advocates remain blind to the variety of outcomes that this principle may yield "on the ground." The unanticipated effects of religious freedom extend to the question of which practices, attitudes, or persons have come to be defined or translated as "religious" in nature. For example, Indian elites have historically defined religion in such a way as to reinforce caste discrimination and inequality (Rupa Viswanath, *The Pariah Problem: Caste, Religion, and the Social in Modern India* [New York: Columbia University Press, 2014]). For an exploration of the cultural and political ramifications of translation in U.S. history, see Tisa Wenger, *We Have a Religion: The 1920s Pueblo Indian Dance Controversy and American Religious Freedom* (Chapel Hill: University of North Carolina Press, 2009), and *Religious Freedom: The Contested History of an American Ideal* (Chapel Hill: University of North Carolina Press, 2017). Talal Asad, *Secular Translations: Nation-State Modern Self, and Calculative Reason* (New York: Columbia University Press, 2018).

29. Elizabeth Shakman Hurd summarizes this scholarship in *Beyond Religious Freedom: The New Global Politics of Religion* (Princeton, NJ: Princeton University Press, 2015), 39, 42.

30. This is not to say that Muslim groups made their challenge on grounds of religious right; see below.

31. Muslims' first, decisive challenge to anti-slaughter laws, which resulted in the Supreme Court decision of 1958, was advanced on similar grounds of livelihood (the plaintiffs were Qureshis, employed in slaughter-related trades) and the nutritional importance of beef. Although the plaintiffs also invoked Eid sacrifice as a "fundamental right," De contends that it was of little concern to the plaintiffs, who had little "interest in making a claim as Muslims." In fact, "in almost every case filed after independence, the petitioners self-identified as butchers, were marked by their names as Qureshis, were found slaughtering the cow for food, or were in the possession of beef" (De, *People's Constitution*, 150, 149).

32. The Wire Staff, "Hapur Lynching Case: SC to Hear Plea After Accused Admits to State Support in NDTV Exposé," *The Wire*, August 7, 2018, https://thewire.in/communalism/hapur-lynching-case-sc-to-hear-plea-after-accused-admits-to-state-support-in-ndtv-expose.

33. Nidhi Dutt, "India's Supreme Court Tackles 'Cow Protecting' Mob Lynching," *NBC News*, October 7, 2018, www.nbcnews.com/news/world/india-s-supreme-court-tackles-cow-protecting-mob-lynching-n911771. The person quoted is Sanjay Hegde, a senior advocate in the Indian Supreme Court and a regular commentator in the Indian press.

34. The practice of untouchability is illegal in the Republic of India, but many are still subject to discrimination and violence.

35. Shraddha Chigateri, "'Glory to the Cow': Cultural Difference and Social Justice in the Food Hierarchy in India," *South Asia: Journal of South Asian Studies* 31, no. 1 (2008): 10–35.

36. Sambaiah Gundimeda, "Democratisation of the Public Sphere: The Beef Stall Case in Hyderabad's *Sukoon* Festival," *South Asia Research* 29, no. 2 (2009): 127–49. For a history, see Anupama Rao, *The Caste Question: Dalits and the Politics of Modern India* (Berkeley: University of California Press, 2009).

37. "Beef festivals" were already a regular form of political assertion by Dalit student groups in south India, including at Hyderabad Central University, Osmania University, and IIT Madras.

38. Kancha Ilaiah, "Beef, BJP and Food Rights of People," *Economic and Political Weekly* 31, no. 24 (June 15, 1996): 1444–45.

39. Scroll Staff, "Gujarat: Una Dalit Family Assaulted for Skinning a Cow in 2016 Converts to Buddhism," *Scroll.in*, updated April 30, 2018, https://scroll.in/latest/877335/gujarat-assaulted-for-skinning-a-cow-in-2016-four-dalit-men-in-una-convert-to-buddhism.

40. Balakrishna Ganeshan, "'Are You Muslims to Eat Cow?': Goons Attack Dalits in Telangana Village on Festival Eve," *News Minute*, January 18, 2018, www.thenewsminute.com/article/are-you-muslims-eat-cow-goons-attack-dalits-telangana-village-festival-eve-74960.

41. The Kisan Mukti (Farmers' Freedom) March to Delhi, November 29-30, 2018, was but one of a series of mass protests by India's farmers; it brought together "the producers of primary agricultural commodities; including Women, dalit, nomadic and adivasi farmers; landowners, tenants, sharecroppers, agricultural labourers and plantation workers; fishworkers, milk producers, poultry farmers, livestock rearers, pastoralists, and collectors of minor forest produce; and everyone engaged in crop cultivation, shifting cultivation, sericulture, vermiculture, and agro-forestry." See the Kisan Charter; on cattle, see item 7. Aditya Nigam, "The Kisan Charter—'Farmers Are Not Just a Residue from Our Past But Integral to the Future of India and the World,'" January 12, 2018, *Kafila Online*, https://kafila.online/2018/12/01/the-kisan-charter-farmers-are-not-just-a-residue-from-our-past-they-are-integral-to-the-future-of-india-and-the-world.

42. On the latter, see Radhika Govindrajan, *Animal Intimacies: Interspecies Relatedness in India's Central Himalayas* (Chicago: University of Chicago Press, 2018), and James Staples, "Blurring Bovine Boundaries: Cow Politics and the Everyday in South India," *South Asia: Journal of South Asian Studies* 42, no. 6 (December 2019): 1135–40; and James Staples, *Sacred Cows and Chicken Manchurian: The Everyday Politics of Meat Eating in India* (Seattle: University of Washington Press, 2020).

43. Cheema, *Constitutional and Legal Challenges*, 11.

44. *Mohammad Hanif Quareshi and others vs. State of Bihar and connected petitions, All India Reporter* 45 (Nagpur: All India Reporter, 1958): 731–56, 735–36.

45. The same is true of the more recent Supreme Court ruling discussed in note 50 below. For reflections on wider issues of constitutional law and religious freedom in the countries of South Asia, see Neeti Nair, "Special Issue: Ghosts from the Past? Assessing Recent Developments in Religious Freedom in South Asia," *Asian Affairs* 49, no. 2 (June, 2018): 199–204.

46. Smith, *India as a Secular State*, 489.

47. Chigateri, "Negotiating," 138.

48. Ibid., 156.

49. Bruno Latour discusses the notional dependence of modern politics on putatively objective scientific facts (*Politics of Nature: How to Bring the Sciences into Democracy* [Cambridge, MA: Harvard University Press, 2004]).

50. The 1958 ruling laid the groundwork for laws restricting bovine slaughter, but the strengthened legislation passed in many Indian states since 2015 is based on a more recent Supreme Court decision, issued in 2005, which eliminated restrictions that the 1958 judgment had put in place, allowing *all* cattle slaughter to be prohibited. *State of Gujarat vs Mirzapur Moti Kureshi Kassab . . . on 26 October, 2005*, accessed April 20, 2018, https://indiankanoon.org/doc/55842.

51. Smith, *India as a Secular State*, 488.

52. *Quareshi vs. State of Bihar* (1958), 750–52, 754; Government of India, Department of Food and Agriculture, *Report of the Expert Committee on the Prevention of Slaughter of Cattle in India* (New Delhi: Manager of Publications, 1955). De discusses the court's use of government reports, though he does not mention this one by name (*People's Constitution*, 159–60).

53. *Report of the Royal Commission on Agriculture in India* (Bombay: Government Central Press, 1928).

54. Although departments were established to create the appearance of colonial expertise, colonial science was largely handicapped by lack of funding, when it wasn't made entirely subservient to the maximizing of imperial profits. David Arnold, "Imperial Science and the Indian Scientific Community," in *Science, Technology, and Medicine in Colonial India*, ch. 5 (Cambridge Histories Online: Cambridge University Press, 2008): 129–68.

55. *Report of the Expert Committee*, 2.

56. Ibid., 2, 40.

57. *Proceedings of the Board of Agriculture in India held at Coimbatore on the 8th December 1913 and following days* (Calcutta: Office of the Superintendent of Government Printing, 1914), 15–17, www.hathitrust.org, http://hdl.handle.net/2027/coo.31924066971635; W. Smith, "Cow Protection," *Agricultural Journal of India* 27, no. 1 (1922): 18–22, 19–20, www.hathitrust.org, https://hdl.handle.net/2027/uc1.b2961345; Royal Commission on Agriculture in India, *Evidence of Officers Serving Under the Government of India*, vol. 1, part 2 (London: His Majesty's Stationery Office, 1927), 31.

58. Imperial Council of Agricultural Research, *Proceedings of the Third Meeting of the Animal Husbandry Wing of the Board of Agriculture and Animal Husbandry in India Held at New Delhi from the 20th to the 23rd February 1939* (Simla: Government of India, 1940), 22; Imperial Council of Agricultural Research, *Annual Report 1937–38* (Delhi: Government of India, 1938), 3.

59. *Report of the Expert Committee*, 45.

60. *Quareshi vs. State of Bihar*, 754–55.

61. Imperial Council of Agricultural Research, *Agriculture and Animal Husbandry in India, 1936–1937* (Delhi: Manager of Publications, 1939), 255.

62. Cassie Adcock, "'Preserving and Improving the Breeds': Cow Protection's Animal-Husbandry Connection," *South Asia: Journal of South Asian Studies* 42, no. 6 (December 2019):1141–55.

63. The colonial position was reiterated by Prime Minister Jawaharlal Nehru and his supporters after independence. Gandhi offered an alternative position that aimed to defuse Hindu-Muslim conflict over the cow, but he did not characterize his as a "secular" solution.

64. The 2020 Annual Report for India can be found at www.uscirf.gov/countries/india, accessed April 15, 2020.

65. In 2019, the Indian government revoked Article 370 of the Indian Constitution, which gave legal rights of political autonomy to the residents of Jammu and Kashmir.

66. "UN Voices Concern Over Violence in India Against CAA, Urges Respect for Freedom of Expression." *The Hindu*, December 18, 2019, accessed June 1, 2020, www.thehindu.com/news/international/un-voices-concern-over-violence-in-india-against-caa-urges-respect-for-freedom-of-expression/article30338241.ece; The Wire Staff, "UN Expert Thinks CAA Has Sparked More Hate Speech, Discrimination Against Minorities," *The Wire* (India), May 20, 2020, accessed June 1, 2020, thewire.in/communalism/un-expert-adama-dieng-caa-hate-speech.

67. Given the basis of Hindu nationalism on the ideology of "Hindutva," which defines Hindu identity in racial or ethnic and cultural terms, rather than in terms of religion, this broad definition of nondiscrimination seems most fitting for the contemporary Indian case.

68. Both the United Nations and the European Parliament censured the police violence unleashed by the state in response to the anti-CAA protests, as well as government efforts to label protesters "terrorists," by recalling the "freedoms of association and expression." NH Political Bureau, "European Parliament Slams Modi Govt for Silencing Activists & Portraying Protesters as Terrorists," *National Herald* (India), May 30, 2020, accessed June 1, 2020, www.nationalheraldindia.com/international/european-parliament-union-slams-amit-shah-says-stop-impeding-and-criminalizing-activists.

Chapter 7

1. Westbrook Pegler, "Fair Enough," *Los Angeles Times*, November 15, 1939. It should be noted that Pegler's column did not appear only in the *Times*. The historian David Witwer notes that, during the 1930s, Pegler's columns "went out six days a week to 174 newspapers that reached an estimated 10 million subscribers." Witwer, "Westbrook Pegler and the Anti-Union Movement," *Journal of American History* 92, no. 2 (September 2005): 527–52, quote from 528.

2. Many of these movements are chronicled by Philip Jenkins, *Mystics and Messiahs: Cults and New Religions in American History* (Oxford: Oxford University Press, 2000), and Charles W. Ferguson, *The New Books of Revelations: The Inside Story of America's Astounding Religious Cults* (Garden City, NY: Doubleday, Doran, & Co., 1930).

3. These trials are described by Marie Failinger, "*United States v. Ballard:* Government Prohibited from Declaring Religious Truth," in *Law and Religion: Cases in Context*, ed. Leslie C. Griffin (Austin, TX: Wolters Kluwer Law & Business, 2010), 33–49.

4. Quoted in Hugh B. Urban, *The Church of Scientology: A History of a New Religion* (Princeton, NJ: Princeton University Press, 2011), 159.

5. Quoted in *Matter of Holy Spirit Assn. for Unification of World Christianity v. Tax Commn. of City of N.Y.*, 55 N.Y.2d 512, 435 N.E.2d 662 (1982).

6. Recent works on American religion exploring these topics include Tisa Wenger, *Religious Freedom: The Contested History of an American Ideal* (Chapel Hill: University of North Carolina Press, 2017); Finbarr Curtis, *The Production of American Religious Freedom* (New York: New York University Press, 2016); Kyle G. Volk, *Moral Minorities and the Making of American Democracy* (New York: Oxford University Press, 2014); David Sehat, *The Myth of American Religious Freedom* (New York: Oxford University Press, 2011); and Winnifred Fallers Sullivan, *The Impossibility of Religious Freedom* (Princeton, NJ: Princeton University Press, 2005).

7. Works on capitalism and evangelicalism include Daniel Vaca, *Evangelicals Incorporated: Books and the Business of Religion in America* (Cambridge, MA: Harvard University Press, 2019); Darren Dochuk, *Anointed with Oil: How Christianity and Crude Made Modern America* (New

York: Basic Books, 2019); Darren Grem, *The Blessings of Business: Corporate America and the Rise of Conservative Evangelicalism* (New York: Oxford University Press, 2016); Timothy E. W. Gloege, *Guaranteed Pure: The Moody Bible Institute, Business, and the Making of Modern Evangelicalism* (Chapel Hill: University of North Carolina Press, 2015); and Bethany Moreton, *To Serve God and Wal-Mart: The Making of Christian Free Enterprise* (Cambridge, MA: Harvard University Press, 2009).

8. Danielle Boaz, "Obeah, Vagrancy, and the Boundaries of Religious Freedom: Analyzing the Proscription of 'Pretending to Possess Supernatural Powers' in the Anglophone Caribbean," *Journal of Law and Religion* 32, no. 3 (November 2017): 423–48; Diana Paton, "Obeah Acts: Producing and Policing the Boundaries of Religion in the Caribbean," *Small Axe* 28 (March 2009): 1–18; LaShawn Harris, *Sex Workers, Psychics, and Number Runners: Black Women in New York City's Underground Economy* (Urbana: University of Illinois Press, 2016); Charles McCrary, "Fortune Telling and American Religious Freedom," *Religion and American Culture* 28, no. 2 (July 2018): 269–306. My thanks to Ahmad Greene-Hayes for pointing me toward this literature.

9. Harry Millis and Royal Montgomery, *Organized Labor* (New York: McGraw-Hill, 1945), 670, quoted in Andrew W. Cohen, "The Racketeer's Progress: Commerce, Crime, and the Law in Chicago, 1900–1940," *Journal of Urban History* 29, no. 5 (July 2003): 575–96.

10. Witwer, "Westbrook Pegler and the Anti-Union Movement"; Cohen, "The Racketeer's Progress"; David Witwer, "The Racketeer Menace and Antiunionism in the Mid-Twentieth Century US," *International Labor and Working-Class History* 74, no. 1 (Fall 2008): 124–47.

11. Upton Sinclair, *The Profits of Religion: An Essay in Economic Interpretation* (Pasadena, CA: Published by the author, 1918).

12. "Spiritualism" in this case refers to "religious movements, more or less organized, whose adherents seek communication with the spirits of deceased human beings," a definition offered by Bret E. Carroll in the *Encyclopedia of Religion in America*, ed. Charles H. Lippy and Peter W. Williams (Washington, DC: CQ Press, 2010).

13. Harry Houdini, *A Magician Among the Spirits* (New York: Harper & Bros., 1924).

14. Julien Proskauer, *Spook Crooks! Exposing the Secrets of the Prophet-eers Who Conduct Our Wickedest Industry* (New York: A. L. Burt, 1932).

15. A. G. Mezerik, "The Foundation Racket," *New Republic*, January 30, 1950, 11–13.

16. "Saintly Profiteering," *Nation*, May 15, 1929, 577.

17. "Churches Should Pay Taxes!," *Christian Century*, April 9, 1947, 454–56.

18. "She Just Sent in $30.20 and Became a Minister," *San Francisco Chronicle*, October 19, 1957.

19. "State Sets Inquiry on Charity Racket," *New York Times*, December 11, 1953; Douglas Dales, "Legislature Gets Bills to Eliminate Charity Rackets," *New York Times*, February 17, 1954.

20. "Expose 'Missions' for Racketeering," *Christian Century*, June 23, 1943, 744.

21. The sociologist Gabriel Rossman has written about the importance of "structural obfuscation" in concealing the exchange of "profane" and "sacred" goods, such as exchanging money for sexual favors. Most of these new religions lacked any such structural obfuscation. Gabriel Rossman, "Obfuscatory Relational Work and Disreputable Exchange," *Sociological Theory* 32, no. 1 (2014): 43–63.

22. Proskauer, *Spook Crooks!*, 130.

23. Richard Mathison, *Faiths, Cults, and Sects of America: From Atheism to Zen* (New York: Bobbs-Merrill, 1960), 21.

24. Ferguson, *The New Books of Revelations*, 9.

25. Ibid., 9.

26. The Comte de Saint Germain was an eighteenth-century French aristocrat with an interest in the supernatural; after his death, he became a key figure in the theosophical canon. Jenkins, *Mystics and Messiahs*, 72–73.

27. Gerald B. Bryan, *Psychic Dictatorship in America* (Los Angeles, CA: Truth Research Publications, 1940), 95–105.

28. Godfre Ray King, *Unveiled Mysteries* (Chicago: Saint Germain Press, 1935 [1934]), 6.

29. Ibid., 134–36.

30. Charles Braden, *These Also Believe: A Study of Modern American Cults and Minority Religions* (New York: Macmillan, 1949), 292.

31. Godfre Ray King, *The Magic Presence* (Chicago: Saint Germain Press, 1935), 72–73.

32. King, *Unveiled Mysteries*, 80.

33. Braden, *These Also Believe*, 270.

34. Fred Lieb, *Sight Unseen: A Journalist Visits the Occult* (New York: Harper & Brothers, 1939), 61–62. The "I AM being," a phrase the Ballards used somewhat loosely, referred to the "electric presence" that was believed to hover a few feet above every human. King, *The Magic Presence*, 32–35.

35. Pegler, "Fair Enough."

36. *The Voice of the I AM*, May 1936, 34–35.

37. Bryan, *Psychic Dictatorship in America*, 51–55, 156–60, 200–204.

38. King, *Unveiled Mysteries*, viii.

39. Ibid., 133.

40. King, *The Magic Presence*, 134.

41. "America's Birthday," *The Voice of the I AM*, July 1937, 33.

42. Pegler, "Fair Enough."

43. "The Great Master Hoax," *The Rosicrucian Digest*, July 1936, 232–36. Edited by H. Spencer Lewis and published out of San Jose, California, the *Rosicrucian Digest* offered articles on the history of Rosicrucianism and occultism as well as advertisements for Rosicrucian merchandise. Pat Deveney, "Rosicrucian Digest," *International Association for the Preservation of Spiritualist and Occult Periodicals*, n.d., accessed December 12, 2018, www.iapsop.com/archive/materials/rosicrucian_digest/index.html.

44. Bryan, *Psychic Dictatorship in America*, 75.

45. Braden, *These Also Believe*, 280.

46. Bryan, *Psychic Dictatorship in America*, 195. After World War II, the journalist Carey McWilliams described I AM in the same terms, as he recalled an audience at one of its meetings "shouting with all the frenzy of a mob of Nazis yelling 'Sieg Heil.'" McWilliams, "The Cults of California," *Atlantic Monthly*, March 1946, 105–10.

47. Bryan, *Psychic Dictatorship in America*, 228.

48. The best work on homegrown "fascism" in this era—and on the fears it inspired—remains Leo P. Ribuffo, *The Old Christian Right: The Protestant Far Right from the Great Depression to the Cold War* (Philadelphia, PA: Temple University Press, 1983).

49. "The Great I Am Runs Afoul of a Cynical Mystic," *Chicago Daily Tribune*, October 14, 1938.

50. "Great I Am Dies of a Heart Attack," *Chicago Daily Tribune*, January 2, 1940.

51. The belief that one's physical body would eventually be raised into a "Pure, Eternal Body of Light" was put forth in *Unveiled Mysteries*, 181–82.

52. Bryan, *Psychic Dictatorship in America*, 63–69.

53. "'I Am' Cult Heir's Finances Aired at Alimony Hearings," *Los Angeles Times*, May 7, 1940.

54. "I Am Leaders Indicted on Mail Fraud Charges," *Los Angeles Times*, July 25, 1940.

55. "Legal Batteries Prepared for I Am Fraud Trial," *Los Angeles Times*, November 25, 1940.

56. Ibid.

57. "I Am Leaders Indicted on Mail Fraud Charges."

58. "Fight to Quash Indictments Pressed by I Am Defense," *Los Angeles Times*, October 1, 1940.

59. "Submarine Plot Enters 'I Am' Case," *Los Angeles Times*, December 18, 1940; "Supernatural I Am Experiment Related at Trial of Inner Circle," January 3, 1941.

60. "Submarine Plot Enters 'I Am' Case"; "I Am Jury Hears Story of Miracle," *Los Angeles Times*, December 13, 1940.

61. "Senator's Widow Tells Court of I Am Secrets," *Los Angeles Times*, December 5, 1941.

62. "I Am Group's Attorney Balks on Brain Adjustment," *Los Angeles Times*, December 21, 1940.

63. "I Am Books Quoted at Trial as Stairway to Ascension," *Los Angeles Times*, December 14, 1940.

64. "I Am Jury Hears Story of Miracle."

65. "Ill in Spite of I Am Aid, Witness Declares at Trial," *Los Angeles Times*, December 28, 1940.

66. "Senator's Widow Tells Court of I Am Secrets."

67. "Preacher Discloses Wisdom Acquired in I Am Presence," *Los Angeles Times*, January 9, 1941.

68. "I Am Solved Mysteries of Life, Young Man Says," *Los Angeles Times*, January 8, 1941.

69. "I Am Movement Teachings Explained by Mrs. Ballard," *Los Angeles Times*, January 15, 1941.

70. "Preacher Discloses Wisdom Acquired in I Am Presence."

71. "Ill in Spite of I Am Aid, Witness Declares at Trial," *Los Angeles Times*, December 28, 1940.

72. "Submarine Plot Enters 'I Am' Case."

73. "Senator's Widow Tells Court of I Am Secrets."

74. "I Am Defendant Tells St. Germain Dictation," *Los Angeles Times*, January 11, 1941.

75. "Cure Attested by Physician," *Los Angeles Times*, January 10, 1941; "I Am Solved Mysteries of Life, Young Man Says."

76. "Mountain Climb with I Am Leader Told by Witness," *Los Angeles Times*, January 7, 1941.

77. Ibid.

78. "Acquittal Refused, I Am Case Goes to Jury Today," *Los Angeles Times*, January 16, 1941.

79. "I Am Jurors Acquit Three, Split on Six," *Los Angeles Times*, January 21, 1941.

80. "Second I Am Trial to Open," *Los Angeles Times*, December 1, 1941.

81. "Mrs. Edna Ballard and Son Convicted by Jury of Fraud," *Los Angeles Times*, February 1, 1942; "Ballards Fined Total of $8400," *Los Angeles Times*, February 18, 1942.

82. "Supreme Court Upholds 'I Am' Fraud Conviction," *Los Angeles Times*, April 25, 1944.

83. Quoted in "Religious Liberty and Fraud," *Christian Century*, May 10, 1944: 383–85.

84. *United States v. Ballard*, 322 U.S. 78 (1944).

85. Braden, *These Also Believe*, 267, 306.

86. David Stupple, "The 'I Am' Sect Today: An Unobituary," *Journal of Popular Culture* (Spring 1975): 897–905.

87. Robert Ellwood, "Making New Religions: The Mighty I AM," *History Today* 38 (June 1988): 18–23.

88. On the *Century*'s place in American religious history, see Elesha J. Coffman, *The Christian Century and the Rise of the Protestant Mainline* (New York: Oxford University Press, 2013).

89. Charles Braden, "Learning from the Cults," *Christian Century*, January 9, 1944.

90. "'I Am' Cult Leaders Indicted," *Christian Century*, August 7, 1940.

91. On the WCG, see David V. Barrett, *The Fragmentation of a Sect: Schism in the Worldwide Church of God* (New York: Oxford University Press, 2013).

92. Sharon L. Worthing, "The State Takes Over a Church," *Annals of the American Academy of Political and Social Science* 446, no. 1 (September 1979): 136–48.

93. Brief of Amici Curiae National Council of Churches of Christ in the U.S.A. et al., *Worldwide Church of God v. State of California*, 1979, from the American Civil Liberties Union Records, MC001, box 1854, "Worldwide Church of God," Seeley G. Mudd Manuscript Library, Princeton University, Princeton, NJ.

94. Anson Shupe, "Sun Myung Moon's American Disappointment," *Christian Century*, August 22–29, 1990; Beth Spring, "With Their Leader in Prison, Moonies Pursue Legitimacy," *Christianity Today*, September 7, 1984.

95. *Hearing Before the Subcommittee on the Constitution of the Committee on the Judiciary, United States Senate*, 98th Cong. 152, 28 (1984) (statements by Sun Myung Moon and Greg Dixon).

96. "In Conversation: Arthur C. Borden, Evangelical Council for Financial Accountability," with Robert Abelman, from *Religious Television: Controversies and Conclusions*, ed. Robert Abelman and Stewart M. Hoover (Norwood, NJ: Ablex Publishing Corporation, 1990).

97. Edward Balleisen, *Fraud: An American History from Barnum to Madoff* (Princeton, NJ: Princeton University Press, 2017).

Chapter 8

1. Jerry Falwell, *Strength for the Journey* (New York: Simon and Schuster, 1987), 334–35.

2. Quoted in Michael Cromartie, *No Longer Exiles: The Religious New Right in American Politics* (Washington, DC: University Press of America, 1993), 52.

3. Quoted in Mark Tooley, *Methodism and Politics in the Twentieth Century* (Anderson, IN: Bristol House, 2012), 222, 224–25; *Annual of the Southern Baptist Convention, 1972* (Nashville, TN: Executive Committee, Southern Baptist Convention, 1972), 72. On the reaffirmations of the 1971 resolution, see *Annual of the Southern Baptist Convention, 1974* (Nashville, TN: Executive Committee, Southern Baptist Convention, 1974), 76. The 1976 resolution was more measured, calling on "Southern Baptists and all citizens of the nation to work to change those attitudes and conditions which encourage many people to turn to abortion as a means of birth control"; but it also affirmed "our conviction about the limited role of government in dealing with matters relating to abortion, and [our] support [for] the right of expectant mothers to the full range of medical services and personal counseling for the preservation of life and health." *Annual of the Southern Baptist Convention, 1976* (Nashville, TN: Executive Committee, Southern Baptist Convention, 1976), 58.

4. Quoted in "What Price Abortion?" *Christianity Today*, March 2, 1973, 39 [565].

5. "Abortion and the Court," *Christianity Today*, February 16, 1973, 32 [502]; quoted in "What Price Abortion?"; Floyd Robertson, *United Evangelical Action*, Summer 1973, 8–11, quotes from 11.

6. For a superb review of the circumstances surrounding the *Green v. Kennedy* case, see Joseph Crespino, "Civil Rights and the Religious Right," in *Rightward Bound: Making America Conservative in the 1970s*, ed. Bruce J. Schulman and Julian E. Zelizer (Cambridge, MA: Harvard

University Press, 2008), 90–105. Crespino correctly identifies this case, together with *Green v. Connally*, as the catalyst for the Religious Right.

7. *Green v. Connally*, 330 F. Supp. 1150 (D. D.C.) aff'd sub nom. *Coit v. Green*, 404 U.S. 997 (1971).

8. "The Moral Majority," undated paper, box 19, Paul M. Weyrich Papers, American Heritage Center, University of Wyoming.

9. Quoted in William Martin, *With God on Our Side: The Rise of the Religious Right in America* (New York: Broadway Books, 1996), 173. As early as February 1979, several months before the formation of an organization by that name, Howard Phillips was using the term "moral majority"; see Letter, Howard Phillips to Jerry Falwell, February 27, 1979, Evangelist Activism, box 15, Paul M. Weyrich Papers, American Heritage Center, University of Wyoming. According to historian Robert Freedman, "The Supreme Court's banning of public school prayer (1962) and legalization of abortion (1973) outraged many evangelicals and fundamentalists. However, few decided to participate actively in politics as a result." He adds: "Weyrich believes that the Carter administration's policy toward Christian Schools was the turning point." Robert Freedman, "The Religious Right and the Carter Administration," *Historical Journal* 48 (March 2005), 236. Michael Lienesch writes: "The Christian conservative lobbyists were originally concerned with protecting the Christian schools from Internal Revenue Service investigations over the issue of racial imbalance." Michael Leinesch, "Right-Wing Religion: Christian Conservatism as a Political Movement," *Political Science Quarterly* 97 (Autumn 1982): 409. On the importance of schools to the nascent Religious Right, see also J. Charles Park, "Preachers, Politics, and Public Education: A Review of Right-Wing Pressures Against Public Schooling in America," *Phi Delta Kappan* 61 (May 1980): 608–12.

10. "'Most Unusual': No Time for a Change," *Christianity Today*, December 17, 1971, 34. Bob Jones III insisted that "there was no connection between the enrollment of this one black student and the major threats facing the university."

11. Paul Weyrich, "The Pro-Family Movement," *Conservative Digest* 6 (May–June 1980): 14.

12. Freedman, "Religious Right and the Carter Administration," 238, 240; Wilfred F. Drake, "Tax Status of Private Segregated Schools: The New Revenue Procedure," *William and Mary Law Review* 20 (1979): 463–512; "Jimmy Carter's Betrayal of the Christian Voter," *Conservative Digest*, August 1979, 15; Michael Sean Winters, *God's Right Hand: How Jerry Falwell Made God a Republican and Baptized the American Right* (San Francisco: HarperOne, 2012), 110; Crespino, "Civil Rights and the Religious Right," 99–100. For a look inside the evangelical subculture, see Randall Balmer, *Mine Eyes Have Seen the Glory: A Journey into the Evangelical Subculture in America*, 5th ed. (New York: Oxford University Press, 2014).

13. Freedman, "Religious Right and the Carter Administration," 240–41, 242; Duane Murray Oldfield, *The Right and the Righteous: The Christian Right Confronts the Republican Party* (Lanham, MD: Rowman & Littlefield, 1996), 100.

14. Quoted in Cromartie, *No Longer Exiles*, 26.

15. Ibid., 173. Falwell declared in his sermon: "The Roman Catholic church is to be commended for their diligent and persistent battle against abortion. They have done far more to my knowledge than any other one segment of our society, to try to stop abortion." Jerry Falwell sermon (transcript), "Abortion-on-Demand: Is It Murder?" Genesis 1:26, 27, February 26, 1978, SE-126, Liberty University Archives.

16. Quoted in Cromartie, *No Longer Exiles*, 52; Dan Gilgoff, "Exclusive: Grover Norquist Gives Religious Conservatives Tough Love," June 11, 2009, "God & Country: On Faith, Politics, and Culture," accessed September 30, 2009, www.usnews.com/blogs/god-and-country.

17. Elmer L. Rumminger, telephone interview with the author, July 17, 2010.

18. Douglas E. Kneeland, "Clark Defeat in Iowa Laid to Abortion Issue," *New York Times*, November 13, 1978; Dick Clark, interview with Bruce Morton, *CBS News*, November 13, 1978. See also Hedrick Smith, "A Pattern of Stability: With Incumbents Faring Well, Results Indicate That Fears of Voter Revolt Were Exaggerated," *New York Times*, November 8, 1978. Allegations later emerged that the white government of South Africa may have illegally contributed money toward Clark's defeat because of his strong stand against apartheid. Wendell Rawls Jr., "South African Role in Iowa Voting Charged," *New York Times*, March 22, 1979.

19. "Religion at the Polls: Strength and Conflict," *Christianity Today*, December 1, 1978, 40–41.

20. Letter, Georgia Glassman to Paul Weyrich, January 26, 1978, box 3, Paul M. Weyrich Papers, American Heritage Center, University of Wyoming.

21. Letter, Paul Weyrich to Daniel B. Hales, December 31, 1978, box 3, Paul M. Weyrich Papers, American Heritage Center, University of Wyoming; Letter, Robert Billings, Christian School Action Inc., to Paul Weyrich, December 6, 1978, box 3, Paul M. Weyrich Papers, American Heritage Center, University of Wyoming.

22. Freedman, "Religious Right and the Carter Administration," 243; Letter, Robert Billings to Paul Weyrich, December 6, 1978, box 3, Paul M. Weyrich Papers, American Heritage Center, University of Wyoming.

23. See Vivien A. Schmidt, "Discursive Institutionalism: The Explanatory Power of Ideas and Discourse," *Annual Review of Political Science* 11 (2008): 303–26. I am grateful to Rogers Smith for directing me to this source.

24. Philip Yancey, "Schaeffer on Schaeffer, Part II," *Christianity Today*, April 6, 1979, 25.

25. Frank Schaeffer, *Crazy for God: How I Grew Up as One of the Elect, Helped Found the Religious Right, and Lived to Take All (or Almost All) of It Back* (New York: Carroll & Graf, 2007), 283, 259, 293; Maddox, interview with the author, Bethesda, Maryland, December 6, 2012. According to his son, Francis Schaeffer had initially balked at bringing up abortion because he didn't "want to be identified with some Catholic issue." Schaeffer, *Crazy for God*, 266. The companion volume for the film series is Francis A. Schaeffer and C. Everett Koop, *Whatever Happened to the Human Race?: Exposing Our Rapid Yet Subtle Loss of Human Rights* (Old Tappan, NJ: Revell, 1979). For a profile of McDonald, see Mark Oppenheimer, "From One Benefactor, Diverse Seeds in Theology," *New York Times*, July 16, 2010. On the ubiquity of "secular humanism," see Tim LaHaye, *The Battle for the Mind* (Old Tappan, NJ: Revell, 1980). LaHaye dedicated the book to Schaeffer. In his paean to Schaeffer, Cal Thomas declared, "No man contributed as much to the conservative side of the ideological battle than did Dr. Francis Schaeffer, who died of cancer last month at the age of 72." Cal Thomas, transcript, *Moral Majority Report*, June 28, 1984, Liberty University Archives.

26. Quoted in William Martin, *With God on Our Side: The Rise of the Religious Right in America* (New York: Broadway Books, 1996), 173.

27. Freedman, "Religious Right and the Carter Administration," 249. According to some accounts, the leaders of the Religious Right also considered Philip M. Crane, U.S. representative from Illinois; Howard Baker, U.S. senator from Tennessee; and Jesse Helms, U.S. senator from North Carolina. See, for example, Memorandum, Anne Wexler and Bob Maddox to Phil Wise, October 22, 1979, "Religious Matters," box RM-1, WHCF-Subject File-General, Jimmy Carter Library. Falwell also confirmed that Connally was under consideration. See Cal Thomas and Ed Dobson, *Blinded by Might: Can the Religious Right Save America?* (Grand Rapids, MI:

Zondervan, 1999), 270. When Tim LaHaye caught wind that some conservatives were considering Connally, he objected vigorously. Writing to Weyrich about Connally, LaHaye said: "He is no born again Christian, is unelectable and has little or no conservative following in his home state." Note, Tim LaHaye to Paul Weyrich, March 2, 1980, Paul M. Weyrich Papers, box 4, American Heritage Center, University of Wyoming.

Chapter 9

1. Heiner Bielefeldt, Nazila Ghanea, and Michael Wiener, *Freedom of Religion or Belief: An International Law Commentary* (Oxford: Oxford University Press, 2016), 31. The international law commentary contained in this book has several excellent sections on complexities at the intersection of women's rights and freedom of religion or belief.

2. 42 U.S. Code § 2000bb–1.

3. Eugene Volokh, "The Individualistic American Law of Religious Exemptions," *Washington Post*, January 19, 2015, accessed May 9, 2020, www.washingtonpost.com/news/volokh-conspiracy/wp/2015/01/19/the-individualistic-american-law-of-religious-exemptions.

4. Ibid.

5. Ibid.

6. Ibid.

7. For an excellent study on international law as it relates to women's equality and freedom of religion or belief, see Nazila Ghanea, *Women and Religious Freedom: Synergies and Opportunities* (Washington, DC: USCIRF, 2017), accessed November 7, 2018, www.uscirf.gov/sites/default/files/WomenandReligiousFreedom.pdf. (Although this report was written while I served as commissioner on the United States Commission on International Religious Freedom, I had no part in drafting the report.)

8. "530D-Letter_FGM Statute," Noel J. Francisco to Congressman Jerrold Nadler, April 10, 2019, accessed July 1, 2019, www.law.georgetown.edu/icap/wp-content/uploads/sites/32/2019/04/530D-Letter-FGM-Statute.pdf.

9. The term "FGM/C" is preferred to "FGM" because, "while such procedures are often referred to as 'female genital mutilation,' 'female genital cutting' has been suggested as a more appropriate term to protect those . . . subjected to FGM/C from humiliation or emotional offense." Donna Mazloomdoost and Rachel N. Pauls, "A Comprehensive Review of the Clitoris and Its Role in Female Sexual Function," *Sexual Medicine Reviews* 3, no. 4 (2015): 254.

10. Will Worley, "Detroit Doctor Faces Life in Prison for 'Carrying Out Female Genital Mutilation on Young Girls,'" *Independent*, April 14, 2017, accessed November 7, 2018, www.independent.co.uk/news/world/americas/detroit-doctor-jumana-nagarwala-life-prison-carrying-out-female-genital-mutilation-young-girls-a7683476.html.

11. Robert Snell, "Up to 100 Girls Cut in Mutilation Case, Feds Estimate," *Detroit News*, June 7, 2017, accessed December 15, 2017, www.detroitnews.com/story/news/local/detroit-city/2017/06/07/feds-estimate-genital-mutilation-victims/102594478.

12. Aarefa Johari, "How I Met My Clitoris, a Bohra Woman's Experience of Khatna," *Daily Pao*, May 19, 2016, accessed November 7, 2018, www.thedailypao.com/how-i-met-my-clitoris-a-bohra-womans-experience-of-khatna.

13. These labels come from Dawoodi Bohra terminology where *khatna* is a term used for both male and female circumcision and *khafd/khafz* is "the specific Arabic term for female circumcision in the community." Mariya Taher, *Understanding Female Genital Cutting in the Dawoodi Bohra Community: An Exploratory Survey* (Sahiyo, 2017), accessed November 7, 2018,

www.28toomany.org/static/media/uploads/Continent%20Research%20and%20Resources/Asia/sahiyo-study_final_12.28.18.pdf

14. Harinder Baweja, "India's Dark Secret," *Hindustan Times*, February 7, 2016, accessed March 4, 2018, www.hindustantimes.com/static/fgm-indias-dark-secret.

15. *United States of America v. Nagarwala et al.* (Eastern District of Michigan, November 20, 2018), USA Criminal Court Docket, www.docketbird.com/court-cases/United-States-of-America-v-Nagarwala-et-al/mied-2:2017-cr-20274-319678.

16. Equality Now, "UPDATE: Disappointment at the U.S. Department of Justice Decision Not to Appeal Ruling in the First Federal Genital Mutilation Case," GlobeNewswire News Room, April 12, 2019, accessed July 5, 2019, www.globenewswire.com/news-release/2019/04/12/1803150/0/en/UPDATE-Disappointment-at-the-U-S-Department-of-Justice-decision-not-to-appeal-ruling-in-the-first-federal-genital-mutilation-case.html.

17. Francisco letter to Nadler.

18. Equality Now, "UPDATE: Disappointment at the U.S. Department of Justice Decision Not to Appeal Ruling."

19. Howard Goldberg et al., "Female Genital Mutilation/Cutting in the United States: Updated Estimates of Women and Girls at Risk, 2012," *Public Health Reports* 131 (January 14, 2016): 1, accessed July 7, 2017, www.uscis.gov/sites/default/files/USCIS/Humanitarian/Special%20Situations/fgmutilation.pdf.

20. Fahrinisa Campana, "In India's Dawoodi Bohra Community, There's a Growing Debate About FGM," *Public Radio International*, August 2, 2018, accessed October 2, 2018, www.pri.org/stories/2018-08-02/indias-dawoodi-bohra-community-theres-growing-debate-about-fgm.

21. Ben Sales, "Alan Dershowitz Explains Why He Is Assisting a Group Accused of Promoting Female Genital Mutilation," *Jewish Telegraphic Agency*, June 12, 2017, accessed September 20, 2018, www.jta.org/2017/06/12/news-opinion/united-states/alan-dershowitz-explains-why-he-is-assisting-a-group-accused-of-promoting-female-genital-mutilation.

22. Adriana Kaplan et al., "Health Consequences of Female Genital Mutilation/Cutting in the Gambia, Evidence into Action," *Reproductive Health* 8, no. 26 (2011).

23. Brian D. Earp, "Does Female Genital Mutilation Have Health Benefits? The Problem with Medicalizing Morality," *Journal of Medical Ethics* (blog), August 15, 2017, accessed September 22, 2018, blogs.bmj.com/medical-ethics/2017/08/15/does-female-genital-mutilation-have-health-benefits-the-problem-with-medicalizing-morality.

24. World Health Organization (WHO), *Fact Sheet: Female Genital Mutilation* (Geneva: WHO, January 31, 2018), accessed March 4, 2018, www.who.int/mediacentre/factsheets/fs241/en/.

25. Mazloomdoost and Pauls, "A Comprehensive Review," 245.

26. WHO, *Female Genital Mutilation: Integrating the Prevention and the Management of the Health Complications into the Curricula of Nursing and Midwifery, A Teacher's Guide*, (Geneva: WHO, 2001), 38, accessed November 7, 2018, www.who.int/gender/other_health/teachersguide.pdf.

27. Mazloomdoost and Pauls, "A Comprehensive Review," 255.

28. WHO, *Fact Sheet: Female Genital Mutilation*. See also Mazloomdoost and Pauls, "A Comprehensive Review," 255.

29. UN International Children's Emergency Fund (UNICEF), *Female Genital Mutilation/Cutting: A Global Concern* (New York: UNICEF, 2016), accessed December 17, 2017, www.unicef.org/media/files/FGMC_2016_brochure_final_UNICEF_SPREAD.pdf.

30. Taher, *Understanding Female Genital Cutting in the Dawoodi Bohra Community*, 17.

31. Ibid., 8.

32. Ibid.

33. Ibid.

34. Kurdstan Rasul and Payam Ahmad, interview by Shokh Mohammad, *Wadi Online*, September 12, 2018, accessed October 2, 2018, https://wadi-online.de/2018/09/12/beschwichtigungen-und-erniedrigungen-das-wadi-team-erbil-im-gespraech-ueber-fgm.

35. WHO, *A Teacher's Guide*, 31.

36. Ibid.

37. Ibid.

38. UN Population Fund (UNFPA), *Female Genital Mutilation (FGM) Frequently Asked Questions* (UNFPA, February 2018), accessed March 15, 2018, www.unfpa.org/resources/female-genital-mutilation-fgm-frequently-asked-questions#age_performed.

39. WHO, *Female Genital Mutilation: Integrating the Prevention and the Management of the Health Complications into the Curricula of Nursing and Midwifery, A Student's Manual* (Geneva: WHO, 2001), 20, accessed November 7, 2018, www.who.int/gender/other_health/Studentsmanual.pdf.

40. Dan Reisel and Sarah M. Creighton, "Long Term Health Consequences of Female Genital Mutilation (FGM)," *Maturitas* 80, no. 1 (2015).

41. G. I. Serour, "Medicalization of Female Genital Mutilation/Cutting," *African Journal of Urology* 19, no. 3 (September 2013): 146.

42. Mazloomdoost and Pauls, "A Comprehensive Review," 255.

43. Mary Nyangweso, *Female Genital Cutting in Industrialized Countries: Mutilation or Cultural Tradition?* (Santa Barbara, CA: Praeger, 2014), 57.

44. WHO, *A Student's Manual*, 17.

45. Mazloomdoost and Pauls, "A Comprehensive Review," 255.

46. Sally Hayden, "'We've Seen Too Many Girls Bleed to Death': Eradicating FGM in Uganda," *Irish Times*, February 6, 2018, accessed September 17, 2018, www.irishtimes.com/news/world/africa/we-ve-seen-too-many-girls-bleed-to-death-eradicating-fgm-in-uganda-1.3382765.

47. WHO, *A Teacher's Guide*, 31.

48. Ibid.

49. Serour, "Medicalization of Female Genital Mutilation/Cutting," 146.

50. Samuel Kimani and Bettina Shell-Duncan, "Medicalized Female Genital Mutilation/Cutting: Contentious Practices and Persistent Debates," *Current Sexual Health Reports* 10, no. 1 (February 21, 2018): 25–34, 26, accessed September 17, 2018, www.ncbi.nlm.nih.gov/pmc/articles/PMC5840226.

51. Ibid., 27.

52. Ibid., 26.

53. Ibid.

54. Mazloomdoost and Pauls, "A Comprehensive Review," 249.

55. WHO, "Health Risks of Female Genital Mutilation (FGM)," accessed September 17, 2018, www.who.int/teams/sexual-and-reproductive-health-and-research/key-areas-of-work/female-genital-mutilation/health-risks-of-female-genital-mutilation.

56. Ibid.

57. Mazloomdoost and Pauls, "A Comprehensive Review," 256.

58. Laignee Barron, "Two Sisters Bled to Death in Somalia After a Female Genital Mutilation Procedure," *Time*, September 14, 2018, accessed September 17, 2018. time.com/5396125/somalia-female-genital-mutilation-death.

59. Hayden, "We've Seen Too Many Girls Bleed to Death."

60. Reisel and Creighton, "Long Term Health Consequences of Female Genital Mutilation (FGM)," 50.

61. Margaret Brady, "Female Genital Mutilation: Complications and Risk of HIV Transmission," *AIDS Patient Care and STDs* 13, no. 12 (December 1,1999): 709.

62. Ibid.

63. Ibid.

64. WHO, *Health Risks of Female Genital Mutilation (FGM).*

65. Lars Almroth et al., "Primary Infertility After Genital Mutilation in Girlhood in Sudan: A Case-Control Study," *Lancet* 366, no. 9483 (July 30, 2005).

66. Nyangweso, *Female Genital Cutting: Mutilation or Cultural Tradition?*, 58.

67. Ibid., 60.

68. Ibid. Nyangweso cites several studies in support of the various medical consequences.

69. Ibid.

70. Rigmor C. Berg, Eva Denison, and Atle Fretheim, "Psychological, Social and Sexual Consequences of Female Genital Mutilation/Cutting (FGM/C): A Systematic Review of Quantitative Studies," *Kunnskapssenteret* 13 (2010): 3, accessed December 15, 2017, www.ncbi.nlm.nih.gov/books/NBK469815/pdf/Bookshelf_NBK469815.pdf.

71. Hanny Lightfoot-Klein, "Prisoners of Ritual: Some Contemporary Developments in the History of Female Genital Mutilation" (Paper, Second International Symposium on Circumcision, San Francisco, CA, May 3, 1991), accessed December 15, 2017, www.fgmnetwork.org/Lightfoot-klein/prisonersofritual.htm.

72. WHO, *Health Risks of Female Genital Mutilation (FGM).*

73. WHO, *A Student's Manual*, 30.

74. Nyangweso, *Female Genital Cutting: Mutilation or Cultural Tradition?*, 61.

75. Alice Behrendt and Steffen Moritz, "Posttraumatic Stress Disorder and Memory Problems After Female Genital Mutilation," *American Journal of Psychiatry* 162, no. 5 (June 2005):1000–1001.

76. Ibid.

77. U. Elchalal, B. Ben-Ami, and A. Brzezinski, "Female Circumcision: The Peril Remains," *BJU International* 83 (1999):103, accessed December 20, 2017, http://onlinelibrary.wiley.com/doi/10.1046/j.1464-410x.1999.0830s1103.x/epdf.

78. Ibid., 30.

79. Nyangweso, *Female Genital Cutting: Mutilation or Cultural Tradition?*, 106.

80. Ibid.

81. Ibid.

82. Ellen Gruenbaum, *The Female Circumcision Controversy: An Anthropological Perspective* (Philadelphia: University of Pennsylvania Press, 2001), 9.

83. Ibid.

84. Elchalal et al., "Female Circumcision: The Peril Remains," 103.

85. Ibid.

86. Nyangweso, *Female Genital Cutting: Mutilation or Cultural Tradition?*, 30.

87. A. Renee Bergstrom, "FGM Happened to Me in White, Midwest America," *Guardian*, December 3, 2016, accessed December 17, 2017, www.theguardian.com/us-news/2016/dec/02/fgm-happened-to-me-in-white-midwest-america.

88. Nyangweso, *Female Genital Cutting: Mutilation or Cultural Tradition?*, 31.

89. Emma Batha, "Interview: U.S. Woman Says Strict Christian Parents Subjected Her to FGM," April 1, 2019, Thomas Reuters, accessed July 5, 2019, http://news.trust.org/item/20190401142012-hf8eu.

90. Nyangweso, *Female Genital Cutting: Mutilation or Cultural Tradition?*, 102.

91. Ibid.

92. Ibid.

93. Ibid., 103.

94. Ibid., 108, quoting Sami Awad Aldeeb Abu-Sahlieh, *Male and Female Circumcision: Among Jews, Christians and Muslims*, Marco Polo Monographs 5 (Warren Center, PA: Shangri-La Publications, 2001).

95. Ibid., quoting Aldeed Abu-Sahlieh, Male and Female Circumcision.

96. Ibid., 108.

97. Ibid.

98. Ibid.

99. Ibid., "quoting Aldeed Abu-Sahlieh, Male and Female Circumcision.

100. Ibid. See also F. E. Peters, *The Hajj: The Muslim Pilgrimage to Mecca and the Holy Places* (Princeton, NJ: Princeton University Press, 1996), 4.

101. Robert C. Gregg, *Shared Stories, Rival Tellings: Early Encounters of Jews, Christians, and Muslims* (Oxford: Oxford University Press, 2015), 14. Gregg uses Brinner's translation of the *History of the Prophets and Kings or Tarikh al-Tabari*, adding: "al-Tha`labi mentions only the piercing of Hagar's ear by Sarah—another tale of the origin of a culturally established practice. Stowasser, *Women*, 47, 147n55, comments on the report in Ibn Kathir's Qisas I, 202, that, in response to Sarah's vow to cut three of Hagar's limbs, Abraham urges the piercing of her ears and circumcision, and says: 'This and similar traditions must be read as religious legitimization of female circumcision. The scripturalist context is important in that Abraham's circumcision, sign of God's covenant, plays a prominent role in the Islamic Hadith.'"

102. Encyclopaedia Britannica Online, s.v. "Fatwa," accessed October 2, 2018, www.britannica.com/topic/fatwa.

103. Nyangweso, *Female Genital Cutting: Mutilation or Cultural Tradition?*, 111.

104. Ibid.

105. Abigail Hauslohner, "A Virginia Imam Said Female Genital Mutilation Prevents 'Hypersexuality,' Leading to Calls for His Dismissal," *Washington Post*, June 5, 2017, accessed October 2, 2018, www.washingtonpost.com/news/acts-of-faith/wp/2017/06/05/virginia-mosque-embattled-after-imam-said-female-genital-mutilation-prevents-hypersexuality/?utm_term=.622f7b206544.

106. Elchalal et al., "Female Circumcision: The Peril Remains," 105.

107. "Muslim Scholars Rule Female Circumcision Un-Islamic," *The Age*, November 24, 2006, accessed January 15, 2018, www.theage.com.au/news/world/muslim-scholars-rule-female-circumcision-unislamic/2006/11/24/1163871589618.html.

108. Philip Pullella, "Pope Condemns Female Mutilation, Domestic Violence Against Women," *Reuters*, February 7, 2015, accessed February 16, 2018, www.reuters.com/article

/us-pope-mutilation/pope-condemns-female-mutilation-domestic-violence-against-women-idUSKBN0LB0JM20150207.

109. Peggy Fletcher Stack, "In a First for a Top LDS Leader, Mormon Apostle Denounces Female Genital Mutilation," *Salt Lake Tribune*, September 28, 2016, accessed October 2, 2018, http://archive.sltrib.com/article.php?id=4381399&itype=CMSID.

110. UNFPA, "FGM Frequently Asked Questions."

111. Ibid.

112. Brief for Islamic Law Scholars as *Amicus Curiae* at 16, *Holt v. Hobbs*, 574 U.S. ___ (2015), May 29, 2014, accessed November 7, 2018, www.scotusblog.com/wp-content/uploads/2017/08/13-6827tsac.pdf.

113. Ibid., 17.

114. *Prince v. Massachusetts*, 321 U.S. 158 (1944).

115. UN General Assembly, Resolution 69/150, "Intensifying Global Efforts for the Elimination of Female Genital Mutilations," February 17, 2015, accessed February 1, 2018, www.un.org/en/ga/search/view_doc.asp?symbol=A/RES/69/150.

116. UNFPA, "FGM Frequently Asked Questions."

117. WHO, *A Student's Manual*, 34–35.

118. Abbey Schubert, "24 States Have No Laws Against Female Genital Mutilation: Here's Why That Needs to Change," *Mic*, July 14, 2017, accessed October 2, 2018, https://mic.com/articles/182161/24-states-have-no-laws-against-female-genital-mutilation-heres-why-that-needs-to-change#.HQcX9GIYN.

119. Ibid.

120. Ibid.

121. Ibid.

122. Ibid.

123. *Sahiyo Newsletter* (Sahiyo, May 2019), https:// mailchi.mp/350466d11300/learn-more-about-sahiyos-work-to-end-female-genital-cutting. Also see Equality Now, accessed June 29, 2020, https://www.equalitynow.org/us_laws_against_fgm_state_by_state.

124. Taher, *Understanding Female Genital Cutting in the Dawoodi Bohra Community*, 7.

125. *A Resource Guide to Best Practice for Sensitive and Effective Reporting on FGC/M* (Sahiyo, 2016), 15, accessed January 31, 2017, https://sahiyo.files.wordpress.com/2016/05/sahiyo_mediaresourceguide_31jan.pdf.

126. Ibid.

127. Taher, *Understanding Female Genital Cutting in the Dawoodi Bohra Community*, 7.

128. Ibid.

129. Ibid., 13–14.

130. Ibid., 7.

131. Absar Ahmad and Aafiya Siddique, "Female Genital Mutilation (FGM): The Unspoken Truth," *Cafe Dissensus Everyday*, April 25, 2018, 3.

132. Taher, *Understanding Female Genital Cutting in the Dawoodi Bohra Community*, 53.

133. Press Trust of India, "Dawoodi Bohra Women's Group Defends *Khafz*," *The Hindu*, August 26, 2018, accessed November 7, 2018, www.thehindu.com/todays-paper/tp-miscellaneous/tp-others/dawoodi-bohra-womens-group-defends-khafz/article24783322.ece.

134. Sales, "Alan Dershowitz Explains Why He Is Assisting a Group Accused of Promoting FGM."

135. Ibid.

136. Kristina Arriaga, "Cutting Young Girls Isn't Religious Freedom," *Wall Street Journal*, August 24, 2017, accessed November 7, 2018, www.wsj.com/articles/cutting-young-girls-isnt-religious-freedom-1503617269.

137. Alan Dershowitz, letter to the editor, *Wall Street Journal*, August 31, 2017, accessed October 1, 2018, www.wsj.com/articles/fgm-is-abuse-culturally-sensitive-or-not-1504201020.

138. "Female Genital Anatomy," Boston University School of Medicine, November 26, 2002, accessed October 8, 2018, www.bumc.bu.edu/sexualmedicine/physicianinformation/female-genital-anatomy.

139. Ibid.

140. Helen E. O'Connell, Kalavampara V. Sanjeevan, and John M. Hutson, "Anatomy of the Clitoris," *Journal of Urology* 174, no. 4 (October 2005).

141. Ibid.

142. Vincenzo Puppo, "Anatomy of the Clitoris: Revision and Clarifications About the Anatomical Terms for the Clitoris Proposed (Without Scientific Bases) by Helen O'Connell, Emmanuele Jannini, and Odile Buisson," *ISRN Obstetrics and Gynecology* 2011 (2011).

143. Naomi Russo, The Still-Misunderstood Shape of the Clitoris," *Atlantic*, March 9, 2017, accessed November 8, 2018, www.theatlantic.com/health/archive/2017/03/3d-clitoris/518991.

144. Ibid.

145. Ibid.

146. Ibid.

147. Complaint at 6, *United States v. Jumana Nagarwala*, No. 2:17-mj-30182 (E.D. Mich. April 12, 2017), accessed October 8, 2018, www.justice.gov/opa/press-release/file/957381/download.

148. Ibid.

149. Ibid.

150. Ibid., 6–7.

151. Ibid.

152. Ibid., 7

153. Campana, "In India's Dawoodi Bohra Community, There's a Growing Debate About FGM."

154. Ibid.

155. Ibid.

156. Maryum Saifee, "I'm a Survivor of Female Genital Cutting and I'm Speaking Out—as Others Must Too," *Guardian*, February 8, 2016, accessed December 1, 2017, www.theguardian.com/commentisfree/2016/feb/08/victim-fgm-speaking-out-cut-genitals-culture-of-silence.

157. Taher, *Understanding Female Genital Cutting in the Dawoodi Bohra Community*, 52.

158. Ibid.

159. Ibid., 40.

160. Ibid., 42.

161. Ibid.

162. Ibid., 44.

163. Ibid., 50.

164. Bridie Jabour, "Australia's First Female Genital Mutilation Trial: How a Bright Young Girl Convinced a Jury," *Guardian*, November 13, 2015, accessed November 7, 2018, www.theguardian.com/society/2015/nov/13/female-genital-mutilation-trial-young-girl-convinced-jury-australia.

165. Ibid.

166. Ibid.

167. Mohua Das, "Bohra Cleric Urges Female Genital Mutilation?" *Times of India*, April 29, 2016, accessed October 4, 2018, http://timesofindia.indiatimes.com/articleshow/52031699.cms?utm_source=contentofinterest&utm_medium=text&utm_campaign=cppst.

168. Jabour, "Australia's First Female Genital Mutilation Trial."

169. Ibid.

170. Masooma Ranavli, "Petition Update: Huge Success for BOHRA Women," *Change.org: End Female Mutilation in India*, February 10, 2017, accessed September 15, 2018, www.change.org/p/end-female-genital-mutilation-in-india/u/19359668.

171. Rina Chandran, "No Evidence of FGM, India Government Tells Court, Appalling Activists," *Reuters*, December 29, 2017, accessed September 15, 2018, www.reuters.com/article/us-india-women-religion/no-evidence-of-fgm-india-government-tells-court-appalling-activists-idUSKBN1EN0QB.

172. "'Women Do Not Live Only for Marriage and Husbands': Supreme Court Speaks Against Female Genital Mutilation," *Firstpost*, July 30, 2018, accessed September 20, 2018, www.firstpost.com/india/women-do-not-live-only-for-marriage-and-husbands-supreme-court-speaks-against-female-genital-mutilation-4851711.html.

173. Ibid.

174. Sanya Dhingra, "Modi Govt Does U-turn on Female Genital Mutilation Days After PM Meets Dawoodi Bohra Head," *ThePrint*, September 26, 2018, accessed November 7, 2018, https://theprint.in/politics/modi-govt-does-u-turn-on-female-genital-mutilation-days-after-pm-meets-dawoodi-bohra-head/124750.

175. Saphora Smith, "Iceland's Proposed Ban on Circumcision Rattles Jews, Muslims," *NBC News*, September 21, 2018, accessed November 7, 2018, www.nbcnews.com/news/world/iceland-s-proposed-ban-circumcision-rattles-jews-muslims-n910541.

176. WHO, *Male Circumcision: Global Trends and Determinants of Prevalence, Safety and Acceptability* (Geneva: WHO, 2007),1, accessed September 20, 2018, http://apps.who.int/iris/bitstream/handle/10665/43749/9789241596169_eng.pdf?sequence=1.

177. American Academy of Pediatrics, "Male Circumcision: Task Force on Circumcision, Technical Report," *Pediatrics* 130, no. 3 (2012), accessed June 20, 2019, https://pediatrics.aappublications.org/content/130/3/e756.

178. Taher, *Understanding Female Genital Cutting in the Dawoodi Bohra Community*, 40–42.

179. Mazloomdoost and Pauls, "A Comprehensive Review," 249.

180. "Female Genital Anatomy."

181. Ibid.; also see WHO, *A Teacher's Guide*, 38.

182. Women Deliver, "*Joint Press Release, Ending FGM/C by 2030: Uniting Forces to Make FGM/C a Practice of the Past*," 2019, accessed June 20, 2019, www.endfgm.eu/editor/files/2019/06/Press_release_WD4.pdf.

183. WHO, *Male Circumcision: Global Trends*, 7.

184. Nyangweso, *Female Genital Cutting: Mutilation or Cultural Tradition?*, 6.

185. Ibid.

186. UN Women, "Sources of International Human Rights Law on Female Genital Mutilation," Virtual Knowledge Centre to End Violence Against Women and Girls, May 2011, accessed March 4, 2018, www.endvawnow.org/en/articles/645-sources-of-international-human-rights-law-on-female-genital-mutilation.html.

187. Ibid.

188. Ghanea, *Women and Religious Freedom.*

189. Arsalan Suleman, "A Necessary Conversation: Debunking Religious Justifications for FGM/C," accessed May 9, 2020, https://berkleycenter.georgetown.edu/responses/a-necessary-conversation-debunking-religious-justifications-for-fgm-c.

Chapter 10

1. 138 S. Ct. 2392 (2018).

2. 138 S. Ct. 1719 (2018).

3. 139 S. Ct. 661 (2019).

4. See Heather J. Sharkey and Jeffrey Edward Green, "Introduction," in this volume, page 1.

5. Ibid., pages 4–5, 9–10, 12–17, 19–21.

6. In a recent religious case where the court denied certiorari on a religious freedom claim from a football coach, Justice Clarence Thomas, Justice Neil M. Gorsuch, and Justice Brett M. Kavanaugh joined Justice Samuel A. Alito's statement respecting the denial of certiorari, which suggested "certain decisions of this Court" stood in the way of valid religious freedom claims that could have been brought. *Kennedy v. Bremerton Sch. Dist.*, 139 S. Ct. 634, 637 (2019) (Alito, J., concurring in denial of cert.); see also *Stormans, Inc. v. Wiesman*, 136 S. Ct. 2433, 2433–34 (2016) (Alito, J., dissenting from the denial of cert.) (suggesting expanding the rights of religious objectors to protect pharmacists who objected to stocking emergency contraception).

7. Protecting the Nation from Foreign Terrorist Entry into the United States, Exec. Order No. 13, 769, 82 Fed. Reg. 8977, 8979 § 5(c) (2017).

8. Ibid.

9. Michael D. Shear and Helene Cooper, "Trump Bars Refugees and Citizens of 7 Muslim Countries," *New York Times*, January 27, 2017, www.nytimes.com/2017/01/27/us/politics/trump-syrian-refugees.html?_r=0 ("[President Trump] ordered that Christians and others from minority religions be granted priority over Muslims").

10. Miriam Jordan, Siobhan Hughes, and Kristina Peterson, "Donald Trump's Immigration Ban Sows Chaos," *Wall Street Journal*, January 30, 2017, www.wsj.com/articles/donald-trumps-immigration-ban-sows-chaos-1485748079.

11. Amy B. Wang, "Trump Asked for a 'Muslim Ban,' Giuliani Says—and Ordered a Commission to Do It 'Legally,'" *Washington Post*, January 29, 2017, www.washingtonpost.com/news/the-fix/wp/2017/01/29/trump-asked-for-a-muslim-ban-giuliani-says-and-ordered-a-commission-to-do-it-legally.

12. Citations for the propositions in this paragraph can be found in Brief of Constitutional Law Scholars as Amici Curiae in Support of Respondents, *Hawaii*, 138 S. Ct. 2392 (No. 17-965).

13. Brief of Amici Curiae Former National Security Officials in Support of Respondents, *Hawaii*, 138 S. Ct. 2392 (No. 17-965).

14. *Washington v. Trump*, 847 F.3d 1151, 1156 (9th Cir. 2017) (*per curiam*).

15. Exec. Order No. 13,780 § 1(i), 82 Fed. Reg. 13,209, 13,212 (Mar. 9, 2017).

16. Taylor Link, "Stephen Miller Admits the New Executive Order on Immigration Ban Is Same as the Old," *Salon*, February 23, 2017, www.salon.com/2017/02/22/stephen-miller-admits-the-new-executive-order-on-immigration-ban-is-same-as-the-old.

17. Press Briefing by Press Secretary Sean Spicer, March 7, 2017, www.whitehouse.gov/briefings-statements/press-briefing-press-secretary-sean-spicer-030717.

18. *Hawaii v. Trump*, No. 17-17168, 2017 WL 5343014, at *1 (9th Cir. Nov. 13, 2017).

19. *Int'l Refugee Assistance Program v. Trump*, 857 F.3d 554, 595 (4th Cir. 2017).

20. Presidential Proclamation No. 9645, 82 Fed. Reg. 45,161 (Sept. 24, 2017).

21. *Hawaii v. Trump*, 265 F. Supp. 3d 1140, 1160 (D. Haw. 2017).

22. In explaining his resolution of the case, the chief justice emphasized a few additional points: (1) the travel ban did not *expressly* refer to religion, (2) there are many potential evidentiary difficulties associated with demonstrating illicit intent, and (3) it was unclear which other actions by the president might also be called into doubt if the court held that this one was tainted by antireligious animus. *Hawaii*, 138 S. Ct. at 2423.

23. *Hawaii*, 138 S. Ct. at 2424 (Kennedy, J., concurring).

24. Ibid.

25. Ibid.

26. Ibid.

27. Ibid., 2433 (Sotomayor, J., dissenting).

28. Ibid.

29. Ibid., 2447.

30. Ibid., 2448.

31. See, generally, Brief for Petitioner, *Masterpiece Cakeshop*, 138 S. Ct. 1719 (No. 16-111).

32. Brief of Floyd Abrams et al. as Amici Curiae in Support of Respondents at 9, *Masterpiece Cakeshop*, 138 S. Ct. 1719 (No. 16-111).

33. *Employment Division v. Smith*, 494 U.S. 872, 884 (1990).

34. See, generally, Brief of Church-State Scholars as Amici Curiae in Support of Respondents, *Masterpiece Cakeshop*, 138 S. Ct. 1719 (No. 16-111).

35. *Masterpiece Cakeshop*, 138 S. Ct. at 1729.

36. Ibid.

37. Ibid. (internal citations omitted).

38. Ibid.

39. Ibid.

40. Ibid., 1731.

41. *Larson v. Valente*, 102 S. Ct. 1673, 1683 (1982).

42. *Ray*, 139 S. Ct. at 661.

43. Ibid., 662 (Kagan, J., dissenting).

44. Ibid.

45. Transcript of Oral Argument at 14–15, Glossip, 135 S. Ct. 2726 (No. 14-7955).

46. See *Hurst v. Fla.*, 136 S. Ct. 616, 626 (2016) (Alito, J., dissenting) ("Although petitioner attacks the Florida system on numerous grounds, the Court's decision is based on a single perceived defect."); *Madison v. Alabama*, 139 S. Ct. 718, 732 (2019) (Alito, J., dissenting) (criticizing counsel for action in bad faith and stating that "the majority rewards counsel's trick").

47. *Bucklew v. Precythe*, 139 S. Ct. 1112, 1134 (2019) ("For example, we have vacated a stay entered by a lower court as an abuse of discretion where the inmate waited to bring an available claim until just 10 days before his scheduled execution for a murder he had committed 24 years earlier.").

48. Editorial Board, "Is Religious Freedom for Christians Only?" *New York Times*, February 9, 2019, www.nytimes.com/2019/02/09/opinion/supreme-court-alabama-execution.html.

49. Emanuella Grinberg, "South Carolina Foster Care Providers Can Reject People Who Don't Share Their Religious Beliefs," CNN, January 23, 2019, www.cnn.com/2019/01/23/politics/south-carolina-religious-freedom-nondiscrimination-waiver-hhs/index.html.

50. Ibid.

51. Dahlia Lithwick, "An Execution Without an Imam," *Slate*, February 8, 2019, https://slate.com/news-and-politics/2019/02/domineque-ray-alabama-execution-imam-first-amendment-scotus.html.

52. 135 S. Ct. 853 (2015).

53. 135 S. Ct. 2028 (2015).

CONTRIBUTORS

Cassie Adcock is Associate Professor of History and South Asian Studies at Washington University in St. Louis. She is the author of *The Limits of Tolerance: Indian Secularism and the Politics of Religious Freedom* (Oxford University Press, 2013).

Kristina Arriaga de Bucholz has spent twenty-five years advocating for religious freedom. She has worked at a U.S.-based public interest law firm and has served as a member of the U.S. delegation to the United Nations Human Rights Council in Geneva, the U.S. delegation to the Organization for Security and Co-operation in Europe, and the U.S. Commission on Civil Rights. She has also served as vice chair of the U.S. Commission on International Religious Freedom. She is a candidate for a Doctor of Philosophy in law at the University of Oxford.

Randall Balmer is the John Phillips Professor in Religion at Dartmouth College, an Episcopal priest, a prize-winning historian, and an Emmy Award nominee. He has written many books, including, most recently, *Evangelicalism in America* (Baylor University Press, 2016) and *Redeemer: The Life of Jimmy Carter* (Basic Books, 2014).

Lori G. Beaman is Professor in the Department of Classics and Religious Studies at the University of Ottawa, where she holds the Canada Research Chair in Religious Diversity and Social Change. She was principal investigator of the "Religion and Diversity Project" and is currently leading "Nonreligion in a Complex Future," a seven-year research initiative involving scholars from Canada, Australia, the United States, Britain, Argentina, Brazil, and the Nordic countries.

Heiner Bielefeldt, a philosopher, historian, and Catholic theologian, is Professor of Human Rights and Human Rights Politics at the University of Erlangen. From 2003 to 2009, he directed the German Institute for Human Rights. From 2010 to 2016, he served as United Nations Special Rapporteur on Freedom of Religion or Belief. His most recent book, written with Michael Wiener, is *Religious Freedom under Scrutiny* (University of Pennsylvania Press, 2020).

Jeffrey Edward Green is Professor of Political Science and Director of the Andrea Mitchell Center for the Study of Democracy at the University of Pennsylvania. A political theorist, he is the author of *The Eyes of the People: Democracy in an Age of Spectatorship* (Oxford University Press, 2010) and *The Shadow of Unfairness: A Plebeian Theory of Liberal Democracy* (Oxford University Press, 2016).

Joshua Matz, who served as law clerk to Justice Anthony Kennedy of the U.S. Supreme Court from 2014 to 2015, is a partner at Kaplan Hecker & Fink LLP and an adjunct professor of law at Georgetown University. With Harvard Law School professor Laurence H. Tribe, he has published *Uncertain Justice: The Roberts Court and the Constitution* (Henry Holt, 2014) and *To End a Presidency: The Power of Impeachment* (Basic Books, 2018).

Daniel Philpott is Professor of Political Science at the University of Notre Dame and a scholar of religion and global politics. His most recent book is *Religious Freedom in Islam: The Fate of a Universal Human Right in the Muslim World Today* (Oxford University Press, 2019). He also promotes global religious freedom as vice chair of the Board of Directors of the Institute for Global Engagement; as a senior associate scholar of the Religious Freedom Institute; and as co-director of the project "Under Caesar's Sword: Christian Response to Persecution," supported by the Templeton Religion Trust.

Leigh E. Schmidt is Edward C. Mallinckrodt Distinguished University Professor in the Humanities at Washington University in St. Louis, where he is part of the John C. Danforth Center on Religion and Politics. His most recent book is *Village Atheists: How America's Unbelievers Made Their Way in a Godly Nation* (Princeton University Press, 2016).

William Schultz is an Assistant Professor of Religions in the Americas at the University of Chicago Divinity School. He is writing a book entitled *Jesus*

Springs: How Colorado Springs Became the Capital of the Culture Wars. He was a Mitchell Center Postdoctoral Fellow during the 2017–2018 academic year.

Heather J. Sharkey, a historian, is Professor in the Department of Near Eastern Languages & Civilizations at the University of Pennsylvania. She is the author of *Living with Colonialism: Nationalism and Culture in the Anglo-Egyptian Sudan* (University of California Press, 2003); *American Evangelicals in Egypt: Missionary Encounters in an Age of Empire* (Princeton University Press, 2008); and *A History of Muslims, Christians, and Jews in the Middle East* (Cambridge University Press, 2017).

Jolyon Baraka Thomas is Assistant Professor of Religious Studies at the University of Pennsylvania. He is the author of *Drawing on Tradition: Manga, Anime, and Religion in Contemporary Japan* (University of Hawaii Press, 2012) and *Faking Liberties: Religious Freedom in American-Occupied Japan* (University of Chicago Press, 2019).

INDEX

ACKNOWLEDGMENTS

As we reflect on work that went into this volume, we have many thanks to extend.

During the 2017–18 academic year at the University of Pennsylvania, the Andrea Mitchell Center for the Study of Democracy sponsored the program that led to this book. We are grateful to the Mitchell Center for making this project possible. We feel especially indebted to Rogers Smith, who founded and for a decade led the Democracy, Citizenship, and Constitutionalism (DCC) Program, which was the forerunner to the Mitchell Center. It was Rogers's idea to dedicate a theme year to the issue of religious freedom. He formed the faculty steering committee for this program and invited Heather Sharkey to lead it. Rogers entrusted direction of the Mitchell Center to Jeff Green, who shepherded the program in the Center's inaugural year. Rogers's vision and commitment over many years set the foundations on which we have built.

We are grateful for the hard work, energy, and vision of the faculty steering committee, whose members spent many hours identifying speakers and planning events for the program that became known as "States of Religious Freedom." Our thanks go to Melissa Wilde, Ram Cnaan, Sarah ("Sally") Barringer Gordon, Michele Margolis, Jamal Elias, and Jolyon Thomas. In fact, Jolyon Thomas became such an energetic participant that he ultimately wrote an article for this volume as well.

A vibrant panel discussion at the National Constitution Center (NCC) kicked off the year's events. We would like to thank the NCC's president and CEO, Jeffrey Rosen, who acted as moderator, as well as the other panelists, Kristina Arriaga (a contributor to this volume), Dan Barker, and David Saperstein.

Several scholars presented outstanding papers in monthly talks within the series. These presenters included Anna Su, Jonathan Fox, and Grace Yukich, along with three others who contributed to this volume: Randall Balmer,

Leigh Schmidt, and Cassie Adcock. Another impressive group presented papers at the end-of-year symposium. These were R. Marie Griffith, Cole Durham, and Mayanthi Fernando, along with five more who contributed to this volume: Heiner Bielefeldt, Daniel Philpott, Lori G. Beaman, Joshua Matz, and William Schultz.

Many colleagues volunteered as discussants and chairs. They responded to papers and raised questions that stimulated lively debate. We are grateful to discussants Vincent Lloyd, Donovan Schaefer, R. Scott Hanson, and Anthea Butler, as well as Sally Gordon, Melissa Wilde, and Michele Margolis from the steering committee. Daniel Cheely, Ronit Stahl, and Jim Hrdlicka chaired panels at the final symposium.

Nancy Ameen did extensive research on the jurisprudence of religious liberty. Two scholars who were PhD students at the time also offered their help. Alon Tam provided research assistance as the steering committee was identifying speakers. Archana Kaku provided editorial assistance in preparing the manuscript for submission.

Matthew Roth gave behind-the-scenes support as the series developed and unfolded. From beginning to end, his steady presence was invaluable, especially as the DCC Program under the leadership of Rogers Smith transitioned into the Andrea Mitchell Center under the direction of Jeff Green.

Even as Penn Press was itself undergoing transitions, its editors were consistently helpful. We are grateful to Peter Agree who advised us in the planning and proposal stages; Damon Linker, who counseled us as we navigated the manuscript submission and referee process; and Robert Lockhart, who offered sage advice as we strengthened the manuscript in response to feedback from anonymous referees and then guided us as we finalized the book. Zoe Kovacs and Noreen O'Connor at Penn Press helped to usher the book through the production process, while at BookComp, Inc. Kathy McQueen provided meticulous copyediting and Jon Dertien advised us as the proofs were going to press. Two referees gave substantive suggestions, and we are grateful for their insights.

Finally, we thank our families for their love and support.

www.ingramcontent.com/pod-product-compliance
Lightning Source LLC
LaVergne TN
LVHW091526200926
848483LV00002B/314
* 9 7 8 0 8 1 2 2 5 3 3 7 5 *